The Island that Dared

The Island
that Dared

Journeys in Cuba

DERVLA MURPHY

ELAND

First published by Eland in 2008
61 Exmouth Market, London EC1R 4QL

Copyright © Dervla Murphy 2008

ISBN   978 1 906011 35 2

Jacket illustration by Laura Carlin
Map © Reg Piggott
Text set in Great Britain by Antony Gray
Printed in England by Cromwell Press

Contents

Illustrations

To all the many Cubans
who helped me on my way

Acknowledgements

Lovine Wilson achieved awesome secretarial feats while swiftly coping with a tedious and incoherent typescript.

Brendan Barrington kindly read the first draft and was generous with shrewd constructive criticism.

Jo Murphy-Lawless as usual contributed enormously in both raw material and moral support. Deborah Singmaster, on a sudden inspiration, brought forth the title.

Stephanie Allen earned my undying gratitude by guiding me towards Eland Publishing. Rose Baring and Barnaby Rogerson provided the sort of encouragement and advice all authors need and a dwindling number receive in the twenty-first century.

Rachel and Andrew put Cuba on my agenda and the former for months worked overtime in cyberspace on behalf of an uncomputerised mother.

To all, my heartfelt thanks.

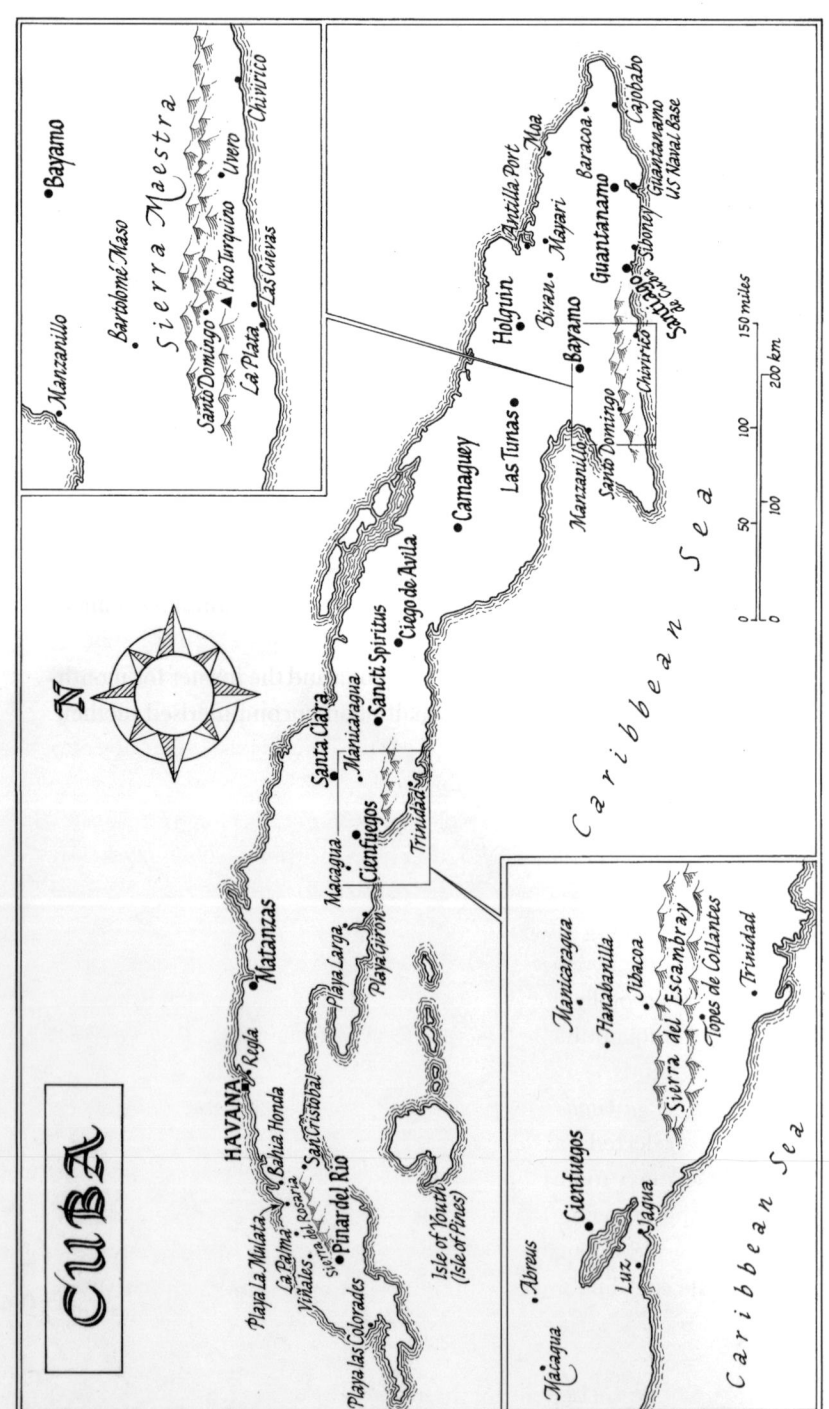

Introduction

In times long past (1973–87) I travelled with my daughter Rachel (born 1968) in Asia, Latin America and Africa; pack-animals assisted us on those months-long treks. In 1993 Rachel met Andrew in Mozambique where both were working as UN volunteers during that country's transition from war to peace.

Fast forward to the autumn of 2005 when my grand-daughters were soon to be ten (Rose), eight (Clodagh) and six (Zea) – old enough to benefit from some real travelling, instead of merely flying from their home in Italy to visit relatives and friends in Wales, England and Ireland. From Andrew came an exhilarating suggestion, a three-generation November wander through Cuba. The island's quasi-Western way of life would not, he judged, overtax his darlings' adaptability and Castroism has brought about a remarkably low crime-rate. But unfortunately this had to be an all-female team; Andrew's job precluded winter holidays and the university vacation months would be intolerably hot.

Everything was easily organised. Low-cost Virgin Air fares were on offer and at the Cuban Consulate in London efficient young women took only seven minutes to process our five visas (£15 each) – thus setting a record, in my experience. Tourism has now replaced sugar as Cuba's main official source of hard currency so it is in the national interest to lower bureaucratic hurdles. Another vitally important source – this one long-established – is the cash-flow, unquantifiable but considerable, from Cuban exiles to their families and friends.

From the *Rough Guide's* list of *casa particulares* (government-approved B&Bs) Rachel selected Casa de Pedro y Candida in Centro Habana and by e-mail booked two rooms for three nights. Beyond Havana we would muddle through; having closely studied our map and guide books, we knew how to avoid the main tourist zones. And Cuba's four thousand five hundred-mile coastline promised that the Trio would not be deprived of sea and sand.

Despite its unique socio-political interest, Cuba was not a country I had

ever considered for a solitary trek or cycle tour; always it's too hot (Siberia
in winter is more to my climatic taste) and topographically it is too tame. I
visualised, not entirely accurately, an island mostly flat and monochrome
(all those canefields!) with only a few low mountain ranges. The Cuban
people, I gathered, were the country's most precious resource, an impression to be confirmed by experience.

I failed to register the Revolution's triumph in January 1959 when I
was in the midst of a prolonged personal crisis that obliterated world
events. However, I do vividly remember the Cuban Missile Crisis of
October 1962. By then I was preparing to cycle to India while everyone
else was, if you believed the media, preparing for nuclear war. I didn't
believe the media and concentrated on sending spare tyres to strategic
points (usually British Council offices) between Istanbul and New Delhi.
Meanwhile Nikita Khrushchev and J.F. Kennedy were sorting things out
without consulting Fidel, which seemed fair enough since he had had no
ambition to host nuclear weapons. Inevitably, however, this ignoring of
their leader caused considerable offence in Cuba; it too loudly echoed
that Spanish and US ignoring of the courageous Cuban army in 1898,
when the Wars of Independence ended. Fidel's accepting of the missiles
was a decision reluctantly taken, as he explained years later. 'By allowing
Cuba to become a Soviet military base the image of the Revolution would
be damaged and we were zealous in protecting that image in the rest of
Latin America.' He was referring to the importance of the Revolution's
being recognised as a one hundred per cent homegrown event, brought
off by ordinary Cubans without any significant outside assistance – financial,
ideological or military.

During subsequent decades, Cuba came to my attention only occasionally:
in 1967 when Ché was executed in Bolivia by CIA-funded militia; in August
1968 when Fidel severely shocked his friends, at home and abroad, by
condoning Soviet brutality in Czechoslovakia; in April 1971 when the poet
Heberto Padilla, winner of a major international literary prize, was bugged
by State Security and subsequently publicly humiliated; in the mid-'70s
when Cuban troops in Angola contributed more than their share to the
defeat of apartheid South Africa's US-backed army. During the following
decades I was impressed by the publication of internationally acclaimed
statistics recording the extraordinary achievement of Castroist health and
education campaigns and in the early '90s it distressed me to hear that the
end of trade relations with the Eastern Bloc was threatening all such
achievements. In Washington that crisis engendered two more anti-Cuba

laws and here one recalls the much-quoted comment of a US diplomat, Wayne S. Smith – 'Cuba seems to have the same effect on American administrations as the full moon used to have on werewolves'.

On 28 September 1990, after all trade with the Eastern Bloc had suddenly collapsed, Fidel announced Cuba's entry into 'a special period during peacetime', an interlude of deprivation comparable to wartime conditions (soon to become generally known a 'the Special Period'). Seven years later the UN Economic Commission on Latin America and the Caribbean estimated that this 'interruption of commercial relations with the Eastern Bloc constituted a loss of markets more severe than that brought about by the Great Depression'.

It could be said that I was starry-eyed (or blinkered?) about the forty-seven-year-old Cuban experiment when our direct flight to Havana took off on 1 November 2005. This family holiday gave me a glimpse of the experiment's complexities and in January 2006 I returned alone for two months – which journey left me somewhat less starry-eyed, though still a staunch supporter of Castroism as it has been evolving since 1990. My final visit (September/October 2007) coincided with Cuba's four-yearly elections and I saw for myself what Professor D. L. Raby had recently pointed out:

> Not only do the Cubans recognise that the Left can no longer afford the mistake of trying to copy a fixed model of any kind, but they accept that the peculiar circumstances of the US blockade and their geographical situation on the doorstep of the imperial hegemony have conditioned and limited their own Socialist democracy.

PART ONE

November–December 2005

Chapter 1

At 11.10 a.m., one hour and forty minutes out of Gatwick, our captain announced, in a bright chatty voice, 'You'll have noticed we've changed direction'. (I hadn't noticed.) Then the voice became soothing. We had a defective engine, the defect so trivial it would be absolutely safe to continue to any other destination. The only snag was that Havana's airport lacked an appropriate maintenance crew.

Rachel and I exchanged raised eyebrows and feigned nonchalance. For both of us this was a novel experience – how unkind of Fate, on the Trio's first long-distance flight! Yet they seemed to accept the situation as part of travelling's rich tapestry and were fascinated by our fuel-jettisoning. Rose, Clodagh and I chanced to be sitting just behind the right wing and for half an hour could see a steady stream of shining kerosene pouring fast from that tank. Clodagh exclaimed, 'It's like a silver sword!' Zea, bred to be frugal, lamented the waste. Rose told her: 'From Gatwick to Havana is four thousand six hundred and seventy-one miles' (she'd been studying her TV screen) 'and all the way we're over the sea. It's *sensible* to waste fuel and go back for repairs!' At which point I realised that she, too, was feigning nonchalance.

Our fellow-passengers, mostly British tourists, made no fuss, were tensely silent or spoke in whispers. The cabin staff, no doubt accustomed to coping with such minor crises, strolled to and fro looking calm and cheerful, offering light refreshments.

Approaching Gatwick, through dense swirling wind-torn clouds, our captain spoke again. We were not to be alarmed by the fire-engines and ambulances lined up to meet us, a standard procedure for an unscheduled landing but of course superfluous in our case. Moments later, as we gained height, that reassuring voice explained, 'Our landing is being delayed by adverse weather conditions'. For twenty long minutes we circled through turbulence while Rose and Zea quietly and neatly filled their vomit-bags.

At 1.10 we touched down, very bumpily, and were instructed to leave no possessions on board. When we had 'deplaned' (who invents these ugly words?) further information would be available.

On our release most passengers at once cell-phoned, excitedly reporting the drama as we were herded down the long corridors. Everyone looked happily relieved rather than frustrated. But soon three grumpy security men blocked our way with a nylon rope barrier. Bureaucratic complications arise when hundreds of passengers are not departing, not arriving, not in transit. For almost an hour we were restricted to limbo, a large space with few seats. The Trio sat on the floor absorbed in *Sudoku* puzzles while their mother and grandmother agreed that the stress of travelling with small children is greatly exaggerated. In general that age-group simply takes life as it comes.

When a ground-staff team eventually rescued us they looked apologetic: we wouldn't be taking off before 8.00 p.m., if then. At a kiosk in the main concourse we each received a fifteen-pound gift voucher for sustenance and promptly I abandoned my descendants, making for the nearest bar. The disappointment was cruel; those vouchers could be exchanged only for food and soft drinks. Meanwhile the Trio, having discovered a spacious play-area, were energetically relating to their contemporaries despite having been up at 4.00 a.m. And Rachel was struggling with a public telephone (we are an anti-cell-phone family) because she wanted Andrew, in Italy, to send an e-mail to Candida, in Havana, explaining that we would not be arriving when expected. For some arcane reason, e-mailing Cuba is much easier than telephoning.

Around the play-area several Havana-bound parents occupied ring-side seats. I sat beside Imelda, one of the few Cubans, a slim, olive-skinned woman looking ill at east in high-altitude garments. She was longing to be home 'where bodies can feel free'. Her extrovert three-year-old son had found the play-area too limited and was roving widely, charming the general public and being followed at a discreet distance by his English father. A family illness had occasioned this mid-winter visit to Yorkshire. When the couple met in 2001 Ted had already been working in Cuba for years. 'Doing what?' I asked – an innocent question, yet Imelda feigned deafness. I was at the beginning of a steep learning curve; beneath their effervescent friendliness, many Cubans maintain a cautious reserve in conversation with unknown foreigners.

Later, Ted volunteered that he was a tourist industry marketing consultant. In his view, Castroism had long been among Cuba's most effective tourist magnets. 'People say, "We must go before it changes", meaning before Fidel dies. Few realise changes have been happening for a decade. They're seeing a country still wearing a Castroist fig-leaf while in rapid transition to capitalism.' I noted Ted's neutral tone; but one could deduce, from his job, that he approved of the changes.

Leaving Rose in charge of her siblings, Rachel and I sat in a nearby bar wondering how, within six hours, we could possibly spend seventy-five pounds on food and soft drinks. Given that sum, or less, Rachel could feed a family of five for a week. Then, collecting the Trio, we toured Gatwick's shopping mall, unsuccessfully seeking wholesome portable foods to sustain us while trekking. In general we boycott the mainstream food industry but this situation called for flexibility; to the Trio's delighted astonishment they were allowed to eat one voucher's worth of mini-yoghurts and mega-ice-creams. ('All full of chemical flavourings and dyes,' their mother grimly commented.) Eventually, in desperation, I proposed a meal, with good wine for the adults, at Gatwick's most expensive restaurant.

By 7.15 the Havana-bound were easily spotted amidst Gatwick's multitude. Anxiously we coalesced beneath the Departure screens and Havana's failure to appear prompted a rising tide of pessimism. Then at 7.50 it did appear (Board Now!) and we all surged towards Gate thirty-two waving our Special Passes – which didn't spare us the X-ray queue. By this stage Zea was half-asleep, riding on Mummy's shoulders, and Clodagh was looking pale and sounding querulous while Rose silently wore her 'I'm a stoic' expression. At the final security check smiling Virgin Air hostesses handed out letters from the Customer Relations Manager regretting that our flight 'had suffered a technical problem' (more delicate wording than 'engine failure') and offering us ten thousand Flying Club miles or twenty per cent off our next Economy ticket.

During that nine and a half hour flight Rose slept quite well, Clodagh slept fitfully and Zea slept so soundly, stretched across her own seat and the maternal lap, that leg cramps kept Rachel awake. To me her avoidance of any movement seemed like excessive solicitude but I reckoned such grandmaternal opinions are best suppressed for the sake of intergenerational harmony. As for Nyanya – I can never sleep in the sitting position though if reclining on a bed of stones (as occasionally happens) slumber comes easily. (Here it should be explained that to the Trio I'm 'Nyanya', the Swahili term for Granny, bestowed on me when Rose was a baby living in Eastern Zaire.)

Peering through the blackness during our descent, it was apparent that Havana is no ordinary twenty-first-century city; instead of the usual energy-wasting glow, dim pinpricks marked Cuba's capital.

In the immigration hall we ceremoniously changed our watches from 5.30 to 1.30 a.m. By then Rachel and I had reached that curious stage of exhaustion when one ceases to notice it (mind over matter? Second

wind?). Rose and Zea were all bright-eyed and bushy-tailed, Clodagh less
so – until she met another eight-year-old with whom she had bonded in
the play-area. The queues were long and slow, each passport and visa
requiring computerisation. Rachel had recently convinced me that computers are *very useful* but I remained aware of their negative effects. The
computerisation of everything – libraries, universities, hotels, hospitals,
government departments, airports – has noticeably lengthened bureaucratic ordeals while encouraging a profligate attitude towards paper use.

Next we trudged through an enormous concourse, past shuttered shops
and restaurants. From high roof struts hung the flags of every nation,
symbolising Cuba's non-aligned stance on the world stage. The Stars and
Stripes and the Keys of St Peter were inconspicuously placed.

While the others waited for our rucksacks I gently prodded the sleeping
young woman in the queueless *Cambio* cubicle and received 1.04 convertible peso (CP) to the euro, the standard rate throughout Cuba. At any
time I could convert these for use in ordinary Cuban shops at a rate of one
CP for twenty-six national pesos (NP). US dollars lost ten per cent in the
exchange; other currencies were commission-free.

We emerged unchecked through Customs though in several Caribbean
countries granny-figures are quite often loaded with drugs. In another
vast space our packaged fellow-passengers were trailing towards their
coaches. 'They all look *too* tired!' commiserated Zea. Soon we were on our
own in this dreary pillared hallway, vaguely resembling an unfinished
Romanesque cathedral and furnished only with a dozen small metal
chairs. Through a glass wall taxis were visible but 3.15 seemed an in-
humane hour to set out for our *casa particulare*. Rose sought a loo but
quickly returned looking non-stoical; it was too awful to pee in . . . For this
unfortunate introduction to Cuba's normally hygienic public lavatories
Hurricane Wilma was responsible; the local water supply had been wrecked
a week previously. When Rachel and Rose hastily took off for the great
outdoors Zea went into a sulk because she hadn't been invited to accompany them and Clodagh complained of (psychosomatic?) dehydration.
This prompted me to explore and discover a small bar in a far corner
where two Customs officers and four Immigrations officers were grumbling
about our delayed flight which had required them to do overtime. Havana
airport's average daily intake of 5,000 passengers normally arrives by
daylight.

Leaving Rachel to counter Zea's sulk I took my first steps into Cuba
with Rose by my side. An airport carpark – even one surrounded by royal

palms and aromatic shrubs – does not provide an enthralling first impression but we agreed that the smells were excitingly unfamiliar and the
sky magical, its stars lustrous on black velvet. The warm stirring of the air
was a mere zephyr and only a rooster duet broke the silence. Rose deduced,
'Here they must have loads of free-range eggs.'

Back in the hallway we found the juniors restored to cheerfulness by
some maternal alchemy and now several other seats were occupied. Two
angry elderly women and a young man (bound for Caracas, said his
luggage labels) were arguing loudly, the traveller seeming both cowed and
defensive. A young Dutch couple had been self-driving around the island
and injudiciously exposing themselves to the sun; tenderly they applied
Savlon to each other's blistered backs. Closer to us, a middle-aged corpu-
lent mulatto was showing an amused interest in the Trio's acrobatics – the
mere sight of all that open space seemed to have recharged their batteries.
When we got into conversation I learned that Senor Malagon was awaiting
a delegation of Canadian agronomists. In a disarming way he boasted
about Cuba's efficient management of Wilma which for six days, towards
the end of October, had flooded eleven of the island's fourteen provinces.
In preparation, 600,000 had been evacuated with their livestock and no
lives were lost.

At 5.30 we approached the taxi rank. All night three vehicles had been
waiting (the sort of veteran cars that send some men into inexplicable
ecstasies) yet there was no competition, no haggling. The first in line was
entitled to us and CP25 was the standard night fare to Central Havana
(to be known henceforth as Centro). Rachel sat in front, practising her
Spanish, while the Trio and I wriggled uncomfortably on the back seat's
broken springs. During that half-hour ride all was predictable: pot-holed
roads, ramshackle factories, Soviet-style blocks of prefab flats hastily
erected in the 1960s.

Shoals of cyclists pedalling to work without lights scandalised the Trio.
'They'll be dead!' said Zea. 'The police will get them!' said Clodagh. 'No,'
said Rose, rapidly adjusting to local realities. 'It's just they've no money
for lamps.'

Centro's bumpy narrow streets, running between tall, dilapidated
nineteenth-century residences, are off the main tourist track; twice we had
to stop at junctions to seek guidance. The dawn greyness was turning
faintly pink when we found 403 San Rafael – our driver looking trium-
phant, as though he had brought off some orienteering coup. We were
piling rucksacks on the pavement when Zea exclaimed, 'Look! Our taxi

has a swan, with big wings!' The driver chuckled and tipped her under the chin. 'Yes, my taxi very old Chevrolet, that very famous swan.'

A high, narrow door swung open, an outer gate was unlocked and it seemed we had arrived among old friends. Candida and Pedro, still in their nightwear, warmly embraced us while volubly registering relief at our safe arrival. The street door led directly into the parlour end of a narrow, sparsely furnished room separated from the kitchen-cum-dining-room by a long, low cupboard supporting bushy house-plants. The front bedroom opened off the parlour; two other windowless rooms opened off a corridor beyond the kitchen. To reach the small communal bathroom one crossed a square hallway at the foot of steep stairs; here more greenery surrounded an antique wrought-iron garden table with chairs to match, all painted white. As our rooms lacked writing space, this was to become my study.

While Rachel was arguing with her daughters about who was to sleep where, Candida poured hot milk from a giant thermos, sliced bread (with apologies for its being yesterday's loaf) and offered mango jam – the Trio's favourite. Then the younger generations tottered off to bed but after three cups of potent coffee I had revived enough to take advantage of Havana's brief morning coolness. An Irish proverb recommends 'the old dog (or bitch) for the hard road'.

Outside No. 403 the olfactory tapestry was complex: defective drains, sub-tropical vegetation, dog shit, cigar smoke, inferior petrol, seaweed, ripe garbage in overflowing skips. Each street corner had its skip to which householders on their way to work contributed bulging plastic bags and empty bottles. Cats crouched on the skip rims, cleverly reaching down to extract fish spines and other delicacies. Two dead rats in gutters proved that some cats had been busy overnight. Dogs swarmed, having been set free at dawn to do what we all do once a day, so one had to watch one's step on the broken pavements. A jolly young woman was selling tiny cups of strong sweet coffee from her living-room window; later, she would do a brisk trade in takeaway homemade pizzas which became popular with the Trio. Further down the street, an older woman was selling ham rolls and over-sweet buns from a plank laid on two chairs in her doorway. She and a neighbour were talking money, the neighbour a grey-haired, ebony-skinned housewife hunkered beside her doorstep, cleaning piles of rice on sheets of *Granma* (Cuba's only national daily, also the Communist Party newspaper).

In the late nineteenth century a sugar-rich bourgeoisie strove to repli-cate the imposing seventeenth- and eighteenth-century mansions of Old

Havana and their residences spread fast beyond the city walls. (These were demolished in 1963 to make way for new housing; only a fragment survives, near the railway station.) San Rafael is one of Centro's almost carfree grid of long, straight streets, every downward slope leading to the Malecón; from their intersections the Straits of Florida beckon – usually a blue sparkle, occasionally a grey-green turbulence. Most buildings are three- or four-storey (a few rise to five or six) and their external dilapidation is extreme. Post-Revolution, this district was taken over by workingclass families and what might tentatively be described as the *petite bourgeoisie*. Since then no restoration has been done; Havana was allowed to decay when Fidel took over, his mind set on improving living conditions for the rest of Cuba, hitherto neglected. Much social history is revealed by Centro's wealth of neo-baroque flourishes around wide-arched entrances or cracked stained-glass balcony windows, and by the strong iron bars protecting both doors and street level unglazed windows; Havana didn't enjoy its recent low crime rate during the centuries when it hogged most of the national wealth. Vivid expanses of Moorish tiles decorate a few façades and, from corners beneath high eaves, ambiguous carved figures lean out: they might represent Christian saints, classical heroes, Spanish conquistadors, Congolese deities or deceased grandparents. Along certain streets most balconies display strangely dressed dolls atop high stools, or little flags mysteriously patterned, or huge sooty kettles filled with coloured sticks – all components of Santería rituals. And long laundry lines of fluttering garments relieve the background drabness; Cubans are obsessive about personal cleanliness and partial to strong, bold colours.

On every street stereotypes appeared with almost ridiculous frequency. Grandads were relishing the day's first cigar, settled in cane rocking-chairs behind wrought-iron balconies high above the pavement. Ebullient schoolchildren in immaculate uniforms – each white shirt or blouse meticulously ironed – converged on their schools before 8.00 a.m. Young men rode bicycles held together with strips of tin, many wearing musical instruments over their shoulders. Older men were already playing dominoes, sitting at card-tables – usually improvised – outside their homes. Neighbours sat on doorsteps or window ledges, arguing, laughing, discussing, complaining, gossiping. Fruit-sellers pushed their homemade handcarts from group to group; when the recycled pram wheels had lost their rubber the rims grated loudly on the cobbles.

Superficially I was back in the Third World, aka the Majority World. But only superficially: no one looked hungry, ragged, dirty or obviously diseased, no one was homeless or neglected in old age. The contemporary Cubans, urban and rural, immediately impress as a self-confident people. Although Castroism has stumbled from one economic disaster to another, for a tangle of reasons, the Revolutionary ideal of equality bred two generations who never felt inferior because they lacked the Minority World's goodies. They appreciated their own goodies, including first-class medical care for all and a range of educational, cultural and sporting opportunities not available to the majority in such free-market democracies as India, South Africa – or the US. As for the third generation, now coming to maturity – I was to find that question marks surround them.

Chapter 2

Since its completion in 1950 (construction was begun in 1901) the *habaneros* have endowed their Malecón with a personality of its own; one can't imagine the city without these four curving miles of promenade, the shimmering sea so close that boys leap over the low wall, diving straight in. Yet the prospect along the shore does not entirely please. A colony of gawky skyscrapers, Havana's tallest buildings, crowd the western end in contrast to the dignified battlements of Castillo de los Tres Reyes del Morro (commonly known as El Morro) on the eastern promontory. In 1589, when King Phillip II realised how important Havana was for the expansion of his empire, he ordered these mighty fortifications to be built – a forty-year task, employing thousands of engineers, craftsmen and peons.

Havana assumed this important because the treasure fleets, returning from Mexico and Peru, could anchor in this safe, spacious harbour while awaiting naval protection for crossing the Atlantic. By the end of the sixteenth century the fleet usually numbered more than 100 vessels laden with silver, gold and emeralds, cargoes much coveted by pirates. The return voyage normally started in June or July, before the hurricane season, and often the earliest arrivals were moored for months. In 1622 a late start proved disastrous; within a day of sailing from Havana in September, twenty-seven ships were mauled by the season's first hurricane which claimed three treasure galleons and five of their naval escort. Over five hundred men were lost. The fleet's assembling was again delayed in 1623 and a sensible decision to 'winter' in Havana caused panic back home; the Spanish treasury now had to face a second year with a grievously depleted income.

The fleets' crews, recruited from all over the Habsburg territories, put their genetic imprint on Havana's rapidly growing population, as is evident to this day. A number were highly skilled craftsmen, employed on ship-repairs, and many settled in Cuba when the island's vast hardwood forests led to ships being built in Havana for the whole Spanish navy, a major industry until the empire shrank in the early nineteenth century.

The Malecón is a slow ten-minute walk from No.403 and when the younger generations bounced back at noon we set off to swim and picnic. My wailing about the debilitating heat gained no sympathy. 'It's *perfecto!*' said

Rose. 'It's why people come to Cuba in November,' said Rachel. 'Nyanya's like an ice-cream!' Clodagh chuckled sadistically. 'She won't last long in the sun!'

The Trio were fascinated by cigar-smoking men with ample bellies sitting on their thresholds wearing only underpants, and by youths practicing baseball catches with a homemade ball and glove, and by an independent trader bargaining with a woman on a fourth-floor balcony who then let down her roped basket to take delivery of four eggs. The fascination was mutual. This fair-haired, blue-eyed trio brought appreciative, affectionate smiles to every face (even the teenagers') and prompted the wrong guess – 'alemana?' As this situation would regularly recur Rachel and I agreed to identify ourselves, en masse, as 'irlandesa' – easier than explaining that the Trio are half-Irish, quarter-Welsh, quarter-English.

At the Malecón's El Morro end, broken concrete steps lead down to sea-level, to what is euphemistically known as 'the people's beach', a long strip of rough pitted rock, painful to walk on in bare feet and uncomfortable to sit on. This shoreline has one odd feature; at intervals of thirty or forty yards oblong chunks have been carved out of the rock, providing safe bathing pools for children. These are explained in Richard Henry Dana's *To Cuba and Back*, a guide-book (I think the first in English) published in Boston in 1859:

> The Banos de Mar are boxes, each about twelve feet square and six or
> . . . eight feet deep, cut directly into the rock which here forms the sea-
> line which the waves of this tideless shore wash in and out . . . The flow
> and reflow make these boxes very agreeable, and the water, which is
> that of the Gulf Stream, is at a temperature of seventy-two degrees. The
> baths are roofed over, but open for a view towards the sea; and as you
> bathe you see the big ships floating up the Gulf Stream, that great
> highway of the equinoctial world . . . These baths are made at the public
> expense, and are free. Some are marked for women, some for men, and
> some *'por la gente de color'*.

Soon the happily splashing Trio had bonded with a group of con-temporaries. We were the only foreigners around; Havana-based tourists swim off the smooth sands of 'developed' *playas* many miles away. The Trio couldn't understand my not joining them in the warm Atlantic; during summer visits to Ireland they are coaxed into the less warm Blackwater River at least once a day. I tried to explain that to me warm water is what you wash in: a swim should be invigorating. Point not taken . . .

We watched two freighters appearing as smudges on the horizon, coming from opposite directions and traversing the bay until they were so close we could discern their rustiness. Havana's port is still important though no longer as crowded as in Dana's day; then vessels had to manoeuvre for space, before unloading hundreds of passengers and valuable cargoes from Europe and the Americas. Now only a few freighters arrive daily, those from Panama carrying (mainly) Asian-made luxury goods for sale in government dollar-stores to Cuba's nouveau riche. Cheap food for everyone comes from Argentina and Brazil; supplies for tourist hotels, including soap and loo paper, come from the EU.

At sunset the Trio's quintet of friends accompanied us part of the way home, all eight girls trotting in single file along the Malecón's wide wall. Children can vault language barriers with enviable ease. Observing this octet, I was reminded of Rachel, aged five, communicating for hours on end with her Coorgi playmates in a South Indian jungle village.

We were led to Parque Antonio Maceo, a dusty expanse presided over by a famous mulatto general, among the most revered heroes of the nineteenth-century wars of independence. Rachel and I made polite admiring noises. Zea bluntly declared, 'It's boring here, why don't they plant grass?' Rose glared at her little sister and said, 'But that man looks interesting.' The octet agreed to meet again next afternoon.

Returning to No. 403 by a different route we passed a few *puestos* (state-run groceries) which the Trio didn't recognise as shops despite their counters and scales. These dismal places – most shelves bare – come to life only when supplies arrive. Then orderly queues stretch away down the pavement, each citizen equipped with much-used plastic bags and a blue *libreta* (ration book, about the size of an EU passport). The basic rations of rice, beans and eggs may be augmented by pasta, cooking-oil and margarine. But always there is a daily litre of milk for children – now up to the age of seven, pre-Special Period, up to fourteen. Those with spare national pesos may buy meat, fowl, vegetables and fruits at farmers' markets regulated by municipalities.

To Fidel's critics, permanent food-rationing proves how hopelessly Castroism has failed. In fact, feeding all Cubans adequately (except during the worst years of the Special Period) has been one of its most remarkable achievements. In 1950 a World Bank medical team estimated that sixty per cent of Cuba's rural dwellers and forty per cent of urban folk were malnourished. No dependent territory is encouraged to be self-sufficient and Cuba was then importing, mainly from the US, sixty per cent of its grain needs, thirty-seven per cent of vegetables, eighty-four per cent of fats, eighty per cent of tinned fruit, sixty-nine per cent of tinned meat, eighty-three per cent of biscuits and sweets. Hunger greatly strengthened popular support for the Revolution. The US embargo, established in response to the revolution, caused dire food shortages until the rationing system, established on 12 March 1962, ensured that no family would go hungry. In Julio Garcia Luis's words, 'Fidel was determined not to allow the law of money and of supply and demand to be imposed, but to ensure justice'.

When my body clock woke me at 2.00 a.m. I read Fidel's *My Early Years*, then at 6.45 strolled alone to the Malecón.

Below El Morro a freighter was emerging from the port, huge and clumsy-looking, vandalising the dusky blue of the dawn as its funnel trailed thick blackness. Already fishermen were sitting at appropriate intervals along the wall, singly or in pairs, watching their bobbing baits. They used only reels; rods are luxury items. As the sun rose through a shoal of rosy cloudlets the sea swiftly changed from a pellucid green to silver-blue. But why so few birds? I associate Atlantic coasts with ornithological abundance. That afternoon, in a Malecón bar, I was told, 'We ate them all, in the early '90s – so they know to keep away from us!' Perhaps a Tale for Tourists? Or perhaps not: that Period was *very* Special . . .

Back at No. 403 the Trio were breakfasting off multiple fresh fruits, Candida's fluffy omelettes, crusty golden bread warm from the neighbourhood baker, imported butter, lashings of mango jam made by Pedro and large glasses of hot honeyed milk with a dash of coffee. *Casa particulares* serve much better food, in both quantity and quality, than even the five-star hotels. But such meals are comparatively expensive so Rachel and I opted for national-pesos breakfasts, eaten in the nearby Fe del Valle Park. Havana's largest department store, El Encanto, once stood on this site. The park is named in memory of a woman who died here when CIA saboteurs set fire to the store two days before the Bay of Pigs invasion in April 1961.

Clodagh, my room-mate, complained after breakfast – holding her nose – about Nyanya's smelly trainers. I assured her that I meant to replace them, ASAP, with strong open sandals. But first I must change euros.

Candida escorted me to the nearest *Cambio*, warning me on the way about *jineterismo*, an unsurprising phenomenon of which she plainly felt ashamed. *Jineteras* and *jineteros* cultivate tourists met in the street, the former offering bodies, the latter offering half-price cigars (some stolen, some counterfeit) or cheap rooms to rent. (Some householders employ touts because by not registering as *casa particulares* they avoid tax). *Jineterismo* evolves wherever tourists congregate in the Majority World but Castroism sees it as a betrayal of the Revolution, and for Cubans – though not for their foreign friends – the penalties tend to be unduly harsh. My enquiries about specific cases met with evasions or contradictory responses.

The *Cambio* lurked in one corner of a dusty, twilit emporium to which national-peso-priced clothing and footwear were irregularly delivered. By the door stood a security guard, uniformed but apparently unarmed, who closely observed every currency exchange. (On later occasions, when I was alone, he insisted that before leaving the premises I must tuck my new wad of convertible pesos somewhere inaccessible.) Candida advised me to convert some convertible pesos to national pesos as foreigners were now allowed to use both, though hard currencies could not directly buy national pesos. Confining tourists to the convertible-peso economy had proved too complicated and not really worth the effort, since few tourists are tempted by what national pesos can buy.

Shopping in Cuba – even in Havana – has to be a hit or miss affair given the erratic supply of all goods. Three meagrely stocked shoe-shops on Centro's main business streets offered only fragile high-heeled sandals (gold or pink), made in China. 'You'll have to go barefoot,' threatened Clodagh. But it was fourth time lucky: the manager of a small shop was unpacking a consignment of sturdy brown leather sandals made in Brazil, price CP21. 'Now you can give your trainers to some poor person,' said Clodagh. But in Cuba there are no people poor enough to make such a malodorous donation acceptable. Moreover, those trainers had both monetary and sentimental value: I had bought them for US$60 in Severobaiskal, my favourite Siberian town. Granted, they were distressingly unsuited to a hot humid climate but I reckoned they might well outlive me and should be left with our winter garments in No. 403 for collection on the way home.

A quest for fruits and peanuts took us to Vedado. (Rachel is a fruit and nut case and has passed that condition on to her children.) Walking the length of commercial Neptuno, we noted that each dollar-store employed two or three unsmiling security men with 'SECSA' emblazoned on their brown uniforms – SECSA being a newish organisation set up to guard banks, *Cambios*, dollar-stores and other repositories of wealth. In Russia, super- and hyper-markets employ their equivalents, bearing side-arms and looking even less smiley as they peer into the shopping-bags of all departing customers. It seems consumerism has become so febrile citizens may no longer be trusted to acquire only what they can pay for.

In a covered market crowds jostled around trestle tables piled with fruit and vegetables – the produce of Cuba's celebrated *organoponicos*, of which more anon. A recent drought had limited the variety available in November; greens were scarce and the Trio lamented mangoes being out of season. Through piped rumbas one could hear the clattering of weights in antique scales and the good-humoured banter of buyers and sellers, the former scornfully identifying defects, the latter denying or justifying them. Two juicy pineapples cost NP30, a large lush papaya NP15 and very many short fat bananas NP1 apiece. Cleft sticks held squares of cardboard on which all prices were clearly chalked and nobody attempted to overcharge us, here or elsewhere. Instead, the girls each received a gift banana.

By chance we found ourselves in one of Vedado's most attractive quarters, near the university. Here, at the turn of the twentieth century, many prominent families built new homes in a ferment of architectural eclecticism and planted magnificent trees – some eminently climbable, irresistible to the Trio. While watching them ascend to giddy heights Rachel and I sat on the pavement scoffing bananas. (From amidst the foliage an invisible Rose shouted 'Don't eat them all!') Behind us loomed a neo-classical mansion, its stucco flakey, cardboard patching its stained-glass window, squat big-belly palms – less common than the royal palm – lining its garden path. Across the street small children were making merry in their kindergarten, the deep verandah and wide lawn of a recently restored Gaudiesque villa. Studying them, we agreed that Cuba's variety of skin shades, and countless combinations and permutations of racial features, make official statistics seem absurd. Who came up with the 'fact' that in 2000 the population was fifty-one per cent Mulatto, thirty-seven per cent White, eleven per cent Black? And what about the missing one per cent? Are they the unrecorded descendents of Cuba's indigenous inhabitants? Or those Chinese who have resisted miscegenation ever since their a hundred and twenty-five thousand or so ancestors arrived as indentured labourers between 1852 and 1874? We also agreed that, aesthetically, the dominant Iberian/African mix has been a sensational success.

Clearing my eyes of sweat, I looked at my watch: 10.50, beer-time for those who rise before dawn – and Rachel, succumbing to Havana's aura, rather fancied a daiquiri. The Trio grumbled slightly on being brought down to earth but were cheered by the mention of Coppelia where they could gorge on ice-creams after we had attended to our alcohol levels. During the descent to La Rampa I recalled that the name Vedado ('prohibited') dates back to the sixteenth century when all construction was forbidden on this slope overlooking the Straits of Florida. Platoons of sentinels were permanently on duty and needed to see the frequently approaching pirates as soon as possible.

In an al fresco bar a dilatory waiter took our order and when the Trio began to roam restlessly Mummy registered guilt about their delayed gratification while Nyanya spoke up for Adult Rights.

It seems socialism brings out the worst in architects – witness the Coppelia emporium, designed by Mario Girona and built in 1966 in the middle of a park that must, until then, have been a blessed antidote to Nuevo Vedado's brash skyscrapers. Constructed mainly of reinforced concrete, it is topped by a single monstrous slab supporting a truncated cone. The six colossal circular ice-cream parlours on the upper floor are subdivided by naked concrete girders – grey and gloomy, seeming to belong beneath a motorway – and by pointlessly placed partitions of tinted glass. The *habaneros* are very proud of this excrescence, the first (and most bizarre) of a chain of Coppelias; all are open twelve hours a day, six days a week, serving affordable ice-cream of the finest *gelato* quality to the general public. In Havana a daily average of thirty-thousand addicts queue happily for hours, without shade. Latterly, however, the Coppelia ideal, like many others, has been tarnished; near the main entrance a small queue-free annex caters for convertible-peso users.

During our fifty-minute wait the naval officer standing behind me (home on a week's leave) spoke of his favourite ports, Murmansk not among them. That led on to the Cuban/Russian relationship when thousands of Soviet troops were stationed on the island for more than twenty-five years. Dryly Nestor said that there had been no relationship; the Soviets kept to themselves, importing their own food and entertainment (if any) and apparently remaining immune to Cuba's charms. I wondered if they were obeying orders or simply found Cubans uncongenial? The latter, Nestor thought – because occasionally groups of Central Asians did venture out to their local Casa de la Trovo. Privately I reflected that the average Russian's deep-seated racism, impervious for seventy years to Marxist egalitarianism, must have inhibited social (if not sexual) intercourse. This suspicion was confirmed later by visits to areas where the Soviets had had bases and left bad memories.

Military precision marks the organising of Coppelia's hordes. Neatly uniformed stewardesses/sergeant-majors stand at strategic points, counting the departing customers, then beckon an equal number to replace them. Should five leave together, and the first five in the queue include only one member of a group of friends, that group must either separate or give way to those behind them. No one seemed to object to this regimentation. But I (otherwise conditioned) felt exasperated when a security guard forbade me to sit on the ledge of nearby railings. Momentarily I was tempted to pull up my trouser leg to show him what long queues in hot weather can do to varicose veins.

Once admitted to the high globe we were directed to a table and Rachel had to join two other queues – to pay for the docket listing our order, then to hand it to a server from whom a waitress soon after took our tray. The Trio pronounced that these gargantuan ice-creams were very good indeed, well worth waiting for – and they, being residents of Italy, are connoisseurs.

Not far from Coppelia we noticed a plaque identifying the site where Fidel first labelled the Revolution 'Socialist' – on 16 April 1961, the eve of the US-sponsored Bay of Pigs invasion.

Surprisingly, the Cubans have no regular siesta-time but that afternoon the younger generations rested briefly while I refuelled in what was to become my favourite Malecón café. Small and shabby, approached by a shaky wooden step-ladder, it was dual-currency; Cubans paid for drinks and one-course meals in national pesos, convertible pesos were expected from foreigners.

Miguel, the manager-cum-barman, kept Hatuey beer, brewed for the national-peso market, under the counter and filled the fridge with Buccanero and Kristal, favoured by tourists. The price difference was slight – NP18 and CP1 – yet my wish to sample Hatuey worried Miguel; he would get into trouble should a snooper from the local Committee for the Defence of the Revolution (CDR) chance to notice a tourist drinking Hatuey on the premises. I could however have lots of Hatuey to take away, concealed in my knapsack. Thus I discovered that this brew is less palatable than the tourists', though equally potent.

On my first visit, the previous day, Miguel had been discussing Wilma with a hurricane-damage inspector. The café, raised above the street, had escaped flooding though it lost one side of its roof – quickly replaced by the municipality. Now his three-roomed home, behind the café at pavement-level, was the problem: a waist-deep torrent had swept through, ruining all the family's possessions. He had a pregnant wife and three-year-old twins yet the authorities were being slow to act. When the inspector had left Miguel glanced around at the only other customers – two young couples in far corners – then confided, sotto voce, 'For the government this place makes tax money, a little home doesn't. In times before – before '92 – all little homes soon got fixed.'

In January I was to hear about Miguel's uncle-sponsored migration to Florida; otherwise I wouldn't feel free to record that conversation.

In some quarters the CDR (Committees for the Defence of the Revolution) have a bad reputation as groups of spies and bullies, ever ready to punish those who fail to uphold Revolutionary standards. While this may not be a baseless slander, it is certainly a wild over-simplification. When Fidel invented the system in 1960 he meant it to affect everyone's daily life as an important instrument of civil defence and socialist reform. The president (unpaid) of each CDR is responsible for three hundred or so citizens (a barrio) and it is his or her duty to find out how people earn their money, what they spend it on, who does or does not march in demos, who is absent from home, where they have gone and why and for how long. We instantly recoil from such a system. Yet whether people are for or against Fidel it seems to be generally agreed that Castroism could not have been so quickly and firmly established, and made to work so well, without the CDR's energetic observing, organising and persuading (or bullying) of their barrios.

Nowadays, out of some eleven million Cubans, at least three million are CDR members, an influential percentage of the adult population. As the state's most significant mass organisation, the CDR is involved in all Public Health campaigns, in school enrollment and attendance, in the National Bank's saving campaign, in arranging barrio study seminars, in checking the quality of services in local shops and reporting defects to the managers, and as crucial links between municipalities and barrios. (That last function helps to sustain Cuba's vibrant version of participatory democracy.)

CDR presidents collaborate closely with the police and can in certain circumstances protect barrio members from over-zealous policing – or, conversely, expose them to it. A minority of presidents are themselves 'counter-revolutionary' and break laws while using their power to silence any who might report them. Much (too much) hinges on the individual president's character. A minority are so dreaded that their barrios feel permanently at war with them. Others are so well-liked and trusted that people go to them with their troubles, emotional or economic. Most are genuinely public-spirited, do their snooping as discreetly as possible and are accepted as an integral part of Castroism.

Early next morning, on our way to 'do' Old Havana, we paused in Fe del Valle Park to watch *ti' chi* enthusiasts (including our host Pedro) being put through their paces by a stern mulatto whose Chinese genes were obvious. Havana has many action-packed corners. On the park's far side primary schoolchildren were having a martial arts lesson, to the Trio's envy.

Pre-Revolution, guide-books described San Rafael's short (pedestrians only) business end as 'elegant'. Now it was being spruced up to include it in the tourist zone, and a central row of unhappy-looking potted shrubs decorated its newly paved length. Formerly fashionable emporiums were being restored by workmen balancing on wobbly scaffolding or demolishing interior walls with sledge-hammers – and without any of the protective gear mandatory in our wimpish world. Two stores had been reopened, on Cuba's emergence from the Special Period, as government-run dollar-shops selling a narrow though gradually widening range of expensive (for Cubans) but usually shoddy imported goods. Others remained boarded up or displayed only a few items of unappealing national-peso-priced stock in fly-blown windows.

For me, Old Havana was a mixed experience. One can agree with UNESCO's 1982 declaration that, as the largest and architecturally richest colonial centre in Latin America, it is part of 'the cultural heritage of humanity'. But most such declarations have dire side-effects. La Habana Vieja is now among the Tourist Board's main assets, second only to the 'developed' beaches, and it grieved me to see young black women in flouncy colonial costumes offering to read fortunes while elderly women, similarly attired, posed beneath porticoed arcades, smoking giant cigars, their placards saying – 'Foto CP1'. A laughing boy, aged perhaps five, was nimbly dancing in a doorway on Calle Obispo, his father on guard against the tourist police but grateful for whatever the child might earn. A pair of slender adolescent girls, wearing bikini tops and leaning over the photogenic balcony of their semi-derelict mansion, shouted and waved at us and suggested 'Camera?' The bands playing near open-air cafés, then passing a sombrero around, were as skilled as Cuban musicians are expected to be but performances aimed at tourists tend to have a sad unspontaneous quality. Prostitution comes in different forms. When 'being Cuban' becomes in itself a tourist attraction, what happens to the Cuban psyche? Cuzco, Bali, Khatmandu, Ladakh and too many other places know the answer.

We made the most of our national pesos, buying from pavement entrepreneurs shots of hot strong sweet coffee, glasses of cold freshly squeezed fruit juices and ice-cream cones for NP1 each. Ham and/or cheese rolls, warm from the baker and generously filled, cost NP5 and substantial home-made pizzas (but the queues were long) NP10 to NP15. Outside tourist restaurants we studied menus and calculated that the most meagre meal for one, minus drinks, would cost NP260 – CP10.

Throughout much of Old Havana motor vehicles are forbidden or restricted and generally Cuba's acute oil shortage (now being eased by Venezuela) has had a benign effect. In 1992 half a million bicycles were imported from China, just as that country was foolishly planning to replace two wheels with four. Then bicycle rickshaws ('bicitaxis') were introduced and at once became popular. Another novelty, for the benefit of tourists who are not supposed to use bicitaxis (though some do) is peculiar to Havana: a small fleet of canary-yellow three-seater covered scooters ('cocotaxis'). Ciclobuses, too, are an innovation, copied from Miami; these can carry several bicycles in metal containers, fore and aft. In contrast are the famous *camellos*, comically humped mega-buses serving distant suburbs; these carry 300 passengers in theory and more than four hundred in practice – including adherents to the outside.

Away from the sea, the Trio showed little interest in Havana, being too young to be excited by its architectural glories, its web of historical associations or its proliferating political question marks. They had long been looking forward to stamina-testing expeditions so now it seemed only fair to move on to the undeveloped (so far) Oriente coast.

Candida and Pedro were adamant that a train journey, our preferred option, would involve cruelty to children. We must do it the tourist way, in a comfortable overnight Viazul coach to Santiago de Cuba. Like most *casa particulares* hostesses, Candida repeatedly exerted herself for her guests beyond the call of duty. Having rung the Viazul office to book our seats, she organised a cut-price taxi to the terminus and arranged for us to lodge in Santiago with her old friend Irma.

Chapter 3

Capital cities and 'the next biggest' tend not to love one another: London and Birmingham, Rome and Milan, Dublin and Cork, Havana and Santiago. Doubtless social anthropologists (maybe psychologists too?) have secured lavish grants to study this phenomenon but in the Cuban case one needs only to know a little history. Santiago was founded as the capital of Spain's new island colony – a very long time ago, but Santiago hasn't forgotten.

When Diego Velazquez de Cuellar came upon a desirable natural port at the foot of gold- and copper-bearing mountains, conveniently close to Jamaica and Hispaniola, he at once set up a central trading station, named it after Spain's patron saint and gave it 'capital' status. That was in 1515. A few decades later when Spain had extracted eighty-four thousand ounces of gold, failing seams put Santiago's importance at risk. So did increasingly audacious pirates – and Nature. After a series of devastating earthquakes Cuba's Governor, Gonzalo Perez de Angulo, moved his head-quarters to Havana, just in time to miss the 1554 sacking and capture of Santiago by French privateers. Their mini-fleet had been able to take the town so easily because of peninsular/creole tensions, already common throughout Spanish America. Santiago's governor, Pedro de Morales, distrusted the local creole militia and, while he dithered about deploying them, his small Spanish-born garrison was overwhelmed. All governors, administrators and regular troops had to be *peninsulares*, most of whom saw creoles as a lesser breed. This uneasy relationship was to colour Cuba's history, often with blood-stains, until Spain handed the island over to the US in 1898.

In 1620 Cuba's total population was less than 7,000, in 1650 it hardly exceeded 30,000. The island attracted few settlers while Spain's continental conquests promised bigger bucks faster. Until the 1760s not many slaves were imported: an annual average of 240 between 1511 and 1762, if we can depend on El Escorial's figures.

The multinational swarms of pirates and privateers who threatened shipping routes for so long resembled modern 'terrorists' in one respect – they occupied a grey area. One monarch's pirate might be another's privateer. To Phillip II, Francis Drake was unquestionably a pirate. Yet in

1570, before his first voyage to the Caribbean, Elizabeth I gave him 'a regular privateering commission'. All privateers were licensed by their governments who appreciated, when war broke out, having privately owned and provisioned ships to reinforce the national navy. (Never mind that those owners invariably ran extensive smuggling operations, usually detrimental to their government's trading. In that respect they were analogous to such twenty-first-century mercenary armies as Blackwater.)

The Governor of Cuba's first duty was to protect the empire's loot from both foreign pirates and creole freelance traders (aka smugglers). Therefore it was decreed, in 1558, that all commerce must go through Havana's port and Santiago dwindled to thirty households. But a generation later its revival began when Cuba was bisected. In military matters the Governor of Havana retained control over the whole island, otherwise the province of Oriente was to enjoy virtual independence under Santiago's jurisdiction. Oriente then incorporated the modern provinces of Guantanamo, Holguin, Las Tunas, Granma and Santiago.

When the defence of Havana became Spain's priority, Cuba's unguarded coastline, fretted with countless small natural harbours, developed into a buccaneers' paradise. Throughout the Hispano-English war (1585–1603) creole cattle ranches and sugar mills were regularly raided. Also, barter flourished; disloyal creoles living hundreds of roadless miles from Havana were delighted to form cordial trading relationships with the empire's foes, exchanging meat and hides for European luxury goods and African slaves.

Oliver Cromwell caused a demographic upheaval when he sailed on to the Caribbean scene in 1655. (He was good at that, as we Irish have reason to remember.) This expedition, to take both Santo Domingo and Cuba, formed part of his 'Western Design' which had to be modified after the Spaniards' successful defence of Santo Domingo. The fifty-five somewhat battered English ships, plus transport vessels carrying considerably fewer than the original 9,000 soldiers, prudently forgot Cuba and set sail for tiny, almost undefended Jamaica. Its seizure served as Cromwell's consolation prize and caused some 10,000 wealthy planters to flee to Oriente, more than doubling its population overnight.

By 1768 Cuba's population had risen to (approximately) a hundred and ten thousand whites, seventy-two thousand slaves, twenty-three thousand free blacks; some of those whites were almost certainly mulatto though not yet named as such. After Haiti's 1791 revolution, thousands of French refugee-planters arrived, complete with slaves and the latest technology.

Most of those refugees invested lavishly in cane growing which became very big business – much too big – for Cuba's future welfare.

In 1662 a fleet of twelve English ships, captained by Christopher Myngs and carrying 2,000 soldiers, easily captured Santiago, sacked the town, demolished the harbour's fortress by blowing up its powder magazine – and then withdrew. This show of force achieved both its objectives by demonstrating that Jamaica would remain an English possession and forging a Santiago-Jamaica trade link. Spain could do nothing to hinder the brisk 'informal' trade in copper, sugar and slaves that soon developed to the mutual benefit of Oriente and Jamaica.

Thus Santiago evolved as a predominantly creole city, resentful of any peninsulare-directed meddling in its commercial affairs. Oriente men led all Cuba's nineteenth-century wars of independence and around Santiago battles were frequent. Many Oriente *campesiños* supported Fidel's guerrillas as they fought the US- and UK-armed troops of Cuba's military dictator, the mulatto Fulgencio Batista Zaldivar. With some justification, Santiago proudly describes itself as the 'the cradle of the Revolution'.

As some of my readers will be aware, I'm not an urban person. Shortly after arriving in a city – any city, however historical, beautiful or politically intriguing – my mind strays towards the exit. So why (I asked myself in the taxi to Viazul) did Havana not have the same effect? Was it because the *habaneros* behave more like villagers than like urban dwellers? I looked forward to spending longer among them on my solo return.

The Viazul terminus has an airport taint. Glossy coffee-table volumes of scenic photographs fill the little bookstall, unappealing souvenirs gather dust in display cases, revolving stands show postcards (printed in Italy) of stereotypical Cuban activities. Spaced-out processed passengers sit in mute orderly rows while new arrivals queue to have each item of luggage weighed, labelled and pushed away on trolleys. Another queue ensures a seat number chit so skimpy one has to concentrate hard on not losing it. From corners, impassive anti-*jineterismo* police watch over all. Our Oriente journeys would, we hoped, be very different – and they were . . .

Many of our fellow-passengers being Cuban surprised me; Viazul was initiated for tourists only. Cuba's sudden dependence on foreigners' hard currency agitated Fidel, who fantasised about protecting Revolutionary standards behind what came to be derided as 'tourism apartheid'. No relevant law existed, yet from 1992–97 Cubans seen in conversation with tourists were often reprimanded and occasionally arrested. Then, a few months before the papal visit of January 1998, the official mood abruptly changed and normal relations became possible. Yet the 'apartheid' policy hasn't sunk without trace. Quite a few Cubans, especially in the provinces, remain uncertain about how they should react to unpackaged foreigners.

Soon after a punctual departure at 6.15 p.m., the Trio were sound asleep and as Rachel studied our map, planning treks, I watched the crimson sun sinking towards a frieze of royal palms and distant factory stacks. Havana's twentieth-century accretions cover many miles and offer nothing distinctively Cuban, apart from numerous Ché Guevara portraits on gable ends and huge wayside hoardings exhorting the citizenry to do their bit to keep the Revolution on course.

As early as the 1930s Cuba was an exception in Latin America, most Cubans being city-dwellers. When tourism's possibilities attracted many more to the capital, Fidel began to have nightmares about mushrooming shanty-towns threatening public health yet he dared not put the hungry Cubans on too tight a rein by forbidding 'change of residence'. April 1997 saw a compromise, a new law restricting job-seekers to one-month absences from their native place: thus, at intervals, all would have a chance to earn a few convertible pesos.

On Cuba's Central highway, built in the 1930s and well maintained, the traffic was light. At 10.15 we parked outside an imitation of a US fast-foodery on the edge of an anonymous town. Here most passengers supped and I sauntered to and fro with an earnest young Australian journalist, tanned and long-limbed and puzzled by Cuba. How come so many *habaneros* were so jolly and welcoming when they were so *deprived*? On the bus he'd been scribbling a list – most couldn't afford *essentials* like cosmetics, detergents, deodorants, nappies, vitamin supplements, shampoo, hair dryers, toasters, electric kettles, cell phones, computers. He loved Cubans, was upset by all those missing essentials, was keen to promote the tourist industry. At the end of a very hot day I had no energy to spare for argument – beyond asking why, given Caribbean sunshine, Cubans should need hair-dryers? (Come to think of it, why should anybody, apart from the manufacturers? For millennia we've been drying our hair without technological assistance.)

Later I reproved myself for not having tried to educate that young man. He had been commissioned to write a series of articles on 'Cuba in Transition' and, as climate change works its way up the political agenda, journalists should be emphasising Cuba's energy-saving habits. Little things do count. When one buys a homemade fruit juice from a pavement seller it comes in a glass to be handed back – not in a 'disposable' mug to be tossed into a litter-bin (or on to the verge). The sheer enormity of 'climate change' deters us from thinking about such minutiae although, cumulatively, they're at the core of the problem.

Throughout the long night I envied my sleeping companions. As grey-ness replaced blackness, low humps replaced flatness – the Sierra Maestra foothills. Now the Trio were awake and hungry and thirsty. Promptly their ever-ready mother provided oranges, nuts and water while I furtively opened a tin of Buccanero – but not furtively enough to avoid Zea's informing the general public, 'Nyanya's having beer for breakfast!'

An extravagant sunrise celebrated our arrival, all gold and crimson, surging upwards from the horizon to fill half the sky. In Santiago's suburbs tropical vegetation almost overwhelmed the solid little tiled houses. Fiacres drawn by smartly trotting horses were taking people to work – or *towards* work, because these vehicles are excluded from the narrow Old City streets.

A dozen taxis, parked at random outside the lucrative Viazul terminus, competed for emerging passengers by playing jolly tunes on their horns. Most were government-registered, their takings therefore taxed quite heavily. We chose an unregistered veteran, bright red where it wasn't rusty. 'Cadillac 1954!' boasted its beaming black owner as he packed our ruck-sacks into the boot where chicken-wire replaced the lost floor.

As we drove uphill Rachel, pointing left, exclaimed, 'There's the Moncada barracks!' Moments later Rose, pointing right, exclaimed, 'They've a Coppelia here, in that park!' Beyond this wide, busy boulevard one descends to the quiet, sloping streets and alleyways of the Old City.

Discreet lògos mark *casa particulares* and No. 197 San Pedro was easy to find, a single-storey late eighteenth-century home, washed pale blue, its finely carved double door opening off the street and protected by an elaborate wrought-iron grill. We were welcomed by Candida's friend Irma – sixtyish, blessed by the sort of bone-structured beauty that changes but never fades, looking elegant in a house-coat. She hugged us on first sight, as is the Cuban way, then led us through a short hallway into a spacious drawing-room, rarely used, where the burnished mahogany furniture was nineteenth-century imperial and the high ceiling, of collar-and-beam trusses, had been copied, we later realised, from Casa Diego Velasquez. Here dozens of frighteningly valuable china ornaments were displayed on window ledges, in wall niches and corner cabinets, on numerous frail occasional tables. They ranged from tiny figurines of courting couples to ornate jugs, tall slim vases, dogs sitting and lying, transparent coffee sets, delicate floral bouquets, birds perched on branches and angels perched on clouds. Urgently I warned the Trio – 'Never *run* through this room!'

In the patio, cooled by much potted greenery, life-size plaster statues of a smiling black couple wore nineteenth-century cane-cutters' attire. On three sides stretched long corridors tiled and pillared, their walls replete with stags' heads. Our accommodation took us aback: two enormous bedrooms, each 'en suite' with two double-beds, bedside lamps, a large fridge and efficient (unless the electricity went off) standard fans. One motive for our journey had been to introduce the Trio to another way of life and this was another way in the wrong direction – incomparably more luxurious than their own spartan home near the top of a mountain in the Dolomites. However, the water supply was sluggish at best, non-existent at worst and the electrical fittings – mostly in unexpected places – made sounds not normally associated with plugs and switches.

The Trio devoured their four-course breakfast in a long narrow dining-room across the patio from our bedrooms. This was also the family living-room where Irma and Antonio watched TV in the evenings, seeming genuinely interested in what Fidel (or Ricardo Alarcón, his possible successor) had to say. In the nearby kitchen, from early morning, Irma's two daily helps were busy – both black, we noticed, as was Candida's cleaning lady. But those relationships were free of any whiff of 'mistress and servant', the women addressing one another as 'compañera'.

On the way to Parque Cespedes Rose noted approvingly, 'Here's much cleaner than Havana'. She was right, Santiago's municipality is either better funded or better managed than Havana's (or both).

Zea observed, 'It's too much hotter than Havana! Why?' The adults didn't know why – maybe something to do with the nearby mountains?

Clodagh scrutinised my face and exclaimed, 'Look at Nyanya's sweat! She's leaving drips behind her on the ground!'

Parque Cespedes (originally, and more accurately, Plaza de Armas) is Cuba's first town square, a space left free of buildings for the convenience of the military, and never encroached upon over four centuries. But would those sixteenth-century town planners recognise it today? Trim shrubs surround neat little flower beds, a few trees provide inadequate shade and as we arrived the grey and red flagstones were being thoroughly swept with grass brooms. While the Trio romped Rachel and I, feeling Viazul-lagged, shared the sparse shade of palms with Carlos Cespedes on his pedestal. 'They're like a litter of puppies,' I remarked, 'the energy seems limitless.' 'Who are you telling!' rejoined their mother.

On all sides stood buildings so often photographed I almost felt I'd been here before. The sonorously named Catedral de Nuestra Senora de la Asuncion, built in 1922 on four-hundred-year-old foundations, has quite a pleasing neo-classical façade but can't compete with Casa de Diego Velazquez. This Andalusia-flavoured stone building has a fortress-like solidity, relieved by many Moorish gratings, and wooden lattice-work shutters and balconies. It took fourteen years (1516–30) to build, as the conquistador's official residence, and in 1965 was intelligently restored. Santiago presents it as Cuba's oldest surviving residence, a claim contested by Havana though it seems not implausible. Less convincing is Santiago's assertion that Velazquez's bones lie beneath the cathedral.

On the Park's west side rises the dazzling white four-storey Hotel Casa Granda, a tourist base since 1920, agreeably conforming to Cuba's eclectic style of colonial architecture. The blue and white Ayuntamiento (Town Hall), simple and dignified, was built in 1950 to replace an earthquake victim but had been designed two hundred years earlier by an anonymous architect whose drawings were found by chance in the Indies Archive. From its short central balcony, on 1 January 1959, Fidel first spoke to the Cubans as their new (twelve-hours-on-the-job) leader.

It was too early in the day for tourists (at no time were they numerous) but on a bench under a weeping fig tree two youths were sharing a cigarette and, we sensed, measuring us up as a possible source of convertible pesos. One joined us adults while his friend asked the Trio where we were staying and how much paying? When Rachel enquired about the nearest *Cambio* both offered to escort her up steep Calle Aguilera. The Trio stayed with me; they were developing a group allergy to queues.

As we lay under a palm drinking pints of water I told the girls about another Trio, Santiago sisters aged eight, nine and ten, whose ordeal is still remembered because Graham Greene recorded it. One night in 1957, soon after their father had joined Fidel's guerrillas in the nearby mountains, they were lifted from their beds by Batista's soldiers and, still wearing pyjamas, carried off to a military barracks to be held as hostages. In Greene's words:

Next morning I saw the revolution of the children. The news had reached the schools. In the secondary schools the children made their own decision – they left their schools and went on the streets. The news spread. To the infants' schools the parents came and took away their children. The streets were full of them. The shops began to put up their shutters in expectation of the worst. The army gave way and released the three little girls. They could not turn fire hoses on the children in the streets as they had turned them on their mothers, or hang them from lamp posts as they would have hanged their fathers. What seems strange to me was that no report of the children's revolt ever appeared in *Time* – yet their correspondent was there in the city with me. But perhaps Henry Luce had not yet made up his mind between Castro and Batista.

Some of Greene's Santiago contacts – including Armand Hart, later to become Fidel's Minister of Education – were outraged by an arms deal then being negotiated: the sale of British fighter jets to Batista's air force. Back in England, Greene prompted a Labour MP to ask a question which brought from Selwyn Lloyd, the Foreign Secretary, an assurance that no weapon of any grade was being sold to Cuba. Months later, shortly before Batista's defeat, Lloyd was cornered and forced to admit that he had indeed sanctioned the sale of several 'almost-obsolete' planes. Allegedly, when this deal went through Britain's Foreign Secretary hadn't yet heard about Cuba's then two-year-long civil war, though all foreign visitors were being confined to Havana province because everywhere else was 'insecure'. *Our Man in Havana* is not entirely a work of fiction.

Rachel was soon back, having been thwarted by one of Cuba's legendary power-cuts; the *Cambio* couldn't open that day. What did I say earlier about the Computer Age? Previously, currency exchanges could take place with the aid of pen and paper.

When the noon heat forced the Trio and me back to our fan-cooled rooms, for many games of rummy, Rachel visited Cuba's most famous Casa de la Trova on Calle Heredia, a few minutes walk from No. 197.

Later, we went shopping and at first were baffled. As tourists it seemed we couldn't buy bread (easy in Havana) and two *tiendas* denied us water – visible in both fridges. That evening Irma explained; when items are in short supply (delivery problems because of petrol problems) regular customers get preference. Fair enough!

Outside one *tienda* a middle-aged mulatta – diminutive, worried-looking – whispered a request to Rachel for CP 0.45 to buy soap. (The monthly ration is rarely adequate.) Because a policeman stood nearby, and begging from tourists is strictly forbidden, Rachel shook her head and moved on – followed by the woman's angry younger companion (daughter?) whose loud abuse included repetitions of '*Puta!*' (whore).

That sound greatly appealed to the Trio who only reluctantly excluded it from their rapidly expanding Spanish vocabulary.

After sunset, during our Happy (childfree) Hour, Rachel and I agreed that Santiago's blacks being so numerous gives the city a special sort of animation while, for both of us, awakening happy memories of African journeys. It seems Cuba's blacks have preserved their cultural identity more successfully than their US cousins; in general their enslavement happened more recently and they form a much higher percentage of the population. Cuba abolished slavery only in 1886 – the last country to do so.

Before Rachel took off for a night of son, salsa and conga we planned an early morning departure for an undeveloped beach – Playa Siboney, twelve miles east of the city.

In the warehouse-like provincial bus terminus hundreds of passengers sat on rows of metal chairs with their bundles by their feet. We were lucky: behind the building a Siboney bus – a vehicle at the other end of the scale from our Viazul coach – was about to depart. Rushing towards it, we found the doorway blocked by a rotund woman brusquely demanding 'chits'. We assumed she meant tickets – but no, one paid on the bus, chits simply entitled one to board it and were issued free from a distant kiosk. Such Soviet-type procedures are now exposing Castroism to ridicule as Cuban youngsters note, and replicate, foreigners' scorn for bureaucracy gone mad. Anxiously the Trio and I watched the bus loading up: would it disappear before Rachel's return? The rotund one seemed not on our side but the black driver, seeing us peering through the door, waved reassuringly and shouted. 'OK!' Relaxing, Zea commented in a discreet whisper on the fascinating (to her) tyre of bronze flesh protruding between the jacket and trousers of the door-blocker's uniform.

This short juddery bus ride (adults NP1, children free) was the Trio's introduction to how the other nine-tenths travel. Zea sat on Rachel, Clodagh sat on me, Rose stood in the tightly packed aisle unable to see out but as ever uncomplaining. Nor could I see much; the bulky man beside me was embracing a large sack of (judging by the rattle) empty bottles and Clodagh obscured the view ahead. Approaching a junction, our neighbours chorused, 'Siboney! Siboney!' – for our benefit. Out in the fresh air Zea asked, 'Why doesn't Cuba make more buses?'

A mile-long tarred cul-de-sac led from the junction to the sea, winding between forested ridges and level scrubland where large piebald pigs rooted vigorously. Only two horse-buses broke the deep silence. Zea loitered to study tiny black crabs in a stagnant roadside creek, then trotted to catch up, tripped on loose gravel – and we all had to pause to commiserate about grazed knees.

A garish new wayside notice briefly alarmed us: HOLIDAY VILLAGE – VILLA TOURISTICA. But this proved to be a local aspiration far from the agreeable reality of wonky wooden trestle tables and benches under a tattered awning overlooking a mile-long crescent of beach – half-stony, half-sandy, uncluttered by 'amenities', fringed by royal palms, sheltered to the east by sheer black cliffs.

Grandmotherhood can induce character change. Although emphatically not a beach person, I thoroughly enjoyed that day. The Trio were ecstatic, emerging at frequent intervals from the clear green sea to report on the marine life seen through their goggles, then being constructive with sand, then underwater again, then shell collecting, then back to the sea, then climbing the low, strangely contorted sea-grape trees. These, scattered along the beach close to the wavelets, provided the only shade. (That evening I wrote in my journal: 'For how much longer will Siboney survive in its simplicity as a naturally beautiful place of sea, sand, shells and silence?')

We had the *playa* to ourselves until two taxi-loads of university students arrived on an end-of-exams excursion, radiating *joie de vivre*, frolicking on the sand, playing waterpolo, swimming so far out that Zea almost panicked on their behalf. 'Will they be able to swim back? Who can rescue them?'

I was alone when two young English-speakers joined me, introducing themselves with an attractive mix of shyness (the age gap?) and that unbumptious self-confidence which I was beginning to recognise as a common Cuban trait. Rene was white, Luis black, both were medical students in their final year. First came the standard questions – 'Which is your country? You like Cuba? You stay how long? You have self-drive car? You like our beer? Now in this month Ireland is all snow?' Then followed, 'Your grand-daughters are beautiful! Where is your daughter's husband? She is beautiful too, why does he let her away to Cuba?'

When it was my turn I asked, 'Will you specialise? How will you choose your first job? Or does the government place you?'

Yes, as graduates they would go where they were told to go. Both had already volunteered to serve abroad in the Henry Reeves Brigade – but that was away in the future, to qualify they must have ten years experience.

'So we'll be thirty-three,' said Rene, 'and probably married and sensible.'

'That means,' said Luis, 'we must find wives also wanting to join the Brigade.'

Rene laughed, slapped his friend on a powerful naked shoulder and said, 'You're lucky, you've found her already!'

Luis looked bashful, then glanced around and pointed to a lithe mulatta doing her *ti' chi* exercises with three friends. 'There she is, a paediatrician by next year, very much wanting to work in Africa. We'll have two babies, then leave them with our parents. Where we go won't be healthy for children.'

That slightly threw me: would Mum be as happy as Dad if separated from her young for so long? Well, maybe so – Cuba's Revolution has bred people with unusual mind-sets.

Rene and Luis boasted about Cuba's contribution to healthcare in remote deprived regions. WHO, they asserted, sends fewer doctors to such areas. (I checked on that: it's true.) Their expressions hardened as they recalled Hurricane Katrina and the US authorities' ignoring of Cuba's offer to send emergency medical teams to New Orleans. 'But we got thanking messages from a few victims,' said Rene. 'Thanking us for *wanting* to help them.' 'Mostly from black victims,' added Luis. 'They suffered worst, like always in the States.'

Rene said, 'As we're talking here having fun in the sun, hundreds of Cubans are freezing up in the Himalayas where that earthquake hit. The Muslim women are pleased, we've so many women doctors – their men won't let other men go near them. We know Pakistan's government works for the *Yanquis* but you can't blame poor people far up in high mountains for that!'

I asked, 'Why is this brigade named Henry Reeves?'

'Because Fidel's not anti-American,' Rene swiftly replied. 'He's not hating ordinary people who must live under criminal governments.'

Luis was more explicit. 'Henry Reeves came from the States in 1869 with other young Americans, to fight with us against Spain. He fought for seven years, got many times badly wounded, kept on fighting, died in a battle. You can see his name on a monument in Havana. Fidel wants us to remember Americans like him. And we do. Tourists from the States all say they feel welcome. They see we don't think they're bad because their government punishes the Revolution. We pity them. And we like the way they trust us, not listening to propaganda saying "communist Cubans hate Americans!" Like Rene said, Fidel tells us *people* are different from *governments*. That day those twin towers were hit, before sunset thousands of Cubans donated blood for New Yorkers.'

The young men offered to show us around the university next morning and suggested 10.00 a.m. But they broke our appointment. Elsewhere, I was to have a few similar experiences with young Cubans spontaneously eager to befriend the foreigner, then thinking better of it – perhaps because someone in authority would disapprove?

By early afternoon the sun had become dangerous, especially for the fair-skinned Trio. On a bluff above the beach we found a friendly, simple convertible-peso restaurant, its half-dozen tables shaded by a towering mango tree. While I attended to my dehydration problem and Rachel sipped daiquiris the Trio stuffed themselves with rice, chicken and grated raw carrot.

Just below us, across the narrow road, a licensed free-standing butcher's stall was surrounded by stray dogs – all pathetically emaciated, to the Trio's distress. Slowly a man cycled into view, towing a bullock's skinned hindquarters and unskinned head in a homemade trailer, on six baby-buggy wheels. Post-Soviet necessity has mothered many inventions centred on the bicycle. The thud of the butcher's cleaver brought men, women and children hastening to the stall, bearing dishes, bowls, pots or pans.

'What will he do with the head?' wondered Zea. 'Hang it on a wall?' suggested Clodagh. 'There's the tongue!' exclaimed Rose, pointing over our balustrade. 'He's selling it all to our waiter friend here, for the restaurant.'

On the way back, seeking to escape the heat-reflecting tarmac, we walked on the verge – a bad idea. Within that grass lurked vicious little thorny burrs which caused much grief when embedded in small feet.

Transport-wise, we were having a lucky day: as the junction came in sight so did a Santiago-bound bus. The younger generations galloped towards it, Nyanya cantering in the rear and Rachel yelling – 'Wait for the granny!' Which it did.

By day three, Rose and Clodagh were familiar enough with the city centre, and at ease enough with Cuba, to move around alone if need be – to return to the loo at No. 197, or be despatched to buy water or, in Rose's case, to linger over the choosing of postcards. Not having to go everywhere as a pack was rather a relief. That evening Rachel and I realised that neither of us had thought for a moment of the 'security' factor. Later I heard about the Mexican wife of a retiring diplomat who pleased her Cuban friends by bursting into tears at a farewell party – because in Havana her children could be let loose to play all day with other children and they wouldn't understand being imprisoned back home . . .

A steep narrowish street of two- or three-storey colonial houses descends to the old market hall, a massive stone building with a wide, curving flight of steps and a high arched entrance, suggesting the approach to some grandee's palace. Inside are two long halls with vaulted roofs, one dedicated to meat, fish, poultry and eggs, the other to fruit and vegetables. We found many counters bare – because of the drought, said Irma. Here were pyramids of oranges – small, green, dry – and good quality bananas, woody dwarf tomatoes, piles of pale brown dried beans, almost identical piles of coffee, ropes of onions and garlic, trays of huge papayas, some cut and sculpted with flies buzzing around their juicy crimson-gold flesh – but no greenery of any sort. The cheerful traders (as many men as women, unlike Africa) welcomed the foreigners, admired the Trio, poked friendly fun at Rachel's Spanish, apologised for having no pineapples, carefully chose for us the least dry oranges and the ripened-to-perfection papayas and advised us to avoid the tomatoes. This was shopping as it should be, human beings relating to one another, 'consumer choice' limited by local circumstances.

Continuing downhill to the waterfront we were greeted by householders sitting on their doorsteps, some men mending shoes or spectacles or trying to heal ailing trannies, some women sewing children's garments or cleaning rice, extracting tiny bits of foreign matter. (Very foreign, all the way from Vietnam.)

The seafront promenade, laid out in the 1840s for the delectation of the local nobility, is low on the list of Santiago's tourist attractions. For some two miles it runs wide and straight between the murky waters of a listless port and a row of tall, grim-looking commercial buildings. A pedestrian walkway bisects this thoroughfare, its line of straggly trees half-shading a few seats in urgent need of repair. At one end is the horse-bus 'terminus', under an ancient ceiba tree, and these long carriages far outnumber motor vehicles. The Trio's suggesting a ride in one caused a slight contretemps between their elders. Horse-buses operate within the national-peso economy and are not licensed to carry tourists. (Havana's tastefully decorated nineteenth-century two-wheelers have special licences.) However, one driver volunteered to break the law for CP5; his four-wheeled twelve-seater was drawn by a large mule and a small horse and had an insecure canvas awning. Rachel then argued that large groups were awaiting transport and it didn't seem fair for us to jump that queue. I saw her point, but I also saw those three hopeful little faces. We compromised. I'd go with the girls, Zea could sit on my lap, we wouldn't be hogging the bus, its driver could have our CP5 (big bucks for him) plus half a national peso from nine others. We waved goodbye to Rachel – still looking disapproving – and trotted off on the sandy equine lane that runs parallel to the tarmac.

Soon it was the Trio's turn to disapprove. Whenever the team's pace slackened they were whipped – just a flick, nothing excessive, but Clodagh muttered, 'He shouldn't beat them!' Rose concurred – 'We're a heavy load, they're doing their best!' Zea said, 'It's very hot, are they thirsty?'

To take everyone's mind off animal welfare I gave them a brief history lesson, pointing to the bay where something hugely important happened on 3 July 1898. As the Spanish fleet sailed out of the harbour it was immediately attacked and sunk by the US navy – and that marked the end of the Spanish Empire. A fortnight later the Stars and Stripes were hoisted above Santiago's palace and General Leonard Wood took over as Velazquez's latest successor.

Three expressions conveyed supreme uninterest. Clodagh said, 'I think the mule's much too thin.' Rose said, 'When there's a drought where can they get enough grazing?' Zea asked, 'Why is it a mule? It has the size of ponies.'

That gave Rose an enjoyable opportunity to be the knowledgeable big sister, explaining the genesis of mules. Then Clodagh asked, 'What happens the other way, when the horse is father?' I explained that that rarely happens; when it does the offspring are known, in Ireland, as jennets. Rose frowned and wondered, 'Why doesn't it happen more? Isn't it easier for a horse to get on a donkey than for a donkey to get on a horse?'

I theorised that mules are a useful tough hybrid whereas jennets are rather feeble, therefore not deliberately bred to suit human needs.

'I'd like to meet a jennet,' said Zea.

Owing to her encumbrances, Rachel had to burn the Santiago candle at both ends – home from the Casa de la Trova or the Casa de las Tradiciones at 2.00 or 3.00 a.m., up at 6.00 a.m. when the Trio swung into action. They and I 'did music' during the day, guided by handwritten notices posted each morning outside the Casa de la Trova, their timing not to be taken too seriously. One might arrive at 11.00 a.m., only to watch an hour-long technological struggle involving yards of flex, electric plugs, the testing of electric guitars and amplifying equipment, the tightening of drums, the tuning of the double-bass, the cleaning of flutes, the altering of music stands. The Trio revelled in all this, especially when invited on to the stage to study the scene in detail. For me (musically reared in an extremely narrow-minded way) overamplification in a smallish room marred an otherwise exhilarating introduction to Cuba's richest heritage.

Two sluggish ceiling fans tried to cool the Casa de la Trova, its slightly raised stage overlooked by a local artist's hectic depiction of the Steps of Padre Pico. In this house lived one of Cuba's most beloved composers, Rafael Salcedo (1844–1917) and until 1995 his home retained its eighteenth-century dignity. Then crass, cut-price renovations were (surprisingly) permitted and the many famous performers whose portraits crowd the walls would grieve to see it now.

Between the stage and the seating (plastic chairs) people danced – anyone in the audience who felt like it, but no more than four at a time. We always sat in front, within touching distance of the performers, and this sense of intimacy is important; one might be at a family party.

One middle-aged couple (white husband, mulatto wife) achieved extraordinary ballet-like gyrations and were 'regulars' – always in the second row, smiling affectionately at one another, then he standing, bowing, formally requesting her partnership while the crowd laughed and clapped. The performances of some young couples were even more overtly sexual but it was the solo dancing of a mulatto youth – small-boned, low in stature, apparently made of rubber – that most enthralled the Trio. Loudest of all was the applause for his performance with a tall big-breasted black girl, her ebony skin gleaming against a scarlet halter and tight green pants. As the band played faster and faster those two achieved an acrobatic-erotic *tour de force* that brought some of the audience to their feet (and perhaps to something else).

All this was more than I had hoped for in Santiago's world-famous Casa de la Trova. Here were ordinary citizens doing what Cubans are supposed to do best, making music, singing, dancing, using their bodies with a joyous, mischievous, provocative eloquence – not for tourists but for fun. Outside the three barred windows, reaching from floor to ceiling, townspeople crowded under the arcade. Beaming old men with sun-worn faces, and eyes brightened by their remembered youth, clutched the bars for hours on end, shouting compliments to their favourite singers. Women carrying shopping-bags paused for some free entertainment on their way home from the market. Youths intently observed the musicians, studying techniques, arguing about styles of play. Uniformed schoolgirls eating lunchtime ham rolls wriggled their hips while commenting on the dancers. One rejoiced to know that this Casa belongs to all of Santiago (entry for Cubans NP1).

Once we joined an early evening session in the tiled patio, a bigger space with potted palms along two walls, a mini-bar at one end and three very obviously dehydrated lavatories at the other. Soon the tourist vanguard appeared, half a dozen bronzed Italians and beetroot-coloured Dutch, all busy with digital and video cameras at CP1 per shot. A tiny nonagenarian white woman – her spine severely curved, limbs withered, eyes sunken, voice quavering – was still able to enjoy dancing. (Her enjoyment couldn't have been feigned.) When she invited the male tourists to dance with her two did so, looking thoroughly uncomfortable, while their partners took photographs. I wished then that I had confined myself to the casual, spontaneous, non-commercial afternoon sessions.

Across the street from No. 197 stands Santiago's celebrated music college (strictly classical) – a fine colonial town house, painted dark pink and navy blue with a view through its pillared chambers to a gracious patio where students relax in the ample shade of kapok and jaguey trees. From Irma's front windows one could hear the students' endeavours and Clodagh, especially, spent many spare moments listening to her contemporaries drawing sounds as of a cat being tortured from their violins – her own instrument of choice. Alternatively, one could stand on the pavement by an entrance – as many passers-by do – listening to orchestral rehearsals or one-to-one tuitions. In our world this might be considered an inhibiting distraction for students but in Cuba lives are shared, privilege is not associated with privacy (an alien concept) and those attentive peripatetic audiences seemed to be appreciated. Throughout our stay the orchestra was struggling with Schubert's Unfinished Symphony and a somewhat confused Clodagh complained, 'They keep on playing the same tune, will they ever finish it?' I explained that the composer himself had left his seventh symphony unfinished, perhaps because he died of typhus fever at the age of thirty-one. Rose looked shocked. 'So he was five years younger than Mum is now!' That inexorably led us into another field of enquiry. 'What,' asked Zea, 'is typhus? Why does it kill people?'

Irma's five-star *casa particulare* had only one defect: no writer-friendly table and chair. Therefore I regularly retreated to a corner café on Calle Aguilera where Mirta, a buxom young black woman with a wide smile and a deep chuckle, provided demitasses of excellent coffee for NP1 and was intrigued by my industrious scribbling. Cubans see no reason to stifle curiosity but discovering my profession scarcely lessened her puzzlement. For all their high literacy rate, most young Cubans are not book-minded.

The café was unlit, its walls panelled in dark wood, its high ceiling smoke-stained. Habitually I sat by one of the barred, unglazed windows and one morning three young men stopped outside on the pavement, staring at my table. After a brief confabulation they entered and shyly offered me NP1 for a pen – the coin on an extended hand. Four pens were visible: blue, red, black and green, all in use when I'm journal-writing, a fetish which perhaps says something about how hard I find it to order my thoughts. Feeling mean and nasty, I apologised for needing all those pens because of being a writer. Gloomily the young men accepted this excuse, one explaining that in Santiago just then there were no pens and when the next delivery arrived they would cost CP1 apiece. Tactlessly I opened my purse to provide CP3. The young men stepped back, gesturing their horror – they weren't *jineteros*, they didn't want a tourist's money, what they urgently needed, *now*, was one pen. I gave them my black and blue pens and accepted NP2.

Usually I was alone in that café, the first arrival, but once, as I was about to leave, fourteen young women assembled outside, looking cowed and sulky, then were led in by a hard-faced older woman. Having pulled two little tables together she opened thick files of rubber-stamped documents containing more figures than words. I ordered another coffee and lingered. The group ordered nothing and on arrival had ignored Mirta. It seemed the young women were guilty of some shared failure, had got their sums wrong, either through incompetence or in an attempt to pilfer. Individually they were challenged, their boss jabbing a forefinger on a page, glaring at them, demanding explanations, hectoring them, plainly enjoying her job. A few muttered defensively, others looked down and said nothing. Only one became angry, raising her voice, half-standing to lean towards the documents and doing a little finger-jabbing on her own account. In response the boss tore up two sheets of paper and snapped something that silenced the angry one who then looked around the semi-circle, seeking support. Everyone avoided her gaze. Next the others were ordered to sign chits which the boss counter-signed and stamped with a large official seal. To me, a café seemed an odd setting for this disciplinary procedure – here was another example of Cuban life being lived in public.

That same morning, on my way down Enramada, Santiago's main commercial street, I heard a dog howling strangely in the near distance and saw a crowd gathering. As I drew closer and the howling became more frenzied, four policemen appeared and herded everyone on to the pavements. A little red garbage van sped past me, a closed van with a smallish door in the back. I could now see the mad (rabid?) dog, a mangy medium-sized lurcher. Mercifully the Trio were not present. Out of the van leaped a very tall man wearing thick dungarees and long leather gauntlets. Seizing the dog by one hind leg he whirled it around and around until it was too dizzy to bite, then tried to open the rear door by flinging the unfortunate creature against it, causing shrieks of pain to replace the howling. When the door remained shut there followed another bout of whirling and flinging, also unsuccessful. I wanted to scream at the nearest policeman – 'Open the bloody door!' At the third attempt it did open, the dog vanished and the indisputably brave dustman pushed one shoulder against it while fighting a rusty bolt. Swiftly he drove away and, glancing around, I noticed many in the crowd looking as queasy as I felt.

That day's quest, for the Casa de las Religiones Populares, took us east from Parque Cespedes, up and then down along Sueno's wide, traffic-free, tree-shaded avenues. This district's art nouveau villas and roomy 1930s bungalows, with tiled facades and colonnaded verandahs, have long since been converted into flats, schools, clinics, kindergartens, government offices. We also passed rows of unassuming old wooden houses ('Caribbean vernacular') recalling the arrival of all those French refugees in 1791. En route I tried to not see the garishly decorated fifteen-storey Hotel Santiago which seems to jeer at a nearby white marble monument to the ascetic Ché Guevarra and the *compañeros* who died with him in Bolivia.

In the Casa de las Religiones Populares, a discreetly crumbling mansion encircled by ceiba trees, the exhibits are not conventionally displayed but carefully arranged, in three rooms, to give a sense of their ceremonial significance. Cuba's popular religions include Santería, voodoo and a cult somewhat ambiguously known as 'spiritism'. Of these Santería is by far the most popular, its adherents outnumbering Christians. It has evolved from a merging of West African cults with elements of Spanish Catholicism, the former the dominant ingredient.

The Trio (being reared as agnostics) were baffled by Santería's interweaving of Christian statues, images and candles with small animal skeletons, a stuffed eagle hanging from the ceiling, weirdly carved walking sticks, intricately embossed drums, cauldrons containing a variety of dead leaves, feathered dolls with forbidding expressions, ebony masks with glaring red eyes and long shaggy manes, votive offerings of fruits, grains and glasses of rum. As we moved from room to room Rose looked increasingly addled while her juniors seemed almost apprehensive. Rachel and I later agreed that this was not our most productive educational effort.

Emerging into the noon heat, the Trio suggested turning towards Coppelia, forgetting Loma de San Juan, a significant small hill which once formed part of Santiago's outer defences. There, on 1 July 1898, fewer than a thousand Spaniards held out for some twelve hours against more than three thousand US troops recruited – according to Theodore Roosevelt, who was present – 'from the wild riders and riflemen of the Rockies and the Great Plains'. This was the only major land-battle of the invasion and Richard Gott records the Cubans' subsequent resentment:

> Calixto Garcia, the rebel commander closest to Santiago, was invited by the Americans to supply troops to divert Spanish forces during the US advance on the city. He sent 3,000 of his men, but none were asked to the subsequent victory celebrations. Cuba was liberated from Spanish control by the American invasion in barely three weeks, yet the Cubans had been fighting for more than three years. They watched bleakly from the sidelines as their victory was taken from them.

Rose chose to celebrate her tenth birthday, on 10 November, by returning to Playa Siboney and the mango-shaded restaurant. Despite a long wait for the bus we were on the beach by 9.00 a.m.

Two hours later the royal palms suddenly became wildly agitated, reshaped by a gale, all their fronds pointing south as masses of low charcoal clouds poured over the Sierra de la Gran Piedra and whiteness flecked the sea – now jade green. We made for the nearest shelter, an improvised café two hundred yards away where the awning was irrelevant because the gale drove the rain horizontally across the tables. Happily the storm passed as quickly as it had arrived and we strolled to the restaurant through a fine drizzle, the slight drop in temperature compensating for the mild discomfort of sodden clothes.

That was a jolly birthday party, if not gastronomically memorable (noodles, pork steaks, grated carrot). Inevitably I recalled Rachel's tenth birthday, celebrated in the little town of Andahuayalas towards the end of our three-month Andean trek. There it took over an hour to find a cake – any kind of cake. That evening we ate steak, onions and chips in a large grotty restaurant lit by an oil-lamp. The bottle of Peruvian wine spotted on the top shelf of a dusty shop was challenging – as was that hard-won sponge cake. But aged ten the symbolism of a birthday cake is what matters.

The clouds began to break up as we returned to the junction, sniffing a medley of strong scents released by the rain: unfamiliar herbs and blossoms, rotting vegetation, ripe pig manure, over-ripe papaya. Outside the long, low junction shed, where locals collect their rations, several groups stood around awaiting transport though no bus was expected for the foreseeable future. Soon a 1950s jeep stopped to pick up two young men carrying tool bags. Some time later an already overcrowded car, minus both rear doors, found space for two slim elderly women. Their fat friend was left behind but her protestations held no rancour. Meanwhile swarms of day mosquitoes were tormenting us though the Cubans seemed indifferent to them. As our itch bumps multiplied, even Rose complained.

Shouts of joy greeted the arrival of an open-backed empty farm lorry and we were urged to climb aboard – easier said than done, for the uninitiated. This was a high truck, without steps, but a strong young man locked his hands together for me and kind arms stretched down to help the Trio. We stood at one side, holding a bar, able at last to appreciate the landscape – and to see Granjita Siboney.

From this little farmhouse Fidel and his hundred and twenty companions, wearing army uniforms bought on the black market, set out by starlight on the morning of 26 July 1953 to assault the Moncada barracks, hoping to equip the Rebel Army by robbing its armoury. Most men were armed only with .22 rifles or shotguns; a few carried heavier weapons. During the previous weeks, as the Movement surreptitiously assembled its volunteers and weaponry on Granjita's two acres, Ernesto Tizol, a poultry farmer who had rented the premises, told the locals that he was building a new battery-hen unit. Now, viewing this tranquil pastoral scene, it seems little has changed since that convoy of motor cars and buses moved off, led by Fidel in a large hired Buick which had just taken him the five hundred and sixty miles from Havana, a black lorry-driver at the wheel, posing as the young white lawyer's chauffeur. Soon more than half those volunteers would be dead. When the Moncada raid failed, many were shot after enduring extreme forms of torture – so extreme that some of Batista's soldiers (not sensitive types) couldn't bear to watch. Moncada's commanding officer, Colonel Chaviano, had demanded ten rebel lives for every one of the nineteen soldiers killed. The rebels had lost six. Several military doctors and junior officers, appalled by what they saw and heard, tried to rescue some of the rebels but were warned not to interfere. One doctor, Mario Munoz, protested so vigorously that he was shot dead. Photographs of the tortured bodies were circulated throughout Cuba and these, like Britain's execution of Ireland's 1916 leaders, did much to help the Revolution on its way – more than the contents of any armoury could have done.

Above Granjita Siboney rises the steep blue bulk of the Sierra de la

Gran Piedra where Fidel took refuge after Moncada, while spotter planes and ground troops sought the surviving rebels. Of the forty who returned to Granjita during the afternoon of 26 July several were wounded and/or demoralised, wanting only to be safe home in Havana. That evening, when Fidel set out to climb the Gran Piedra (four thousand feet and precipitous) only nineteen followed him and only two, Oscar Alcade and José Suarez, were able to stay the course until 1 August. Then, at dawn, sixteen Rural Guards found the fugitives asleep in a remote hut. When a corporal suggested killing them on the spot half a dozen men eagerly volunteered for the firing squad. Rural Guard conscripts were black and uneducated and favoured Batista, a mulatto former sergeant, rather than these white middle-class rebels. Just in time, Lieutenant Pedro Sarria realised what was about to happen and ordered the Guards not to fire. Aged fifty-three, he had been among the courageous minority who attempted to halt the Moncada torturing. When he died in 1973 his funeral was attended by both Fidel as President of Cuba and his brother Raul as Commander-in Chief of the armed forces.

At a junction halfway to Santiago we joined two weary-looking women sitting on empty sacks. All around stretched undulating pastureland, yellowish-brown when it should have been green, and in the distance co-op dairy buildings were visible, our lorry's destination. In Havana we had heard about the drought, Cuba's worst since 1901. Some two million citizens, out of eleven point two million, were currently dependent on water-tankers. Forty-two of the island's two hundred and thirty-five reservoirs were dry, the rest were down to thirty-two per cent capacity, on average.

The Trio fretted as desperate horned cattle pushed their heads under a wire fence to reach the unappetising roadside growth. Soothingly I remarked on these bullocks' fine condition; their glossy golden-brown coats suggested ample supplementary feeding.

The first bus ignored us; it was packed to danger point and swayed erratically as it took a nearby bend. I admired the Trio's reaction to life as it is lived by the average Cuban: no whining though by this stage all three looked exhausted. The next bus stopped only when the women ran after it, shouting what may have been voodoo curses. A genial mulatta offered Zea a seat on her lap, the rest of us stood. At the terminus I suggested a taxi but in unison the Trio said – 'No! Walking is better.' Their age-group readily absorbs parental standards: if walking is feasible one simply doesn't use motor transport. I hope that in ten years hence they won't be competing for men with Porsches. Back at base they enjoyed an unexpected reward. Generous Irma had baked a fruit and cream birthday cake, as large as it was luscious; by then she had the measure of their appetites.

Cuba and rum go together, like Scotland and whisky. 'The cheerful child of sugar cane,' wrote Fernando Campoamer, one of Ernest Hemingway's drinking *compañeros*, and this child, though born in Haiti, was reared in Santiago. The industry's development at first alarmed those who imagined that Haiti's slaves must have been rum-empowered to kill so many of their French owners before driving the survivors into exile. But in time the *santiagueros* became proud of their association with Bacardi rum.

The Rum Museum riveted the Trio with its graphic displays showing in detail how rum is made, from the planting of cane to the bottling, corking and labelling of the refined finished product. I was more interested in a short history of the Bacardi distillery. It seemed suggestively noncommittal and prompted me to probe on my return to Ireland.

In the late 1850s, when Germany and France began to extract cheap sugar from beet, the US suddenly became Cuba's main customer, able to name the price, and many Oriente planters and merchants found themselves on or near the breadline. But not the Bacardi family, who plunged into the rum alternative.

In 1862 a French-born distiller, José Leon Boutillier, transferred his equipment and expertise to the brothers José and Facundo Bacardi who then registered a liquor company, 'José Bacardi y Cia', in Santiago's Town Hall.

Twelve years later, Facundo bought out his brother and Boutillier, and eventually two of his sons, Emilio and Facundo Jnr, inherited the distillery. In 1894 their immensely rich brother-in-law, Enrique Scheug – part-educated in England and with City experience – joined the partnership.

Bacardi was among the few Cuban companies to profit from the island's satellite status. Their official historian records:

> The US assisted Cuba in gaining independence and Cuba, among its many gifts in return, gave North Americans a taste for the tropical spirit made in Santiago de Cuba: BACARDI Rum. In the climate of turn-of-the-century US protectionism, Bacardi thereby gained a foothold in a market that it would carefully cultivate.

Only the naïve were puzzled when the fateful Eighteenth Amendment to the US Constitution left Bacardi undamaged, though Prohibition outlawed the production, sale, import and consumption of alcohol. The ingenious gangs initially known as bootleggers, then as the Cosa Nostra, operated with the least hindrance on what they called 'the rum route': Jamaica, Cuba, New Orleans.

On 5 December 1933, when Prohibition ended, Cosa Nostra millions had been swirling around the US for some twelve years, leaving tell-tale stains on the bank accounts of a few powerful politicians, senior security service officers and eminent churchmen. Early in 1934 Batista's friend, Mayer Lansky, a gambling consultant and much-feared Cosa Nostra leader (almost on a par with Lucky Luciano and Al Capone) was granted the exclusive right to run Cuba's casinos, legally established, after years of controversy, in 1919. Opposition had come from two disparate but some-times overlapping sources. Florida's tourist industry feared competition, religious leaders feared US citizens being further corrupted in Cuba, already notorious for 'naked women gyrating on a public stage' (entrance fee, less than a dollar). Hearing of Lansky's new job Lucky Luciano, soon to feature prominently on the Cuban scene, proclaimed triumphantly, 'This is Cosa Nostra's first opening in the Caribbean!'

Throughout the 1930s Bacardi expanded fast and their transnationalism bothered some Cubans, including the academic economist Jacinto Torras. He complained in 1944:

> The current Bacardi company denies in practice [its] pure Cuban history . . . Bacardi has lied again in seeking to justify the transfer of its factories to foreign countries. Bacardi has said that they have never stopped marketing rum from Cuba in the US, but the statistics say something else . . . According to the US Department of Trade, Cuban rum represented fifty-two per cent of imports in 1935, only seven point three per cent in 1940.

During prohibition José Bosch, generally known as 'Pepin', had joined the very extended Bacardi family by marrying Enrique Scheug's daughter. Pepin it was who organised the post-war distribution of Bacardi – from Finland to the Lebanon, from Switzerland to Korea. Meanwhile, back in Santiago, things had turned nasty.

The Rum Museum's director, Pepin Hernandez, has one very unhappy memory. In the 1950s Pepin Bosch persuaded his Santiago staff workers to invest in a new company, Minera Occidental, at US$10 a share – big money for a Cuban distillery worker. As a new company, about to lessen unemploy-ment, Minera had no taxes to pay on imported machinery and materials. When the company was declared bankrupt, not long after, Pepin Bosch bought up the imported goods for a short song and the investors were left with worthless share certificates. Following Pepin Hernandez's father's death, several of those certificates were found and the son resolutely confronted Bosch, claiming their value. He was told to come back with a document, signed by his father, nominating him as the rightful heir.

By then the *santiagueros* were no longer grateful for whatever crumbs might fall from the Bacardi table, yet most felt genuinely shocked by the kidnapping of a small boy, Facundo Bacardi Bravo, in February 1954. Immediately Santiago witnessed Bacardi-power in action. When Pepin Bosch contacted the US consul a helicopter arrived from the Guantanamo naval base, soon followed by a plane from Miami carrying an FBI team. Within twelve hours the child had been rescued and the two kidnappers shot dead. Both were youths employed by the Bacardi family as domestic servants. Neither was armed.

Under President Carlos Prio (1948–52), Pepin Bosch (by then the Bacardi company's president) became minister of finance and Cuba's budget thrived. Mayer Lansky was now the US Mafia's second-in-command and millions of dollars were being laundered on the island. The historian Enrique Cirules has written: 'From the 1930s up to 1958 no political event of magnitude or any great business deal took place in Cuba without the presence of Lansky's hand or attention.'

General Batista's 1952 coup d'etat left the rum trade undisturbed yet Cuba's loss of its 'democratic' fig-leaf made the Bacardis uneasy; in 1957 they moved their company headquarters from Santiago and re-registered its trademark in the Bahamas. This was not the end of Bacardi in Cuba, however, as will become evident in a later chapter.

Rachel and I share a certain squeamishness (probably ill-advised) about needlessly exposing small children to the worst aspects of human nature. Therefore, in the Emilio Bacardi Moreau museum we steered the Trio past a display of slave-controlling neck-chains, heavy leg-irons, barbed whips and those chopping-boards on which the most unruly were deprived of feet or hands or arms. Such mutilations took place on Calle Carniceria (Carnage Street) in front of large crowds.

The museum's structure, a very fine neo-classical building, is its best feature. We all preferred the Museo del Carnaval, its three jolly rooms crowded with elaborate costumes, colourful banners, an amazing range of comical papier mâché masks and the musical instruments of several West African kingdoms – most conspicuous the *tumbadoras*, leather and wooden drums taller than the Trio, each intricately decorated with patterns unique to a particular *cabildo*. (The *cabildos* were societies for the preservation of African music, languages, religious beliefs and medical lore.)

On the eve of our departure for the coast Rachel packed while the rest of us 'did a Coppelia' and enjoyed the adjacent fun-fair. Its hand-operated machinery looked more nineteenth than twentieth century but the Trio happily swung up and down, or around and over, on contraptions that would panic the most laid-back EU Health and Safety inspector. However, we were assured that all such equipment is regularly checked, is not as life-threatening as it might seem. Cuba's enforced disregard for appearances goes with an admirable concern for its citizens' welfare – especially the junior citizens.

On the way back we needed to acquire extra national pesos. The long *Cambio* queue was being supervised by a power-enjoying SECSA guard and only three might enter at once. When my turn came he inexplicably ordered me to give way to the person behind. 'Why?' wailed a hot and thirsty Zea. 'You were here first!' 'I don't think he likes tourists,' said Clodagh. 'Or maybe,' suggested Rose, 'that person is his friend?' I tended to agree with Clodagh.

In the Casa de la Trova one of Rachel's numerous dancing partners had organised an unregistered 'taxi' (his friend's Buick) to take us to the truck-bus terminus. Raimundo would pick us up at 4.30 a.m.; a vehicle might leave for Chivirico, some forty-four miles west, at 5.00 or 6.00 or 7.00. We told Irma we didn't know exactly when we'd return; our plan was to trek along the coast, and a little way into the Sierra Maestra, for ten days or so.

Irma, looking worried, asked, 'What will you eat?' In our ignorance we assumed we'd eat whatever the locals ate. We had a lot to learn.

Chapter 4

To the kindly Irma, the Trio's mother and grandmother must have seemed quite callous; despite Rachel's protestations, she insisted on rising at 4.00 to feed our victims in preparation for their ordeal.

Raimundo arrived punctually, a tall black youth with the physique of a prize-fighter and the smile of a happy angel. Heaving our two rucksacks over the back seat, he explained that the boot couldn't be opened. (Only two rucksacks: we weren't callous enough to burden the Trio on their first trek.) Mother and young fitted comfortably into the back and as I sat in front Raimundo warned me not to shut my door; it must be held ajar, no door could be opened from the inside – 'all handle gone!' And there was another complication: the engine wouldn't ever start while the bonnet was down. Raimundo chuckled about this, as one might affectionately mock a dear friend's idiosyncrasy. Having raised the bonnet he switched on the engine, leaped out to close the bonnet and off we went. The others had collapsed into uncontrollable giggles, a response to all those little hitches which pleased Raimundo, matching his own light-hearted attitude.

Slowly we descended to the sea-front, through bumpy unlit streets, the Buick's senile springs prolonging those giggles. Now I had two tasks: holding the door ajar while cherishing a bulging bag of bananas irrationally provided by Rachel to sustain us on our way. These had ripened fast overnight, my nose told me, and needed protection from bumps.

In the terminus – a converted warehouse, its three doors lorry-sized – scores of passengers occupied long rows of chairs. They had evidently spent the night in situ and lacked the usual Cuban joie de vivre. Mistakenly we took three front row vacant seats, only vacant because three mulattas were chatting to friends at the end of the row. Vehemently they reclaimed their space and we, muttering apologies, moved to the back row where five chairs were free and peopled rearranged themselves to allow us to sit together. A black mother was changing an infant's nappy while a wailing toddler pulled at her slacks. When the blonde Trio's arrival distracted him Rose tactfully worked on that, earning a grateful smile from his mamma.

We assumed that the vehicle parked outside was bound for Chivirico though no one seemed sure about this. Cuban truck-buses are just that: long trucks, tarpaulin-roofed and open-sided, fitted with four rows of narrow metal benches. Standing passengers pack the slight spaces between them, hanging on to the roof struts if need be.

Until 5.30 some men continued to doze, most women busied themselves packing up their few possessions, several children had to be taken out to pee, two grey-haired men beside us argued over a shared cigar (who was drawing most from it) and we ate bananas.

When our driver appeared we were left staring as a wave of bodies surged towards the truck, even the fattest women leaping over chairs as though in a hurdle race. This was not a queue situation. Arriving last on the pavement, we saw the vehicle being besieged. Young men and women swarmed up the sides, using the wheels as footholds; old folk were being hoisted through the back, children dragged between the bars – or passed up like parcels. We hesitated; already the truck looked overfull, for us to find space seemed impossible. But when our hesitation was noticed many voices urged us on; in petrol-starved Cuba the faint-hearted get nowhere – literally. Hands reached down to take our rucksacks before we scrambled up the metal steps at the back. A woman sitting beside the steps made room for me by vigorously pushing at the man on her left, then Rachel and the Trio were lost to view. I was lucky, able to see all. They couldn't see beyond the nearest bodies.

Now the private enterprise food vendors appeared: women laden with kettles of strong, hot, sweet coffee and buckets of water in which to rinse cups, young men selling ham rolls and beef fritters, old men selling roasted peanuts in newspaper cones. When a power failure left the street in darkness business continued to be brisk, by starlight, for half an hour, during which several newcomers somehow inserted themselves into non-existent spaces. By dawn-light I noticed a young couple embracing near the steps – he a handsome white policeman, trying to be cheerful, she a beautiful mulatta allowing tears to trickle. Twice she obeyed a female (maternal?) voice summoning her aboard, twice he successfully begged her to descend for another tight lingering embrace. She stayed with him until the departure signal, our 'conductor' rattling a thin chain; once it had been hooked across the steps no one was allowed to enter or leave.

Truck-bus fare-collecting takes time. As the conductor couldn't possibly penetrate the interior he walked around the vehicle, gathering pesos through the open sides, those sitting within reach passing on the coins of the inaccessible. Cheating is out, would involve an intolerable loss of face. This forty-four mile journey cost me NP3 but when I tried to pay NP9 for the Trio my neighbour explained that children travel free. Elsewhere in

Cuba I was to observe that animals do not travel free; the fare for a goat or a pig is half a national peso.

Beyond Santiago's down-at-heel dockside factories this narrowish coastal road was in good repair, except where Wilma's floods had torn the tarmac or recent landslides had strewn rocks from verge to verge. The calm sea shone a translucent emerald until the sun rose amidst a scattering of cloudlets – gold-fringed pink, then briefly crimson. Nearby, the dusky blue Sierra Maestra were gaining height. On wide palm-dotted pastures, rising to meet the mountains, grazed small flocks of sheep. Horses, mules and donkeys were tethered or fenced close to the few one-storey dwellings; pigs and dogs roamed free, as did hens, turkeys, guinea-fowl, ducks.

We met an antique bus and three open farm lorries whose many passengers were perched precariously on high loads of sacks or lumber. Fidel must feel bitter about the post-Soviet transport shambles. In 1985 he spoke to the Brazilian economic journalist, Joelmir Beting, and described his reaction to the workers on a major construction site being crammed into seatless trucks when travelling long distances to visit their families: 'I asked, "How many buses are needed – thirty? We're going to try to get them. We'll use the ones we have in reserve." I suggested building a campsite near the project so their families could visit them and rest with them . . . Of course, the agencies responsible for the project needed more resources and direct support; they got it . . . What interests me is taking care of the men. A worker will feel more interested in the project if he has decent conditions and sees that his work is appreciated and that there is constant concern about his human and material problems.'

On visiting this site, near Cienfuegos, Beting commented, 'I realised that knowing the Commander is keeping an eye on the work is a great incentive.' And the men got their thirty buses – until that family campsite was built.

During the 1960s Cuba imported no cars. To Beting Fidel explained, 'Both the economic and trade blockade to which we were subjected, and our own priorities, channelled resources to other sectors, such as health and education. Whatever automobiles we import mustn't adversely affect social needs.'

Beting then remarked that 'Brazil produces two thousand five hundred litres of alcohol from every hectare of sugar-cane – enough to meet a car's need for a year.'

Swiftly Fidel replied, 'Just imagine how many hectares of sugar-cane are needed for so many cars! It's sad to think of all that land being used to feed cars, not people.' Twenty-two years later, he again made that point in conversation with Hugo Chavez – several months after thousands of Miami Cubans had danced in the streets because they believed he was about to die.

We passed two undeveloped little beaches, ten and twelve miles from Santiago, where at week-ends the city folk enjoy themselves in their non-consumerist way. The truck's first stop was at Chivirico where we and a dozen others disembarked beside an unwalled mini-park which merged into Playa Virginia. The Trio, having been seriously squashed and over-heated for two hours, stared longingly at the sea. But my immediate concern was that bag of bananas; I had failed adequately to protect it so three kilos of pale brown mush needed to be eaten without delay. An adult dispute followed. Rachel peered into the bag and said, regretfully, 'I think we'll have to give them to a pig.' (Two sows were scavenging in the near distance.) I protested that the bag had been clean to begin with, therefore the contents could be scooped out and eaten without hazard. Usually the Trio support their mother but on this occasion they sided with me. As we sat on a stone bench, slurping nourishment from amidst black skins, Rachel pointedly departed the scene, balancing on a wobbly duck-board laid across a lake of sticky post-Wilma mud. We saw her enter a bakery, then emerge empty-handed; in this town foreigners couldn't buy bread.

Wilma had left its muddy marks everywhere and the park's mutilated palms and dishevelled shrubs would take some time to recover. Even concrete seats had been damaged as the sea raged towards the road. Playa Virginia, a mile-long public beach, was littered with withering fronds, the remains of a fishing-boat, someone's hall door and a few washed-up tree trunks (climbing frames for the Trio). This strip of coarse brown sand, between a bank of loose stones and the water's edge, in no way resembles Cuban beaches as depicted on postcards. To the east, a high, steep, wooded promontory concealed three small all-inconclusive tourist hotels; to the west a short chain of mangrove cays extended from the shore. As we undressed beneath a grotesquely gnarled tree bearing strange fruits, two kind young men left their chess game in the park to warn us against swimming near the cays, an area of powerful undercurrents.

Along this west coast only Chivirico caters for tourists yet despite those hotels we saw no other foreigners in the town, nor any shops selling beach equipment and souvenirs. Here we have serious 'tourist apartheid'. The hotels run their own shops, control the best local beaches and charge non-residents (ordinary Cubans) a daily CP10 admission fee – a humiliating exclusion device. On hearing this I winced, remembering the pride with which, in January 1959, the Revolutionary leaders opened Cuba's beaches, clubs, parks, race courses, golf links and other public spaces to all citizens free of charge – the easiest and one of the most popular reforms, soon to be followed by fifty per cent reductions in rent, electricity and telephone charges.

With Buccanero in mind, I had already investigated the bungalow-style *tienda*, newly painted white and standing alone on a grassy rise opposite the park: opening hours, 11.00–1.00 and 4.00–6.00. At 11.05 we were on the doorstep, planning to buy emergency rations for our trek. But alas! This *tienda*'s edibles were limited to maize crisps (dyed orange and red), packets of six sweet biscuits from Argentina, chewing-gum from Brazil (does that count as an edible?) and toffees sold singly at half a convertible peso apiece. Glass-topped cabinets displayed imported plastic toys, children's garments, two boxed sets of tin cutlery and a few enamel dinner plates. Behind the counter a high shelf held five dusty bottles of Scotch and two of London Dry Gin.

'There's *nothing* for us to eat!' lamented Rose. 'But Nyanya's OK,' said Clodagh, indicating a tall fridge amply stocked with Buccanero. I stuffed ten tins into my rucksack and we followed Rachel to the *agromercado*, not far up a side road. Too late, alas, too late! Beside a few palm-roofed trestle-stalls a notice nailed to a fence listed prices and hours of business: 8.00-10.00 a.m.

Back on the main road we paused beside a very old woman squatting under a ceiba tree, her posture oddly grasshopper-like, her black skin hanging loose as a garment, her bright eyes lively, a basket between her feet. She was selling another unfamiliar fruit – four inches long, oval-shaped, with a kiwi's skin, sweet red flesh, a huge shiny brown stone and an acrid smell. 'Like a dirty stable,' commented Clodagh, declining to sample one. The others promptly spat out their first bites, to the old lady's amusement. I nevertheless bought ten, not an extravagance at a fifth of a national peso each.

Even in Cuba swimming sharpens the appetite and a hunger mutiny threatened. Rose looked gloomy, Clodagh peevish, Zea rebellious. 'There must be a restaurant,' said I. 'You speak without conviction,' said Rachel. But there was one, separated from the road by another mud-lake and opening at noon. Rose looked at her watch and proposed twenty minutes of rummy to take minds off grumbling stomachs. I excused myself, by then reduced to a sweat-producing zombie.

Soon after I noticed a girl leaving the bakery with an armful of saucer-sized 'ship's biscuits' – flat, hard, golden-brown. In Havana I had been able to buy their like and, because the instinct of child-protection overcomes even heat-lassitude, I now hastened hopefully across the duck-boards. An anxious Rose accompanied me; being at a rapid growth stage food was pivotal to her thinking. Happily no *libreta* was required and, exercising restraint on behalf of the locals, I bought fifteen for NP30. 'Five each!' exclaimed Rose though I had been mentally calculating 'Three each'.

In the lean-to restaurant – built against a co-op store missing half its roof – local electricity rationing had stilled the ceiling fan and the dumpy, grumpy waitress wore a sweat-band. Wide spaces separated the eight four-person tables, their oil-cloths frayed but clean. (In Fidel's Cuba cleanliness comes a long way before godliness, and is almost obsessionally emphasised as part of the national health-care programme.) We were the first arrivals, soon followed by two urban-looking men carrying briefcases and three svelte young women clutching thick files: touring government officials, we surmised. The waitress served them first, perhaps by way of reminding us that, strictly speaking, foreigners should be ejected from a subsidised national-peso food outlet. But for the Trio, we might well have been ejected; our proper place was in one of the tourist hotels.

The communal menu was an oblong of cardboard, handwritten in pencil. Impatiently Zea said, 'Let's look at the book' – she's not accustomed to eating out. The 'book' listed only *arroz con frijoles* and stewed or fried pork: heavy going when it's 88°F in the shade. Observing the lavish helpings, Rachel rightly judged that three orders would suffice. Eventually plates heaped with white rice appeared, and bowls of soupy kidney beans to be poured over it, and large slabs of fried pork – fifty per cent fat with the bristles in situ. I never eat lunch and this fare did not tempt me to abandon the habit of a lifetime. Later I was to regret not stoking up; in rural Cuba the wise eat when they can. Meanwhile we were all absorbing pints of water; the waitress kept an eye on our glasses and topped them up repeatedly – for free, though in *tiendas* bottled water costs CP0.85 per litre. Our bill came to NP44, much less than two euros.

Back on the beach my bloated companions were only fit for rummy and, anyway, the heat dictated passivity until 3.00-ish.

Our plan to follow the sandy shoreline was soon thwarted by mangroves. A path led up to the treeless and heat-reflecting road; as we plodded along I felt like an egg in a frying-pan and Clodagh complained about the sea's being invisible. 'With luck,' said Rachel, 'we'll soon get back to it.'

Where the terrain began to slope slightly up I fell behind to consult our map. Alarmingly, it showed the road swinging inland for several shadeless miles. Catching up with the others I remarked brightly, 'At least there's no traffic.'

Zea scowled, transcended her anti-motor conditioning and said, 'I'd *like* traffic! We might get a lift. I'm too *hot!*' Her sisters looked as though they rather agreed with her but made no comment, having a clearer concept of the purpose of this holiday.

Then came a long, high bridge spanning a river-bed some seventy yards wide. The drought had reduced this river (nameless on our map) to separate streams winding erratically between boulders and patches of scrub. Rachel paused, studied the cliff path leading down from the road and said, 'Rivers lead to seas – let's follow it.'

'*Yes!*' yelled the Trio in unison. At once they bounded down an almost perpendicular path like so many goats. Their mother, overloaded with bottled water, proceeded more cautiously. Their grandmother, overloaded with beer, and mindful of the friability of septuagenarian bones, sought a stout stick before descending. At the base of the cliff five little boys, building a mud fort, stared at us in silent astonishment. Then a horseman appeared from under the bridge, riding bareback, wearing only shorts and a sombrero, trying to lassoe herons. He ignored us.

Released from that hellish road, our spirits soared. The main stream glowed through deep pools between high boulders. 'This is *fun!*' shouted Rose, leaping from boulder to boulder. Clodagh and Zea each went their own way, Clodagh slipping often on slimy green stones in swift shallow water, Zea pausing, as is her wont, to examine various mosses and tiny rock plants. (Her paternal grandmother is a botanist.) The burdened adults sought the easiest way forward between streams – not all that easy, balancing on large loose stones. Where the streams converged the current strengthened and Zea tended to wobble while fording. So did I, despite my stick, and Zea, noticing this, waited for me and said, 'I'm not very stable but I'll try to help you.' The sort of remark that sticks in a grandmaternal memory.

Hereabouts the challenges multiplied. Around a sharpish bend the river-bed abruptly narrowed to thirty yards or less and the water's power and depth forced us into a thorny mangrove swamp. Undaunted, the Trio squelched ahead and were small enough to dodge the thorns that lacerated their elders. On half-slipping into the swamp I yelped for Rachel to rescue the Trio's supper – those precious ship's biscuits in my cloth shoulder-bag.

Soon, in the distance we could hear a rhythmical rattling roar. 'That can't be the sea!' exclaimed Rachel. A few hours previously, in Chivirico's sheltered bay, wavelets had been gently hissing on to the sand. But since then a strong wind had arisen and along this exposed flat coast the Atlantic was turbulent. Emerging from the bushes we caught up with the Trio and stood in awe of towering white breakers crashing on to a natural causeway of big stones and small boulders.

It took us some moments to realise we were in a trap of sorts. Contradicting Rachel's reasonable assumption that rivers flow into seas, this depleted river here became a murky lagoon, some eighty yards long and sixty wide, separated from the sea by the causeway. On either side sandy beaches were visible but mangrove swamps intervened. I glanced at the sun: not enough daylight remained for us to retrace our steps to a grassy campsite by the bridge. And being put to bed on a muddy path might overtax the Trio's adaptability. They of course could swim across the lagoon to one of the beaches – but what about the laden adults? Luckily my stick was long. I waded in, having first prudently undone my rucksack's waistband, and before each step tested the depth. The bed was unnervingly uneven, yet Rachel and I were able to wade through, circuitously, while the Trio swam to the eastern beach, Rose pulling Zea on to the six-foot-high causeway. From there they watched us slowly zig-zagging across, rarely more than crotch-deep though two waist-deep spots saturated my money-belt. 'You are silly!' chided Rachel. 'You should've put it in your rucksack.' As she helped me on to the causeway we heard the Trio rejoicing about another swim.

'No!' I shouted – they were already scampering towards the waves and this sloping beach had an undertow threatening even to adults. Rachel however looked sceptical about my diktat and I recognised the dawn of her 'I'm on the girls' side' expression. She hates to disappoint her offspring and also has strong views (possibly inherited) against over-protectionism. When planning for Cuba I had stipulated that she must be the sole leader and decision-maker but on this one occasion I went into reverse gear and ordered – 'No child is to go *near* those waves until Mummy has tested them!'

At once Mummy dumped her rucksack and approached the high water mark, a ridge of sand and stones now being washed over by this full moon tide. Momentarily she viewed the breakers as they advanced, crashed, seethed – then withdrew, dragging the shale with them, making a rasping rumble. Happily she felt no need to immerse herself before supporting my embargo.

I sat down, opened a Buccanero and drank to this momentous initiation ceremony, the Trio's first night camping without a tent, under the stars. We had chanced upon a magnificent site, overlooked by the Sierra Maestra's intricate arrangement of wooded spurs and peaks, never far from this coast. No dwellings were visible. Dense groves of sea-grapes and dwarf palms hid the swamp and bleached tree skeletons, carried here by who knows which hurricane, decorated the long shore, its eastern extremity marked by a grassy promontory. Nearby, to the west, three-hundred-foot limestone cliffs jutted ruggedly into the sea, now tinted by a flaring sunset.

'This is blissful!' I exulted. 'Clever Mummy, leading us down the river-bed!'

The Trio, however, had practical concerns. 'Where are we sleeping?' asked Clodagh.

'Right here,' I replied, patting the coarse sand beside me.

'But there's stones everywhere!' protested Zea.

'There *are* stones everywhere,' said I with Pavlovian pedantry.

'We can clear them away,' said Rose, looking consciously virtuous as she set about that task.

Clodagh followed suit and observed – resignedly, not complaining – 'They're heavy.'

Zea moved closer to her mother – busily unpacking – and said craftily, 'I'm too small for heavy stones.'

'They're not *that* heavy,' I argued. (Zea, being abnormally muscular for her age, can cope with huge weights when it suits her.) I added, 'Poor Mummy! All afternoon she's been carrying a *really* heavy load!' But of course Mummy cleared Zea's space. You can't lose if you're the youngest.

We decided to save the ship's biscuits for breakfast and while the Trio dined off emergency ration organic raisins, imported from California via Ireland (shameful food miles!), the adults drew sustenance from Buccaneros. Only then did we notice that we were not alone on the beach. A distant bonfire glowed through the dusk and a figure was approaching, walking close to the waves. He stopped a few yards away, greeted us shyly, then expressed concern: he had come to warn us against the ravenous swamp-based mosquitoes. We were invited to join his fishermen's camp, they would be keeping an anti-mosquito fire smoking all night. Thanking him effusively, Rachel explained that the niños were too tired to move on, then showed him our homeopathic insect repellent. He nodded, looking unimpressed, but said no more. He seemed very shy.

Half-an-hour later we were all asleep, our lullaby the tumultuous Atlantic, no more than ten yards from where we lay.

When my bladder roused me a full moon stood overhead and the world seemed brighter than at noon in Ireland on a rainy November day. For some time I walked to and fro by the foaming, gleaming waves, adding to my collection of those memories that enrich one forever. As Nicolas Bouvier noted of such moments, in his classic *The Way of the World*, 'Life dispenses them parsimoniously; our feeble hearts could not stand more.'

Then, gazing down at the sleeping quartet, I had another of my vivid flashbacks – to a tentless, full moon night on a mountain-top in Cameroon in 1987 (exactly half Rachel's lifetime ago, our last long trek together). Waking to re-tether our pack-horse, I spent moments gazing down at my daughter, wondering what the future held for her. And now I wondered what it held for the Trio. Given this century's problems, maybe it's best that I'll never know the answer.

My itchy bites kept me awake and soon I heard diverse whimperings. Clodagh had also been mosquito-ravaged, was too hot and very thirsty. Zea was equally thirsty and much troubled by sand in her bag. Patiently Rachel provided water, applied more repellent, shook out sand, made soothing noises. Looking back, I don't recall myself being so calm and tolerant when travelling with only one small child. Those humane genes must come from somewhere else.

At sunrise, as we broke camp, Zea announced, 'I don't think I like living without a house.' Rose threw her a sympathetic look and predicted, 'You'll get used to it.'

'I do like it,' said Clodagh. 'It's nice staring up at the sky. The mozzies are nasty but they come into houses too. They were in our room in Havana.'

I had begun to feel twitchy about Rachel's plan to seek a path on the western beach. A high tide was pouring powerfully across the causeway into the lagoon: how could we keep our balance in that current on a surface of shifting stones? I was about to suggest returning to the road by another route when two fishermen, smelling strongly of wood smoke, overtook us. They knew precisely where to step – and *when*, in relation to the ebb and flow. Having greeted us briefly they summed up the situation, carried the Trio across, then offered me a supporting arm – without which I would certainly have been swept into the lagoon. Only Rachel, with the aid of my stick, made it alone. Our silent rescuers showed no curiosity about this daft family. Muttering 'adios' they hurried ahead and were soon scrambling on to a ledge at the base of that limestone cliff and casting lines from their reels. Already we could see that the cliff presented an insuperable obstacle: we were doomed to turn inland.

Here the backdrop of trees concealed another long lagoon, this one algae-lidded and of unguessable depth. Searching for an upward path we wandered along its edge, through thickets of leafless thorny bushes. Then Rose found faint footprints leading up a sand-dune to scrubland dotted with cowpats.

'We can try to buy milk from the cows' owners,' said Rose.

'Listen!' exclaimed Clodagh. 'Cocks are crowing, maybe we can buy eggs!'

Firmly I dampened such hopes. 'These Cubans have nothing to spare for foreigners.'

'Why haven't they?' demanded Zea. 'In Italy we're foreigners but our friends next door give us milk and eggs and cheese.'

For a few moments Rachel struggled bravely with comparative economics in simple language – until the Trio raced off in pursuit of a spectacular butterfly.

Soon we were ascending on a rough winding track, its hedges of tall green weeds sprouting minute pink blossoms, delicately scented. We passed several *bohios*, set back from the track – simple dwellings, tiled or frond-roofed, almost invisible among the royal palms and giant banana plants. No one appeared though salsa was pulsing from several radios, activating Rachel's hips. Pigs, poultry and lurchers abounded, the dogs nervous of strangers, not bred to guard property.

Clodagh asked, 'Can we stay all day on paths like this?' Her mother replied, 'We'll try to.' But I felt pessimistic and my future solo ventures into the high Sierra Maestra proved that continuous paths are indeed quite rare.

Within an hour we were back on the road, a few miles beyond and above the bridge. In the comparative cool of the morning, with a strong breeze off the sea, we enjoyed that corniche climb below high, multi-coloured cliffs – beige, pink, yellow, rust-red. On our left small bushy trees hid the ocean and a wide grassy verge allowed comfortable walking.

All the traffic was equine, as many mules as horses, most in splendid condition, glossy and happy, unlike their overworked Santiago cousins. Briskly trotting pairs drew canopied carriages (homemade, no two alike), rarely overloaded. Youths cantered on sprightly ponies, slow open carts were piled with sacks, a woman astride her horse's rump balanced a wicker basket of bananas on the saddle, pack-mules were almost invisible beneath their burdens of firewood and charcoal, a family sang as they went – father in the saddle, mother and toddler behind, Zea-sized son clutching their horse's mane. A cowboy, complete with lasso on pommel and shiny spurs, outpaced the rest. Some saddles and bridles were elaborately beautiful, the status symbols of a motor-free world.

Where this gradual climb ended the Trio were at first more interested in raisins than in the panorama ahead. Far below stretched a narrow valley, its exuberant vegetation vividly lush, and for miles beyond – as far as one could see – silver cliffs, sharp and sheer, rose from a sparkling sapphire sea.

'It's all too rocky!' complained Clodagh. 'Where can we swim?'

Rose heaved a melodramatic sigh. 'Seems we'll be stuck on this road all day.'

'And it's getting near the too hot time,' Zea grimly reminded us.

Rachel reassured them, indicating the flat land where the corniche ended. 'Somewhere there we'll surely find a cove.'

During our descent my main concern (unspoken) was food: how to find it. Adults can live off their fat for several days but the Trio couldn't be expected to keep going on handfuls of raisins. I foresaw starvation aborting this trek. We should have listened more attentively to Irma.

Down on level ground, at 11.15, Zea voiced what we all felt – 'I'm *boiling*!' Here undulating pastureland separated the nearby foothills from the coast and we paused by a rudimentary gate on our left. The pathlet beyond traversed a grassy slope and led to a *bohio* dwarfed by its palm grove.

'Let's go this way,' urged Clodagh. 'I can hear a beach.'

'But the path goes to someone's home,' objected Rose, always punctilious on such matters.

'We can go round the house,' argued Clodagh. 'We won't disturb them.'

'We'll be quiet as a mouse,' guaranteed Zea.

I looked at Rachel – what would our leader decide?

At this crucial moment Miguel appeared, trotting eagerly towards us along the verge, a small wiry mulatto with a big smile and a big heart, wearing only white cotton shorts and sandals. Introducing himself, he stroked the Trio's uncombed locks (one doesn't waste the cool hours on toilettes) and offered water, shelter, *cena* (an evening meal). 'I'm a teacher in this school' – pointing to a solitary building on a ridge-top – 'and I live in this house' – pointing to the *bohio*. 'Now is too hot to march, you must rest by the sea with coconuts.'

It later transpired that Miguel shared the tiny *bohio* with his mother, his eight-year-old son Raul, his sister and her nine-year-old daughter and two-year-old son. His dentist wife was on a two-year 'internationalist' mission to Venezuela, based in a high village near the Columbian border. One can understand why Cuba's medical and educational teams are such a success in the Majority World's remoter regions and are so praised for their adaptability. They bring with them Minority World skills but take in their stride living conditions that our pampered aid workers would find intolerable.

Just beyond the empty *bohio*, where we left our gear, we were suddenly on a beach. This cove must have been a buccaneer's favourite – concealed from above by dense palm groves, its half-mile crescent sheltered to east and west by high wooded promontories. Miguel helped Zea over a barrier of hurricane detritus, then set about providing refreshment. Well-aimed stones brought down three coconuts, with his machete Miguel topped them and, when we had drunk the milk, shells were split and bits used to scoop out the white jelly lining. Coconuts come free, scarce pesos must be spent on the mandatory boiling of water. Countless discarded shells lay under the trees: acceptable fast-food litter.

Now the sea was subdued, only a slight swell recalling the night's tumult, and the swimming Trio were soon joined by Raul. When they all emerged Miguel encouraged his son to speak English with the visitors, a suggestion not adopted. Later, I noticed the four conversing at length in whatever hybrid language children devise for themselves.

In mid-afternoon Miranda appeared – Miguel's sister – looking worried. She welcomed us enthusiastically, then the siblings retreated to the *bohio* and twenty minutes later Miguel returned to announce a change of plan. Miranda was worried because only *casa particulares* are legally entitled to entertain foreign guests. Therefore we must move to their father's *bohio*, also near the shore but west of the cove. It no more resembled a *casa particulare* than Miguel's home so what was going on? Were local politics (in Cuba even more opaque than elsewhere) somehow involved? Perhaps Father belonged to this zone's CDR and could give himself permission to break the law. When Miguel gallantly offered to carry both our rucksacks I handed over mine – now tragically light, minus Buccaneros.

For the building of Father's three-roomed *bohio* enough concrete blocks had been available to raise half a house, neatly plastered and white-washed with a tin roof. The more attractive half, of rough-hewn planks, had a red-tiled roof. When Hurricane Dennis badly damaged one plank wall, jagged scraps of rusty corrugated iron, washed ashore by the hurricane, were used to replace it. The floors were of polished cement, flimsy six-foot partitions served as interior walls and curtains served as doors. The unglazed windows had wooden shutters but no insect screens. Two cane rocking-chairs, a long bare wooden bench and a TV set furnished the living-room. A double-bed and a large unsteady cupboard filled one bedroom, the other held only three charpoy-type beds.

We were graciously received by Father, a well-built, broad-browed, soft-spoken man in his fifties, several shades darker than his café-au-lait children. Grandad, a tall, thin, vigorous octogenarian seemed shy of us; he looked pure Creole, his strong regular features recalling portraits of those eighteenth-century grandees appointed to rule Cuba. The island's racial mix increasingly fascinated me, a mix only acknowledged as an advantage when Castroism fostered pride in being Cuban.

When we were shown to the double-bedded room Clodagh frowned and wondered, 'Where will our friends sleep, if we're in their bed?' Rachel insisted that we could sleep outside, that we liked camping under the stars. As Zea began to contradict her, expressing a preference for a bed in a house, Rose said 'Shush!' Then Father decisively dismissed our scruples and Zea relaxed.

On the back verandah stood a wooden trestle 'dining table', its 'chairs' a few shaky stacks of crates. Nearby was the charcoal fuelled mud-stove, built on to the outer wall and recently augmented by an electric rice-steamer which shared the living-room's one socket with the TV set. A freighter-load of Chinese rice-steamers had been recently imported by the government and made available to all Cubans at affordable prices. After sunset the whole *bohio* depended on that room's solitary 15-watt bulb. The pathway to the plank earth-closet (roofless and doorless) led through a banana grove but was now blocked by one of Wilma's royal palm victims which Miguel would deal with as soon as he could borrow a suitable saw. When Rachel sought the loo Grandad hurried after her to provide a few squares of newspaper.

With this family we immediately felt at home, being readily accepted as oddities and causing no alteration in the domestic routine. As Raul showed us around the compound I noticed two hens on the table, industriously pecking. Soon after, Grandad could be seen shooing them off before pouring rice and spreading it widely, then carefully flicking aside bits of grit.

Meanwhile Miranda was drawing water from the very deep well, its contents disconcertingly murky but safe to drink when boiled. Beside it grew two spindly orange trees, their fruit small, bitter and dry. Raul warned the Trio not to enter the grassless paddock, shaded by several spreading mango trees, where six white short-horned cows and a black bull spent the hot hours. At sunset Raul drove the cows on to pastureland and fed grass clippings from the roadside to the bull. In contrast, a small flock of slim, long-legged sheep – light brown with dark brown lambs – then returned home to another fenced paddock. 'Are you sure they're sheep?' asked Zea. 'They look more like goats!'

Next came the excitement of our supper being hunted. Miguel, Raul and one of four dogs pursued a hen all around the compound before cornering her. When Miguel had swiftly strangled her Miranda immersed the corpse in boiling water, then plucked and gutted it – and two sows quarrelled over the guts.

The sow's mate, a massive boar, was confined in a small smelly sty, roofed with banana fronds, and was allowed out only to beget piglets. When Miguel complained, 'He can be very dangerous!' I thought, 'Wouldn't you be dangerous if imprisoned in darkness unless procreative?' The sows and their numerous offspring roamed all over the compound and far beyond, eating a prolific weed found in shady places.

As Richard Gott records, pigs arrived in Cuba with the earliest Spanish settlers, many of their progeny escaping and wandering all over the island. Soon pork had become, as it remains, an important source of protein. From the natives of neighbouring Haiti, Cuba's 'Indians' learned how to preserve meat for sale to pirates and smugglers – first dry it in the sun, then lay it on a rack (known in the native language as a 'boucan' or 'buccan') above a smokey fire of green leaves and sappy branches. 'Those who prepared and sold the meat were referred to as "boucaniers" or buccaneers.' Thus 'the word became associated with the pirates themselves, the men who brought home the bacon.'

While the aged hen was being simmered to tenderness, Miguel, Raul and several other children led us to the nearest beach – under mango trees, through a bean field, across an acre or so of desiccated pasture. We forded a clear shallow river just below its homemade dam, the locals' bathroom and laundry. Again the wind had strengthened (evidently an afternoon phenomenon) and white breakers were being driven towards an exposed shore from which a line of dark battlemented rocks extended far into the ocean. This sand was unusually soft and deep and Zea flagged, requesting a piggy-back. Intuiting my silent disapproval, Rachel reminded me, 'She's not yet six!' I forebore to remind her that when not quite five she herself had to negotiate the jungle paths of Coorg for many miles without piggy-backs.

Craving a little solitude I fell behind the rest and strolled by the waves, enjoying an orange and purple sunset (presaging thunder, said Miguel) while thinking backwards, as is my wont. This district's sadly eroded state has a pre-Revolution cause. All the coastal land west of Santiago once formed part of the Hacienda Sevilla, belonging to the cement-making and ship-building Babun brothers, from the Lebanon. They also exported mahogany and cedar, stripping the mountains of magnificent forests, now replaced by almost valueless secondary growth. Perhaps the Babuns had second sight; fourteen months before Fidel's victory they sold their hacienda for a million dollars. Three Babun sons, eclectically named Santiago, Omar and Lancelot, soon after joined the CIA's surrogate 'régime change' militia and in 1961 went ashore at the Bay of Pigs. Other Sierra Maestra *latifundos* belonged to the aristocratic (sort of) Cespedes family, to several members of the Castillo family and to the New Niquero, Cape Cruz and Beattie Sugar Companies. The local *campesiños* grew coffee, burnt charcoal and lived permanently on the brink of destitution. Traditionally, hereabouts, food cultivation was limited to river beds – where their configuration permitted it.

On our way back we saw Father having his evening bath in the dam, soaping himself all over. 'You like to wash?' asked Miguel. 'This soap you can use' – a touchingly generous offer, given the soap shortage. We declined it, being less keen than the Cubans on personal hygiene and feeling adequately cleansed by the sea.

In the dusky compound we watched a bedtime ritual, much squawking and fluttering and pecking as hens and cocks flew and climbed to their perches high in a mango tree. Clodagh marvelled – 'I didn't know hens can *fly*! Ours can't.' 'Because we chop their wings,' explained Rose. Zea asked, 'Is the dead hen cooked yet?'

It was and in near darkness we sat around the table and were urged to help ourselves from the rice-steamer and a battered tin saucepan. Only two tin plates and three spoons were available; fingers replaced knives and forks. Given a skinny hen and a starved Trio, Rachel and I restricted ourselves to token spoonfuls of rice and delicious gravy. A basin of water and a threadbare towel stood by the table for hand-washing before and after. Having made all the suitable noises, we retired as the family sat down to ample helpings of rice and beans. The Trio had stripped the chicken bones even of their gristly bits.

On the narrow floorspace between bed and wall Rose and I spread our flea-bags amidst a lively population of giant cockroaches, happily not noticed by Rose who slept instantly. When all three were asleep Rachel and I conferred in whispers about a suitable farewell gift; it's stressful being capitalists in a society conditioned not to think in terms of profit. We were carrying no presents (a major mistake) and because this affectionate, demonstrative family was treating us not as tourists but as new friends we feared money might strike a discordant note. Yet we couldn't leave without contributing something to the household. And after all this wasn't a traditional rural Muslim community with a strict 'no payment from guests' code. We decided on CP20, to be discreetly slipped from Rachel to Miranda as we left – 'for the children'.

The family's addiction to *Yanqui* films on TV kept us adults awake until midnight and thereafter our slumbers were uneasy. Clodagh and Zea frequently kicked Rachel and I sweated in my bag but was deterred by those hyperactive cockroaches from lying *on* it. At dawn we quickly packed up but Father insisted that we must wait – the Trio must have milk for breakfast. Clearly an immediate departure would have given offence: we had to resign ourselves to losing the cool hours. In our room Rachel furtively fed raisins to the again hungry Trio. *Desayuño* consisted only of very sweet herbal tea, two chipped enamel mugs being filled from that battered saucepan and passed around casually as people went about their morning chores. Before dressing for school, Miranda's daughters herded the sheep to their grazing while Raul fetched the cows. Father and Miguel went first to the dam; twice-daily ablutions are de rigueur. Before following them Grandad fetched firewood while Miranda cleared the stove, dumping its ashes in the long-drop, an effective and environmentally sound 'air freshener'.

Pedro arrived then, a handsome youth wearing baggy jeans and a baseball cap and riding a piebald mare with foal at foot. He had come to collect milk and offered the Trio rides. Zea hesitated when her turn came, then objected, 'There's no saddle, I might fall off!' 'Don't be *silly*!' snapped Rose. 'She's not going to gallop!'

Meanwhile Father was milking, squatting by the pail, quietly crooning, leaning his head against a hind leg. 'Why doesn't he have a stool?' wondered Clodagh. 'Daddy sits to milk goats.' 'Different countries have different habits,' pronounced Rose, looking wise. Zea had long since fallen for Miguel and was now watching him washing the churn by the well, scouring it with handfuls of sand, a procedure which might disturb EU dairy inspectors. Then pails of frothy warm milk were poured into the churn through a sieve and I envied the Trio. Milk straight from the cow is my second-favourite drink.

At departure time (8.15) Zea rightly remarked, 'It's nearly too hot already.' We walked close to the cliff edges where noisily pounding waves flung spray so high that momentary rainbows fascinated Zea, usually the first to notice such fleeting details. Cacti – mainly prickly pear – bristled along the cliff tops and low grassy foothills sloped up from the road with many rocky outcrops. Few dwellings were visible but numerous livestock grazed high up – mingling together, not in fields – and over all circled Cuba's omnipresent turkey vultures, unlovely but useful. Although the Sierra Maestra closely accompanies this coast, rising to eight thousand feet and more, the visual drama is lessened by an odd feature – natural terracing, each terrace six or seven hundred feet high.

Where the road briefly curved inland barbed wire fencing appeared on our left, displaying little 'Military Zone' notices. Soon we saw an army barracks, no bigger than a villa but flying the flag. At my suggestion we hurried past in silence. 'Camping wild', as the ridiculous phrase has it, is illegal in Cuba, hence our need to avoid official attention as much as possible. In fact the only sign of life was a young woman hanging nappies to dry on a line strung between two basketball stands without nets. However, three large raised vegetable beds, well tended, indicated troops in residence.

By 11.15 all were wilting and as we approached a Dennis-shattered bus shelter I suggested waiting for motor transport to Uvero, the nearest possible source of food. Apart from those rotting bananas, I had eaten almost nothing since leaving Santiago, Rachel's Chivirico lunch was two days past and the Trio's breakfast milk intake, though generous, seemed an aeon away to them.

This short-haul open lorry, uncrowded by either people or sacks, dated from the Khruschev era and its rattling precluded conversation with our jolly fellow-passengers. Around the first corner we turned on to a winding, shady track and had to crouch to avoid overhanging branches. Banana plants at varying stages of growth surrounded a few concrete post-Revolution dwellings. We stopped outside a large compound – sending teenage pigs squealing into the undergrowth – to deliver an elderly man and his sack of manioc. Plaintively Clodagh asked, 'Why can't we *stay* on paths like this? It's so nice and cool!' I pointed ahead: the track ended below a precipitous terrace accessible only to goats. As the lorry turned (a tricky manoeuvre) two mothers carrying babies hurried towards us, relieved to get a lift to Uvera's polyclinic where the infants were due to have some inoculation. Come economic hell or high water, no Cuban baby goes uninoculated.

Ten minutes later, in a straggling little town, the driver refused any payment and directed us towards the restaurant, one of a row of drab two-storey 1960s houses set back from the road. At 12.30 p.m. it was firmly closed: peering through the window we saw four tables on which chairs had been upturned. The next-door state bakery sold unlimited fresh lime juice, served ice-cold in small jam jars for NP1. Its day's stock of ship's biscuits was gone but we rejoiced to see, on otherwise bare shelves, two long yellow-brown cakes, each weighing half a kilo and costing NP10. These were stodgy and over-sweet (I sampled a fragment) but the Trio fell upon them as Rachel asked if there were any more, or anything else edible. No, not until mañana, but sometimes the *tienda* across the road stocked tinned food. Leaving the Trio under a mango tree finishing those revolting cakes, Rachel cruised around in search of fruit while I investigated the *tienda*. Even in Rachel's estimation, our current state of malnutrition would surely justify the purchase of those junk foods we had so improvidently spurned in Chivirico. But Uvero's residents, lacking tourism-generated convertible pesos, apparently couldn't afford junk food. They could however occasionally afford beer and ruthlessly I bought the entire stock of nine half-litre tins. The amiable and very beautiful young woman behind the counter assumed that I was on my way to Uvero's Rebel Army monument – some way up a hillside, guarded by a stately grove of royal palms. But I lacked the energy to pay my respects and anyway the others weren't interested.

Uvero earned its place in the history books on 28 May 1957 when it was the scene of a guerrilla victory described by Ché Guevera as having 'a greater psychological impact than any other in the history of the war'. Yet this battle lasted only two and three-quarter hours. A small wooden barracks almost on the beach, beside an enormous Babun lumber storehouse, was defended by fifty-three Batista troops and attacked by eighty guerrillas. These included one US citizen named Charles Ryan and Celia Sanchez, the first woman to fight in the Rebel Army's front line. A doctor's daughter from nearby Media Luna, Celia had supplied most of the weaponry used on this occasion. The Batistas lost fourteen dead, another fourteen captured, nineteen wounded – and six who ran away. Six guerrillas were killed and two seriously injured. In our day of proliferating small (and not so small) arms, and the indiscriminate bombing of 'suspected terrorist' homes and villages, Cuba's civil war seems a mere skirmish.

Ché wrote:

This battle was one of the bloodiest of the revolutionary war. It was an assault by men who had advanced bare-chested against an enemy protected by very poor defences. It should be recognised that on both sides great courage was shown. For us this was the victory which marked our coming of age. From this battle on, our morale grew tremendously, our decisiveness and our hopes for triumph increased also. Although the months which followed were difficult ones, we were already in possession of the secret of victory. This action at El Uvero sealed the fate of all small barracks situated far from major clusters of enemy forces, and they were all closed soon after.

The victors took with them to their mountain hideouts the fourteen prisoners (soon to be released: their nuisance value was considerable) and a loggers' truck with all the medical equipment and weaponry they could collect. Then as now, but for different reasons, Uvero was not where one stocked up on food.

Some of the easiest Sierra Maestra tracks were (and still are) those gouged out by loggers. Throughout this area the Rebel Army received much help from a childhood friend of the Castro brothers, Enrique Lopez, who worked for the Babun brothers – close friends of Batista & Co.

Rachel's cruising had been fruitless and we held an emergency meeting under the mango tree. Without food we could walk no further. Our guide-book mentioned a *campismo* with canteen at La Mula, some ten miles to the west. Most *campismos* are off-limit for tourists but surely three starving children would soften official hearts – Cuban hearts being peculiarly susceptible to juvenile charms.

'Let's swim before we hitch,' pleaded Rose, echoed by her sisters. That cake had worked wonders. But Uvero's sloping beach proved swimmer-unfriendly just then: romping waves were ebbing too fast. Back on the road, our luck changed; a grossly over-crowded truck-bus was about to depart for Pilon, via La Mula. Boldly we forced our way on, having got the message that every stationary truck-bus is a challenge to be overcome.

A large black man took Clodagh on to his knee, I took Zea on to mine, Rachel and Rose stood. The young woman who formed the other half of a Rose sandwich guessed our destination and was sympathetic. She doubted if the *campismo*, wrecked by Dennis, had yet reopened. But perhaps we'd be allowed to sleep there because of the niños . . .

We were put down on a long bridge spanning a gorge between high spurs, their bases palm-fringed. Here began another cornice and below lay the *campismo*, looking dormant, its wide gate closed. Most of the concrete cabins had new tin roofs. Slithering down a dusty embankment we surmounted piles of hurricane débris, found an opening in the damaged fence and were not warmly welcomed by a pot-bellied caretaker with a crew cut and a livid diagonal scar across his golden-brown back. No, we couldn't camp here and there was no food – or electricity, or running water. Nor could we swim (tempting waves sparkled twenty yards away) because Dennis had piled tons of mingled seaweed and tree-trunks against the malecón. And there was no nearby beach. At this point a Trio riot might have been forgiven but all three stoically accepted how things were, shared a litre of water (happily we'd been able to refill our bottles in Uvero's bakery) and asked for their *sudoku* books and pencils. Grudgingly, the caretaker had agreed to our heat-dodging in the spacious circular pavilion, furnished with new café tables and surrounded by badly mangled palms. When functioning, this simple *campismo* must be an attractive spot. Where else in the world are such affordable resorts now provided by the government?

Rachel and I pondered the ethics of the situation. If we waved a CP20 note (a fortune in rural Cuba) would the caretaker suddenly find himself able to feed us? Probably yes, but perhaps only by depriving others of their rations. The *libreta* system undoubtedly works; we saw no Cubans anywhere looking undernourished. (Only during the worst of the Special Period did malnutrition strike, for the first time since 1959.) It would therefore be cruel ('unethical' too weak a word) for relatively rich foreigners to rock the rationing boat.

In a report for the organisation 'Sustain', by Courtney Van de Weyer, we are reminded that in Britain, from 1940–1953, 'Rationing resulted in a restricted, yet nutritious, diet for the wider population. Limited as it was, it is often suggested that the British population has never been healthier than during those years. Certainly infant mortality decreased and children's general health improved. The rations provided the poor with more protein and vitamins, and the rest of the population ate less meat, fats and sugar.'

Rachel now proposed going backwards for a mile or so to a tiny cove glimpsed from the truck-bus. There we could swim, eat raisins and sleep before continuing west to Las Cuevas, the next village. If it proved foodless we'd have to admit defeat and take a vehicle – if possible onwards to Marea del Portillo, otherwise back to Santiago.

The Trio approved of that little cove, its patch of sand separated from the ocean by a climbable rock barrier through which waves surged to form a pool some three feet deep and fifteen yards wide. Our arrival was observed by a young woman who immediately hurried down from her hillside *bohio*, with toddler at foot, to warn us that beyond the barrier flowed dangerous undercurrents. Appalled by the notion of our camping out she invited us to stay – but tentatively, uneasily, not with Miguel's light-heartedness. We hesitated, thinking 'rice and chicken'. She would however be taking a risk by entertaining us and she looked quite relieved when we declined her invitation.

A low headland, grassy and scrubby, overlooked our cove to the east and there I found an ideal – by my standards – campsite. The Trio had other standards. 'It's not level,' objected Rose, 'we could roll over the edge while we're asleep.' 'There are lumpy stones under the grass,' reported Clodagh after an inspection. 'The grass has prickly things in it,' added Zea.

Rachel and I, underfed and short-tempered, ignored all this, unrolled five flea-bags and said, 'Bedtime!' We then finished the Buccaneros, slapping at mosquitoes while a swollen golden moon slid upwards through diaphanous streamers of cloud. Nearby rose some of the Sierra Maestra's highest ridges along which, on the night of 27–28 May 1957, Fidel led the amateur Rebel Army to attack Uvero's barracks. Following a loggers' track, in total darkness and moving silently as cats, it took them eight hours to cover the ten miles from their La Plata camp.

In *Reminiscences of the Cuban Revolutionary War* Ché recalls that at other times the Rebels endured extreme thirst and hunger:

> We rationed our water – and with what precision! We distributed it in the eyepiece of a pair of field-glasses; nothing could be fairer. Coming to a mountain torrent we threw ourselves to the ground and drank for a long time with the avidity of horses. We would have continued but our stomachs, empty of food, refused to absorb another drop. We filled our flasks and kept going.

> Elsewhere, one man was reduced to drinking his own urine and Ché, a chronic asthma sufferer, unsuccessfully tried to coax water from a damp rockface with his breathing apparatus. Now and then minute residues of water were found in parasite plants. And when Fidel and two of his men became separated from the others, and had to hide in a canefield for several days, they survived by chewing and sucking the cane stalks.

At dawn the others were somewhere else, not where their bags had been laid. Rachel, I deduced, had had a testing time, coping with Rose's paranoia about falling off the cliff and Clodagh's absurd sensitivity to a few pebbles. Only Zea and I were feeling bouncy after a sound night's sleep. With no breakfast to delay us, we were marching west by 6.45 as the sky behind us brightened.

Here was an austerely beautiful corniche. Its sheer naked cliffs – streaked ochre, silver, pink – towered above us as we walked by a narrow pebbly verge, devoid of vegetation, overhanging the dazzling blue sea. This sparsely inhabited area generated little traffic of any sort. We often rested and doled out raisins but those cliffs acted as storage-heaters and by 10.00 exhaustion threatened.

'Let's have a long rest,' begged Clodagh. 'Where?' demanded Rose. 'There's no shade.' 'I'm hot enough to *die*,' announced Zea. 'Best to keep going,' said Rachel, 'Las Cuevas must be close.' And it was.

Around the next bend the corniche ended in a short, wide valley where a few score scattered dwellings, linked by stony paths, clung to steep slopes. Alas! there was no beach; fifty feet below the road rough seas swirled over sharp rocks. Here the Trio took refuge under a row of puny wayside trees while their seniors foraged.

Las Cuevas was dusty, grey, arid and quiet; occasionally a distant figure appeared as we passed the polyclinic, local government offices and a school with the customary playground bust of José Martí, leader of the 1895-8 independence struggle against Spain – reminding me of the BVM statues once common in Irish school grounds. Only water was available in the bakery where a memorably handsome young man interrupted his domino contest to fill our bottles – for free. He regretted having no ship's biscuits, or anything edible, and informed us that Las Cuevas is shopless.

Rachel broke the bad news to her hungry offspring. 'Seems it has to be Marea de Portillo or back to Santiago.' I marvelled as the endlessly resourceful mother produced a box of coloured chalks and at children's limitless energy. Short of food and sleep, having just walked eight miles – the last hour in punishing heat – the Trio now set about chalking the tree-shaded bit of road and playing hop-scotch. Their parents, I suggested to Rachel, could make lots of money by using them in a TV advertisement for Californian organic raisins.

A trickle of energetic foreigners passes through Las Cuevas, one of the officially approved starting points for the ascent of Pico Turquino, Cuba's highest mountain (1,974 metres). Yet the few villagers who strolled past didn't stop to chat, restricting their greetings to silent nods. Unsupervised tourists are still treated with caution in some rural areas.

Sitting on the gravely ground, using rucksacks propped against trees as backrests, Rachel and I laid bets on when/if a vehicle would appear and in which direction it might take us. To the west the corniche continued for miles, curving around those radiator cliffs, and once a truck came into view, galvanising us. A false hope, its destination was local. When the hop-scotchers gave up at noon Zea and I settled to rummy, the others being in *sudoku* mode. Not long after an elderly man approached – wiry and fine-featured, wearing a kind expression and an air of authority. Shaking hands with Rachel and me he addressed us both as compañera and introduced himself as Wilfredo. (First names are the norm in Castro's Cuba; the President being universally known as 'Fidel' is not quirky.) Were we waiting for public transport or expecting a friend to arrive? If no vehicle came we could sleep in the Turquino National Park rangers' hut: he pointed to it, on a ledge beyond the village. Meanwhile would we like some refreshment? A milky hot chocolate drink? Fresh orange juice? Like puppies at feeding time the Trio yelped with excitement.

Wilfredo lived in a larger-than-average white-washed house high above the road and we watched him taking a short cut, nimbly leaping from boulder to boulder. Forty minutes later he descended on a path, bearing litre jugs of hot chocolate and ice-cold pure orange juice – costing a mere NP20. In *tiendas* tins of imported drinking chocolate are wildly expensive but many Cuban villagers grind their own cocoa berries.

During our four-hour wait two licensed taxis passed, one going each way, their passengers staring in astonishment at the displaced persons by the wayside. Then at 2.40 that local lorry reappeared – bound for El Maja, a village so small we'd hardly noticed it on our ride to La Mula. From there, Wilfredo assured us, a dawn bus departs for Uvero – whence an afternoon truck-bus usually (though not always) departs for Santiago.

Six others climbed on to the lorry's load of wooden stakes and the driver invited me into the cab. Our situation puzzled him. From where, how and why had we got stranded in Las Cuevas? My explanation that we had walked most of the way from Chivirico because we enjoy walking left him even more puzzled. On arrival in El Maja I offended him by opening my purse. He made a dismissive gesture and said something derogatory about *capitalismo*. After that, when riding in farm lorries, I suppressed my capitalistic impulse to pay for transport.

El Maja, too, was shopless but I faintly hoped for some other source of beer – perhaps a private enterprise household selling Hatuey? Wandering alone up a side road I discovered that there is more to El Maja than meets the main roader's eye. Several laneways wind between detached or terraced post-'59 one-storey homes. These dreary little dwellings lack the charm of *bohíos* but are supplied with electricity, indoor loos, showers and fridges, evidence of Fidel's wish to modernise rural Cuba. I stopped everyone I met (two men, three women) to ask my 'cerveza?' question. All emphatically said 'No!' and conveyed disapproval of my mission. Possibly Ché's influence persists in these communities. When setting standards for the Rebel Army, after its victory, the ascetic Ché wrote:

> Just as it was in the Sierra, the Rebel must not drink, not because of the punishment that may be inflicted by the disciplinary organism, but simply because the cause that we defend – the cause of the poor and of all the people – requires us not to drink, so that the mind of every soldier is alert, his body agile, his morale high. He must remember that today, as yesterday, the Rebel is the cynosure of all eyes and constitutes an example for the people. There is and can be no great army if the bulk of the population is not convinced of the immense moral strength we possess today.

No mere rhetoric, this. When the Rebels became the rulers of Cuba in January 1959, all observers were astonished by their orderly behaviour. The English historian Hugh Thomas puts it well in his monumental *The Cuban Revolution*:

> There was anxiety lest . . . the successful revolution should spawn endless minor gangster forces roaming violently across the country. In the event, there was little private settling of scores, an almost unparalleled development in such situations in Cuba; and one has only to think of the end of the occupation of France to realise the extent of this achievement by the Cubans.

When I rejoined the others, looking grumpy, Clodagh exclaimed, 'Poor Nyanya! She *needs* beer!' Rachel hid her own yearning and said primly, 'It's good to give our livers a rest now and then.'

Again we went backwards, for a mile or so, to a sheltered beach where mountainous sand dunes would conceal our camp from the road and the swimming was safe and the Trio's mosquito nets could be hung from low sea-grape branches. In the shade of those trees Rachel and I studied the map at length, debating various possibilities, then hatched a new plan. Having bought enough tinned food for a nine-day trek (the Trio would have to do some of the porterage) we'd take a bus to Baracoa and roam through its surrounding mountains on secondary roads. In that much more fertile region bananas at least would be plentiful and to date our nocturnal experiences had been reassuring; it seemed easy to get away with illegal camping.

I unrolled my bag near the waves and for an unforgettable hour lay watching a multicoloured display of distant sheet lightening. We associate lightning with thunder; to me there was something ethereal, mysterious, almost mystical about those spasms of silent brilliance flaring among cloud banks on the far horizon.

Before dawn Rachel was busy dismantling mosquito nets with the aid of her forehead torch.

'It's dark!' grumbled Zea. 'Why are we awake?'

'Because the bus goes early,' replied Rose, 'and if we miss it we must walk to Santiago.'

'I could easily walk,' said Clodagh. 'But Mummy and Nyanya are too empty, they won't eat our raisins.'

As we struggled through the deep loose sand of those high dunes I thought about Ché's September 1958 marathon expedition from the Sierra Maestra to Las Villas province. His second-in-command, Camilo Cienfuegos, afterwards recorded:

Forty days of march, often with the south coast and a compass as the only guide. During fifteen days we marched with water and mud up to the knees. Travelling by night to avoid ambushes . . . During the thirty-one days of our journey across Camaguey we ate eleven times. After four days of famine we had to eat a mare.

Ché himself recalled that on the banks of the La Plata river, three miles from Las Cuevas:

We ate our first horse . . .

The horse was more than a luxury meal; it was also testing the men's capacity to adapt. The peasants in our group were indignant and refused their ration. Some considered Manuel Fajardo a virtual murderer, for he was the man chosen to slaughter the animal since he had been a butcher in peacetime . . . That tired old horse constituted an exquisite feast for some and a test for the prejudiced stomachs of the peasants, who believed they were committing an act of cannibalism as they chewed up man's old friend.

At the bus stop a crowd of thirty or more – mainly young people – had already gathered in the half-light. Although it wasn't a queue-shaped crowd one young woman made it plain, politely but firmly, that as the latest arrivals we just might be left behind. Seemingly buses and truck-buses have different boarding conventions. As the sun rose No. 7 appeared, a small Cuban-made model with unglazed windows, broken doors and metal seats. By then we were no longer the latest arrivals and the same young woman saw to it that the newcomers didn't 'jump' us. Queues don't have to be queue-shaped to work.

At numerous junctions, where mountain tracks joined the road, passengers got on and off; twice the driver had trouble starting a US-born engine that may well have been aged when transplanted to this bus body.

By 8.30 we were back on Playa Virginia where rummy filled the gaps between swims. The bakery opened at 10.00 but it wasn't a ship's biscuit day. The *tienda* opened at 11.00 but had been drained of its monthly ration of cerveza. At noon we were first into the restaurant but lean pork was off the menu and despite (or because of?) being so 'empty' I found my mound of rice, mixed with chunks of bristly fat, hard to take.

Lest the truck-bus not stop for us on the main road we walked to its terminus shed, a shadeless uphill mile from the restaurant. That journey – as crowded and much hotter than our early ride from Santiago – tested everyone's stoicism to the limit.

Irma was not even slightly surprised to see us back on her doorstep several days ahead of schedule.

Chapter 5

As the Viazul coach (there is no Santiago-Baracoa alternative) hooted through an agreeable rush-hour – fiacres, bicycles, children thronging to school – a row of hundred-foot royal palms stood out blackly against a blood-red sunrise and Clodagh said, 'I'd like to paint that!' Two couples, Canadian and Swedish, were looking forward to a taxi trip from Guantanamo city to Cuba's most piquant tourist attraction, Mirador Los Malones. From that high platform the US naval-base-cum-concentration-camp may be observed through a telescope sardonically provided by the Cuban army. Our other fellow-passengers were bound for various towns en route; only *los irlandeses* went all the way to Baracoa.

Beyond the city gentle blue hills overlooked wide pastures and Rose observed that the numerous cattle were much bonier than their coastal cousins. Cuba's early settlers had rejoiced to find the island so well suited to stock-raising and Europe's craving for cheap leather soon made the creoles rich. Annually throughout the 1570s, twenty thousand hides were legally exported; illegal trading probably doubled that figure. By the end of the seventeenth century enormous ranches covered areas later given over to cane, coffee and tobacco. Until the 1820s cattle and tobacco remained dominant, though by then Cuba's three thousand ranches and five thousand tobacco farms were competing with one thousand colossal sugar mills and two thousand *cafetales*.

The Trio exclaimed in wonder as we drove through a fragment of dense forest, some trees liana-draped, some sustaining complexities of epiphytes like fantastical hanging baskets. Along the shaded roadsides tall coffee bushes thrived but too soon this interlude was over.

Although the Revolution has done much to lessen Oriente's disadvantages it remains Cuba's poorest region, the countryside mainly populated by blacks. Most are descended from the thousands of Jamaicans and Haitians who, in the late nineteenth and early twentieth centuries, sought work on Cuba's expanding cane plantations. Their isolated thatched *bohios* peep out of thriving banana groves and, despite the petrol shortage, school buses still serve their children – taking some to the nearest town and those from remote homesteads to weekly boarding-schools.

During each short stop the Trio commented on this area's comparative abundance of food. Wayside stalls sold homemade buns and pizzas or hefty pork sandwiches prepared while you wait, the juicy joints being dexterously carved with rapier-like knives. Said Rose, 'We should've trekked around here.'

In these smallish towns only an occasional Flamboyant or almond tree, or a piled fruit stall, brightened streets of (mostly) one-storey houses, their unpainted façades of weather-bleached wood, mangy stucco or dismal concrete. Paint had been virtually unobtainable since 1992. Front gardens were rare but on some pillared verandahs flowering shrubs were carefully cultivated in leaking cauldrons, cracked jugs, a damaged drawer, a dead fridge. Such towns can sound and smell truly rural – cocks crowing in the background, pigsty aromas drifting on the breeze – but for obvious reasons Cuba lacks picturesque old villages.

Always slaves were accommodated (imprisoned) on their owners' land. Then, after emancipation in the 1880s (it was a gradual process), those with access to a little plot – as tenants, sharecroppers or squatters – built individual isolated *bohíos*. So did small farmers, mulatto and white, and any casual labourers who could find a site of no interest to the *latifundistas*. Throughout large areas there were no churches, primary schools, shops, cottage hospitals, medical dispensaries or sports fields – those institutions around which European villages coalesced. In the towns, built along main roads with perhaps a few unpaved back streets, lived merchants and wholesalers, lawyers, doctors and teachers (not many) and the local administrators and security forces (too many). *Bohío* dwellers walked or rode to the towns to shop, meet friends, and, if literate, collect their mail, normally addressed 'care of' a merchant; the government provided neither post offices nor deliveries to scattered homes.

On the narrow road between Navarrete (originally a cattle-ranchers' town) and Guantanamo city we caught up with a snail-slow Cupet oil-tanker, small and rusty, trapped behind a sedate bullock-cart with truck-wheel tyres. Over the next few miles, until we came to a junction, the ambling bullocks Ruled OK, their cigar-smoking driver feeling no need to whip them for the benefit of motor vehicles. To me, a comforting incident: but our driver muttered imprecations. By this stage the Trio were asleep, their devoted Irma having roused them at 5.00 a.m. to allow time for a three-course breakfast.

We skirted Guantanamo, a city chiefly notable for its proximity to the US base. Founded in 1796 to accommodate French colonists fleeing from Haiti, coffee stimulated its rapid development. The refugees rejoiced to find ideal conditions for their favourite crop on Santiago's hills and in the valleys between Guantanamo and Baracoa. By 1803 they had planted one hundred thousand bushes and by 1807 four million were flourishing on a hundred and ninety-one *cafetales*. Unfortunately coffee farming is labour intensive and the sugar industry was also booming and not enough blacks had migrated from Haiti. As the slave trade quickened the Sociedad Economica, representing Cuba's most powerful landowners, urged Madrid to sponsor white immigration. One of its most influential spokesmen, Francisco Arango, designed a scheme to 'whiten' rural areas by establishing ready-to-use villages for immigrants. Cuba's then captain-general (governor) liked this plan and in 1817 Madrid agreed to tempt poor Spaniards with land grants and tax concessions; the scheme was to be funded by an import tax of six pesos on each male slave. Between 1818 and 1821 more than fifty-six thousand males were unloaded at Havana and one could do a lot of colonising with three hundred and thirty-six thousand pesos. Yet those carefully scattered villages, visualised by Arango, never materialised. Instead, the towns of Cienfuegos, Mariel and Nuevitas were founded in unpopulated areas.

By 1830 Cuba's population was reckoned to be more than half black, counting legally freed slaves and *cimmarones* (runaways who hid in the forests and mountains.) The landowners became increasingly twitchy; their ever-expanding plantations urgently needed more and more slaves – who might any day 'do a Haiti'. In Madrid, Cuba's rulers, foreseeing just that, proposed ending the slave trade to all Spain's Caribbean colonies. As Eric Williams has written:

> The emancipation of the slaves in French Saint-Domingue and their establishment of the independent republic of Haiti, recognised by the Great Powers, elevated the slave revolt from the field of island politics to the sphere of national policy and international diplomacy.

In 1832 Daniel O'Connell, the Irish campaigner for Catholic Emancipation, put it more graphically in the British House of Commons:

> The planter is sitting, dirty and begrimed, over a powder magazine, from which he will not go away, and he is hourly afraid that the slave will apply a torch to it.

Around this time the annexationists emerged, grouped around José Antonio Saco, a polemical journalist and, in our terms, activist. These men, loosely associated with the Sociedad Economica, were the first Cubans to think of their island not as a fragment of Spain that chanced to be in another hemisphere but as a place with its own distinctive character, traditions and needs. Saco excoriated the government's multiple ineptitudes; after the loss of most of its empire Spain was unable adequately to govern itself, never mind its remaining colonies. Yet independence never occurred to this group; they advocated annexation to the US where slave-owning was still respectable. Contemplating the imminent emancipation in the British Caribbean, Saco wrote:

> The colonisation of Cuba [by whites] is urgently required . . . It is necessary to counter the ambitions of 1,200,000 Haitians and Jamaicans who seek her lovely beaches and unused lands; it is necessary to neutralise as far as possible the terrible influence of the three million blacks who surround us – and the millions to come by natural increase who will drag us down in the near future in a bitter, bloody holocaust.

Gaspar Betancourt Cisneros, a planter who wrote under the pseudonym El Lugareno, heartily agreed and was even more specific. Cuba needed to be settled with 'superior beings' – Saxons and Germans. Luckily those beings have begun to arrive only recently, as tourists.

Beyond Guantanamo city the level terrain was dusty and brownish-green, the Sierra del Purina a blue-grey blur along the horizon. Here and there brightly clad teams of men and women were slowly swinging machetes in weedy former canefields, clearing corners for vegetable plots. On expanses of over-stocked grassland authentic cowboys, driving cattle to some invisible source of water, brought me back to Christmas Day 1938. In that distant era children didn't write demanding letters to Santa but waited hopefully, relying on his prescience. And sure enough, on Christmas morning I morphed into a cowboy and spent the day galloping around on a stick shooting dangerous wild animals. Even then it would have been held politically incorrect, in an Irish household, to shoot Red Indians – our fellow-victims.

Down at sea-level, marshland bordered the road on our right where scrubby ridges concealed Guantanamo Bay. Rachel spotted a barely legible sign to Caimanera, a town within walking distance of the infamous base – but one is advised not to walk, this area being densely mined. Anyway visitors (even Cubans) need special permits to pass the road-block. For generations Caimanera's residents have been employed by the US marines, to-ing and fro-ing morning and evening. Pragmatic inconsistencies abound in Cuba. Given the island's long-standing unemployment problem – especially acute in this barren region – it made post-Revolution sense to allow Cubans to continue to work for the occupying forces, earning dollars. Because those workers are witnesses to the 'American way of life', Havana supplies all the townspeople with extra rations. The Irish might label Fidel 'a cute hoor', which may be taken as compliment or insult.

Owing to a population of giant lizards (Caimans), now extinct, the indigenous Tainos called Guantanamo Bay 'Caimanero' – as do many contemporary Cubans. Christopher Columbus landed here in 1494 and with dull accuracy renamed it Puerto Grande. Although the largest harbour on Cuba's southern coast, its snags deterred permanent settlement. Prodigious swarms of yellow-fever-bearing mosquitoes plagued its shores, Europeans found its temperature intolerable at all seasons (those enclosing hills!) and its hinterland was infertile. Yet when Admiral Edward Vernon seized Caimanera for Britain in 1741, promptly renaming it Cumberland Bay, he despatched a favourable report in the first flush of conquest. 'I think this spot the best chosen for a British settlement of any in this island and am glad to find the Americans begin to look on it as the Land of Promise already.' Those Americans were six hundred would-be settlers from the Thirteen Colonies.

Soon the admiral was having second thoughts. His ambition had been to march overland to take Santiago – and eventually Havana and the whole island, as Jamaica had been seized a century before. But the Spaniards were waiting nearby with a mixed force of whites, blacks, mulattos and Tainos, all of whom knew the terrain intimately. That knowledge was crucial. The much more numerous invaders, including one thousand Jamaican blacks, didn't get far along the track to Santiago – the almost exact predecessor of the road we were on. Confined thereafter to the Bay and prevented from foraging for food, with hundreds of yellow feverish men to be medicated or buried every day, Vernon had no choice but to lead his eight warships and forty transports back to Jamaica.

In 1898, as General William Rufus Shafter led a fifteen thousand-strong US invasion force towards Oriente, he studied accounts of the Vernon disaster and decided to put his men ashore much closer to Santiago. An expeditionary force of one thousand had already landed at Caimanera and been punished by the Bay's Spanish defenders before escaping to join their Cuban allies in the Sierra.

Incidentally, Bush II is not the first US leader to hallucinate about God Almighty's role in military matters. A *Harpers* journalist accompanying ('embedded with') the Shafter armada quoted one of the Generals on board – 'This is God Almighty's war and we are only His agents.'

When Shafter's force arrived the freedom-fighters had been courageously at war for three years and the Spaniards were weakening. Some Cuban historians argue that the local troops didn't need help; others regard this as an open question no longer worth debating. In any event, having delivered the coup de grâce, the invaders ignored Cuba's military and civilian leaders, made their own arrangements with the Spaniards and presented themselves to the world as victors entitled to set up a military dictatorship. During the next four years Washington's Men in Havana controlled Cuba's political scene. Their puppet-in-chief was Thomas Estrada Palma, lately resident in the US where he hobnobbed with agents of the administration particularly interested in Cuba's economic future. Estrada led the constituent assembly, elected in December 1900 to draft a new constitution and undisguisedly a Washington creation, like its twenty-first-century equivalents in Kabul and Baghdad. Six months later the assembly members voted (by fifteen to fourteen) to include the infamous Platt Amendment as an annex to their embryonic constitution – an Amendment already incorporated into US law on 2 March 1901, *before* the Cuban vote.

The Amendment's first two paragraphs dealt with US control over Cuba's foreign policy and public finances. The third allowed US forces to intervene in Cuban domestic affairs whenever they judged it necessary 'to protect US interests'. The fourth outlawed any criticism or analysis of 'all acts of the US in Cuba during its military occupancy thereof'. The fifth and sixth dealt with disease control and the legal future of the Isle of Pines, now the Isle of Youth off Cuba's south coast. The seventh entitled the US to set up permanent military bases on the island – hence Guantanamo Bay.

Fifteen assembly members accepted Platt only because the alternative was a continuing military occupation; they acknowledged that they had voted for 'a restricted independence'. General Juan Gualberto Gomez, one of the black leaders of the War of Independence, was blunter. He voted against Platt, declaring that it would 'reduce the independence and sovereignty of the Cuban Republic to a myth'. Which it did, until 1 January 1959. Although the Amendment was repealed in 1934 it had by then poisoned Cuba's body politic and the repeal in no way affected the status of Guantanamo Bay as leased property.

In the early 1960s, when the US Joint Chiefs of Staff were frantically seeking a justification for again invading Cuba, they suggested staging a series of lethal attacks on US citizens and interests – all to be blamed, using CIA-concocted 'evidence', on that diabolical Castro. This lunatic project included a plan to simulate a Cuban attack on Guantanamo Bay, employing Cuban exiles to sink a ship by way of deceiving the international media. Havana soon became aware of all these plans, which may partly explain why none was directly implemented.

On 1 May 1964 Fidel emphasised, in his Labour Day speech, that Cuba would never use force in an attempt to reunite the island:

> The base was there when the Revolution triumphed, it is an old problem from half a century ago . . . We have stated that we will never resort to force to solve the problem and that has always been the position of the Revolutionary Government. Because we know those shameless imperialists, we have followed the policy of not giving them any pretext for their plans. We can take whatever time is necessary to discuss and resolve this old problem.

During the 1960s Fidel made some major mistakes but he was too experienced a soldier to bite off, militarily, more than he could chew. Besides, even verbal agitation about reuniting the island would have deflected people's energy from the task in hand – improving their own living conditions.

Our driver took a cigarette break and bought a sack of bananas in the tiny town of Yateritas; state-owned banana plantations, well weeded and watered, cover many nearby acres. When we continued the Caribbean Sea was coruscating beside us, separated from the road by a narrow shore of jaggedly pitted limestone. Gazing across this dazzling water towards the prison, I sent telepathic messages of sympathy to its wretched inmates and winced to remember the methods used to entrap so many 'unlawful combatants'.

To your average Afghan US$5,000 is a small fortune and that was the 'bounty' offered to anyone who handed a 'terrorist' over to US forces or their allies – allies like the criminal Rashid Dostum whose private army was not dedicated to making Afghanistan 'safe for democracy'. In David Rose's chilling exposé of 'Gitmo' (the US pet name for their base) he explains:

> It was enough for 'evidence' merely to assert that an individual was a Taliban fighter or a member of al-Qaeda, and he would be on his way to Gitmo. In the statements made by prominent administration officials . . . evaluation was replaced by tautology. If you were in Guantanamo, it was because you had been captured on the battlefield

and if you had been captured on the battlefield you must have been with the Taliban or al-Qaeda. Entirely missing was any attempt to ascertain, in the case of each prisoner, whether any of these claims was true . . . Hundreds of 'Gitmo' prisoners were absolutely innocent of the least involvement in anything that could be reasonably described as terrorist activity. They ended up there as a result of military-intelligence screening procedures, in Afghanistan and elsewhere, that were flawed and inadequate, made still worse by the use of woefully poor and virtually untrained translators.

Notoriously, the 'unlawful combatant' concept was invented by the Bush II administration to put its captives (imprisoned on leased territory over which the US has no sovereignty) beyond the protection of both the Geneva Conventions and US law. It could also be applied to those 'Coalition' troops who invaded a sovereign state under false pretences in March 2003 to secure US control of Iraq's oil. Personally I would like all homicidal combats to be regarded as 'unlawful'. But that's another debate for another generation – perhaps the Trio's?

The fuzzy notion that 11 September 2001 so traumatised the US administration that it lost its moral compass is sometimes advanced to explain (even excuse) Guantanamo Bay and the US forces' indifference to massive civilian casualties in Afghanistan and Iraq. Some people forget that exactly a decade before '9/11', in September 1991, Haiti's elected president, Jean-Bertrand Aristide, was ousted by a US-sponsored military junta who slaughtered uncounted thousands of his supporters in full view of the world media. Hitherto, the Bush I administration had forcibly repatriated Haitian asylum-seekers; now this programme was put on hold for two months to give the shocked media time to move on (they usually recover quickly from such shocks). Meanwhile the junta's mass-murdering had increased mass-migrations in small boats. As many as six thousand were simultaneously at sea and repatriation was equivalent to a death sentence, as the UN High Commission for Refugees and many other observers pointed out. Various legal bigwigs agreed with Professor Kevin Johnson of the University of California who repeatedly denounced 'the Executive Branch's unlawful treatment of the Haitians'. Eventually, after a shameful Supreme Court judgement in favour of the Executive Branch, the Haitians' champions secured a grim compromise: imprisonment on the 'Gitmo' base for an indefinite period (almost two years in some cases) instead of instant repatriation.

Scores of tents were hastily erected, encircled by barbed wire and swarming with rats, snakes and scorpions. The tents leaked and there were no lavatories, washing facilities or exercise areas. According to the *New York Times*, 'The military and Coast Guard emphasise that theirs is a humanitarian mission'. (Just as NATO's bombing of Kosovo and Serbia was 'a humanitarian intervention'.)

Soon rumours of mistreatment were rife but hard to confirm; the military discouraged visitors. Their anodyne press briefings provoked several independent journalists (now a seriously endangered species) to seek access to Guantanamo Bay through the courts. Thereafter Ingrid Arnsen of *The Nation* interviewed someone who had been imprisoned (or 'detained') for thirteen months and who eloquently contradicted the mainstream US media's depiction of Gitmo as 'a haven for refugees':

> Since we left Haiti last December we've been treated like animals. When we protested about the camp back then, the military beat us up. I was beaten, handcuffed, and they spat in my face. I was chained, made to sleep on the ground.

Some of those prisoners were personally known to Paul Farmer, Professor of Medical Anthropology at Harvard Medical School. In *Pathologies of Power* he wrote:

> In the eight months following the coup, the US Coast Guard intercepted thirty-four thousand Haitians on the high seas; the majority of these refugees were transported to Guantanamo . . . Officials charged with upholding US law could intercept refugees, take them to a US military base, and openly declare any action taken there above the law. Neither the hypocrisy nor the irony was lost on the Haitians.

As public unease increased, the administration felt obliged to 'explain' Guantanamo. A legal team loyal to Bush I was directed to develop an argument based on flagrant contempt for both US laws and internationally accepted norms. For the first time, Washington was anxious to make it clear that the US does not *own* Guantanamo Bay – it has jurisdiction over the territory but no sovereignty.

Time passed. In 1994 thousands of Cuban 'rafters' were held in Guantanamo; they had illegally fled towards Florida from the privations of what then looked like an indefinitely prolonged Special Period. In 1996 an unknown number of Chinese would-be immigrants were flown to Guantanamo from Bermuda and imprisoned under appalling conditions before being sent home via Mexico. In November 2001 the first 'terrorists' arrived. 'Where,' I asked Rachel, 'do you think the next consignment will come from?' Her reply was seemingly trite – but only seemingly. 'Wherever oil or gas supplies are imagined to be most at risk.'

The Trio awoke in time to marvel at the stark arid beauty of this coastal road – their first view of semi-desert, the vegetation gaunt cacti. On our left, beyond expanses of harsh red earth, miles of high golden cliffs were fissured and erosion-sculpted. Ahead loomed the richly-forested bulk of the Sierra del Purial, an obstacle so formidable that no road linked Baracoa to the Caribbean Sea coast until the 1960s. The road begun under Batista was abandoned when the workers' union demanded a fair wage.

At Cajobabo we turned inland. This town's fame far exceeds its size; here, in 1895, José Martí and Maximo Gomez came ashore to launch their three-year War of Independence. At that date – and until 1959 – no road served Cajobabo; it depended on sea transport. Now it marks the beginning of Cuba's most spectacular motor-road, La Farola – 'the beacon'. It seems a poet named it, seeing its improbable engineering feats as beams of light, flowing through space.

The abrupt transition from semi-desert to riotously lush greenness (a myriad shades of green) feels unreal, like moving from one dreamscape to another. And – I speak as a mountain connoisseur – this sierra's configuration is unique. The mountains rise not to peaks but to long serrated ridges – scores of ridges, so close-packed that canyons rather than valleys lie between their almost sheer slopes, seamlessly clothed in subtropical forest.

Frustratedly I lamented, 'We should've walked this stretch!'

Rose frowned, said nothing. Zea observed, 'It's a very long hill!' (That I couldn't dispute: some eighteen miles up, before the twelve-mile descent to Baracoa.) Clodagh calculated, 'We could've walked slowly for four days, camping at night.' Rose viewed the precipices on both sides and noted a lack of off-road camp-sites. The consensus seemed to be that Nyanya was fantasising.

On the way down we passed a few clusters of *bohios* and at intervals could glimpse slivers of blue sea. 'When can we swim?' asked Clodagh. 'In about an hour,' replied Rachel. 'I want to eat first,' said Rose. 'Then you can't swim for *ages!*' Zea reminded her. 'Maybe there won't be anything to eat,' warned Clodagh. 'Maybe the restaurant will be closed.'

Baracoa's location protected it from Fidel's ardent industrialisation campaign and at sea level the suburban streets seemed more rural than urban. We were driving along the Malecón, past little houses where dogs played on flat roofs, and a youth was wearing a six-foot snake corpse around his neck, and Mickey Mouse cartoons decorated the walls of a children's play park. I had fallen in love with Cuba's oldest town before we reached the bus terminus on the tip of a mini-promontory, where Irma's friend Beraldo was waiting to guide us to his *casa particulare*.

Chapter 6

Near Baracoa, in 1492, Christopher Columbus became the first European to set foot on Cuba. On 3 December he eulogised in his diary:

> I climbed a mountain and saw a plain sown with *calabaza* and so many other native vegetables that it was a joy to behold. In the centre of the plain was a large village . . . houses looking like tents in a camp, without regular streets but one here and another there. Within they were clean and well-kept, with well-made furniture. All were of palm branches, beautifully constructed . . . The multitudes of palm trees of various forms, the highest and most beautiful I have ever seen, and an infinite number of other great and green trees; the birds in rich plumage and the lushness of the fields make this country of such marvellous beauty that it surpasses all others in charms and graces . . .

The villagers were Tainos, skilled farmers, potters and weavers whose many coastal settlements have recently been identified by the Archaeological Society of Baracoa. Other excavations, near Mayari, show that Cuba was inhabited as early as 5000 BC by hunter-gatherer cavepersons who migrated from the mainland by canoe. The Taino, comparative newcomers, seem to have been more advanced than the indigenes. They introduced Columbus's crewmen to tobacco smoking, their cave drawings include a sophisticated map of the solar system and their society was classless. In 1530 one Spanish chronicler, Martirde Angleria, reported the Taino belief that 'the earth as well as the sun and water were common property, and that there should not exist among them *mine* nor *yours*'. This was a ridiculously primitive attitude to Europeans determined to make everything in sight *theirs*, completely excluding the Indians. (I dislike using 'Indian' to describe any American or Caribbean natives – it's such a silly misnomer, commemorating Columbus's obsessional insistence that he had arrived in Asia. But when a usage has been so generally accepted for so long inverted commas look equally silly.)

The Tainos were peaceable, not at first inclined to challenge their mysterious visitors. ('They are very free from wickedness,' wrote Columbus.) However, the colonists' plans became disturbingly obvious in 1511 when Velasquez was dispatched from Hispaniola (now Haiti) to conquer Cuba. At once resistance was organised by Hatuey, a Taino caique from Hispaniola who, in 1503, had witnessed Spanish atrocities on his own island, then fled with his followers to the mountains around Baracoa. For years he organised guerrilla warfare (long before the term was invented) against Velasquez's settlement on the shore, thus inspiring other communities to defend their homes and land. Then one of his own betrayed him, tempted by a 'bounty'. The Spaniards made much of his capture, took him hundreds of miles to Bayamo, displaying him on the way, then with maximum publicity burnt him at the stake. Of course there was a Franciscan friar in attendance, offering baptism; a repentant Christian criminal could enjoy an eternity of bliss, after the brief ordeal of being roasted to death. Hatuey declined the option, preferring to avoid an eternal association with Spaniards.

Reading Richard Gott's *Cuba: A New History* (an exhilarating display of scholarship as entertainment) I was dismayed to learn that Ireland contributed dogs to the conquest of Cuba. 'Hunting dogs were among the most fearsome weapons used by the Spaniards in the early days. Irish greyhounds were introduced on to the island, and bred to search out and slaughter the Indians.' Here I suspect a mistranslation: surely those dogs were wolfhounds? At that date both wolves and wolfhounds operated in Ireland and the much smaller greyhounds (even smaller then than now) would have been far less effective murder-machines.

These man-hunts, and the Spaniards' guns and horses, terrorised and demoralised the defenceless Tainos and other Indians living along the Cuban coast. ('Shock and Awe' operations were not invented by the Pentagon.) An angry Fray Bartolomé de las Casas, the illustrious Dominican 'Protector of the Indians', recorded, 'Some began to flee into the hills, while others were in such despair that they took their own lives. Men and women hanged themselves and even strung up their own children.'

The abuse of man's oldest friend spread to Central and North America. In 1539 Hernando de Soto sailed from Havana to Florida accompanied by 'very bold, savage Irish dogs' and his secretary elucidated what might have been, to some of his readers, an unfamiliar word. ' "*Apperrear*" (to throw to the dogs) is to have the dogs eat him, or kill him, tearing the Indians in pieces.' Also from Havana, thirty-six hounds and twelve handlers were deployed to help 'ethnically cleanse' Nicaragua's Mosquito Coast.

In 1763, when the English Colonel Henry Bouquet was pursuing North American Indians, he enviously wrote, 'I wish we could make use of the Spanish method. To hunt them with English dogs, supported by Rangers and some light horse, who would, I think, effectually extirpate that vermin.'

A generation later, in 1795, the Havana authorities displayed white solidarity by sending a killer dog team to Jamaica where the maroons had launched yet another rebellion. By then, in Cuba, hounds were often used to track and recapture runaway slaves. For this job another, more rigorous, training was required; you wouldn't want to risk having expensive slaves eaten.

Baracoa is said to be one of the few corners of Cuba (Bayamo is another) where Taino genes are still visible to the discerning eye. The rapid elimination of Cuba's Indians is questioned by Richard Gott. Given their number in 1500 (estimated at about half a million), and the remote expanses uncontrolled by the Spaniards for centuries it does seem likely that isolated communities survived for much longer than conventional historians allow. As late as 1901 an American anthropologist, Stewart Culin, photographed a few settlements of pure Taino in hard-to-reach valleys near Baracoa.

In the sixteenth century certain vested interests were involved. Imperial Spain's arm had been twisted by the passionately pro-Indian Las Casas whose books, translated into all the major European languages, were on bestseller lists for years. These shamed Madrid into decreeing that no Indians anywhere were to be deprived of their communal lands. In reaction, Havana asserted that as Cuba's Indians were virtually extinct all their land could be colonised with a clear conscience. By the nineteenth century, as Richard Gott explains, 'Progressive Cubans were happy to downplay the survival of the Indians since those who sought to praise and promote Cuba's Indian heritage were usually conservative racists who wanted to . . . downgrade the contribution of the black African element in the population.'

Few women had accompanied the pioneering Spaniards and throughout their empire white fathers and Indian mothers bred many *mestizos*. During the first half of the sixteenth century these became a distinctive strand in Cuba's population while in Hispaniola, the Spaniards' original Caribbean colony, a 1514 census lists forty per cent of the settlers' officially recognised wives as Tainos. For unofficial partners, the percentage was around ninety. Most *mestizos* spoke Spanish and used their paternal names but for a long time remained reluctant to abandon their maternal culture.

Other interesting progeny came from the unions, permanent or temporary, of Taino women and escaped slaves who had eluded the hounds. In inaccessible locations these formed *palenques*, independent communities some of which survived into the twentieth century, having provided sustenance and shelter to generations of freedom-fighters.

Outside Baracoa's bus terminus no vehicles waited – not even horse-buses or bicitaxis. Most passengers walk to their destinations which can't be too far away. Following Beraldo through two narrow streets of single-storey houses I found it impossible to think of Baracoa (population forty-two thousand) as a city. On the little pillared verandah of No. 137 Isabel – plump and white-haired – greeted us with open arms, then led us into the living-room furnished only with three cane rocking-chairs, a dozen potted plants and a large TV. To the left was the family bedroom; ahead, beyond a curtain, the small kitchen-cum-dining-room and off that an even smaller guest room with less than a yard between two double-beds. By night the loo-bound had to step over me in my bag – or, more usually, fall over me. To gain a *casa particulare* licence, Beraldo himself had added a tiny bathroom (shower cubicle and loo) sparsely populated by cockroaches after dark. The ballcock often needed Rachel's expert manipulation: my timid interventions only made things worse. A back door led to a small concrete yard-cum-utility room, softened by a lovingly cultivated jungle. Over a capacious stone sink hung a sociable budgie who engaged in prolonged dialogues with his owners as they gutted and filleted fish for sale at the Saturday morning market. (Beraldo was a part-time fisherman.) A steep shaky ladder gave access to the flat roof of a neighbour's annex where Rachel and I – in retreat from the TV – enjoyed our evening beers.

When we registered for three nights, explaining our plan, an argument ensued. At first we assumed that Isabel and Beraldo were merely being over-protective when they chorused 'No! Impossible to trek to Jauco!' But the problem was real: Guantanamo Bay's proximity. Although Baracoa district doesn't feel like a military zone, part of it is just that – and the rest is a Reserva Biosfera, forbidden to unguided visitors whether Cuban or foreign. Our friends were adamant that hereabouts we couldn't get away with camping and no *bohio* dwellers en route would dare to shelter us. Or if they did – being moved to pity by three tired children – it would be unfair of us thus to overtax Cuban hospitality.

I thought positive, recalling Columbus's encomium about Baracoa's environs, and we booked in for nine nights.

Downcast, Rose asked, 'What are we going to do with all that tinned stuff?'

Pretending not to be downcast I promptly replied, 'Eat it on long day-trips around Baracoa – up in the mountains, along the coast.'

Clodagh also thought positive. 'Then we needn't take our rucksacks, Mummy can carry enough for one day.'

Zea urged, 'Let's go for a swim *now*!' At not quite six one lives very much in the present.

On our way to the beach we walked half the length of the Malecón, away from its western end which has been slightly marred by three five-storey residential blocs, ugly evidence that Fidel's housing reforms neglected no corner of Cuba. A large, well-equipped playground separates these blocks from long rows of little houses, some receiving post-hurricane attention. On flat roofs women often wash clothes while their menfolk sit nearby puffing cigars.

One can imagine Columbus's rejoicing as he first sailed into this wide bay. Its sheltering green hills stretch far into the ocean and El Yunque ('the anvil') rises some eight miles away to the south-west. This conspicuous limestone outcrop – 1,885 feet high, about a mile long and one-third of a mile wide – was for centuries a navigators' delight. Now we were walking east, towards low ridges that merge into close-packed, forested mountains dominated by two pointed peaks known (some might think irreverently) as St Teresa's breasts.

Near Columbus's statue (not a thing of beauty) we descended to the main beach, passing a long, low Wilma-stricken café, closed for repairs. Baracoa remains as yet 'undeveloped', though several ominous plans lurk in pipelines. Near the Malecón this *playa* is overlooked by houses losing their stucco, built almost on the sand; numerous fowl peck amidst the squalid surrounding litter. Then comes a mile-long beach, smooth and golden, strewn with exquisite shells and a magical variety of bright stones: red, yellow, green, pink, orange, purple. This *playa* offers a choice of swimming places, the turquoise Atlantic or the olive-green Rio Miel, a river flowing parallel to the beach before quietly joining the sea. Here the sea is so shallow that the Trio preferred the Miel, its red-earth banks crowded with almond trees and glossy coconut palms. Next day we discovered a more distant, deep-water cove.

Baracoa's charm is independent of its architecture; Cuba's 'oldest town' lacks impressive colonial buildings. The tourist brochures present it as the island's first religious and political capital but this more than slightly overstates the case. True, Velasquez founded Cuba's first European settlement here in 1511, naming it 'Nuestra Señora de la Asuncion de Baracoa'. However, he soon moved his capital to the more accessible Santiago, leaving Baracoa with little to show for its moment of glory. During the next two centuries nothing of architectural consequence happened, apart from three forts built between 1739 and 1742 in reaction to increasing Anglo-Spanish hostility and pirate activity. As a convenient harbour for lone ships trading with Havana, Baracoa became largely dependent on smuggling pigs, poultry, honey and precious woods – irresistible pirate-bait. French corsairs first plundered the port in 1546 and frequently returned thereafter.

No. 137 was just around the corner from Antonio Maceo, the 'mainest' (as Zea said) of Baracoa's two main streets, both long and straight and lined with nineteenth-century two-storey buildings raised high above road level to reduce hurricane damage. For lack of public lighting those broken, arcaded pavements could be tricky after dark and caused the Trio much anxiety on my behalf. ('Watch out Nyanya! There's a bit missing!' 'Careful Nyanya, here's a big *hole!*' 'Slow down Nyanya, you've got to *jump* over a drain!')

Antonio Maceo leads to Independence Park, not really a park but a laurel-shaded concreted triangle. Here an idealised (one suspects) bronze bust of Hatuey faces the Catedral de Nuestra Señora de la Asuncion – of modest dimensions, its pink-wash faded, its squat twin towers more military than ecclesiastical, its windows Moorish. Built in 1833 on the site of its 1512 predecessor, hurricanes and post-Revolution indifference have left their mark. The imperial religion soon waned when its rich flock migrated to Florida, its *peninsulare* shepherds were banished to Spain and Fidel nationalised all Cuban schools. On our Sunday in Baracoa only a few dozen worshippers attended Mass but the recently restored Evangelical church, large and bright, was thronged three times – the afternoon service for children – and those enthusiastic hymn-singers could be heard on the Malecón.

We set off early to find the deep-water cove, on the far side of the eastern promontory, following a sandy shaded path between the sea and the Rio Miel. Here tiny agitated crabs scuttled to and fro in apparently pointless perpetual motion and Zea wondered, 'Are we scaring them?' Footprints and bicycle-tyre marks led us to a wooden pole stuck in the mud to help those who couldn't easily leap aboard the estuary ferry, a broad-bottomed canoe serving hamlets hidden amidst jungle on and beyond the promontory. This is a busy route (fare NP1); we used it three times and always had to queue. The canoe seats six plus cargo: a bicycle, or a new fridge, or a sack of something, or a trussed piglet – or, on our first crossing, the motorised wheelchair of a legless young man who was gently lifted aboard. Cuba's care for all its disabled citizens is not exaggerated. Where else in the Majority World does a government provide free wheelchairs for peasants living in the back of beyond? The black ferryman, small and grey-bearded, wore his sombrero at a rakish angle and sang softly as he punted: a plaintive air, in time with the graceful, seemingly effortless swaying of his supple body.

On the other side gallant hands were extended to hoist the *abuela* on to a long causeway, half its planks missing, its width just permitting bicycles to be wheeled. A step-ladder led to a wider causeway where little boys sat fishing. Meanwhile the canoe was putting the legless young man ashore where his backyard met the water.

We passed four *bohios*, their sows and piglets rooting along the edge of a mangrove swamp or rolling in ponds of green and black liquid mud. Overlooking the track a scrubby precipice swarmed with goats and loudly bleating kids. 'Are they losing their mothers?' Zea asked anxiously. 'Don't think so,' I replied. 'They're just looking for attention the way small things do.' Zea frowned up at me, rightly suspecting an unkind dig. When we hesitated at a junction a buxom young woman paused in her chopping of plantains to direct us up a steep path traversing a rocky hillside. Outside a battered two-roomed *bohio* a litter of kittens played with the tail of a tolerant lurcher, while several small, sturdy golden-skinned children, sharing a homemade wooden tricycle, paused to stare at the Trio and giggled shyly when greeted.

The path widened on level grassland separating us from the invisible sea. There stood an assembly of royal palms, far apart, rising to 120-130 feet and taking regality to its limit: silver-grey boles flawlessly smooth and straight, elegantly drooping five-yard fronds glistening emerald against an intensely blue sky.

'They look like very high concrete posts,' Clodagh prosaically observed.

On our right vegetation only half concealed high terraced cliffs, weirdly eroded, pitted with caves. One free-standing rocky outcrop, a cylindrical towering mass swathed in vines, eerily resembled the temple ruins of some forgotten people. A not too fanciful thought: many local caves and grottoes contain petroglyphs, and more recent rock carvings, indicating their religious significance for indigenous tribes. I could have spent hours wandering happily along this track but the Trio were swim-fixated.

'Where's the sea?' demanded Rose. 'How do we get to it?'

Ernesto soon answered her question. He overtook us on his way to the shore, dragging a handcart to collect sand; a second storey was being added to the family home. Tall and well-built and copper-coloured, with an aquiline nose and deep-set green eyes, he eluded racial labelling – as do many Cubans. (Not all Spanish colonists were pure-bred Caucasians; the Moors had been around for several centuries and by 1500 more than one hundred thousand African slaves were toiling in Andalusia.) On invitation, the Trio gleefully hopped into the handcart for a short ride to the beginning of the faint cove pathlet. Without Ernesto, we might never have found it. He invited us to visit his home on our way back, then took another path with his cart.

Here traces of military activity surprised us, concrete trenches prepared soon after the Revolution when a US-sponsored invasion was expected. But the invasion happened on another shore, in 1961, at the Bay of Pigs.

One approaches Paradise Cove (my name for it) through a belt of ancient, wind-twisted trees where piles of sharp rocks obstruct the path – so sharp that they must be climbed with care, as Zea found out the hard way. But she is not one to wail for more than a moment about bleeding knees. Then comes another line of defensive trenches scarcely forty yards from the sea; invaders trying to sneak ashore via this secluded cove would be easy targets, trapped between cliffs. The 'beach' is no more than a patch of coarse Wilma-littered sand sloping down from the trees to a short channel in the rocky shore. There the waves' back-pull was strong enough to be exciting but not dangerous, though Rachel had to time the ebb and flow for the Trio lest they might be thrown against the channel's rough walls. Immediately the water was deep and, while swimming, the cove's long protective ridges of volcanic rock looked like mythical monsters with snouts uplifted from the surging foam.

It was easy to spot Ernesto's house; not many locals could afford a second storey. His parents' home was a cream-washed 1960s dwelling from which the younger generations had recently moved to the new 'upstairs'. Soon, he explained, an outside staircase would replace the unnervingly flexible ladder leading to a balcony-in-progress. Sitting around a long palm-wood table (made by Ernesto, smelling new), we drank ice-cold guava juice and ate *cucurucho*, a toffee-like Baracoa specialty served in a cone woven of palm fibre. Our hostess listed the ingredients: grated coconut, ground cocoa beans, guava, banana, honey. The stock of cones in the fridge suggested 'cottage industry' but our attempt to buy half a dozen failed. Unless licensed to run a *casa particulare*, Cubans are strictly forbidden to trade in cocoa, coffee, coconut; all must be exported to earn hard currency.

When Ernesto offered to guide us around the caves of the nearby National Park (entrance forbidden without a guide) we arranged to meet at the junction two days hence.

As we were being punted back across the estuary, at sunset, I decided that if exiled from Ireland (for leading a revolution against the Celtic Tiger?) I'd settle in Baracoa. A silver sheen lay on the still water as our tiny canoe silently glided through a tranquil space encircled on every side by dense greenery. A simple scene: no bright colours or dramatic cliffs – but ineffably beautiful under a dove-grey evening sky.

Baracoa's weather was kind to me; sometimes the clouds never broke all day and as the temperature dropped my energy level rose. Occasionally it even *rained* – cool, delicious rain . . .

On long day-trips into the forest we had no fixed destination – just wandering from mountain to mountain, we assumed that if we didn't lose sight of the sea for too long the town would be accessible by sunset. Rachel has an acute sense of direction, not inherited from her mother, and a feeling for the terrain's idiosyncrasies enabled her to sense when an unpromising path was in fact the right one. Often we followed streams instead of paths, clear sparkling streams, their beds a treasure-trove of minuscule multicoloured pebbles. Once we came to a short waterfall, cascading into a deep pool where the Trio swam and competed to find the biggest of the umbrella-shaped leaves that decorated the banks. Rachel and I swigged Buccaneros while admiring those three lithe naked bodies being energetic. When I took photographs, as fond grandmothers are wont to do, Rachel issued a grim warning. 'Don't have those developed in London or you might end up in court.'

In inhabited areas most streams have laundry-pools where convenient rocks serve as washing boards and women gather; sometimes their songs and laughter led us to a stream. Twice we saw water being collected by muscular teenagers (boys and girls), each carrying two buckets on a yoke. Both Beraldo and Ernesto expressed concern about the predicament of those *campesiños* should the drought worsen and their streams dry up. As it was, some Baracoa households had become dependent on water-tankers delivering a ration every other day. Local ecologists were making the obvious deduction. They quoted Professor Enrique del Risco, a founder member of Cuba's Institute of Forest Research:

> Forests are responsible for the infiltration through soil of most rain water, then stored underground to supply little by little the different water courses. The destruction of forests has much to do with today's large-scale floodings and the fact that many rivers that used to flow

year-round are now intermittent. The Cauto River, the largest of the Cuban archipelago and deep enough for navigation along most of its course until the nineteenth century, came to be just a stream.

On levelish land, between the mountains, we came upon a few lack-lustre cacao plantations – the trees ungainly, the long pods lumpy and drab though a few had half-opened to reveal scarlet beans. Cacao has flourished hereabouts since its introduction towards the end of the seventeenth century when the *peninsulares* unkindly identified it as 'well-suited to Cuba's workers, needing little care'. It never spread island-wide but became one of Baracoa's main nineteenth-century exports. The others were meat, beeswax, coffee and bananas, those last the most lucrative crop. By 1900 more than three million hands were being sold annually to the US.

Most slopes were too steep to be inhabited but we sometimes passed a *bohio* on a ledge, or clusters of three or four dwellings. Twice we met firewood-laden horses, their owners at first taken aback by the out-of-place foreigners, then quickly asking if we were in trouble – lost? With worried frowns they listened to Rachel's explanation – we were simply enjoying Baracoa's beauty – then urged their horses on, looking unconvinced and likely to report our presence to their CDR president. For Rachel and me, those hikes were slightly overshadowed by our awareness that as foreigners we should not be roaming alone. For the Trio, being warned to keep quiet as we passed *bohios* added to the fun: they relished the drama of silently skirting 'dangerous' areas. And then they discovered a new thrill: one-tree-trunk bridges across narrow ravines. *Slim* tree trunks, at that – not Nyanya's idea of fun. But happily those short cuts were avoidable by going a long way round. In Nepal and Laos, where there were no long ways round and the ravines were very much wider and deeper, I straddled the tree trunks and 'rode' across.

Thrice our rambles were curtailed by low, sagging wire fences hung with faded little boards saying 'Military Zone'. Beyond those signs, Bernaldo had warned us, land-mines might lurk. If travelling alone I wouldn't have taken those warnings too seriously but grandmotherhood (not to mention motherhood) activates caution. We never once saw a uniformed soldier, nor did I see many identifiable soldiers elsewhere in Cuba, perhaps because of Fidel's 'rectification' programme. After the 1984 US invasion of Grenada, when the Reagan administration was considering repeat performances in Nicaragua and El Salvador, Fidel decided to arm all Cubans of a suitable age instead of depending on a regular army. This was a reversion to 1960s thinking; until Cuba foolishly modelled its economic planning and defence system on the Soviet Union's, the government had believed that all citizens should share in the Revolution's defence.

To equip the new 'Citizens' Army' Cuba tripled its imports of military hardware, then trained more than three million men and women. To ensure a 'rapid reaction' should the US invade, weapons were distributed throughout the island – to each small town, to each city zone and mountain hamlet, to farms, factories, universities, hospitals. At a date when 'rectification' was seen to be essential because Soviet-style planning had bred major problems, this arming of the population astonished many Cuba-watchers. No leader not sure of the support of the vast majority of citizens would dare to put them in control of arsenals stashed in every corner of the country.

Returning home one afternoon, our zig-zagging red earth path suddenly brought us on to open ground – the forest long since felled, only orange trees and banana groves surrounding pathside *bohios*. Pausing for a final snack, we were directly overlooking the town, its buildings half-smothered by its trees. Under a cloudy sky the iron-grey Atlantic was white-flecked, its cats' paws becoming rollers near the rocky shore, then rearing up to drench the malecón. From our height it seemed the whole coastline had been trimmed with white lace.

When three *campesiño* women appeared, slowly ascending, their leader waved at us from a distance. Balanced on her head was an enormous cloth-wrapped bundle; this African skill has survived in Cuba and ever since our arrival the Trio had been practising it. ('Very good for their deportment,' commented Rachel.) An older woman carried two tin pails heaped with pig-feed, vegetable refuse from El Castillo – originally a Spanish fort, now a tourist hotel, visible far below on a ridge above the town centre. The third and youngest woman was doubly loaded: a year-old son on one hip, a half-sack of rice over the other shoulder. Beaming, they stopped to admire and caress the niñas' blonde hair, a ritual to which the Trio had by now become accustomed. As Rachel was satisfying their friendly curiosity a young man came bounding down the path, causing the babe to wriggle and gurgle ecstatically. When handed over he was vigorously kissed, while he as vigorously tugged at the paternal curls. I glanced at his mother, hoping she would also hand over that sack of rice. But no . . . Swiftly Pappa carried his son home, tossing him in the air as they went, leaving Mamma to toil in his wake.

Ten minutes later an elderly man came hurrying after us to present the Trio with half a dozen oranges. Another of those slightly awkward situations – a gift, or was he hoping for a 'convertible'? One can only play it by intuition. Afterwards, Rachel and I agreed that his courteous manner and kind eyes suggested 'gift'. Pesos might have been regarded as a hurtful misinterpretation of a generous gesture.

The National Park to which Ernesto led us was not yet a tourist attraction. No sign marked its rusty barbed wire fence, interwoven with forest under-growth, and the high, crudely-made plank gate refused to open. Cautiously we climbed over, glad of Ernesto's help, then for an hour walked in single file through green coolness. (That was one of those blessed days when the sun never shone and occasionally it rained.) At intervals a balancing act was required when the path became a knife-edge ridge of volcanic rock. Ernesto provided refreshment by kicking off his shoes, swarming up the forty-foot naked bole of a coconut palm, hacking off three nuts with his machete and flinging them down after warning shouts. The Trio were mesmerised – and felt challenged. Our future hikes were slowed by frequent attempts to 'do an Ernesto', success only limited by shortness of limb.

Approaching the caves, I chickened out; my head for heights, never good, has been kiboshed by age. From ground level the entrance – some-where very far up on a sheer cliff – was invisible behind veils of ferns and vines. A ladder made the first stage possible: after that you were on your own. Typically, Clodagh led the way (no cliff too sheer for her!) and having seen everyone safely up I went on my way, not displeased to be alone in the forest.

It seemed there were *bohios* nearby; I had soon passed four high hillocks of coconut shells, a common sight around hamlets. Many trees are multi-purpose, palms notably so. The royal palms' hardwood goes both to build and to furnish *bohios* (and other houses), its fronds thatch them. From the fibrous bract *campesiños* make slippers, baskets to be carried on the head, *cucurucho* cones and containers for tobacco, after the leaves have been cured on palm-wood racks, The bract's heart, always a valued food, is now revered for its association with the Rebel Army; at times Fidel's guerrillas were largely dependent on it. When grazing is scarce, cattle and horses make the best of green palm leaves and cattle (though not horses) accept the trunk's pith. In many areas the pigs' staple diet consists of royal palm nuts and, because palms flower perennially, they keep honey bees in non-stop production. Palm oil goes into the making of soap (when it's not being exported to earn hard currency) and a distillation from palm tree roots is the traditional remedy for diabetes. Perhaps in recognition of this versatility, Cubans generally obey the new law protecting palms though most such constraints are ignored. Fifteen varieties are native – three particular to Baracoa's rain forests – and a few exotics have been introduced. As the national symbol, incorporated in the Republic's seal, the royal palm has been much praised in verse and prose by esteemed writers, but literary outpourings butter no parsnips and all Cuba's palms urgently needed protective legislation. The population was drastically diminished, post-Revolution, by new dams and reservoirs and the mechanisation of agriculture.

Were I allowed only one adjective to describe Baracoa it would have to be *green*. Countless *shades* of green, countless green *shapes* and *textures* – from the palms to the massive ceibas, from riverside groves of the wide-spreading, long-leaved balsa to the gangling sea-grapes, from sprawling mangroves to blowsy banana plants and their wispy young, from gigantic kapoks with flanged roots to that absurd cactus with a slender six-foot stem topped by a solitary oval fruit – looking, from a distance, like a road-sign that might say 'STOP' or 'ONE WAY'. And then there are the mosses and vines and ferns and rare, mysterious rain forest oddities. Baracoa's mountains even *smell* green, to my nostrils, though the Trio mocked me when I said so.

The descent from the caves was an easy pathlet but when I suggested my entering at that end Rachel firmly said 'No' and the Trio supported her. Evidently the walk through had been vertigo-inducing, even for them.

On the way to the next excitement the forest thinned and tall coffee bushes surrounded a hamlet where half-naked hens scratched in the undergrowth. (On first seeing these birds we pitied their diseased state; in fact they are a distinct breed brought to South America many centuries ago by Chinese voyagers.) Two women waved and smiled at the Trio, Ernesto knew everybody and some banter was exchanged. Not long after, in a more open area of high rocks and bushy thickets, our path abruptly ended at the mouth of a deep dark underground cavern filled by a lake, one corner just visible from above. Huge boulders, damp and slippy, formed a natural stairway and that water, guaranteed 'frio' by Ernesto, did look tempting. Yet I again became a separatist to guard our rucksack; the two youths crouching in nearby bushes, not showing the usual Cuban friendly curiosity, made me uneasy.

Ten minutes later, as I sat on the top boulder listening enviously to the Trio's joyful squeals and splashings, there came a sudden commotion –

angry shouts as the youths ran on to the path pursued by a uniformed
Park Ranger wielding a short truncheon. He didn't chase his quarry but
approached me with a reassuring smile, apologising for the annoyance,
describing the two as 'bad boys'. Then he looked at his watch, explained
that we must be out of the park by 5.00 p.m. and shouted down to Ernesto.
It seemed odd that a park so vaguely fenced and gated should have strict
opening hours and a uniformed Ranger. But Cuba's like that . . .

Casas particulares date from 1993 when a desperate government allowed
Cubans to possess and spend dollars – and to earn them, by renting spare
rooms, running private taxis, making and selling souvenirs, setting up
roadside food stalls. Self-employment was in again, accompanied by the
unannounced visits to *casas particulares* of Immigration Police, Public Health
inspectors, Tourist Board agents. As the average Cuban home might not
satisfy the average foreign visitor, the authorities set standards of modest
comfort which usually required a certain initial investment, often made
possible by US-based relatives. (In 1995 Cuba absorbed some four hundred
and fifty-seven million US dollars, partly family remittances, partly the
spending money of holidaying Cuban-Americans.)

All our hosts complained about the licence fees – US$5 per night for
each bedroom whether or not the room is occupied, plus US$85 for a
monthly licence to serve meals. A US$1,000-fine punishes unlicensed
letting, an inability to pay that fine entitles the State to confiscate the
property – something rarely done. These fees and fines fund the provision,
by local authorities, of homes for young couples trapped with in-laws in
cramped accommodation.

All families must retain one bedroom for their own use and not allow
more than four guests per room, a rule that usually doubled our lodging
costs. Each *casa particulare* is supplied with a register in which every
conceivable detail must be entered and the docket signed by both host and
guest. Even on our first morning in Havana, when Rachel was swaying
with exhaustion, this time-consuming routine had to be gone through
before she retired, lest some inspector find two rooms occupied by unrecorded foreigners.

In 1993 families with spare rooms, and with relatives among the diaspora,
were already privileged and on gaining their licences they became even
more so. In an uneasily defensive speech, during the October 1997 Fifth
Party Congress, Fidel implicitly recognised Cuba's new class division and
referred to *casas particulares*:

Some people decide to live crowded together, some out in the garage, here or there. What we have to do is regulate that. If a number of citizens receive an income that way, on the basis of making a personal sacrifice or because they've got excess house space, that's not a tragedy for the Revolution. It's not going to suffer because someone has a certain income.

We had wondered, when booking in to No. 137, if the Trio equalled two adults, thus legalising five to a room. On our sixth evening we got home to find Isabel and Bernaldo being interviewed by a tall thin young man who, as we entered, was scrutinising the open Guest Register with compressed lips. All three were standing in the living-room, looking unrelaxed, and an awkward silence fell as we appeared. Rachel hustled the Trio through to our room – they puzzled by Isabel's failure to fuss over them, ask how far we'd walked, pour fruit juices, assure herself that no one had been sunburnt. The interview then continued, *sotto voce*, and soon the inspector left. There had been a small problem, Bernaldo admitted, but now all was well and we could stay another three nights, as planned.

Had the inspector just chanced to call or had someone informed him that five foreigners were staying in a *casa* known to have only one guest room? We thought the former more likely: surely a complaint would have led to our being immediately evicted? But the latter remained a nasty possibility – though there's a certain lack of logic in describing it as 'nasty'. When it suited us, we were grateful for Cuba's law-abidingness. And that inspector, or anyone who might have 'informed', was entitled to enforce a not unreasonable law.

Although Baracoa has scarcely been industrialised, for topographical reasons, it does have a cigar factory and a gigantic chocolate factory, opened in 1963 by Ché Guevara and Raul Castro and soon deservedly famous for the quality of its output. Therefore the Trio had been promised lots of chocolate – not a normal part of their diet – on arrival. But (a cruel disappointment!) none was available, apart from bars in disguised wrapping being furtively sold by elderly men and those we were advised to avoid. Then Rachel heard that a factory shop sold to tourists (only) and on her day off (something every mother needs) the Trio and I endured a two-mile main road walk through Baracoa's one dullish district – deforested land, afflicted by the beginnings of ribbon-building. Our timing was peculiarly misfortunate; all the gates were locked and groups of dejected workers sat around on the forecourt playing dominoes or morosely reading *Granma*. That very morning the factory had been closed for lack of spare parts and no one knew when/if it would open again.

Trudging back, we invented a guessing game inspired by the sight of a horse-bus driver stopping to remove a tyre-rubber shoe. Some Baracoa equines go unshod, some are shod with rubber or iron and those options sound quite different. Our competition involved identifying an approaching equine's footwear and the Trio generously made allowances for Nyanya's being aurally challenged; one of my correct guesses equalled two of theirs.

At the Trio's request we turned aside to visit Baracoa's Archaeological Museum which cleverly occupies small caves on the second and third terraces of a high embankment near the town centre. Within this shadowy complex of limestone caverns religious ceremonies and burials took place over many pre-colonial centuries. Several skeletons have been left exactly as the archaeologists found them, in the foetal position; each is surrounded by pebbles, their size and colour indicating the deceased's status and age group. A spiral staircase leads from level to level and in the lower cave dim lighting made the skeleton of *Megalonus* look quite creepy. Poor Megalonus, a giant tree sloth, has long been extinct; the Tainos liked their meat course and Megalonus was not speedy. Most of the many Taino artefacts were baffling since I couldn't read their labels. But one row of wooden spatulas, hanging below an electric bulb, had a legible label; before communicating with their gods the Taino were obliged to purge themselves and they used spatulas to induce vomiting.

'Disgusting!' exclaimed Rose. 'I use my fingers,' remarked Clodagh, 'if I feel I must vomit.' 'What's "purge" mean?' asked Zea.

On our way down to the Malecón we passed three boys shouting triumphantly under a tree, one with a very long, thick, brown and green snake draped around his neck.

'Is it alive?' wondered Zea.

'Can't be,' said Rose. 'They'd be scared of it, not wearing it like a scarf!'

'Poor snake!' mourned Clodagh. 'Are they so happy because they killed it?'

'Probably,' I replied. 'That's horrible!' said Zea. So I had to explain a harsh fact of life in subsistence economies. The Cuban boa, the largest snake in the Greater Antilles, is harmless to man but not to poultry. Therefore it may soon go the way of Megalonus.

This left the Trio unsatisfied. Rose argued, 'People could make runs for their hens, like Daddy does for our ducks.' 'Yes!' agreed Zea. 'We don't kill all the foxes because they eat ducks.' Clodagh looked sombre, then reminded us – 'But we have friends who kill foxes *for fun*.'

At which point, to my relief, Mummy appeared in the distance and all three raced towards her. She had spent a gruelling two and a half hours in the bus companies' offices, being repeatedly passed from Viazul to Astro and back again. She hoped, but it wasn't yet certain, that our seats were secured for the day after the morrow.

We sat near Columbus's statue, watching the rush-hour traffic: many crowded horse-buses, bicitaxis carrying people or sacks, mule-carts piled with coconuts or bananas. Soon the Trio were suggesting a bicitaxi ride – 'Just to see what it feels like,' said Clodagh. 'You two needn't come,' added Rose. 'There's only room for us in one taxi.' Briefly their elders hesitated; but to have shaken the Trio's trust would have seemed not only over-protective but downright wrong. We beckoned an amiable young man whose scarlet tricycle had a snow-white awning. Surprisingly, his price for a half-hour ride was NP20; despite Baracoa's tourist-flow he wasn't yet thinking in convertible pesos.

Waving off the happy Trio, we wondered where Baracoa's tourists flow *to* . . . Almost every day we had seen a luxury coach with curtained windows taking its cargo to the out-of-town Porto Santo hotel. And twice we'd seen those cargoes being led around the town centre, looking slightly weary and more than slightly bemused as their guides 'sold' them the Revolution in broken English. We never saw them elsewhere; presumably that town centre tour was *it* – they had done Baracoa. Safely back in their hotel, they could splash in the pool's familiar chlorine-scented water, recline with daiquiris on the terrace and photograph sunset over the bay before packing up in readiness for an early departure and the next two-night stand. Mass-tourism's rate of increase is disturbing on several counts, not least because it reduces people and places to consumer items.

To go directly from Baracoa to Havana by public transport is not possible. However, I relished our return journey to Santiago with Norma as my seat companion – a congenial Bush-defying *Yanqui*, a botanist with a special interest in El Yunque's two carnivorous plants, its *Coccothrinax yunquensis* (an endemic palm) and its *Podocarpus*, among the world's oldest plant species. Despite her bona fide academic purpose she had been refused permission to travel to Cuba and, if detected on the island by US agents, could be fined US$10,000.

'But I guess I'm OK, they wouldn't dare take me on, I've a global name.

It could all go to the Supreme Court, Dubya has no right to restrict a US citizen's freedom of movement – it's unconstitutional, fascist stuff.'

As we passed close to Guantanamo Norma quoted George Clemenceau – ' "The United States is the only nation in history which, miraculously, has gone directly from barbarism to degeneration without the usual interval of civilisation".' She added, 'And Clemenceau was dealing with Wilson – what epigram would he have hung on Dubya's US?'

Norma provided a morsel of good news from the outside world; nineteen thousand non-violent protesters had just staged a vigil – organised by 'SOA Watch' – at Fort Benning, Georgia, where the US Army School of the Americas (SOA) runs torture courses for thousands of foreign (chiefly Latin American) military and police officers. By 2001 this educational establishment had aroused such public concern that it became WHISC, the Western Hemisphere Institute for Security Cooperation. Norma laughed angrily. 'The phrase "security cooperation", that's supposed to make torture acceptable – *inevitable*, for "homeland safety"! The name change was a sop to the House of Representatives who wanted to close SOA and hold a congressional investigation. That was a bi-partisan move, defeated by only ten votes.'

SOA Watch was founded in 1990 by a Maryknoll priest, Roy Bourgeois. 'It's done most, of all the groups, to stir public worry about WHISC. In 1990 Roy and two other vets – former US officers, in your speak! – did sixteen months in federal jails. Punishment for protesting peacefully against hundreds of Salvadoran soldiers then being trained at the Fort. Roy himself won a Purple Heart as a Navy officer in Vietnam. And the others, the Liteky brothers, also got decorations. They're not softy pacifists, they're just against soldiers being trained as torturers.'

I said, 'So quite a few of you – millions, in fact – have stopped off on the way from barbarism to degeneration.'

In Santiago we learned that all Cuba was preparing for a week-long 'strategic exercise' led by the army and involving, in one way or another, most able-bodied civilians. The first such exercise had taken place a year previously in reaction to the launch of Bush II's 'Commission for Assistance to a Free Cuba'. The commission's chairman was Colin Powell, then Secretary of State, and its chief advisors included Condoleezza Rice, then head of the National Security Council, and senior CIA operatives, Pentagon officials and representatives of most government departments. When its 450-page 'Report to the President' was publicised on 6 May 2004, Cubans took particular note of a recommendation to expand 'the Cuba budget' to $41 million, the extra funding to benefit anyone likely to expedite 'regime change'. The Report's third chapter explains:

> Lessons learned in Afghanistan and in Iraq, the former Soviet Union, and other countries would inform whatever US assistance to the Cuban constitutional reform process is requested.

At once Ricardo Alarcón, President of the Cuban National Assembly, noted that the commission openly advocated 'dominating Cuba and putting under US control the economy, the services and all social activities – in effect, completing the annexation of the country, which would barely be left with some imaginary local authorities, totally subjected to a foreign power.'

The Trio were touchingly put out because our overnight journey to Havana precluded an adequate seventy-fourth birthday party for Nyanya. When a severe chest infection felled Rachel, our last two days in Cuba were sadly Mummyless. Yet we managed to enjoy ourselves; it seemed I missed the invalid more than her offspring did. A return to Coppelia was inevitable, then more swimming below the Malecón and the discovery of Callejon de Hamel, an alleyway not far from No. 403 where the Trio revelled in expansive Afro-Cuban murals, at once amusing, mysterious and wildly colourful. My delayed birthday party was a gargantuan lunch in one of the Barrio Chino's good-value Chinese restaurants. Even Rose couldn't clear her plate so I had to improvise a doggy-bag, the 'dogs' being my companions at supper-time.

Candida looked both pleased and worried when I booked a room for 17–20 January 2006 – worried because she thought it inappropriate for an *abeula* to roam alone in the Escambray, the Sierra Maestra and the Sierra del Rosario. Solo travelling disconcerts the gregarious Cubans, especially when the traveller is past her sell-by date.

I, too, had mixed feelings about my return. Cuba was now so closely associated with a light-hearted family holiday that changing gear might be difficult. Yet part of me eagerly anticipated that change; without the Trio I wouldn't have to worry about food supplies, landmines, staying too long in museums, travelling by train, getting lost, being arrested. As a traveller, I'd be back to normal.

This holiday had been an experiment of sorts, my first journey with the adult Rachel. When last we trekked together, in Cameroon in 1987, she was only legally an adult, aged eighteen. It pleased me that now, when she was the leader, we remained on the same wavelength as travellers, wanting to do the same sort of thing in the same sort of way. And again I marked the peculiar value of a shared sense of humour; with nobody else do I laugh as much as with my daughter, a bond dating back to our Baltistan trek. Then she was aged only six but we both saw the funny side of various set-backs, like having to survive for days on apricot kernels, and thinking our morning tea tasted odd because before daylight I'd filled the kettle from the wrong bucket. When the temperature is -40°F one doesn't go out to pee . . .

PART TWO

January–March 2006

Chapter 7

In January I zig-zagged back to Cuba via Miami, Key West and Jamaica. Miles Frieden, Director of Key West's Twenty-fourth Literary Seminar, was responsible for this circuitous route. My London-Miami return ticket cost the Seminar three hundred and twenty pounds, my Miami-Jamaica-Havana return ticket cost me five hundred and eighty pounds. Thus was I directly exposed to the US embargo which since 1961 has been condemned fourteen times by the UN General Assembly.

After 11 September 2001 the US administration shovelled billions of dollars into its new Department of Homeland Security. So why were ten of Miami airport's twenty immigration stalls closed at 1.00 p.m. when two flights had just arrived from London and one from Lima? That cost-cutting gave me more than ninety minutes to absorb a singularly unwelcoming atmosphere. Obese black-clad security officers carrying large guns strolled around surveying us all as though we were prisoners in transit who might at any moment make a dash for freedom. As the silent jet-lagged queues slowly shuffled forward, immigration officers snapped at those, like me, who coped clumsily with the finger-print and eye-print equipment. What happens to all those millions of records? Exactly what purpose do they serve? Were I to join al-Qaeda now, and return to the US in 2011 as an octogenarian terrorist, would an immigration officer immediately pounce on me? Seems unlikely . . .

All the airport staff were other than Caucasian. During the flight I had talked with an aged Miami resident, another varicose veins victim so we met while taking exercise. He was tall and stooped and brooding, with watery blue eyes and a toupee. In the past decade, he informed me, Miami has been infested with many thousands of 'illegals' from Columbia, Peru, Brazil, Panama, Puerto Rico, Venezuela, Nicaragua – 'all those places'. They deal in drugs, they smuggle, forge, cheat, mug, rape and murder. But when he agitates, demanding their deportation, he's told they're needed because Cuban-Americans breed slowly and dodge all the dirty jobs. But of course the Cubans stay in control, politically and economically, and that's unlikely to change – the administration trusts them. (As well it might: their votes – plus the non-votes of those deviously excluded from the register – put Bush II in the White House.)

When stereotypes come alive one feels illogically taken aback: and I was soon to meet a few more.

At Miami airport an immigration queue delay caused me to miss, by five minutes, my 3.00 p.m. Greyhound bus to Key West. Next departure, 7.00 p.m. – what to do with this four-hour wait? A quick trip to the city centre? No, bad idea when jet-lagged: to face down-town Miami one would surely need reserves of resilience. Moping through acres of concourse I noticed a Cuban 'Hair Stylist' and drifted in for a trim.

While snip-snipping the senior 'stylist' introduced herself: Bertha, forty years an exile. In response to my murmuring that forty years is a long time to be away from home she looked ahead: with luck her three children and seven grandchildren could move soon to Havana. 'That crazy man is nearly ninety (*sic*), when he's gone we'll be free.'

'But will they want to move?' I asked. 'Weren't they all born here? Marvellous of course for them to visit, I only wonder if they'd want to settle in Havana?'

Bertha bristled. 'We had a fine apartment in Vedado, when there's democracy we can get it back. My children know they're *Cuban*. There's going to be big opportunities, reconstructing. They can be happy working on that.'

'And will you return with them?'

Bertha hesitated, frowned, sighed. 'I figure I'm too old to leave my home. But I'll be free to vacation with them.' I nodded sympathetically, wondering how the younger generations really felt about Granny's vicarious urge to return.

Bertha had taken it for granted that a European tourist would be anti-Castro and so did the Miami-born mulatto who sat beside me in the Cuban Bar where he seemed to have spent some time. Five minutes into our conversation he was proclaiming, 'That island is *my* place, not belonging with Communists! My grandmother stays in Havana – very old, soon one hundred. She dies, he dies, I go back and live in her home. Four big rooms, in Centro, here I never get money for more than two rooms.'

'What's your job?'

'I mend electrics, that's a good job for Cuba. They have no men with this training, nobody *educated*.' When he suggested that I might stand him a rum and coke I ordered a coffee instead.

Two hundred years ago Key West, then known as Caya Hueso, was no more than a coral and limestone reef, some four miles long by one and a half miles wide, without arable land or fresh water, populated by flamingos, deer and turtles, conveniently free of indigenes – or anyone else. In 1819 John Whitehead, son of a New Jersey banker, happened to notice this reef. He had just survived a shipwreck and when the captain of the rescue vessel praised Caya Hueso's natural harbour (wide, deep, sheltered) Whitehead quoted his friend John Simonton – 'Capitalists will always go where profit is to be found.'

This harbour, a mere ninety miles from Cuba, promised much profit if developed as a naval and commercial port. True, Florida and its keys were Spanish possessions, as they had been for over three hundred years, but the US was gleefully watching that empire's decline and Whitehead was prepared to wait. He didn't have long to wait; in July 1821 Spain formally transferred Florida to the US.

Key West's history is so short that every drama counts; my town map marked the spot, near Fort Taylor, where Narcisco Lopez's failed 1850 expedition came to its climax. Lopez (born in Venezuela) was a former Spanish army officer and governor of the Cuban province of Trinidad who had been inspired to change sides by Bolivar's plan for Cuba's liberation. Early one May morning a crowd gathered to watch his steamer, *Creole*, being pursued by the Spanish gunboat *Pizarro*. As the gunboat came almost within firing range the steamer slowed and seemed doomed. The anti-Spanish crowd groaned in sympathy. Then suddenly black smoke began to pour from the *Creole's* funnel and her wheels rapidly revolved: the crew had stoked her with crates of bacon and hacked-off bits of her woodwork. She escaped into the harbour leaving the frustrated *Pizarro* 'a few yards away, with port holes open, and broadsides grinning, like the fangs of a bloodhound balked of his prey'. So wrote an over-excited observer.

Key West gave Lopez and his 'gallant band of liberators' a tumultuous welcome. He and his officers were lionised by the town's leading families while the *Creole's* Cuban crew intimidated the respectable Spanish residents and looted saloons and grocery shops.

Fifteen months later, at Havana's Playa el Morrillo, Lopez led two hundred and twenty-three men against one thousand three hundred Spaniards and killed their commander, General Enna, before being captured with fifty of his followers. They were shot and Lopez was garrotted beneath the Punta fort. Hundreds assembled to witness his strangulation and the authorities, oddly enough, allowed him to address them – 'It was not my wish to injure anyone, my object was your freedom and happiness'.

Cuba's Ten Year War (1868–78) overtaxed the Spanish garrisons and 'volunteers' – murderous bands of white racists, mostly not long arrived from Spain – were recruited to terrorise the population. Throughout the 1870s their atrocities drove thousands of asylum-seekers to Key West and among the earliest migrants was Vicente Martinez Ybor, a wealthy Spanish cigar-maker based in Havana. He reacted to the 'volunteers' by opening a branch factory across the straits and when the authorities, suspecting him of disloyalty, put him under 'volunteers' surveillance' he moved himself, his family and all his assets to Key West. His factories employed generations of exiles and soon the island's economy was suffering. All over the US, Key West-made cigars (the tobacco of course Cuban) were outselling their Havana-made rivals because they were free of import duty.

By the 1890s more than one-third of Key West's 18,000 residents were Cuban, their community centre the San Carlos Hall. The original building was the starting point for Key West's cataclysmic 1886 fire; spread by a gale, it roared for hours from one street of wooden buildings to the next and most of the town centre was lost. Then as now, conspiracy theories flourished in the sub-tropical climate; many accused Spanish government agents of arson, without any direct evidence.

This charge, however, was not wholly implausible. Key West had become important to the Cuba Libre movement after the Ten Years War when the clandestine Cuba Convention began to organise another armed uprising. The Convention's leaders were war veterans; its members were academics, businessmen and professionals with a leavening of factory workers. As this Cuban colony donated more than its share to help buy weapons, boats and supplies, the burning of its cigar factories and colossal tobacco warehouse seriously depleted Cuba Libre's coffers. Before the fire, at a fund-raising meeting in a packed San Carlos Hall, even the lowest-paid workers eagerly donated dollars and ladies impulsively unpinned brooches from their bosoms and slid rings off their fingers. One American, Colonel F.N. Wicker, Key West's Collector of Customs, contributed US$100 (then an enormous sum) to 'strengthen the sinews of war' – in defiance of the official US façade of 'neutrality'. Next day the Spanish Consul informed Washington, by telephone, and the day after Colonel Wicker was sacked – also by telephone.

Soon after, Havana charged Carlos Aguerro, a Key West Cuba Libre leader, with 'rapine, arson, highway robbery and murder'. His extradition was sought but a US District Court refused the application because the alleged offences were associated with a revolutionary movement. Aguerro's friends carried him on their shoulders from Key West's packed courthouse and thousands of cheering Cubans formed a procession behind him through the town centre. He then armed a schooner, was joined by a dozen other patriots and sailed for Cuba confident of being reinforced on arrival. Within hours of landing he and his followers had been, as the Spanish put it, 'exterminated'.

A decade before the fire Carlos M. de Cespedes, son of the Great Liberator, was elected Mayor of Key West. By 1892 it had been realised that the Cuban colony here produced shrewd politicians as well as keen revolutionaries though most tended to vote for friends, relations or colleagues, feeling no particular affinity with either US party. Accordingly, both Democrats and Republicans ran Cuban candidates, all of whom were elected, leaving Monroe County without even one American representative. But this, interestingly, caused no discernible bad feeling in Key West.

My map also marked the spot where José Martí landed on Christmas Day 1891. Cubans thronged the banner-draped dock, cheering and singing, waving flags, weeping for joy. All Key West's exiles – men, women and children – soon belonged to one of the Partido Revolucionario Cubano (PRC) branches, controlled by a central committee of veterans. For the next three years, until Martí ordered military action to begin on 24 February 1895, those clubs collaborated in the various tasks assigned them. It helped that most Key Westers were, like Colonel Wicker, on the Cuban side.

The most conspicuous monument in Key West's cemetery is the *USS Maine* plot, its bronze statue of a solitary saluting sailor surrounded by twenty-seven white marble headstones, simple and nameless. Only twenty-seven, though two hundred and fifty-eight US sailors were lost when the battleship *Maine*, at anchor in Havana harbour, blew up on 15 February 1898 and quickly sank.

Two months earlier the *Maine*, apparently on her way to pay a courtesy visit to Havana, had docked at Key West and on Christmas Eve, when the crew hung illuminations from bow to stern, thousands crowded the shoreline marvelling at this jolly display of advanced naval technology. Key West's elite then entertained the officers while the crew made merry in taverns, gambling saloons and (we can assume, though the coy local historians don't say so) *burdels*.

In January the mood changed. From Havana came news of anti-American rioting and when the rest of the US North Atlantic Squadron joined the *Maine* many suspected that this Squadron was not so far south merely to take part in warm-water exercises. But nothing could prepare them for the news telegraphed from Havana on 15 February. As the *New York Herald* reported, 'Key West is in the deepest gloom'.

The future President Theodore Roosevelt, then Assistant Secretary of the Navy, blamed a Spanish mine and wrote in his diary: 'The *Maine* was sunk by an act of dirty treachery'. The Spaniards insisted, 'Undoubtedly an accidental internal explosion'. In the 1970s, when US Admiral Hyman Rickover closely re-examined all the evidence, he agreed with the Spaniards. But in 1898 no US citizen would accept this explanation. (At least, none who dared to speak out; there must have been a questioning minority.) Inflamed by a stridently nationalistic press, the public clamoured for revenge and on 25 April the US declared war on Spain – a war long under consideration, but the *Maine causus belli* ended all dithering.

Earlier in April, when volunteers were besieging every recruitment centre, John Black Atkins landed in New York and reported to the *Manchester Guardian*:

> The United States flag was everywhere hung across the streets and from the windows. Warlike sentiments and war bulletins were stuck in the shop windows. Men and women and dogs went about the streets wearing American medallions or 'favours'. Bicycles were decorated with the national colours as though for a fancy dress parade. Everywhere one saw the legend 'Remember the Maine!'

Does that remind you of anything?

On 9 April three passenger steamers from Havana docked at Key West, each perilously overloaded with US citizens. They had been seen off by hundreds of Cubans yelling, 'Get out, *Yanqui* Satan!' Illogical hostility, you might think, when the US was about to declare war on Spain. But those demonstrators were well aware that the *Yanquis* did not have Cuba's liberation at the top of their agenda.

Exactly half a century before, in 1848, President James Polk had offered Spain one hundred million US dollars for Cuba and six years later President Franklin Pierce upped the offer by thirty million US dollars. But Madrid wasn't interested and emphatically said so – whereupon President Pierce's European diplomatic corps advised him, 'If Madrid refuses to sell, then, by every law, human and divine, we shall be justified in wresting it from Spain if we possess the power'. At that date Washington was unsure of possessing the power and took no formal military action. Instead, filibustering increased. 'Annexationists', from both Cuba and the US, were often willing to sponsor a few hundred adventurers to land on the Cuban coast where they would, it was hoped, be joined by thousands. In fact few 'rebels' ever turned up, being hopelessly disorganised and disunited until Martí asserted his leadership in the 1890s.

Many of Key West's rich Cubans hastened home when the Spanish withdrew (four hundred and seven years after Columbus landed at Baracoa), some to take high office in the new republic. Gradually the colony dwindled, but in 1960 new migrants arrived and turned the San Carlos Institute into a Cold War battleground. Built by the Cuban government in the 1920s, it became the only US public school (in the transatlantic sense) maintained by a foreign power. Because it was for the education of Cuban children, it was also among the earliest racially integrated schools in the US. Conspicuously Cuban-Spanish, San Carlos stands out on Duval Street like an exiled bit of Havana. The lobby's majolica tiles are quite stunning, the auditorium is splendid in a restrained way and the curving mahogany staircase leads to a long, high-ceilinged library where any bibliophile interested in eighteenth- and nineteenth-century Cuba would convulse with excitement.

In March 1961 the San Carlos directors proved their loyalty to Washington by cutting all links with Havana and spurning their regular annual subsidy, which Fidel was willing to maintain. A month later, Key Westers were baffled to see gigantic US Navy destroyers ('half the size of our island!') anchoring off-shore. Then the journalists arrived, packing every hotel and bar, poised to leave for Cuba to cover its rescue from Communism. When the Bay of Pigs invaders were defeated within seventy-two hours, the destroyers sailed away, leaving the journalists to deflect public attention from Washington's humiliation by filing reports of colourful anti-Castro demonstrators marching up and down Duval Street.

During the following decades many Cuban migrants landed on Key West's docks, either off their own usually unseaworthy small boats or having been rescued from rafts by Coast Guard vessels. As most chose to move on to Miami, Key West's present colony is small and not easily accessible to visitors.

I was lucky to meet Mario in the famous 'Five Brothers Grocery', a Cuban corner shop, pokey but stocking an extraordinary variety of goods. From the Brothers' mini-kitchen come delicious Cuban sandwiches, made while you wait, and Key West's best *café con leche* (why it's famous). In a long queue Mario stood behind me and at once communication was easy. Then we relaxed with our horrible polystyrene cups on the bench outside and I remarked on the wholesome absence of such throwaway 'conveniences' in Cuba.

Mario had left Havana in 1970, aged twenty-five, and settled in Key West because he detested Miami's anti-Castroism. 'I felt like I was living in an unhealthy swamp with no good air to breath. I'd left for the same reason you, as a writer, would have left. You wouldn't be happy in a country where you couldn't express all your true thoughts and feelings. Still I admire the good the Revolution was doing for most – my bad karma, being in the repressed minority! So I sailed away not hating *el comandante* but seeing no space for me in his world. You could meet many like me in Miami but having to keep quiet, not allowed *not* to hate Castro! More repression! In Key West there's space for all sorts.'

That evening I supped with Mario in his bungalow on Atlantic Boulevard and was given the addresses of four Havana families with whom he has kept in touch and occasionally visited – before Bush II tightened the embargo screws.

Obeying numerous 'Détour' signs, my Greyhound bus approached Miami airport circuitously through what seemed to be a war zone. Deep yawning craters and long wide chasms were overlooked by mountains and ridges of jagged rock and raw earth from which protruded palm tree carcasses and shreds of picket fencing. Three lines of towering, thick, concrete pillars marched in parallel through this desolation. Hamlets of prefab metal huts squatted amidst patches of mangled shrubs. Scarlet or canary yellow machines, the size of small cathedrals, moved to and fro between the pillars, ponderously purposeful. 'A highway extension,' explained the driver. So in a sense this was a war zone: the internal combustion engine versus The Rest.

Check-in time for my Kingston flight was 6.30 a.m. next day and Key West friends had advised me to endure the Airport Hotel, in January the cheapest available.

At 4.00 p.m., on a bus to 'downtown', my fellow-passengers were gum-chewing airport workers, sitting separately, four plugged into their i-Pods, two frenetically texting. In Cuba, deprived of such gadgets, they would have been animatedly conversing, whether or not acquainted. Electronic communications, I've come to realise, significantly impede my work as a wandering writer primarily interested in people. Where strangers converge – queuing for something, or sharing public transport – it used to be easy to gather 'raw material' and sometimes to establish a more than transient relationship. Not any more. Nowadays most strangers are equipped to remain strangers, each individual encapsulated within his/her personal circle. Of course I exaggerate, everywhere there are exceptions – but not many.

Near the end of Seventh Street I disembarked, city map in hand, and deduced that I was seeing downtown at its worst, on a Sunday afternoon. In this district of wide, almost deserted streets, often in the shadow of elevated motorways, the buildings were drab and featureless, all the shops shut – their windows massively protected – and an odd quietness prevailed. The few pedestrians were ill-clad Latinos, drifting around in small silent groups or slumped on pavement benches sharing bottles of something unlabelled. I paused beside a young seated couple feeding water to their baby from a half-naggin rum bottle with teat attached. Did they know of any nearby source of cerveza? For a moment they stared at me, expressionless. Then the young woman laughed, said something that made her partner smile and pointed to a nearby arcade, under a motorway. Within that long tunnel I saw three pot-bellied rats running across overhead struts. Two premises were open. In a dingy Cuban café, beneath fly-blown tourist posters of Havana, threadbare, unshaven elderly men played dominoes. Opposite, in a large general store, Spanish-language newspapers and magazines filled the rack by the door and I was the only customer. My arrival seemed to be ignored by the young mulatto store-keeper but his eyes followed me and this displeased his small son, sitting on the counter; they had been playing some computer game. The little fellow wore his Sunday best, a military uniform with a row of medals across his chest. Beside him were a toy radio-telephone, gas-mask and machine-gun. (Was he being groomed for another invasion of Cuba?) As US beer is drinkable only when unavoidable, I bought a European brew. Like many Cuban-Americans, the storekeeper spoke no English and didn't even try to understand my halting Spanish.

Turning back towards Seventh Street I quickened my pace, suddenly feeling a mite twitchy about being still on foot, downtown, after dark – the sort of feeling one never has, at any hour, in any district of Havana. When an agitated woman joined me on the bus-stop seat as the sun was setting, this twitchiness seemed excusable. With one hand she held together a torn blouse, the other was clutching the waistband of a long flounced skirt.

'They took my belt too!' she said. '*Fuck* them!'

Gloria had a developing black eye and a badly grazed cheek. Two Latino youths had observed her buying hash ('only three puffs') from a regular contact, followed her a little way, punched her in the face, pinned her to a wall and taken the hash, US$20, her cell phone and Walkman. 'I only had a Walkman, I can't afford an i-Pod.'

I opened one of my tins and as we shared it Gloria talked non-stop. 'I'm an exception here in this city, a *white* real American, born here in Miami, always *staying* here! I'm a graduate, a mortician, fully qualified to embalm – it's a three-year course. I'm an educated person, it's because I've bad habits I lose jobs. Who wants to be aged forty-eight on food-stamps, only a trailer to live in with two butches and they fight all night . . . They go for shoot-ups, I go for hash when I can get it. Heroin's fuckin' deadly, I hate it. What do you go for?'

I admitted to being archaic, only going for alcohol and nicotine. Gloria looked sympathetic and pronounced, 'Alcohol's the *worst*, killed my parents in their fifties. Takes big pressure to make me drink – like now, after being hurt.' Gingerly she touched her eye and cheek-bone. 'This evening I might be drunk!'

I wondered how someone on food-stamps could afford to get drunk. But then Gloria, even at forty-eight and despite her 'bad habits', remained physically an attractive woman.

Chapter 8

From thirty thousand feet up, Cuba looked endearingly small; approaching one coast, the other was already visible and gazing affectionately down I could identify certain lakes. On the drought-brown land pale threads linked towns – long, straight, shadeless roads, crossing the island's flat centre. Cuba is often spoken of as the answer to a cyclist's prayer (lack of motor traffic, lack of hills) but this cyclist likes hills and does not like Caribbean temperatures. So I had decided to rely on public transport and my feet.

Air Jamaica had recently acquired new owners who tended to over-invest: so said the *Miami Herald*. Our airbus was less than half-full and at 9.30 a.m. ersatz champagne was served in tumblers by tall bony air hostesses wearing supercilious smiles and too much make-up. Those unaccustomed to champagne for breakfast had to pay US$1 for a half-litre of water. At any hour I dislike champagne (even the real thing) and I fumed inwardly, remembering the cost of the ticket. Then I brooded over 'freedom of movement', a concept allegedly dear to White House occupants. It's preposterous that I, an Irish citizen with a valid Cuban visa in my passport, should have to fly over the island before returning from Kingston.

At Montego Bay most passengers 'deplaned' and I talked with Roberto, a plump, slightly foppish young man who had been doing sums on his laptop all the way from Miami. He, too, was Havana-bound, the son of émigrés going to visit two granduncles. The embargo allowed that if he spent no more than US$50 per day in Cuba.

I laughed. 'Who checks? How can the US authorities know what you spend?'

Roberto also laughed and made a rude gesture. 'It's all plain crazy! This embargo's bad for American business and good for Castro. He can go on punishing Cuba and blaming the imperialists. Not that it's much important now, he'll soon be gone.'

I asked, 'Would you want to live in Cuba?'

'Me? Live there? Hell no! Though I guess my parents would. They left in '80 – Mariel people. They've not been back so they keep sorta sentimental about Havana. This is my second look, I know how the place is after fifty years of a one-man power-trip! I've good contacts for when there's

democracy but I'm no way sentimental about that shitty city. I'll be a useful
link for my bosses, coming and going, making more contacts – never *living*
there!'

As we were fastening our seat-belts I asked, 'Are you sure most Cubans
want US-style democracy?'

Roberts stared at me, suddenly suspicious. Was I on the wrong side? His
face tightened as he replied, 'Wouldn't you want freedom if you'd grown
up shit scared of Communism?'

I nodded. 'For sure I would. It's just that the Cubans I've met don't
seem shit scared of anything. Discontented, maybe, wanting more consumer goods and reasonable public transport. But that's another issue.'

En route for Kingston, we flew low over green, densely populated
Jamaica, its steep red-earth tracks winding up and down between ridge-
top hamlets. Norman Manley Airport, guarded by the blue bulk of nearby
mountains, felt like an extension of the US and was being elaborately
extended, with scaffolding and cranes and ladders and orange nylon
fencing and 'NO ADMISSION!' notices all over the place. My English
travel agent had assured me that passengers in transit can avoid the
immigration queue – are dealt with at a separate desk – and that my name
would be on the 'In Transit' list. But it wasn't. Patiently I queued at that
desk, only to be told, brusquely, to join the immigrants' queue. Then
another set-back: I hadn't filled in my immigration form on the plane –
why not? It should have been handed to the officer at the immigration hall
entrance for processing before I presented my passport. *Why* hadn't I
filled it in? Meekly I explained that I'd been told I didn't need to . . . *Who*
told me I didn't need to? Who was trying to dodge Jamaica's immigration
laws? The vibes were bad. 'You have disrespected Jamaica's rules!' A
scowling official thrust a form into my hand – so roughly that it crumpled –
and sent me to the back of a long queue. By then two more flights had
come in.

All this surprised me. Most countries dependent on tourism at least
feign a welcome where the foreign currency flows in. It also disappointed
me; I'd been looking forward to encountering Jamaicans on their home
island, in charge of their own affairs. Then I reminded myself that no
airport brings out the best in either passengers or staff; I would surely get
a more favourable second impression in Kingston – ten miles away. I swore
aloud on discovering the next complication. Because I'd got my boarding
card for Havana I must now accept the 'in transit' status previously denied
me and spend six hours hanging around an airport where the outside

temperature was 85°F, the natives were morose, the kiosk bookshop stocked unreadables and 'extensions' had closed the bar.

Fast forward to 5.00 p.m. when I made my way to an overcrowded departure lounge and spotted six English businessmen en route to Havana. Eavesdropping, I gathered they had been conferring with Cuban-American colleagues and were hopeful of clinching a few tourism-related deals. British (official) loyalty to Bush II has limited UK investment in Fidel's 'repressive' state, leaving Spaniards, Italians and Canadians to take the biggest slices of the Cuban cake – such as it is. But individual entrepreneurs refuse to miss an opportunity because of that silly old embargo.

Our boarding cards showed that flight JM 0061Y, originally scheduled to depart at 6.30, had been re-scheduled to 8.30, boarding time 8.10. But at 6.40 an Englishman on his way back from the loo chanced to notice a screen announcement confirming Flight JM 0061Y's 6.30 departure 'On Time'. Consternation! We dispersed, rushing hither and thither, demanding reliable information. Two Air Jamaica officials, tracked down with difficulty, confirmed the confirmation. The Englishmen then let their upper lips hang loose and had a collective tantrum. My reaction was different; as someone secretly afraid of flying (never mind the statistics) I went tense and wondered – if Air Jamaica can't get its scheduling sorted out, what about remembering which screws need tightening? Moments later a third official came striding towards us, his uniform several ranks more important than the others'. He was grey-haired and very tall and he spoke softly and looked infuriatingly amused. There was no need to fuss, it was a minor error, some screen operator hadn't got a message, we should have relied on our boarding cards. 'Enjoy your flight!' said he, before disappearing through a nearby doorway marked 'NO ADMISSION'.

An hour later we were aloft in a three-quarters empty airbus being offered more ersatz champagne. (Who, where, had over-produced?) Roberto recalled a more realistic thirty-seater having previously done the eighty-five mile Kingston-Havana hop.

At José Martí Airport a sour young immigration officer, reeking of cheap scent and sporting black nail polish, needed to align her mind-set with the Tourist Board's. My visa seemed to trouble her – I'd spent November in Cuba, why was I back so soon? Truthfully I replied, 'Because I love your country!' Then a small reluctant smile replaced the frown and her computer received my details.

As we left the airport it was raining, heavily and persistently, to the horror of the Irish couple with whom I was sharing a taxi. They came from

Co. Galway, where it rains most of the time, and had been holidaying in
Jamaica. 'Our daughter have a very big job near Kingston with the past
two years. Every month she's off to Cuba for a week-end – loves this place!
She's booked us into a lovely old hotel that used to be some famous
person's house – some Spaniard built it. But we didn't expect *rain!*'

Our driver, Orestes, spoke fluent English; his day job was teaching the
language. 'Nobody expects January rain,' he said. 'And it's bad for the
cane harvest, though now that doesn't much matter. It's symbolic: cane
out, tourists in! Cuba's changing fast.'

'For the better?' I suggested.

Orestes glanced at me over his shoulder and laconically replied – 'Too
soon to judge.'

When he had helped to carry the couple's ludicrously bulky luggage into
El Comendador and we were on the way to San Rafael I asked, 'Is there any
fear of US meddling, after Fidel?' (I was being deliberately tactless.)

'None,' Orestes stated flatly – a monosyllable indicating that Cuba's
future leadership was not up for detailed discussion with tourists.

Centro felt like my Cuban home territory – its decrepitude of no concern
to UNESCO, its streets almost traffic-free, many of its residents recognising
me, welcoming me back, enquiring about the missing niños. The dogs,
too, wagged their recognition, especially Pluto, the white Scottie (a Scottie
with minor modifications) who quietly dominated San Rafael's canine
population, sitting on his door step looking lordly.

On my way to visit Anna and Fabian Ramose (Mario's friends) I saw
fewer tourists than in November though January and February are Cuba's
most comfortable months. A coolish wind tempers day-long sunshine and
occasional rain storms lay the dust. (Admittedly, that dust becomes a lot of
mud.)

Many of Old Havana's ancient mansions are so obviously falling apart
that one ascends a nobly sweeping staircase with trepidation, wondering
when that semi-detached roof-beam on the left will at last obey the law of
gravity, or when a certain crumbling, bulging, rain-stained gallery wall,
retaining vivid patches of floral friezes, will finally let itself go. These slum-
like vistas reinforce the strolling tourists' conviction that Cubans live close
to destitution on their average monthly wage of two hundred and NP49
(US$9.58), a figure repeatedly quoted to 'prove' Castroism's failure. Using
the peso/dollar exchange rate, without explaining Cuba's economic
realities, is a perniciously effective propaganda device.

Assume a family of four, the parents between them earning NP498. (Whatever the job, men and women earn equal pay.) At the time of writing their average monthly expenses were:

Rent	NP26.60 ($1.02) – if they belong to the fifteen per cent of Cubans who do not own their home.
Electricity	NP13.60 ($0.52)
Cooking gas	NP 7.63 ($0.29)
Telephone	NP 6.25 ($0.24)
Water	NP 1.30 ($0.05)
Food rations	NP45.56 ($1.75)
Total	NP100.98

Since the Special Period the food ration has lasted no more than a fortnight and must be supplemented in state-run markets or by private trading, in national pesos, with individual food producers.

The Ramoses lived in a notable mansion, its richly carved doorway wide enough to admit a carriage and pair. Their three-roomed, third-floor flat was approached via a cracked marble staircase overlooking a vast shadowy courtyard with disintegrating Seville-tiled wainscoting. In Old Havana's 'apartment blocks' it jolts one suddenly to exchange the external imperial decay for the socialist ambience of the individual flats, always neat and clean and simply furnished.

The Ramoses received me with incredulous delight; Mario was a much-loved friend but their links were few. When I had delivered his gifts we drank coffee on the balcony, its wrought iron railing intact, its plank flooring rotting. 'You watch where to put the foot,' warned Fabian. I remarked that since November the pace of demolition had quickened; nearby we could see a new open area, strewn with rubble and garbage and overlooked by high Baroque ruins (too ruinous for restoration) awaiting 'the ball'. Recent changes troubled this mulatto couple, both born in Old Havana – Fabian three weeks early, in January 1959, his mother having been over-excited by the Revolution's success. Rumour had it that their mansion might be deemed worthy of conversion to a tourist hotel. Neither could tolerate the prospect of living elsewhere, though Mario had offered to arrange for their migration.

Fabian had lost his permanent job in 1998 – yet another factory closure for lack of spare parts. Since then he had been doing odd jobs. 'A few days this place, one day that place, then nowhere for more days.' As a museum attendant Anna had access to a few convertible pesos (tips) and their daughter also operated on the fringes of the tourist industry as a laundress at the Santa Isabel Hotel. Both parents were ashamed of their student son's wish to migrate to New Jersey. He was doing well at university and Cuba needs all its talented young people – and deserves their loyalty, Fabian pointed out, having provided them with good physiques and a first-class education.

That introduction set off a chain-reaction, as Mario had foretold. Fabian said I must visit their friends Mirta and Carlos in Centro, where Mirta said I must visit her cousins Paula and Ernesto in Vedado.

Mirta and Carlos occupied half a three-storey residence designed to exclude as much sunlight as possible. They needed that space for an extended family including Mirta's mother and the four orphaned children of Carlos's brother; their parents, while tending a tobacco field, had been killed by lightening in a brief freak storm.

When I arrived, at sundown, seven schoolchildren were doing their homework around a long mahogany table in what would once have been the salon; improbably, a cut-glass chandelier remained in place. To one side, high narrow doors gave access to large windowless bedrooms. Ahead, a passage-like patio, partially glass-roofed, led to the kitchen-living-room from which one could see, through an archway, the much bigger patio where Mirta grew vegetables, in three raised beds, for the local market.

Carlos, a policeman, seemed initially not quite at ease with the foreign writer. Rosa, our interpreter, their beautiful and vivacious sixteen-year-old daughter, was very happy to exchange homework for a rare opportunity to practice English with a native speaker. We sat in the kitchen, drinking coffee, while Mirta ironed seven school uniform blouses and shirts for the morrow. Gradually Carlos relaxed enough to question me about the Irish police. He'd heard that in Britain and Ireland ordinary policeman carry no guns. So why do the citizens respect them? Mirta – a jolly, fat, forceful woman – pre-empted my reply. 'Maybe that's why!' And she darted a quizzical look at her husband.

Rosa asked, 'Do Irish people like Fidel?'

I had to be honest. 'Most don't have a view. To them Cuba's simply a holiday place suggested by a travel agency – sunny, cheap, great for music. They don't understand Fidel's Cuba.' Carlos cracked his knuckles and growled, 'That's because of *Yanqui* propaganda.'

I suspected that Rosa might have reservations about Fidel which would never be voiced in her father's presence. When I invited her to accompany me back to No. 403, ostensibly to admire photographs of the Trio in Cuba, Carlos at once quashed the idea – to the evident indignation of both Rosa and her mother.

Isabel came next on my list; we had met in November as I queued for bread outside a San Miguel bakery. A sallow, wispy little woman, aged fiftyish, her demeanour that morning seemed oddly twitchy. She feigned to ignore me while taking a furtive interest in my exchanges with the other shoppers, then on the way home I realised that she was following me. Out of sight of the bakery she laid a hand on my arm, stared up at me intently and half-whispered in English, 'You can visit me in my home? I need to talk with a foreigner. But I'm watched.' Swiftly she looked around, her expression hunted, then fumbled in a pocket for a scrap of paper. 'Take this, find me here. Remember, tell no Cuban you're visiting me. Don't say my name to your friends in your *casa*.' The handwriting was educated.

'Sorry,' I said, 'tomorrow we fly home.' When Isabel's face crumpled, pathetically, I added, 'But I promise to visit you in January.' Again gripping my arm Isabel exclaimed, 'Thank you! Thank you! Remember, don't write to me – *ever*!' I watched her hurrying away, head bent as though all eye-contact must be avoided.

Her address took me to the sixth floor of an exceptionally run-down Centro tenement (c.1890). In the hallway I confronted an antique twenty-person pulley-lift, its mechanism visible through iron bars, its groans and squeals unsettling. In fact such lifts are meticulously maintained, like the fun-fair equipment in Santiago; a building's residents being bottom-of-the-pilers makes their safety no less important than anyone else's. (In theory there is no 'pile' in Cuba, in real life Revolutions can't overcome individual limitations.) However, at that date my research had not en-compassed municipal virtues so I chose the stairs. Sections of the rusted wrought-iron banisters hung loose or were missing and in the dim light one had to watch one's step while negotiating loose chunks of marble cladding. The five landings gave access to long galleries overlooking an unadorned rectangular courtyard that seemed dark despite its canopy of blue sky. Ten narrow doors opened off each gallery, the flats' numbers crudely chalked on the wall and often indecipherable because of falling plaster. This whole building looked as though it had been neglected not merely since 1959 but from its date of completion.

Isabel's flat was distinctive; chewing-gum blocked the keyhole and the small barred window was not curtained like the rest but tightly boarded up from inside. In response to my rapping a half-frightened, half-angry voice asked '*Nombre y appelidos?*' After much drawing of bolts and clinking of chains I was admitted and rapturously greeted.

Such a cramped flat would demoralise me within days. In a rural setting a *bohio* housing eight or ten is tolerable: life simply overflows to the Great Outside. Confinement to two cupboard-sized rooms (shared with Toni, a large adult son) on the top floor of an urban tenement must be hellish, especially if one is neurotic about spying neighbours. The unlit outer room was furnished only with a sofa-bed, an incongruously large dining-table on which Toni slept, and a lavatory behind a curtain. The inner room's window, barred and unglazed looked towards the gleaming, twink-ling Straits of Florida. The sink was multi-purpose: washing up, laundering, food preparation, personal toilets. Garments hung behind a curtain of Vietnamese rice sacks. A pressure-cooker stood on a gas-stove, there was no need for a fridge or larder; food disappeared as soon as bought. Catholic icons, untainted by Santería, occupied a shelf above two metal chairs.

We sat on the divan in semi-darkness and Isabel, without preamble, asked me to memorise a telephone number in Geneva and a message to her Swiss ex-husband – to be written now. When I had learned it off by heart it would be flushed down the loo. The poor woman was even more deranged than had been apparent on the street.

Paula and Ernesto (both black) shared the roomy basement of a ram-shackle 1920s villa with their undersized dachshund and long-haired Alsatian, the latter serving as a couch for the former. A ceiba tree's roots gave character to the living-room; every year, Ernesto explained, he had to repair that wall. Yet the ceiba was regarded with much affection, to fell it would be unthinkable. Anyway, given those roots' radius, the villa might come down with it. This was a happy family, the parents very proud of both of their sons' baseball achievements.

On my second visit the Lavíns (fluent English-speakers) confided their deep dissatisfaction with Fidel's 2003 decision to again restrict private enterprise. Paula, a high school teacher, had then been running a one-woman hair-dressing salon, after school hours, for four years.

'He's trying to "purify" the Revolution,' said Ernesto in a scorn-laden voice. During the truly desperate Special Period, impurities had to be permitted. Then, as Ernesto put it, 'Cheap Venezuelan oil made things less desperate and *el comandante* got scared, saw capitalism poisoning "our

Revolution", little business people being not so poor as others. Taxes got worse and silly rules and regulations made small enterprises too hard to run.'

Paula sighed gustily and said, 'It's crazy! And makes corruption worse – more need for bribes, more black markets. We know fourteen Trade Ministry inspectors visited that store near the harbour, where 2,000 tonnes of food got lost. Not one noticed anything missing! Last week Raul, our vice-president, said corruption in government departments is like a cancer spreading from our knees to our neck.'

Ernesto's brother had migrated to Florida in 1992 and returned ten years later. 'Here we grow up feeling equal, he didn't like feeling unequal. He had more comfortable living but only a factory job and he's a math graduate. He got into bad debt, the rents are so high. Even before the Revolution, blacks didn't have the same problems here as in the States.'

'Not the same,' said Paula, 'but bad enough. How many blacks went to university?' (Both she and Ernesto were graduates.) 'Even with Fidel, how many blacks have been high in government?'

Ernesto gestured impatiently. 'Isn't that because mostly we don't like politics? I like more my researching and my students.'

I asked, 'What's your brother doing now?'

'Can't you guess? By day lecturing in the university, by night working in Hotel Anglaterre. His tips get him ten times his university pay. It's all gone mad, his official job his hobby, his night work feeding the family. But he's happier than in Miami.'

Castroist Cuba has its old-fashioned aspect, much derided by those who see this as yet another symptom of authoritarianism/tyranny. Paula showed me a Ministry of Education 'directive' containing the Youth Code, to be imprinted on tiny minds by parents, then reinforced at school. 'Children should at all times display correct social behaviour and understand that they have a fundamental obligation to love their parents, and respect their teachers, professors and all adults in general.' Parents and teachers are urged to present 'our grandparents' courtesy as the standard to be upheld. This includes men opening doors for women, offering to carry heavy burdens and other such quaint customs (of Spanish rather than African origin) which of course incense feminists. Personally I warm to a code promoting grandparental standards.

Walking home, I passed Coppelia and briefly missed the Trio. Then I remembered a conversation with a Cuban journalist at Santiago's Viazul terminus at the end of November. Fidel had just launched another anti-corruption campaign during a speech at Havana University. The journalist recalled that since 1992 *el comandante* has been arguing that the cancer of corruption, rather than external opposition, killed the Soviet Union. And now, he warned the students, Cuba's economic revival was being undermined by widespread dishonesty at every level. I remembered that 'every level' when, over the next few months, *Granma* reported the replacement of five out of the Party's fourteen provincial leaders. Also, a young member of the twenty-one member Politburo was publicly sacked, accused of 'abuse of authority' and 'ostentation'.

That evening there was another prolonged *apagón* (power failure), these being not least among Cuba's post-Soviet tribulations. For their guests, *casa particulares* provide portable battery-powered strip lighting, less privileged households make do with small smoky kerosene lamps. Few people complain within earshot of a foreigner – out of loyalty to Castroism? Or because disloyalty is felt to be imprudent? In individual cases a casual visitor can't presume to judge how that cookie crumbles.

Certain it is that Cuba's chronic *apagón* problem had engendered an admirable government policy: Cubans pay higher rates for electricity the more they use, an energy-saving device that favours the poor. Incidentally, the World Wildlife Fund, in their *Living Planet Report 2006*, praised Cuba as the only country at present 'developing sustainably'.

Following another Mario contact, I spent an afternoon at the university with a group of English language students (five male, three female) and found them predictably cagey on the topic of domestic politics. Instead, they took me out of my depth with their knowledge of English Literature in its historical context. I soon realised that quite complicated messages about contemporary Cuba were being conveyed by references to Shakespeare's relationship with Elizabeth I's court, Milton's successful opposition to press censorship, the involvement of writers in eighteenth-century English politics, Byron's Greek escapism, Dickens' exposure of social evils and Evelyn Waugh's exposure of social frivolities.

Towards sunset we dispersed and I sought the nearest café, as is my habit, immediately to record the afternoon's impressions. There I was observed, writing rapidly, by the Milton specialist and his girlfriend. They paused to stare at me, looking alarmed. That was an odd moment: alarm seemed to become hostility before they went on their way. Why? They knew my profession and writers take notes. Or was I imagining things? Occasionally, in Castroland, I did doubt my antennae.

Another odd moment occurred the next day. In November I became a regular customer at a small *tienda* on arcaded Galiano; if Jorge noticed my approach he at once opened the fridge and with a big grin placed six tins of Buccanero on the counter. (He, too, seemed bothered by my solo return; loose-cannon *abuelas* do flummox the family-oriented Cubans.) On this occasion, when I coincided with a youth who spoke uncommonly fluent English, Jorge encouraged a conversation and his young woman assistant requested a photograph of the Trio, with whom she had established a rapport. I was closely questioned about the Northern Ireland Peace Process; my lack of enthusiasm for Riverdance disappointed everyone; we debated the respective merits of Guinness and Buccanero. An elderly man, born in Santiago, joined us and was gratified by my fondness for his native city. Then a fourth customer arrived to buy two packets of pasta – an entirely unremarkable man, but at once the atmosphere changed. Clearly Jorge didn't want him to observe our fraternising and I departed without the usual friendly farewells.

To those not pressed for time almost everywhere one wants to go in Havana is accessible on foot and I only once tried to take a bus. That involved waiting on Padre Varela Street for forty minutes; some of my eighteen companions had been in situ for more than an hour and were beginning to grumble. The bench seated a mere half-dozen but on my arrival a shaven-headed youth, wearing a spruce check shirt and carefully patched jeans, politely surrendered his space.

Despite President Chavez's oily largesse, Havana's traffic remained sparse enough for dogs to be independent and I watched a large, well-fed piebald mongrel happily bounding along this main thoroughfare. He was the quintessential Heinz; usually one can theorise about a mongrel's family tree but his defied speculation. Near the bus stop he paused, looked back – and waited for his owner, a stooped little black man on crutches. As he caught up Heinz wagged an absurd tail (both curly and plumed) in a congratulatory way, then bounded another fifty yards ahead and waited again. Soon after a dachshund appeared, sitting upright in the handlebar basket of an obese elder whose breathing was audible as he slowly pedalled up Padre Varela's hill, his carrier loaded with bananas. In all districts of Havana, up- or down-market, dachshunds are by far the commonest pure breed. Flawless pedigrees give them only a minuscule monetary value but are a matter of great pride among their own coterie.

Looking at my watch, I reckoned a forty-minute wait, plus my companions' patience-test, entitled me to report that in January 2006 Havana's public transport was inadequate. I then walked to Casa de las Americas.

This much-admired (though not by me) Art Deco building could be a Mormon Church and was built within four months in 1959. It houses a cultural institute founded by Haydee Santamaria, one of the Revolution's most celebrated heroines, its purpose to forge bonds between artists and writers from all over Latin America. I had been invited there by Mario's friends Nicanor and Sofiel, an anthropologist, and his marine biologist son who specialises in the protection of coral reefs. 'Such work,' declared Sofiel, 'is two-way important. For the planet's health and Cuba's wealth. When our tourist industry gets more clever it can earn more from our reefs if we can keep them alive.'

Nicanor proudly claimed Taino blood. 'Just a few drops, five generations ago, but I value those drops. They make me feel more Cuban than most Cubans. That's a silly way to talk for someone in my job – too sentimental . . . I don't care!'

In Sofiel's view, the Cuban identity 'would have been much harder to grow' (his disagreeable phrase) 'if the Indians survived as a group. I mean, seeing themselves as the rightful owners, thinking the rest of us should feel guilty. The way it is, we're all from somewhere else – whites by choice, blacks by force. So Cuba's what we've made together even if we didn't want to be together.'

Dryly I pointed out that the growth of US and Canadian identities has not been stunted by the survival of numerous Indian tribes as actual or potential guilt-promoters.

'It's different there,' said Sofiel. 'Northern European settlers were more efficient than the Spaniards and had mixed motives, not all about mining. They never depended on Indian labour like the Spaniards did. I'm thinking Latin America – Peru, Bolivia, Mexico, those sorts of places. The English started their colonies a century after Columbus. In Cuba Europeans were only learning how to be imperialists. They killed the Indians before seeing how much they needed their labour. Where Indians survived, will those countries ever get to grow our sort of unity? Since the Revolution we're happy about Cuba being ours – black, white, mulatto just feeling *Cuban*! No Indians in corners making tensions!'

'You forget something,' Nicanor said to his son. 'There would be tensions if most of a certain class hadn't left soon after the Revolution. And there's been background tension because some of those want to come back, to make a coup.'

'*They* don't want to come back,' scoffed Sofiel. 'They're doing OK where they are. It's the *Yanquis* want to come back and that doesn't give me tension. We're ready for them!'

As we talked on, I opined that the rest of the world urgently needs to learn from Cuba how best to cope with climate change. Then I began to suspect that Nicanor was taking a professional interest in me. He remarked that foreigners' impressions of Cuba must be conditioned by the baggage they bring with them, not only in the narrow pro- or anti-socialism sense but as regards personal preferences and standards. I agreed. Given my aversion to how the world has changed within my lifetime, naturally Cuba charmed me – increasingly, day by day. Its genial air of shabbiness and the level of physical comfort (lowish) matched what I'm used to in my own home. And where 'People Before Profit' is no mere slogan but a way of governing, the level of psychic comfort is very high.

'Do you feel depressed' – probed Nicanor – 'by the monotony of the shops and the media and ideological hoardings all over the place?'

'Quite the reverse!' I retorted – and explained how liberating it is to have ingeniously exploitative advertising replaced by exhortations to be loyal to the Revolutionary ideals, work together for the common good and so on.

'I wish,' said Nicanor, 'our hoardings were as successful as yours! But yours encourage human weaknesses while ours try to overcome them.'

Sofiel indicated a long line of black and white photographs, much enlarged, hanging above the café tables. These showed people thronging Havana's streets in late January 1959 when guns were numerous and obvious. 'Study the faces,' urged Sofiel. 'See the difference?'

The difference was startling. Those expressions ranged from bewildered to scared, tired, sad, hungry, timid, defiant. The Cubans were awaiting the fruits of their Revolution. Sofiel said, 'When you compare then and now, you know our hoardings *have* worked!'

In 1859 Richard Henry Dana described the latest addition to Cuba's racial mix. On Havana's streets he noticed 'men of an Indian complexion, with coarse black hair. I asked if they were Indians, or mixed blood. No, they are coolies! Their hair, full grown, and the usual dress of the country which they wore, had not suggested to me the Chinese; but the shape and expression of the eye make it plain. These are the victims of the trade of which we hear so much. I have met them everywhere, the newly arrived in Chinese costume, with shaved heads . . . I must inform myself on the subject of this strange development of the domination of capital over labour. I am told there is a mart for coolies in Havana. This I must see, if it is to be seen.'

That same year Lord Elgin, recently appointed Britain's 'special pleni-potentiary' to China, excoriated Britain's two main opium-trading com-panies, Dent and Jardine. Both also traded in slaves, labelled 'indentured labourers'. His Lordship did not approve of 'Kidnapping wretched coolies, putting them on board ships where all the horrors of the slave trade are re-produced and sending them on specious promises to such places as Cuba'.

Many died at sea but between 1853 and 1874 a hundred and thirty thousand or so were delivered to the cane plantations. At Havana's mart they fetched US$400 apiece and during their eight years of indentured labour they were poorly fed, given two suits of clothes annually and paid a monthly wage of US$4.

In 1902 General Wood, Cuba's US administrator, prohibited this trade; it hampered his ambition to entice thousands of Spanish settlers, to make Cuba an island safe for whites. However, when the price of sugar soared, during and after the First World War, many more Chinese arrived illegally.

Meanwhile, in the early 1870s, a separate contingent of voluntary Chinese settlers had arrived from California. These were merchants, keen to invest their savings in Havana where they grew the island's first mangoes (a sensational and lasting success) and added the cornet to the African drums and rattles, and to the trumpets, trombones, clarinets and guitars that make up a typical Cuban band. Barrio Chino soon developed, a compact, self-sustaining district with its own shops, newspapers, theatre and restaurants. In general whites scorned the Chinese and blacks hated them; the outlawing of marriages between blacks and Chinese was scarcely necessary. Yet the latter, like the Taino, have made their subtle genetic mark. Peter Marshall notes: 'It is not uncommon to see a person with green oriental eyes, straight black Indian hair, African features and a light brown skin. The Cuban population is a living testimony to the beauty of racial mixing.'

To celebrate the new millennium Barrio Chino (close to San Rafael) was gaudily restored at China's expense. Again restaurants line its narrow streets (pedestrians only, the décor theme-parkish) but by now few of the residents look Chinese. In an enormous courtyard the Cuba-China Friend-ship Society sponsors a daily *ti' chi* session, regularly attended by Pedro. My being uninitiated astonished him – *ti' chi* is popular throughout Cuba – and one dark morning we set off together, taking care to avoid the pavement's deep holes. When Pedro pushed open a wicket gate in a high wall we exchanged Centro's dinginess for scarlet and gold – streamers and wall-hangings and an outsize Chinese flag all glowing by the light of two tall lamps. Sessions begin with the raising of Cuba's flag on a ten-foot staff – a ceremony prolonged that morning, with some loss of dignity, by tangled cords.

Our teachers were a burly middle-aged Chinese woman and a slim young mulatto with Chinese eyes. Both wore nylon track-suits and the female of the species was much stricter than the male. She took the advanced class, including Pedro, and barked her criticisms. The young man made allowances for tyros' clumsy wobblings and advised us kindly. Those scores of enthusiasts represented a complete Cuban cross-section: all skin shades, all bodily shapes from muscular wiriness to flaccid fatness, all age-groups – the senior an eighty-three-year-old black woman, a new recruit seeking relief for her rheumatism. The junior was a possible for the Beijing Olympics, a white teenager apparently made of rubber. Here was another example of that most agreeable feature of Cuban social life, the mingling of generations. This has a two-way civilising effect, helping older people to remain sympathetically interested in youthful concerns while the young benefit from what their elders have learned the hard way. Our exclusive 'Youth Cult' – a notoriously lucrative segment of the consumer society – has the opposite effect, dividing communities into apprehensive oldies hurrying to get home from Bingo before the swearing young come stumbling out of their pubs and clubs.

I found *ti' chi* mentally quite exhausting, despite all the movements being so simple, slow and gentle. Yet at the end of two non-stop hours I was simultaneously feeling extra-energetic and ready to fall into a deep sleep – very odd. When I sought a tape of the hauntingly beautiful accompanying music none was available; this is not a commercial enterprise.

A political spiel followed, translated for me by Martin, a retired physics professor who uncannily resembled José Martí. We were reminded that the CIA/US Interests Section continue to use agents disguised as tourists in their new 'Transition to Democracy' campaign – why some Cubans clam up when vigilante-types notice them making friends with (as distinct from being polite to) foreigners. As we left, Martin spoke with Pedro, then invited me to drink coffee in his Vedado home – to which he cycled while I followed on foot.

This top-floor flat, mainly furnished by books, overlooked a large garden where a black man, bare to the waist, was digging in a leisurely way.

'I moved when my wife died,' said Martin. 'Two rooms are OK for me, I exchanged with a big family, making a little arrangement about meat – the grandfather is a farmer. It's illegal to profit on housing but now everyone does illegal things, they were going crazy here with growing kids!'

I asked who was responsible for garden-care.

'Elba, whose family once owned the house. She lives in the ground-floor flat – chose to stay when most of her kind left. She's adaptable, many could have stayed if they'd accepted change. Fidel never wanted to drive out the bourgeoisie en masse. No one was evicted from their home. Some were even allowed to keep a second home in the country or by the sea – *if* they shared it. This house is typical, made into four flats, one for the original owners. As that generation dies out – Elba was born in this very room in the 1920s – all becomes state property. That's the big change, no one can inherit wealth, we're all expected to earn our living. People could keep their interest from Cuban investments but the US embargo blocked interest from foreign investments. When houses and farms were confiscated the state pension system started, with compensation paid in regular fixed monthly instalments. Elba's family estate was big so she's always been able to afford one servant and a gardener – which surprises a lot of visitors to communist Cuba!'

At noon we graduated from coffee to rum and discussed Guantanamo Bay where Martin's father, a Cuban naval officer, spent thirty-two years. In 1958 he retired and before long had become a *fidelista*. He lived another thirty years and latterly admitted to a troubled conscience: he hadn't actively participated in the routine torturing of anti-Batista prisoners but he knew what was happening . . . His son and I then discussed the use of the word 'crime' to describe the misdeeds of 'authorised forces' – a long discussion.

Martin was amused by my reaction to the 'Commission for Assistance to a Free Cuba' and its appointment of Caleb McCarry as 'Coordinator' – his first task to tour European capitals enlisting support for the Commission.

'How dare they?' I furiously demanded. 'And to admit publicly they're investing millions in "regime change"! Why does the US still feel such a rabid compulsion to subjugate Cuba?'

'Partly wounded pride, no one else has successfully defied them for so long. Most commentators miss the point, calling it *Fidel's* defiance. He's no superman, able to stand alone against "the colossus of the north" – Martí's phrase, now become a boring cliché. Don't get too overheated about this Commission, nobody associated with it understands our Revolution so it's not as dangerous as it sounds. Fidel succeeded because most Cubans wanted to go where he was leading them. What's condemned as his 'dictatorship' seemed benevolent to the average citizen. Yes, it was flawed by accepting the Soviet model, and handicapped by the *Yanqui* blockade – but still better than anything we had before.'

Martin's attitude didn't reassure me, especially when the Commission's Second Report (July 2006) recommended 'eighty million dollars over two years to continue developing assistance initiatives to help Cuban civil society realize a democratic transition. The Commission also recommends consistent yearly funding of Cuban democracy programs at no less than $20 million on an annual basis thereafter until the dictatorship ceases to exist.' Among a population of eleven million, eighty million dollars could be destabilising. On almost every page of this Report the phrase 'free and fair election' recurs, often three or four times.

Cuba has of course been here before. In 1900 Elihu Root, a Republican lawyer, was chosen by Washington to organise the island's future. He agreed with General Wood, the military governor, that 'the mass of ignorant and incompetent people' should be excluded from voting in Cuba's first post-colonial elections. A restricted suffrage of literate males over the age of twenty, possessing at least two hundred and fifty dollars' worth of property, or who had fought against Spain, kept the electorate down to five per cent of the population. This would ensure 'democratic' backing for annexation – or so thought Root and Wood. However, the formerly rich class, supposedly in favour of union with the US, didn't bother to vote. Its members were indifferent to Cuba's future, only concerned to salvage what they could from the imperial wreckage and get out. The pro-independence parties won, enraging Root and Wood. Drastic action was needed. In Root's view, the US was morally obliged to set up 'a stable and adequate government' before withdrawing the troops. (Just as it is a century later, in Afghanistan and Iraq.) He wondered how to 'get rid of the adventurers who are now on top' – i.e., the Cubans' elected representatives. Thus was born the Platt Amendment of unsavoury memory.

In the 1901 Cuban Presidential election Tomas Estrada Palma, a US citizen born in Cuba, was elected unopposed. Bartolome Maso, the anti-Platt candidate whose popularity far exceeded Estrada's, withdrew when General Wood stacked the electoral commission by appointing five Estrada supporters.

The February 1904 elections for the National Congress exposed Cuba's inability to run a 'free and fair' election campaign. The Republicans,

Estrada's party, were the more adroit fraudsters but their victory was not acknowledged by the Liberals, who boycotted Congress.

Estrada ran again in December 1905, massively supported by Washington's man in Havana and opposed by the Liberal's José Miguel Gomez, Governor of Santa Clara. Once more the opposition candidate withdrew, deterred by the tension in the air and the fast-accumulating evidence that Estrada's re-election was a certainty, no matter how many voted for Gomez. Thousands of thwarted Liberal supporters then resolved to oust the government; twenty-four thousand men, the majority black, set out from Pinar del Rio and one Havana journalist referred to 'the butchers of Africa' seeking revenge. When the insurrection became countrywide Estrada begged for US military intervention. Instead, President Roosevelt despatched two negotiators to Havana, to reconcile the Liberals and Estrada, but the latter wasn't interested in reconciliation. By 1906 he needed the Marines to protect his position.

Soon Estrada resigned, leaving Cuba ungoverned because his cabinet had to follow suit. Hastily Roosevelt sent in the Marines 'to establish peace and order'. Then Charles Magoon arrived, a lawyer who had just completed his term as Controller of the Panama Canal Zone and was to spend the next three years as Cuba's de facto colonial governor. His main tasks were to oversee the training of a new army and the construction of new legal and electoral systems. This last challenge was taken up by Colonel Enoch Crowder, a military 'hero' renowned for killing Indians (New Mexico's Apache in 1886, four years later the Sioux led by Sitting Bull). 'Crowder's Rules' applied to the 1908 elections won by the Conservatives, a party put together by Crowder, using all the bits of the old Estrada coalition.

In 1916 Mario Menocal y Deop, a Cornell-educated sugar multi-millionaire, shamelessly bent Crowder's Rules to ensure his re-election as Conservative President. The votes cast far outnumbered the registered voters, the Liberals again rose up in their wrath and the Marines returned for six years.

Before the next election, President Menocal urged Colonel Crowder to manipulate the electoral law, so that he could bend it so deftly no Liberal would notice. Crowder spent eighteen months on 'amendments' – to no effect. When the Conservative Alfredo Zayas claimed victory in November 1920, the Liberals demanded a replay, supervised by what are now known as election monitors – appointed by President Wilson. This demand was granted but extreme violence disrupted the new campaign, causing the

Liberals to abstain. Zayas was once again declared President, in May 1921, a month before the total collapse of Cuba's banking system. In April the National Bank's controlling shareholder had hanged himself from his flat's balcony. Many other bankers then scarpered and the few remaining banks (mostly US) threatened to follow unless Crowder were appointed US ambassador to Havana.

Zayas held office until 1924 when at last a Liberal was elected: Gerardo Machado y Morales, whose campaign had been funded by his US boss, head of the unscrupulous and immensely powerful Compañia Cubana de Electricidad. Machado soon turned Cuba into a military dictatorship and in 1928 didn't bother to call an election but announced that he had given himself another six years in office. Ambassador Crowder overlooked this constitutional hiccup and advised the State Department to do likewise, praising Machado for affording the US 'the closest possible co-operation'.

When a 1933 revolution had got rid of Machado there were several more failed experiments with parliamentary democracy. Improbable coalitions, juntas and alliances came and went, as did interim Presidents, US advisors, coup plotters and Mafia bosses. A new word was minted to describe Cuban politics: *Gangsterismo*.

This was the Batista era. For quarter of a century Fulgencio Batista, in 1921 a nineteen-year-old private in the army, controlled Cuba – playing various roles. The first mulatto to rule the island, he presented himself as a *genuine* Cuban, being of – allegedly – Indian, Spanish, African and Chinese descent. In the late 1930s the hitherto illegal Cuban Communist Party (only distantly related to Fidel's Party) was admitted to the political arena. At this stage Batista needed their support.

The 1939 Constituent Assembly elections gave the Autentico Party and its allies forty-one seats, Batista's party and the Communists thirty-five. This Assembly produced a new and vastly improved constitution with a promising social-democratic flavour. Henceforth all adults over twenty could vote – even blacks and women. Trades Unions were given a civilised degree of power and racial segregation was outlawed (easier written than done). Race-based political parties of course remained illegal; the fear of 'a black republic' never faded. One US resident of Havana, Ruby Hart Phillips, commented in her diary on Batista's influence: 'Sergeant Batista really is good but he'd better be careful those negroes don't get the idea that the island is completely theirs and go out to help themselves to anything in sight.'

The sergeant became President in 1940 and for four years maintained his popularity by respecting (more or less) the spirit of the new constitution. Yet in 1944 his rival, Grau San Martin of the Autenticos, won by a huge majority; US corporate interests, and others allergic to social-democracy, had funded his campaign. At first it seemed he might betray his sponsors but soon he took a sharp right turn and split his own party by opposing a new Communist-led labour organisation, the Confederation of Cuban Workers. To prove beyond doubt his value to his backers, he ordered an army captain to shoot Jesus Menendez, the black leader of the powerful sugar union.

Following the Autenticos' split, Eduardo Chibas (an eccentric on the scene, because honest) founded the Partido Revolucionario Cubano Ortodoxo and stood for the Presidency but lost to the Autenticos' Carlos Prio Socarras. The Prio government, according to Julia Sweig, was Cuba's 'most polarised, corrupt, violent and undemocratic'. In August 1951, at the end of one of his weekly anti-Prio broadcasts, Chibas declaimed – 'Sweep away the thieves in the government! People of Cuba, arise and walk! People of Cuba, awake! *This is my last knock on your door!*' He then shot himself while still on air and died soon after. An accident, some said: but broadcasters don't normally fiddle with loaded revolvers in an absent-minded way. One of the shocked listeners was a twenty-five-year-old law student named Fidel Castro Ruz.

In the run-up to the 1952 Presidential election Batista was limping along in third place; it was time to give up pretending to play the democracy game. His coup in the small hours of Sunday 10 March was efficiently managed. At once the universally detested Prio became an asylum-seeker in the Mexican embassy and no guns were needed, except for show. Most Cubans felt relieved to have Batista again in control – never mind his not, this time, being elected. He soon 'suspended' most of the new constitution, yet diplomatic recognition came quickly from the governments of Latin America and Europe – and, not much later, from the US.

By this date Cuba had become the world's largest sugar producer and the US took sixty-five per cent of its exports and provided some seventy-five per cent of imports. Two mightily wealthy men controlled the sugar market: Francisco Blanco and Julio Lobo. Blanco was among Batista's most valued 'financial advisors'. Lobo's fourteen mills, fed by one hundred thousand acres, brought in an annual fifty million dollars which financed Havana's Riviera and Capri hotels, among other projects. Tourism flourished, much of it underpinned by Batista's Mafia friends who ran the major casinos.

Shipping, banking and radio also contributed to the Lobo coffers. Meanwhile, in Peter Marshall's words, 'the majority of the population eked out a subservient and miserable existence'.

When Fidel and his *compañeros* considered Cuba's future they 'had doubts about the value of the electoral process in the Cuban context', as Richard Gott dryly puts it. Comparing the state of the island between 1900 and 1958, and 1959 and 2006, it is indeed very difficult to sustain an argument for the 'electoral process in the Cuban context'. John Gray puts it all in a politically incorrect nutshell:

> Modern states exist to meet enduring human needs, among which security from violence and recognition of cultural identity are as important as they have ever been. No state that fails to meet these needs is likely to survive for long . . . Popularly legitimate states need not be democracies. Where a move to democracy might involve weakening government, an authoritarian régime is often seen as more legitimate . . . Nor does a state need to promote prosperity to be accepted as legitimate. Prosperity is not so much a requirement of legitimate government as one of its consequences. Where vital human needs for security or recognition are not met, rising incomes yield political instability . . . The mass of humanity cares more about security than it does about prosperity. States that deliver safety are more legitimate than those that promise wealth.

In November Rachel and I had noted the scarcity of uniformed police and soldiers in Fidel's 'dictatorship'. However, on the eve of my departure for Santa Clara (20 January) police were swarming throughout Havana, in twos and threes and fours, foot-patrolling the main streets, standing on every other corner, frequently checking ID cards. The explanation: a mega-demo, planned for 24 January to protest against Radio Marti, broadcast from Miami and relayed from the US Interests Section on the Malecón. Fidel would, at intervals, mingle with the million or so marchers. The logic of this explanation escaped me. How could those checks prevent an assassination attempt? Was it likely that the assassin would be strolling around Havana exposing himself to suspicion and arrest? But then, I know nothing of security measures. Better-informed people assured me that the authorities knew what they were doing.

I dawdled, observing police-public relations, and sensed no hostility on either side. By international standards this force seemed amiable enough and acceptable to the *habaneros*. One does however hear talk of another force, not in uniform and less acceptable and amiable. Such talk is always in whispers.

On that same day I witnessed, for the first and last time, violence on a Cuban street. Mild violence, yet startling (and a bad omen?). Suddenly an open space not far from the Capitol was filled with rioting high school pupils. Scores of angry boys and girls were using boots and fists to attack one another, then threatening the few teachers seeking to quell the riot. This racing mini-mob knocked over one frail old lady and when a young man rushed to her assistance, shouting indignantly, he was kicked on the buttocks. I looked around: where were the police, moments before so obvious? They had vanished, chosen not to become involved. That evening I was told the school in question had become polarised, some pupils regarding their exam results as unfair (bribery!), others furiously denying this. Then, in a move that shocked everyone, both factions felt free to take their disagreement on to the streets.

In Santa Clara I discussed this incident with an aged member of the bourgeoisie who had 'stayed on'. She saw those angry students, and the failure of the police to intervene, as a good omen. 'Now there is much bribery, a new thing within our educational system. I like to see students resisting it. It's not good that they kick and punch, other forms of protest would be better. But if nobody listens to their words, I prefer action to passively accepting corruption. After acceptance comes participation . . . Yes? Is it so in your country?'

I had to admit that it is so – very much so – in my country.

Chapter 9

In 1837 Cuba acquired Latin America's first railway, originally laid to serve certain cane plantations, then gradually expanded to its present 3,030 miles. Yet Havana's imposing station is almost tourist-free for reasons which soon become apparent. At 'Information' a chatty, elderly woman told me that the only service to Santa Clara was the thrice-weekly *especiale* to Santiago; it would depart next day at 2.15 p.m., arriving in Santa Clara four hours later, leaving me time to find my friends' house before sunset – new English-speaking friends, met on the Malecón and impulsively hospitable.

Whether you're running a democracy, a dictatorship or an international institution, bureaucracy constipates efficiency. For years Fidel has been condemning the Cuban variety, to no effect; even during the Special Period, with its particular urgent needs, the Faceless Ones resisted most reforming efforts. Cubans are of course the main victims, often on a daily basis. Tourists usually escape this net, woven of illogicality, but free-range travellers are soon enmeshed. For instance, Havana's railway ticket office is a brisk ten minutes walk away from the station itself – why? Moreover, there are *two* offices in separate buildings, one for Cubans, one for foreigners – why? Arriving at 12.50, I was told to return at 1.15; one's ticket must be bought within the hour of departure – why? Then, having queued twice in that vast office, one has to queue again, within the station, for the ticket to be 'Confirmed'.

In the spacious concourse, high and wide, the seating seemed like a planning error: long rows of black metal chairs were welded to the floor and packed close together à la cut-price airlines, leaving open expanses between blocks. A six-foot barrier and locked gates allowed no access to the four deserted platforms. A tall, slim young woman wearing a smart sky-blue uniform labelled 'Security Service (Private)', guesstimated that the Santiago *especiale* might leave at 5.00-ish. She and her three colleagues appeared to be in lieu of a police presence. Watching them, I again noted the cold, almost disdainful persona assumed by many Cuban petty officials (including staff in government *tiendas*) when dealing with the public. Is this attitude, so unlike the average Cuban's relaxed friendliness, a result of Soviet training? Or is it a symptom of the tension that has come to exist between frustrated citizens and agencies now often despised as corrupt?

Obviously nobody expected this *especiale* to depart at 2.15. My many fellow-passengers looked settled and resigned; most families were lunching, sharing saucepans or bowls of rice and black beans and pork fat. Some men played chess or dominoes while their wives dozed, others read *Granma* with close attention – surprising to me because Cuba's only daily news-paper is the Party's voice. Small extrovert children romped around the open spaces, making new friends as they went. A happy mixed family occupied the seats opposite mine, in the next block – white wife, black husband, toddler son was happy if left free to wander. Only his maternal grandfather, an army officer, was allowed to restrain him: pick him up and carry him round while grandad's cap was repeatedly removed, tried on, then flung to the ground with a chortle. As the overhead clock registered 2.30, 3.30, 4.30, no one seemed disgruntled. Beside two of the platforms long trains stretched away into the distance looking as though they had been stationary for months if not years. And maybe they had.

At 4.10 the *especiale* arrived from Santiago and hundreds disembarked; many carried a musical instrument, some wheeled bicycles. When our departure was announced queues formed at four gates, each line confined between metal bars as in a cattle-crush. Then came a delay, caused by several pairs of porters pushing long handcarts piled with cargo for Santiago. Shouting and laughing, they raced each other along the broad hundred-yard expanse between barrier and buffers, their loads wobbling precariously. Unsmiling young women eventually unlocked the gates and closely scrutinised each ticket and ID document. They wore the railway uniform of purple shorts and tunics with black tights and absurdly high-heeled shoes. Although foreigners must travel first-class I had trouble finding my allotted place; all the coaches had gone unpainted for decades. Excitedly chattering groups were being guided to their seats by other uniformed women one of whom led me to a carriage with torn upholstery and mud-coated windows. My only companion was Raimundo, tall, lean, distinguished-looking and very black. A history professor, specialising in colonial Africa, he spoke fluent English.

At 5.15 our engine hooted hoarsely and as we moved, almost imper-ceptibly, I remarked that we should reach Santa Clara by 9.30. Raimundo looked sceptical and said, 'Maybe'. Then we stopped, still under the station roof. Raimundo, sorting through papers in his briefcase, glanced at me and chuckled.

For twenty minutes nothing happened. After we had backed to our starting position nothing continued to happen. Again all the platforms were deserted, apart from one jovial railway official engaged in private enterprise, selling delicious sausage rolls, more sausage than bread. I offered CP1 for a roll and received NP12.10 change – perhaps a measure of how little the railway is used by tourists.

At 5.50 we moved again, very slowly. At 6.10 we stopped again. Raimundo closed his briefcase, took off his spectacles and made enquiries. Our engine had broken down, decisively, and must be replaced. As this news spread other passengers laughed uproariously, tuned up their guitars and began a sing-song. Standing in the corridor, watching our engine being detached, I was joined by an effervescent mulatta teenager who offered me a swig from her half-bottle of rum. 'Have a drink! Cuba transport bad for tourists, Cuba rum good!' Accepting her offer, I was conscious of Raimundo's disapproving stare. As the defunct engine passed us, on the next track, passengers crowded to the windows leaning out to cheer and clap ironically. Raimundo smiled at me and said, 'That's how we survived the Special Period.'

Our replacement engine got going at 6.55, groaning reluctantly as we left the station. Beyond the suburbs shanty homes huddled close to the track – as shanty as any I've seen in the Majority World yet the residents look better nourished than their equivalents elsewhere. For years past many Cubans have had to struggle to supplement their rations but for most it's possible to do so, by being persistently ingenious and/or devious.

Beyond flat scrubland the sun was sinking and when Raimundo calculated that we were unlikely to reach Santa Clara (170 miles from Havana) before midnight I decided to sleep in the waiting-room until dawn.

Soon the only glimmers of light came from the stars and our engine's weak beam; even in the first-class coaches no one had a torch. 'This train years ago lost its illuminations,' Raimundo resignedly remarked. I closed our door, to reduce the salsa decibels, and we stretched out, giving thanks for an uncrowded compartment, and discussed Ché's Congolese débâcle – an almost forgotten fragment of history which Raimundo had closely studied. Then he told me about Santa Clara's origins. For all Cuba's sparse population and distance from the motherland, Spain's Inquisition didn't spare the colony. In 1682, in the prosperous little town of Remedios, when a priest detected demons by the dozen he summoned Inquisitors from Havana to organise the 'trial' and incineration of 'the possessed' and the torching of their homes and property. This operation prompted many terrorised residents to flee thirty miles inland and found Santa Clara.

At 12.20 my escort handed me on to a long platform, lit by one feeble bulb, and we were about to seek the waiting-room when Tania came hurrying towards us, arms outstretched apologising for the unreliability of Cuban trains. Raimundo looked immensely relieved; he hadn't approved of my plan – not for security reasons, but because he refused to believe an *abuela* could sleep soundly on a floor. The little plaza outside the station, a busy horse-bus terminal during the day, was deserted and the few others who had disembarked were crossing the tracks, heading towards those famous sub-urbs where Ché's troops won the Revolution's final battle. For a mile or so Tania and I walked through silent, empty, starlit streets of eighteenth-century dwellings – a pleasing introduction to a provincial capital (population some 210,000). We kept to the middle of the road, my companion reminding me that 'broken pavements need daylight'.

No. 374 was a small, two-storied terraced house not far from the central Parque Vidal. A boisterous puppy greeted us and Tania warned me to leave nothing within Mesa's reach; he was teething in a manic way and never out of trouble, chewing cushions, towels, rugs, shoes and – his major crime – the lower leaves of Tania's beloved house-plants. His playmate, Tigre, a four-months-old-kitten, was often gently dragged across the tiled floor by the tail or a leg, to her evident delight. If ignored for too long she sought Mesa out, then lay on her back extending two forepaws towards his nose. Tigre's mother, a sedate smoky blue Persian, spent most of her time atop a tall bookshelf, looking inscrutable. In my room (leading directly off the living-room, which led directly off the street) another kitten was curled up on the bed, paws over eyes. Tania's embarrassed exclamations trailed away when she heard that normally I sleep with one cat on my pillow and another between the sheets.

Santa Clara is both dignified and jolly, handsome in the centre, dishevelled in an insouciant sort of way around the edges. It is compact enough to be walkable, culturally enthusiastic enough to support regular theatre, ballet, orchestral, jazz and film festivals. Horse-drawn vehicles are numerous, motor vehicles few – and restricted in the centre, where boys play baseball on the streets. This is a city with a strong personality, a place content to be itself – which irritates would-be developers eager to 'realise its tourist potential'. As yet most tourists arrive by coach, have lunch, 'do' Ché's Memorial, then go on their way to Havana or Trinidad.

On my first morning I aroused much friendly curiosity by joining a slow-moving thirty-person queue outside a co-op bakery. (The state-run sort require a *libreta*.) Fifteen minutes later I reached the doorway, just in time to see the last loaves leaving the shelves and a huge dough-laden trolley being pushed into an room-sized oven. The pleasant mulatta behind the counter advised us to come back in thirty-five minutes.

As I rambled around, a few householders were drawing water from a standpipe that needed vigorous pumping. One skinny, stooped *abeula* was hardly up to the challenge and, noticing this, a passing youth braked his bicycle and went to her assistance.

No noisome skips pollute Santa Clara; instead, thin plastic bags appear beside doorsteps each morning to the delight of wandering dogs. Then street sweepers come on the scene equipped with hand-barrows, wide grass brooms and enormous dust-pans – both men and women smoking the sort of cigars we associate with London clubs. These do not, as I had at first assumed, fall off lorries. Outside Santa Clara's cigar factory one can stand on the pavement, by the unglazed, barred windows, watching work in progress – every cigar handmade and Perfectionism Rules OK. 'Defectives' (their defects minuscule) may be legally bought by the locals at CP3 for twenty-five. And one local was kind enough to sell on to me, making an illegal CP2-profit.

Despite all the street sweeping (it happens thrice daily) rats are quite numerous, especially at dawn and dusk, scuttling in and out of the sewage pipes that emerge from under houses in the older districts. When I returned to the bakery, and admired its three cats, I was told they were famous as Santa Clara's best ratters.

At the end of December 1958 the city centre was, not for the first time, a battlefield – Ché's guerrillas versus Batista's National Army. Yet Parque Vidal seems scarcely changed since its creation in 1925: even the brass street lamps have survived, and the bust of Colonel Leoncio Vidal, marking the spot where this Independence War hero fell in 1896. Within the park guasima trees, poinciana and royal palms surround gay flower-beds and shapely miniature shrubs while sparrows drink from a gently splashing fountain. On every side neo-classical buildings recall Santa Clara's nine-teenth-century sugar-based prosperity. Only the 1950s Libre Hotel – lime-green, eleven storeys, on the south-west corner – offends the eye. One magnificent mansion (1810) now holds the Museum of Decorative Arts; the Provincial Governor's palace has become a library; the Teatro de la Caridad (The Theatre of Charity, 1884, simple but stately) remains a theatre. It was presented to the city by an heiress celebrated for her munificence, Martha Abreu de Estavez, who also provided a hospital, a fire station, an astronomical observatory, an electricity station and four public bathhouses. The theatre is so named because it incorporated a casino, ballroom, restaurant and barber shop – all run to raise funds for the local poor. Most of those were black and, until 1894, not permitted to share the whites' promenade around the square's periphery where stout railings enforced the colour bar.

Nowadays the park has good vibes. Adults saunter or sit, enjoying it; children romp with dogs and balls and are treated to goat-cart rides; teenagers gather after dark to make music, dance, sing *guajiras* (topical lyrics, often with a sharp edge). Their elders applaud them and sometimes display their own dancing skills. Only the goat-carts bothered me – drawn by three grievously over-worked billies, twelve or fourteen children being crammed into each cart as though in training for truck-bus rides. When given a rare break, the billies lie on the tarmac looking done in. But then, their owners have children to feed . . .

Sitting on an elaborately wrought iron bench (very 1920s) I took out my tattered paperback copy of Ché's *Reminiscences of the Cuban Revolutionary War* and re-read the last few pages:

Santa Clara is the hub of the central plain of Cuba. It is a railroad centre and possesses an important communication network. It is surrounded by low, bare hills, which the enemy troops had already occupied . . . We had a bazooka but no rockets, and we were fighting against ten or more tanks. We realised that the best way of combating them was to go deep into the densely populated neighbourhoods where tank effectiveness is considerably diminished . . . On December 29 the battle began . . . The police station fell, along with the tanks that had defended it. The prison, the courthouse, and the provincial government headquarters fell to us, as well as the Grand Hotel [now the Hotel Libre] where the besieged men continued their fire from the tenth floor almost until the cessation of hostilities . . . We succeeded in taking the electric power station and the entire northwestern section of the city. We went on the air to announce that virtually all Santa Clara was in the hands of the Revolution. During the morning of January 1st we sent Captain Nunez Jiminez and Rodriguez de la Vega to negotiate the surrender of the Leoncio Vidal Barracks, the largest fortress of Central Cuba. The news was astonishing; Batista had just fled . . . We immediately contacted Fidel, told him what was happening . . . The rest is well known. Several days later came the installation of Fidel Castro as Prime Minister of the Provisional Government.

Pre-Revolution, rich people lived in the streets around the park, their substantial homes not in the palatial league but quite imposing, with graceful arched doorways and decorative stonework. Most have been converted to flats, some shelter very extended families, the majority are reasonably well maintained.

On one such street I paused outside a smallish, half-restored Protestant church, built in 1923, abandoned in 1960, recently reopened. It had neither windows nor doors and a stage instead of an altar. Seeing rows of empty chairs at the back I slipped in, unnoticed by the congregation of one hundred and fifty or so – mostly whites, from babes-in-arms to great grannies. All the women wore hats and everybody was more expensively dressed than average (even allowing for 'Sunday best'). From a distance rousing hymn tunes had been audible and a four-man band sat behind the handsome mulatto preacher who wore a thick red sweater and neatly creased black trousers. For some ten minutes he spoke slowly and clearly before suddenly speeding up to reach the climax of a homophobic sermon; one didn't need fluent Spanish to get the message. Repeatedly he struck his left palm with his right fist and his eyes glistened strangely. I wondered – 'Is this fear or hate or both?'

As the congregation left, each being greeted at the exit by the pastor, I lingered; with luck I might meet an English-speaker who could fill in the details I'd missed. In fact the pastor himself spoke English and beamed down at the foreigner while vigorously shaking my hand. Had I understood his message from God? No? Quickly he stepped on to the pavement and shouted after a departing parishioner. This stocky young man, unusually attired in a pin-striped suit, was introduced as Luis, an apprentice pastor always happy to translate God's message.

We strolled along Independencia, the main commercial street, where on this Sunday forenoon several *tiendas* displaying new imports were attracting excited throngs – the majority window-shoppers. At each exit purchasers had their bags emptied, and the contents checked against receipts, by SECSA men whose body language was aggressive. 'You see?' said Luis. 'We have a police state!'

In Parque Vidal we sat on a bench munching roasted peanuts bought from an obese black *abuela* who made some teasing remark that annoyed Luis. (In this city one senses that many inhabitants have a village-like awareness of each other.) My companion took his task seriously, having established that my soul was not saved. Here was a precious opportunity to rescue an old woman (just in time!) from a painful eternity. Listening to him, I was reminded of my one exposure, many years ago, to a famous (subsequently infamous) US televangelist.

Luis's homophobia was nonetheless chilling for being utterly banal, not to say illogical. He believed that God sent AIDS to punish homosexuals who are somehow responsible for the deaths of millions of heterosexuals all over the world. The Vatican imposes celibacy because most RC priests are perverts who wouldn't want to marry anyway and the celibacy façade conceals their vice. All homosexuals molest little boys. When communities ignore the scum in their midst, they're tolerating sin. God wants the scum identified, shamed, excluded even from peripheral jobs in education, health care, tourism, sports clubs – anywhere they can deprave others. In the past Cuba had ways of controlling homosexuals, now the police have gone soft on them. Even in Santa Clara, in the El Mejunje community centre, they feel free to run their own discos!

While transmitting this message from the sort of god one can do without, Luis stared into my eyes as though attempting hypnotism. 'You understand how it's dangerous? Some governments now let them *marry*! It's bad for women's rights, having men replacing them! And money wasted on AIDS treatments leaves less for good patients!'

It was time for me to show my hand. I asked, 'Why should Cuba's government continue to discriminate against homosexuals when such relationships, between consenting adults, have been legal here since 1979?'

Luis looked aghast. My tone must have conveyed more hostility and contempt than was intended. Abruptly he stood up, muttered something about my being blind to God's design and hurried away.

Cuba's homophobia served (and in some circles still serves) as a big stick with which to beat the Revolution. People forget that in 1959 Britain had not yet had its Wolfenden Report, New York had not yet had its Stonewall riots and in numerous countries homosexual acts were serious crimes. Cuba's 1938 Social Defence Code, based on Spanish law, imposed a six-months sentence, or an equivalent fine, for 'habitually engaging in homo-sexual acts' or 'creating a public scandal by flaunting homosexuality'. (That last prohibition I can sympathise with, recalling the uses to which, for example, some of San Francisco's public spaces are put; most citizens of any country don't wish to observe either homosexuals or heterosexuals in action.) The deviant sons of Havana's rich were often exiled to some distant land by parents intent on protecting family honour. Other parents less rich but similarly driven, maintained the fiction, between themselves and with the neighbours, that their sons and their partners were 'just good friends'.

Under Batista, ordinary decent Cubans felt humiliated by their country's status as a 'paradise' for grossly affluent tourists and celebrities and as a secure base for US gangsters. In the 1950s at least ten thousand women (some estimated fifteen thousand) staffed the 'paradise's' brothels and escort agencies and an early Revolutionary project was to turn them into seamstresses. Given training for alternative employment they could (as indeed many did) become 'respectable'. Then lines got crossed. Why not do a similar job on homosexuals? Rescue them from decadence, enable them to become 'real' men . . . But this project proved less successful than seamstress-training.

In 1961 a fanatical determination to clean up Havana inspired Operation Three Ps – pederasts, prostitutes and pimps. (Not all prostitutes had by then gratefully embraced their sewing machines.) This campaign promoted an ominous shift of the bureaucratic mind-set. Homosexuals, always regarded with contempt, now came to be seen as enemies of the state – dangerous bits of nonconformist grit in the sensitive Revolutionary mechanism. In Cuba, as elsewhere, such men and women were prominent on the academic, literary and artistic scenes and could have contributed much to the New Cuba. But most were rejected. Their thoughtful input would have complicated things and Fidel et al., intent on immediately improving daily life for the masses, had no time to spare for long-term analyses of where the Revolution might be going. Yet Fidel himself felt no personal aversion to 'deviants'. One of his closest friends (they met at university) was Alfredo Guevara, generally known to be a (discreet) homosexual, who went on to become a member of the Central Committee of the Communist Party and head of the internationally acclaimed Cuban Film Institute.

Homegrown homophobia was reinforced by Soviet influences. In 1934 Stalin had recriminalised homosexuality, a decade or so after it had been decriminalised by the first Bolshevik government. When Samuel Feijoo, a notoriously homophobic intellectual, returned to Cuba from a leisurely tour of the Soviet Union he proclaimed that 'deviance' was no more among the Russians. By implementing 'revolutionary social hygiene', Communism has excised the vice. In *El Mundo* (15 April 1965) he wrote, 'No homosexual can represent the Revolution, which is a matter for men, of fists and not of feathers, of courage and not of trembling'.

That same year the dual-purpose Military Units to Aid Production

(UMAP) were set up within Camaguey province where the conversion of ranches to canefields was being slowed by a dire labour shortage. UMAP's grim second purpose, as explained by the Castroist historian, José Yglesias, was 'to take care of young men of military age whose incorporation into the Army for military training was considered unfeasible. Young men known to avoid work and study were candidates; so were known counter-revolutionaries; and also immoralists, a category that included homosexuals'.

These forced labour camps represented a regression to slavery. Captives received a token wage of seven pesos a month and in their limited time off could visit the nearest town only under military escort. The Nicaraguan author, Ernesto Cardenal, a former Sandanista Minister for Culture, re-corded some inmates' complaints. 'We worked surrounded by a barbed wire fence two and a half metres high.' A few camps, no worse than the rest, held homosexuals only. Most held a volatile mix including con-scientious objectors (Seventh Day Adventists and Jehovah's Witnesses whose homophobia is legendary) and 'lazy' heterosexuals, macho men temperamentally averse to Party diktats. Homosexuals were often severely 'punished', especially those whose behaviour was defiantly provocative, and some commentators have put them on a par with Stalin's and Hitler's victims – a tendentious comparison, as Ian Lumsden has emphasised in *Machos, Maricones and Gays*. 'The extermination of Jews in Germany was a monstrous and unique operation that was nevertheless consistent with the Nazis' racist ideology. In contrast, the persecution of homosexuals and other minorities in Cuba completely contradicted the humanist and liberating values that had motivated the Revolution.'

During the late 1960s most 'deviant' artists, dancers and writers lost their State-funded jobs and were compelled to 'Make a New Cuba!' by the sweat of their brow. It didn't count that they had been gladly contributing their talents to the Revolution's cultural development. Observing his homeland from abroad, the novelist Guillermo Cabrera Infante argued at this time that homophobia *per se* was not the real problem. That lay in the Ministry of Education's compulsion to 'contain any form of deviance among the young' in order to preserve the population's 'monolithic ideo-logical unity' as the keystone of the revolutionary structure.

UMAP, unlike most 'Make a New Cuba!' projects, was implemented as furtively as possible and lasted less than three years. Protests from the Cuban Union of Writers and Artists, backed by angry cohorts of Mexican and European intellectuals who hitherto had lauded the Revolution, hastened its end. But the decisive intervention came from Rawuel Revuelta, a leading actress who had been a Popular Socialist Party activist in the Batista era, when support for that party was hazardous. Following the banning of her own Teatro Estudio, because of its high quotient of homosexuals, she became aware of UMAP and denounced it to her close friend Comandante Rene Vallejo. As Fidel's personal physician, he was well placed to expose the viciousness which had developed in these camps. Fidel reacted promptly, appointing Captain Quintin Pino Machado to close the camps. That procedure took a year, forced labour being so crucial to the reform of Cuba's agriculture, but under Captain Machado conditions at once began to improve.

In 1975, after a harsh decade which wrecked many lives and careers, Cuba's Supreme Court was allowed to award financial compensation to those who could prove 'wrongful dismissal'. Amando Hart then took over the Ministry of Culture and replaced the worst homophobic excesses by restraints found all over Latin America including 'liberally democratic' Costa Rica. However, most homosexuals had long since become emotionally (if not politically) counter-revolutionary and they eagerly joined the government-authorised 1980 exodus to Miami. Among more than a hundred thousand disillusioned and 'maladjusted' (to the Revolution) migrants were several thousand genuine criminals – a black practical joke on Fidel's part. The 1979 Penal Code (facetiously misspelt by some commentators) had decriminalised homosexuality and now *Granma* printed a smugly unpleasant editorial: 'Even though in our country homosexuals are not persecuted or harassed . . . there were quite a few of them in the Mariel boatlift, in addition to all those in gambling or drugs who find it difficult to satisfy their vices here.'

Post-Mariel, Amando Hart's reforms quickened the pace of change. Yet a rocky and disputatious road stretched from 1979 to the Penal Code's 1989 revisions, then on to Santa Clara's El Mejunje disco – and the screening of *Fresa y Chocolate* in April 2007 by Cuba's Permanent Mission to the UN. My invitation listed the 'awards won' and gave a synopsis:

> Diego, a cultivated, homosexual and skeptical young man, falls in love with a young heterosexual communist full of prejudices and doctrinary ideas. First come rejection and suspicion, but also fascination. *Fresa y Chocolate* is the story of a great friendship, that is, a great love between two men, which overcomes incomprehension and intolerance.

In June 2007 I remembered Luis when Mariela Castro, Raul's daughter and Director of the National Centre for Sex Education, proposed to the fifth International Congress on Culture and Development a reform of the Family Code to grant to gays and lesbians the same housing, patrimonial inheritance, civil and adoption rights as heterosexual couples.

Said Mariela Castro, 'I can't guarantee it will reach parliament this year. That's our hope but it doesn't depend on us and of course is facing a great deal of resistance. The clause on adoption meets the heaviest opposition. We have inherited a model of a patriarchal family, and are unable to break with that model, but we have to. The political will exists to eliminate all forms of discrimination in our laws.'

It must be admitted that I, if Cuban, would oppose the adoption clause. Growing up in the twenty-first century will be confusing enough without having unisex parents.

Cuba's reputation for homophobia exacerbated the international con-troversy surrounding Castroism's rapid reaction to the AIDS threat. Using the quarantine regulations which had already enabled the eradication of several diseases, the Health Ministry promptly locked up all who tested positive. To me the logic of AIDS prevention justified this; while isolating many as yet in perfect health, it also provided them with the most favourable environment for maintaining good health while protecting their fellow-citizens from infection. The original sanatorium/jail, some twenty miles from Havana, was a fine old hacienda in spacious grounds surrounded by high concrete walls. Santiago de las Vegas ('Los Cocos' for short) had been in military hands since 1959 and was chosen as the national AIDS quarantine centre in 1985 because almost all Cuba's first batch of seropositives were young soldiers just back from serving as *internacionalistas* in Africa. Initially the isolation programme was run as a military operation and Fidel's critics abroad lamented this 'totalitarianism'. Yet most Cubans readily accepted the quarantine centre; they had every reason to trust their Ministry of Public Health. In 1983, when AIDS was little understood in any country but blood-borne infection was suspected, that Ministry banned the importing of factor VIII and, as a precaution, destroyed twenty-thousand units of blood products. Had the French, Chinese, US and various other governments been equally alert, thousands of haemophiliacs' lives would have been saved.

By the late 1980s US newspaper headlines had become hoarsely con-demnatory: 'Cuba's AIDS Centre Resembles Prison' – 'Cuba's Callous War on AIDS' – 'Cuba AIDS Quarantine Center called "Frightening"'– and so on and on. As the AIDS virus is not air-borne, the more pedantic Cuban officials objected to Los Cocos being described as a 'quarantine' centre. It was, they explained, a sanatorium for the close epidemiological surveillance of the inmates who received rigorously supervised medical treatment. It was also a research centre where new drugs were being developed and tested.

Within less than a year the original score or so of infected soldiers had been joined by a similar number of civilians, mostly homosexuals whose seropositive status had been discovered in their local clinics. The army doctors, already stressed by their soldier patients' increasingly perplexing symptoms, now had to cope with their homophobia. Segregation was called for, including restricted access to recreational facilities for the civilians – men not readily amenable to military discipline. They continued to complain about the soldiers' (never the staff's) nastiness and in 1988 the Ministry of Defence begged the Ministry of Public Health to carry this can of intractable worms.

Jorge Perez, director of the in-patient unit of Havana's Institute of Tropical Medicine, was then invited to run Los Cocos. After some hesitation he accepted, on his own civilian terms; the sanatorium must come under the aegis of his Institute and he must be left free to devise another sort of AIDS control program. Nine years later he told Paul Farmer, a Harvard Professor of Medical Anthropology, 'I saw that Cuba had a chance that many other countries did not: a small number of cases, and the public health capacity to intervene definitively to prevent a major epidemic.'

Under Perez, Los Cocos' high walls were razed and the 'internees' became 'residents'. The physiological necessity for 'safe sex' was explained in simple laymen's terms but in graphic detail and with harrowing illustrations. Equal emphasis was given to the seropositives' moral responsibility to safeguard others. Then some asymptomatic residents were allowed to return by day to their workplaces or their university halls and several were encouraged to practice their professions *in situ*, seropositive doctors and nurses taking charge of the infirmary and the laboratory.

All returning *internacionalistas* were screened, a routine ante-dating the AIDS crisis to prevent the resurgence of eradicated diseases. More and more seropositives came home, and increasing numbers of civilian homosexual and bisexual cases were diagnosed, the majority with North American or European associates. When Los Cocos overflowed, its grounds sprouted many small, air-conditioned residential units equipped with cooking facilities and colour TV. In 1993 Dr Perez made residential treatment optional but not many 'chose freedom'; coping with the Special Period was easier under the Health Department's wing.

The establishment of sanatoriums in each province coincided with the beginning of the Special Period when funding for most projects was drastically reduced. Happily the bureaucrats listened to Dr Perez's argument – were shortages of food (the Special Period's main hardship) allowed to weaken seropositives, while their numbers increased for lack of the sanatorium regime, Cuba couldn't avoid a major epidemic. Thus it came about that in Cuba the virus has so far been controlled. It is currently estimated that less than point one per cent of Cuba's adult population is infected with HIV, compared to a global estimate of some one per cent.

All this starkly illustrates Castroism in action. The infected individual had no choice. Off to a sanatorium! – as inexorably as a convicted criminal goes off to prison. However, since Cuba's healthcare system is not financially constrained the authorities could combine incarceration with the provision of everything needed to prolong seropositives' lives. And, astonishingly – because Cubans are not culturally disposed to sexual restraint – most people did listen when the spread of AIDS through unsafe sex was presented as a moral issue.

In conversation with the director of a provincial sanatorium I found him taking the seropositives' passivity for granted. 'Why should they expect *choice* about how to react to their misfortune? If they look across at Haiti they can see where that gets people – it's now with the Western hemisphere's highest AIDS rate. And that's after UNAid set up an expensive programme there years ago.'

In 2002 the US publicised its plan to donate fifteen billion dollars, over a five-year period, to the developing world's AIDS-protection needs. Five years later we learned that most of those dollars had been squandered either on agency 'overheads' or on Bush II's surreal campaign to defeat the virus through encouraging abstinence.

That evening an *apagón*, affecting just a few streets, halted my diary-writing.

'The embargo,' explained Tania. 'We can't get enough spare parts, again and again our electricians have to patch things up.'

We sat on the doorstep in the gloaming, attended by Mesa and Tigre, watching the western sky turn from old gold to plum to steel grey. Tania recalled the worst of the Special Period when almost every day, owing to the oil shortage, *apagones* struck, often lasting for eighteen hours. It became slightly easier to cope when electricity was rationed and each district forewarned. Since 2003 all electricity has been generated by Cuban oil (too sulphuric to be refined into petrol) and now most *apagones* are brief.

Soon a little van rattled into view, laden with a prodigiously long ladder. 'Let's watch,' said Tania and around the next corner we joined one of several animated groups, some sitting on their thresholds or window ledges, others lounging against walls. They had gathered to admire a lean, nimble, grey-haired man, festooned with tools, who swarmed up the ladder, held steady by his mate, and for over an hour struggled with a dottily tangled mass of wires linking two metal posts that soared above the house tops. He was working by starlight only and occasionally violet sparks ran to and fro along the wires causing the spectators to gasp fearfully or giggle nervously. Tania nudged me and said, 'Don't worry, he knows his job. It's taking so long because he's inventing the cure. Each *apagon* is different, he has to be creative.'

The evening traffic consisted of horse-buses, each with its mandatory oil-rag burning in a tiny tin hanging low from the rear axle. As the street lights suddenly went on we all cheered and clapped our hero and when the ladder had been swiftly folded and loaded the van sped off – to another *apagon*, Tania said, on the far side of the park. She added, 'Embargo problems bring out the best in Cubans' – a point missed, over the past half-century, by ten US administrations.

At first I had found Cuba's Ché cult, which reaches its full flowering in Santa Clara, rather irritating, even slightly distasteful. For propaganda purposes some aspects of his story have been blurred – unsurprisingly, yet I felt this dishonoured his memory. In the Prologue to *Reminiscences of the Cuban Revolutionary War* he encouraged his fellow-survivors to record their own recollections and added, 'I ask only that the narrator be strictly truthful. He should not pretend, for his own aggrandisement, to have been where he was not, and he should beware of inaccuracies'.

In December, on my way home with the Trio, I met in London a venerable Cuban to whom I confided my unease. Señor C— had known Ché as a member of the first Revolutionary government, before he himself became disillusioned with Castroism in the '70s and retreated to Europe. In his view, 'This cult is a sort of transference. Fidel never wanted a personality cult to form around himself – at least not the usual sort, obvious and banal. But he thought Cubans needed a contemporary hero figure so he gave them Ché, a twentieth-century back-up for Martí. Another thing, Ché soon became a world hero, the most attractive face of the

Revolution – literally. After his "romantic" death, it was clever to keep him in the public eye, everywhere, not just in Cuba.'

A cynical view? Or a shrewd comment? I'm not qualified to judge. But my initial unease had faded by the time I reached Santa Clara.

Born in Argentine, as a two-year-old Ché suffered his first asthma attack and all his life he demonstrated, as do many asthmatics, the extraordinary power of mind over matter. His mother (Celia de la Serna, of Spanish descent) recalled, 'His father slept sitting on Ernesto's bed because he weathered the breathless attacks better sleeping with his head resting on his father's chest. I taught him his ABC but he could not attend school regularly. His brothers and sisters would copy the lessons and he did them at home.' (Ché's father, Ernesto Guevara Lynch, was a civil engineer of part-Irish descent.) Despite this sporadic schooling, Ché graduated as a medical doctor in 1953 at the age of twenty-five. And then – a delicious irony – the Argentinean government judged one of the twentieth century's most celebrated guerrilla soldiers unfit for military service.

Ché, a prolific and talented writer, penned numerous essays, lectures and TV talks while a member of the government. Amidst those hundreds of pages – explaining the ideological background to the Revolution's military success and striving to boost the workers' morale while urging them to try harder – one can discern signs of dissatisfaction with Cuba's pace of change. Ché was an impatient idealist, stressing the need for leaders to remain in touch with the masses while not himself taking their limitations into consideration. As leader of the Department of Industry he dealt harshly with Cuba's militant trade unions who, in the bad old days, had wielded surprising power and secured for their members better 'terms and conditions' than were normal in Latin America. The man who declared himself willing to (and did) lay down his life for the poor of the earth was accused of hypocrisy when he told Cuba's workers:

> You have to get used to living in a collectivist regime and therefore cannot strike . . . You must understand the need to sacrifice an easy demand today to achieve a greater and more solid progress for the future . . . Should workers have to go on strike because the state assumes an intransigent and absurd position, it would be a signal that we have failed, it would be the beginning of the end of our popular government. But the state will ask for sacrifices from the working class.

In fact Ché's demands were not unreasonable three years into the Revolution, given two hundred thousand jobless. For everyone to benefit from this radical social upheaval, some of the better-off trade union members had to accept reduced privileges. Nobody's wages were lowered but annual bonuses regardless of output, and sick leave without evidence of sickness, were abolished. For the ensuing friction and confusion, education was the remedy. Workers must be brought to understand that now they were living in another sort of political entity. Dissent was *out*, equity was *in*. For the first time, national sovereignty was genuine, a fact readily appreciated as people came to experience the benefits of nationalising the means of production. Commitment to jobs, central to the delivery of revolutionary promises, increased spectacularly when Cubans realised that they were no longer working for the owners of private property but for a state that belonged (at last!) to them. An observer from New York State University, Professor Marifeli Perez-Stable, quotes a cigar worker in 1962 – 'When a Cuban feels honour and pride in his heart for his nation, this means more than material benefits.' And a brewery worker happily commented, 'Never before has there been such fellowship between the workers and the administration and other Cubans.'

As an anti-capitalist, Ché unfailingly practised what he preached. All the royalties from his best-selling *Reminiscences of the Cuban Revolutionary War* went to the Writers' Union with a brief note: 'I cannot accept a cent from a book that does nothing more than narrate incidents from the war. Do whatever you wish with the money.' Declining a fee for lecturing at Havana University he explained, 'For me it is inconceivable that a monetary remuneration be offered to a leader of the government for any kind of work. Among the many recompenses I have received, that most important is that of being considered part of the Cuban people. I could not evaluate that in pesos or centavos.' In a letter to Fidel, written before Ché set off on his risky mission to the Congo, he noted that his family in Cuba would inherit nothing material but that was okay; the state would provide housing, education and medication for his four young children. To them, two years later, he wrote tender farewell letters from Bolivia when his survival seemed unlikely. The eldest received a separate letter, being of an age to carry the Revolutionary torch. 'Remember, there are still many years of struggle ahead and even when you are a woman you will have to play your part.' Aleida Guevera is still playing her part, working as a paediatrician in the most needy corners of the Majority World and helping to run the William Soler Children's Hospital in Havana.

In 1965 Ché's apparently abrupt decision to leave Cuba and resume his guerrilla career generated durable rumours. Anti-Castroites gloated over an 'inevitable' falling out between two tough young men, 'natural rivals for power'. It was knowingly asserted that Fidel, being the tougher of the two, had 'banished' Ché. (Perhaps even had him eliminated? He had vanished without trace . . .) To those who knew both men, such flourishes of pop psychology lacked all credibility though for a time the rumours did have a certain destabilising effect within Havana's body politic.

In its early days, Cuba's Revolution was for export. Its military success excited that minority of Bolivar believers to be found in every generation, throughout Latin America, since the Liberator's death. Cuba's new leaders, especially Fidel and Ché, were happy to be in this export business. During the '60s a guesstimated two thousand Latin Americans studied guerrilla warfare in Cuban training camps, to the Soviets' dismay. The Kremlin disliked armed insurgency not directed by the Kremlin. And here were these Cubans messing things up in a region designated by the Politburo (bearing the Monroe doctrine in mind) as best subverted by go-slow, non-violent political operations under KGB supervision. (A chilling book, *The Mitrokhin Archive II* by Christopher Andrew and Vasili Mitrokhin, incidentally illuminates the KGB/CIA affinity – two sinister organisations having much more in common with each other than either has/had with the ordinary decent citizens of their respective countries.)

Cuba's revolutionaries were genuine internationalists, as they would prove in the decades to come, and seen from the Caribbean in the 1960s Africa looked like another continent ripe for a Cuban-style revolution. But of course it wasn't. Ché's longing to build a global opposition to Capitalism Rampant completely baffled the Africans they had set out to help. Those Congolese had never heard of the IMF or GATT or the CIA/KGB or Marx or Milton Friedman. They didn't know what Ché was talking about and he didn't know what they were feeling about. Their conflicts and objectives, based on important (to them) tribal differences, and concentrated within comparatively small areas, were millennia away from the concept of revolution as an intercontinental process unifying the poor of the world. Blank stares greeted Ché's talk of replacing predatory foreign corporations with disciplined African work-forces capable of sustaining, by their productivity, an economy that would provide for the welfare of every citizen. After three frustrating and humiliating months Ché and his one hundred and twenty highly trained guerrillas (all black) retreated the way they had come, by boat across Lake Tanganyika.

When his *compañeros* had hurried home, glad to be shaking the African dust off their boots, Ché lodged in the Cuban embassy in Dar-es-Salaam for two months, editing his Congo diaries. At heart he preferred the pen to the gun and it is as a writer that he most appeals to me. *The African Dream*, unpublished until 1999, is his best book – perhaps because he knew, while working on it, that for political reasons it wouldn't be published within the foreseeable future, if ever. It is searingly honest and innocent of political correctness. No one comes out of it well: not Ché, not his *compañeros*, not their Congolese allies – least of all Laurent Kabila who, decades later, reappeared destructively on the world stage. In *The African Dream*'s final paragraph we read:

> Up to now, Kabila has not shown that he possesses any (leadership) qualities. He is young and it is possible that he will change. But I will make so bold as to say, in this text that will see the light of day only after many years have passed, that I have very great doubts about his ability to overcome his defects in the environment in which he operates.

That was written in January 1966. Thirty-one years later Kabila – his defects still in place – ousted General Mobutu.

The African Dream allows us great intimacy with Ché and some readers may be shocked by the nakedness of his own cultural imperialism. He was, after all, a man of his time, a Latin American with little knowledge of other continents, lacking the flexibility essential for this self-imposed task of helping Africans. He also lacked the hypocrisy used by many contemporary leaders to disguise their racism. Had he been in a position to influence those Congolese tribes, he would have hustled them away from their own traditions and into our industrialised world as relentlessly as any colonial power or modern development agency. In an epilogue mingling sadness and bewilderment he acknowledges 'hostility on the part of the population' and wonders:

> What could the Liberation Army offer these peasants? That is the question which always bothered us. We could not speak here of dividing up the land in an agrarian reform because everyone could see that it was already divided; nor could we speak of credits for the purchase of farm tools, because the peasants ate what they tilled with their primitive instruments and the physical characteristics of the region did not lend themselves to credit-fuelled expansion. Ways would have to be found of *fostering the need to acquire industrial goods* (which the peasants were obviously willing to accept and pay for) and therefore a need for more widespread trade. [My italics.]

Ché's Bolivian venture has been variously described as hot-headed, callous, arrogant, romantic, irresponsible, melodramatic, unrealistic. Reviewing *The Bolivian Diaries* in 1968, less than two years after their author's death, I chose 'just plain daft'. (That was ten years before my own three-month trek in the roadless High Andes, which gave me rather a different perspective.) The English translation was published by Allen & Unwin, a guarantee of its authenticity, as the critics noted, though in fact Daniel James' Introduction is lamentably tendentious. The Cuban edition, distributed free throughout the island, became the Ché cult's keystone. It was incomplete – heavily censored – as Fidel admitted at the time; 'image-building' had not yet been so named but *el comandante* well understood this ancient process. Thus 'The Diaries' became an inspiration for generations of Cubans who imbibed carefully selected quotations with their mothers' milk – and thereafter were exposed to them on everything from exercise-book covers to *tienda* wall posters to gigantic wayside hoardings.

By now the genesis of Ché's last campaign has been forgotten by most people. Bolivia was chosen not because its minuscule Communist Party was champing at the revolutionary bit but because Ché had in his sights all five of its bordering countries (the domino effect). With Fidel, he had decided that 'Bolivia will sacrifice itself so that conditions for revolution can be created in neighbouring countries. We have to make Latin America another Viet Nam.'

The eighteen experienced Cubans in the 'expeditionary force' expected the peasantry to support them as the Sierra Maestra villagers had eventually supported Fidel. But uninvited foreign forces, whether Cuban guerrillas or US marines, have trouble 'winning hearts and minds'. Instead of flocking to Ché's standard these Bolivian villagers were scared by the incomprehensible arrival in their remote mountains of strange long-bearded men (the indigenous Indians are not hirsute) who set about digging inexplicable tunnels and couldn't speak their language. Ché's attempt to learn Quechua was irrelevant; the tribe amongst whom they found themselves spoke Guarini which not even the Bolivian guerrillas knew. These peasants didn't want to fight anybody but when the shooting started they usually sided with their own army, informing them of the invaders' movements.

For all his callous talk about 'another Viet Nam', and his insistence on the value of guns to social reformers, the mature Ché was a hesitant man of violence. Nor did he urge his team, in Bolivia, to be ruthless. Given a tiny revolutionary 'army', hoping to outwit a professional (though inept) national army, one might have expected him to kill at every opportunity. Not so, however. His diary records occasions when he couldn't bring himself to shoot vulnerable young conscripts who presented easy targets. On 3 June – 'At 1700 an Army truck came by, with two little soldiers wrapped in blankets in the bed of the vehicle. I did not feel up to shooting them, and my brain didn't work fast enough to take them prisoner, so we let it go by'. On 20 June – 'The officer is a Second Lieutenant of the police that was sent with a carabinero and a teacher who came as a volunteer . . . His mission entailed a long trip for which they allowed him only four days . . . We considered killing them but then I decided to send them back alive'.

The uncensored *Bolivian Diaries* is a movingly honest record of a tragically ill-planned campaign. It is also a gripping adventure story. For eleven months the guerrillas endured extreme hardship amidst one of the Andes' most formidable ranges. For days they went without food or water, were lost (together or in two anxiously wandering groups), had to use machetes to clear the way on jungly pathless slopes, had to retrace their weary footsteps when thwarted by sheer precipices, had to make rafts to cross wide rapid rivers in which a few *compañeros* were drowned and several precious weapons lost. Meanwhile the Bolivian army was tracking them, ineffectually, until reinforcements arrived, troops specially trained and equipped by the US army for the Ché-hunt.

The day after their quarry was wounded and captured the CIA conferred with the military junta in La Paz who then ordered Sergeant Mario Teran to kill his prisoner. Expediency demanded Ché's murder. As a Cuban government representative, he had addressed the Organization of American States, the 1964 UN Conference on Trade and Development, the UN General Assembly, the Organization of Afro-Asian Solidarity meeting in Algiers. Internationally, he had made his mark as a passionate spokesman for the voiceless. Had he been brought to trial millions, already enthralled by his deeds and words, would have listened attentively to his speech from the dock. And many would certainly have been inspired to take up where Ché had to leave off – shades of Nelson Mandela's Rivonia peroration. A helicopter took his body to a small hospital in the hill town of Vallegrande where the open-eyed corpse was photographed and identified by a Cuban-American agent of the CIA, known as 'Eduardo Gonzalez', who had directed the Ché-hunt. Almost forty years later, in that same hospital, a blind octogenarian, a retired army sergeant named Mario Teran, had his two cataracts removed by a Cuban opthalmic surgeon, one of a team of twenty providing free medical care to the local *campesiños*.

In 1960 Ché had spent months in the Soviet Union being feted and to some extent brainwashed. But only to a limited extent; thereafter he presented himself as an internationalist Marxist rather than as a Kremlin-controlled Communist. He openly criticised Soviet imperialism, finding it too similar, where foreign aid was concerned, to the capitalist version. Genuine Communists, argued Ché, would provide stringless aid to un-developed countries – how else could the poor be freed from their trap? Doubtless this straight talk partly explains the Soviet reaction to his death. All around the world pro-Soviet journalists and broadcasters used his ignominious (as they interpreted it) end to prove the Kremlin's point that in Latin America armed insurgency was not the way forward.

Observing the World Bank, the IMF, GATT et al., as they deftly manipu-lated the Majority World, Ché accurately foretold the consequences. Our current proliferation of books dissecting the stratagems employed by Capitalism Rampant would not have surprised him. Long before the Washington Consensus was declared, he clearly saw that pattern emerging.

In our day, Ché would of course rank as a terrorist. So how come this idol of the rebellious '68-ers, this Marxist gunman, this purveyor of violence and sedition, was eulogised in a variety of unexpected quarters? I quote from US reviews of *Reminiscences of the Cuban Revolutionary War*, published in the mid-'60s:

A tremendously interesting and illuminating document . . . tells much about the character and personality of the protagonist: *Washington Evening Star*.

The absolute truth, putting to shame the pretenders and privileged of the contemporary world. I think it is bound to have powerful meaning to the youth of America: *Collegiate Press Service*.

Impossible to read and not know one is in the presence of a rare being, a man of principle: *Commonweal*.

A fascinating picture of a man caught up in what he considered an idealistic process, the saving of a Latin American country from tyranny: *Atlanta Journal*.

If Guevara had spent his time at the typewriter instead of leading revolutionaries, then the world would be hailing a new giant in literature: *Cleveland Press*.

Thus was Ché's fervent adherence to Marxism indulged in the midst of the Cold War. His extraordinary qualities were recognised, even by those whose way of life would have been demolished had his thinking prevailed, and despite his active promotion of armed insurrection against Washington's satellite regimes. Now he would be relentlessly demonised, his integrity impugned and his ideals scorned – a disturbing measure of how intolerance has gained momentum under the aegis of 'the new imperialists'.

The Cuban Missile Crisis of 1962 prompts a similar comparison. In those days world leaders exchanged real, personal letters and, reading the correspondence between John F. Kennedy, Nikita Khrushchev and Fidel, one is struck both by the courteous wording (even when the writer is angry and/or frightened) and by the efforts being made to see the other point of view. Granted, that fraught atmosphere – with nuclear weapons pointing in every direction – made diplomatic tip-toeing and whispering seem advisable. Yet one senses that the civilised tone of those exchanges also had to do with the personalities involved. An equivalent crisis, given the aggression-glorification and coarse phraseology of the present US admini-stration, would be unlikely to have a non-violent ending.

Had President Kennedy survived, he and Khrushchev might have radically changed the Cold War chemistry, to the arms industry's detriment. And Fidel believes that the Cuban-US relationship would almost certainly have benefited. As he said in an interview with Ignacio Ramonet:

> Kennedy was a man courageous enough to introduce some changes into US policy . . . The day he was killed I was talking to a French journalist, Jean Daniel, whom Kennedy had sent to me with a message . . . so communications were being established . . . His death touched me and grieved me. He was an adversary, of course, but it was as though I'd lost a very capable, worthy opponent . . . His assassination worried me too because when he was taken from the stage he had enough authority in his country to impose an improvement in relations with Cuba. That was palpably demonstrated in the conversation I had with Jean Daniel who was with me the very instant we heard of Kennedy's death. As the 'ifs' of history go, that's quite a biggie . . .

Some January nights can be blessedly chilly and I approached the Ché Memorial at dawn through a silver-grey fog, dense enough to obscure Ché until I was standing directly below José Delarra's bronze statue – water-bottle on hip, one arm in a sling, the right hand rather casually carrying a rifle. Then the rising sun created an eerie optical illusion: as the mist thinned and shifted, it seemed that Ché himself was moving.

This statue was erected on the twentieth anniversary of Ché's death.

Ten years later his bones, and the remains of seventeen other guerrillas, were flown from Bolivia and interred in a simple mausoleum behind the monument, a building that could easily be overlooked. Tania had shown me photographs of countless thousands watching Ché's coffin being lowered from an aeroplane while an army band played *Suite de las Americas*. 'Emotions were mixed,' she recalled. 'My generation, we wept . . . For younger Cubans, Ché had been as remote as Martí, then suddenly he became real because of his coffin! Real because he was dead! Soon many of them wept too. Other youths became jubilant in a belligerent way – all very interesting. A sociologist colleague of mine wrote an essay about the different reactions. Everyone noticed how *sad* Fidel looked. Through the worst times, Ché was his best friend.'

I had thought I was alone but now a patrolling policeman appeared in the distance, at the end of his eight-hour shift. As he saluted me amiably I wondered if he really spent the night pacing to and fro on that long, high, concrete platform supporting both Ché's statue and its attendant bas-relief depicting the Battle of Santa Clara. The expansive Plaza de la Revolucion looked neglected, most of the benches broken, the star-shaped flower-beds weed-dominated, the conspicuous ornamental fountains de-funct, their basins half-full of litter. Far away around the periphery, house-sized hoardings showed Ché in various moods and poses; some had been not only weather-beaten but vandalised, which perhaps explained the twenty-four hour guard. One can imagine the iconoclastic fury with which some of today's frustrated young non-consumers might attack Ché's memorial.

Back on the platform, approached by steep flights of steps at each end, I waved at the new cigar-smoking policeman, then sat at Ché's feet to scribble in my diary:

Ever more urgently our planet needs Ché's vision of the New Man to be realised. It's easy to mock that vision, to assert that human nature can't be renovated. But the average human being is *led*, this way or that. Comparatively recently we in the Minority World have been led (most of us) to reject people being tortured or burnt at the stake, children being forced down mines or up chimneys, overt slavery, segregated blacks, jailed homosexuals. Those changes required the evolution of New Men and Women, new ways of thinking. Ché's ideal of people working not only for themselves but for the general good may seem a more fundamental challenge to human nature – but is it? By definition 'the general good' benefits most people. Working towards it would thwart only the minority who thrive within the Growth Society, feeling free to disregard the majority.

I'm not often drawn by big occasions, when crowds gather to celebrate something momentous. Yet here and now I'm deciding to return to Santa Clara in October 2007 for the fortieth commemoration of Ché's death.

No. 374 was a polyglot household – Tania speaking English, her son Ed fluent in French, his wife Carmel able to get by in German, their son and daughter, aged ten and twelve, attempting Mandarin Chinese at school – despite having heard a rumour that Chinese children must spend fourteen years learning how to write. Ed and Carmel lectured at Santa Clara university, Cuba's third largest, described by Tania as 'our city's main industry'. Conviviality happened in a minimally furnished kitchen behind the living-room. A crowded *organoponico*, visible from the kitchen window, produced more than enough vegetables to feed the family. Proudly the children informed me that in 2005 urban Cubans had grown over four million tons of vegetables. On their way home from school they collected supplementary feeding (weeds) for the four hens who scratched, clucked and laid at one wire-fenced end of the small garden.

In the 1980s, Tania remembered, eggs were plentiful enough to be unrationed and factory chickens were part of the weekly meat ration and also available on the open market through a cafeteria chain ('Pio Pio') modelled on Kentucky Fried Chicken. But many of those birds, including 'starter chicks', and almost all their feed, were imported. Come the Special Period, the government distributed chicks to be raised free-range and bred from – hence the numbers of happy poultry now foraging all over rural Cuba.

Cuba's Revolution was the opposite of green, whatever shade that may be. ('Orange!' I hear some of my Irish friends shouting.) If Fidel read *The Silent Spring* in 1963 – quite likely, given the breadth of his reading – he didn't heed Rachel Carson's warnings. He and Ché and their advisors truly believed in agriscience and the land and people of Cuba have suffered accordingly. From the Soviet Union came thousands of massive, soil-compacting machines and countless tons of hazardous chemical inputs accompanied by platoons of agronomists – whose domestic record Fidel should have scrutinised before bowing down before them.

Thirty years on, when the Special Period ousted agriscience, not much knowledge of traditional farming remained to be resuscitated. Most labourers were descended from slaves who had cultivated efficiently within their homelands' subsistence economies but, within a generation or two, had lost skills no longer relevant. Although Cuba has always been capable of amply feeding itself from its own soil the imposed monoculture prevented that.

Even before the Special Period, some outspoken young agronomists had been blaming their leaders' ex-colonial mind-set for a too respectful acceptance of Soviet advice, given by 'experts' totally ignorant of local conditions. By the early 1980s Fidel & Co. had begun to fear that Cuba was en route to catastrophe, being so dependent on food imports, and from then on 'the Alternative Model' of agriculture was encouraged. When the necessary research was funded, factions formed. The keen young researchers advocated and devised microbial formulations, biofertilisers and biopesticides non-toxic to humans, the Soviet-revering Agriculture Ministry bureaucrats scorned their discoveries. A prolonged controversy ensued, incidentally contradicting the widespread notion that Fidel ruled as an all-powerful tyrant. A Castroist government is in fact a complex institution; Fidel's backing for the young researchers secured their funding but did not enable them at once to defeat the bureaucrats. Victory rewarded them only when COMECON cut all trading links with Cuba.

When the going got tough Fidel didn't hesitate to admit his past mistakes. Addressing the fifth Congress of the National System of Agriculture and Forestry Technicians, in 1991, he avoided fudging the issue as our politicians invariably do when their great schemes come unstuck:

> The food question has the number one propriety. We must produce more food without feedstocks and without fertilisers. Keep one idea clear: the country is without feedstocks and fertilisers. All plans based on fuel availability must be cut practically in half; half of what the country consumed in normal circumstances. We have bred one hundred thousand new oxen, we are breeding a hundred thousand more. Even if we have to subsist on vegetable protein, we cannot eat the oxen because we need them to cultivate land. The ox does not just save fuel: the ox can perform tasks that would be impossible for a tractor, raising the productivity of human labour. Even when the Special Period ends, the role of the ox in Cuban agriculture will not be totally over. We must convert farming into one of the most honoured, promoted and appreciated professions. Our scientists will create resources that will one day be more valuable than sugar cane. Now more than ever, the phrase 'economic independence'

has meaning. We will achieve it through miracles of intelligence, sweat, heart and the consciousness of humankind.

Shades of Ché! This direct talking to the public helps to explain how Castroism survived the Special Period. As Tania boasted, 'He was like Britain's Churchill, during World War II! He got people feeling though the situation was desperate they could win!'

At that stage, what are emphasised as some of the worst horrors of 'Communist Cuba' were used to good effect: state control of the food supply and the media, plus a population amenable to being organised from the centre for the common good.

When we moved to the living-room, in time to hear the end of Fidel's evening communication, I remarked, 'He looks and sounds much stronger that in November.'

Tania smiled. 'He knows how much we need him, with McCarry touring Europe!'

Caleb McCarry contributed significantly to Haiti's 2004 'régime change'. Recently on Radio Four I had heard him explaining his European mission – 'It's my job to persuade our allies to support opposition to the Castro dictatorship *within* Cuba.'

We watched preparations for the morrow's protest march against Radio Marti. Men using street plans and pointers explained where and when groups should assemble, which streets (including San Rafael) would be closed to traffic from 6.00 a.m. to 6.00 p.m., where to find first-aid posts, how to summon ambulances, which routes to follow when dispersing. Civilian monitors would be responsible for crowd control – a revealing reversal of the procedure in our democracies where demos require the deployment of extra police units. Radio Marti's transmissions began during the Reagan era and have become ever more seditionary, prompting many with serious reservations about Castroism to close ranks around their leader.

When Carmel asked why I hadn't remained in Havana for this event I explained – 'Friends warned me tourists may not march, will be confined to certain supervised vantage points'.

Next day the family were at first amused, then impressed by my seven-hour TV marathon – 8.00 a.m. to 3.00 p.m. 'You take your job very seriously,' said Ed, not realising that I was riveted by this skilfully presented TV spectacular. It took all of those seven hours for one point four million Cubans to pass the US Special Interests ten-storey block. Every sort of Cuban processed cheerfully along the Malecón, waving little flags, chanting slogans, singing songs, blowing whistles, carrying toddlers on shoulders, linking arms with shuffling oldies, sharing bottles of water, munching peanuts, occasionally leaping in the air or performing an impromptu dance. The anti-Radio Marti chanting became strident as people approached its source – strident but not threatening. We saw several close-ups of groups grinning broadly while shaking clenched fists at 'Special Interests'. If there were angry frowns, we weren't shown them.

Thrice Fidel descended from his podium to walk with the crowd, holding himself erect, vigorously striding out for a hundred yards, not looking like a man who five months later would be in intensive care. As he spoke with those who chanced to be around him, nobody seemed in the least awed – as I most certainly would be, were we to meet. Is this a consequence of 'no personality cult'?

As the hours passed I found myself wondering how to interpret such demos. Many would assert that I was looking at rigorously regimented Cubans doing what they had been ordered to do, fearful of staying at home. Or had they been conditioned to see these mass rallies-cum-fiestas as a fun day off work or school and a proud expression of *cubania*? If they weren't enjoying themselves they deceived me – and surely the cameras could not have been manipulated to avoid all discontented faces? Then I thought, uneasily, 'Perhaps Cuba really is a uniquely one-man show, Fidel still holding it together?' – even after the Special Period hardships, after the dual currency revival of class divisions, after the birth of a generation to whom the Revolution is history, not perceived as their own achievement . . .

Was this demo's message being heard across the Straits of Florida? Here were thousands of men and women, all trained to use guns, displaying their resentment of US interference in Cuban affairs. They may covet the tourists' designer clothes, digital cameras, iPods, scuba-diving equipment – yet most remain protective of their Cuban identity. Military intruders, inhibited by world opinion from bombing a Caribbean island into sub-mission, would find themselves up against 'insurgents' of a very different calibre from Iraq's. The comparison is allowable; in both cases the name of the game, on Washington's own admission, is 'régime change'. And the united Cubans (united against the US threat to the republic's indepen-dence, whatever their domestic squabbles) would form a resolute and disciplined defence force.

When I said as much to the family, Tania observed that the Bush II administration is not known for its sensitivity to world opinion. And Carmel apprehensively pointed to the Ukraine, Georgia and Azerbaijan as obvious examples of what cleverly spent dollars could achieve. But Ed dismissed the notion that eighty million US dollars (the sum of tax-payers' money by then at the Commission's disposal) could divide and conquer a Cuba so aware of the Revolution's benefits, however critical of its restraints.

Tania added, 'It's sure the *Yanquis* couldn't even try to set up a government run by returned exiles, like they tried in Kabul and Baghdad. That's when rivers of blood would flow!'

By then my hostess and I had established a certain rapport and when we were alone I ventured to ask, 'Can you guess how many of those marchers remain loyal, in their hearts, to the Revolution, to Fidel's internationalism, to Ché's "New Man" ideal? How many would have marched spontaneously against Radio Marti?'

Quietly Tania replied, 'We don't ask ourselves such questions. If we could ask them we'd be living in another sort of country. Maybe better than what we have, maybe a lot worse.'

During the demo Elián Gonzales and his father Juan Miguel had briefly joined Fidel on the podium and been rapturously cheered – the beautiful six-year-old child now a handsome fourteen-year-old youth. To Tania I mentioned my disapproval of this too-famous boy being kept in the limelight for an apparently petty motive: to remind Miami's fanatics of their defeat.

Tania corrected me; the motive was far from petty, Elián's extraordinary seven-month ordeal had given him a no less extraordinary and permanent political/social significance.

'Mostly,' said Tania, 'such dramas get blotted out soon by something new. But our reaction to Elián's tragedy actually *changed* Cuba, gave the whole country an injection of vibrant *cubania*, reinvigorated the Revolution. Cintio Vitier wrote a poem to Elián about the *Yanqui* bungling and one line says – "What fools! They have united us forever!" Foreign reporters said the government forced us to make a fuss but not so! It was an explosion of passion and debate and patriotism – spontaneous, all over the island, among all sorts. Psychologists and philosophers, factory and farm workers, artists and lawyers – gathering impromptu in streets, schools, conference halls, warehouses – everywhere! After three weeks our television started a series of *Mesas Redondas*, Round Tables, and millions watched qualified people looking at every side of the crisis. With Elián safely home, *la Batalla de Ideas*, our Battle of Ideas, grew out of those programmes. And that led to what we have now, *Tribunas Abiertas*, Open Rostrums, big open-air meetings all over Cuba for people to plan and communicate and argue about all sorts of social and cultural activities and political worries like the Miami Five – how to help them and their families? That's why Elián has to be noticed and cheered and loved! He was the catalyst for this renaissance of the Revolution.'

That evening we had yet another conversation about the fostering of dissident groups by CIA agents and their infiltration by Cuba's State Security officers. Again I felt a time slippage: socialism and capitalism still playing their Cold War spy games but on a shrunken stage – one little Caribbean island instead of two hemispheres.

Santa Clara university is privileged by location, its tranquil campus some seven miles from the city, wide parklands separating the faculties, a variety of mature trees shading the pathways. This campus has been much extended since Ché established his base here, on the eve of the Rebel Army's famous Last Battle, yet further extensions are urgently needed. In the hostels, four must share a small room; in the canteen, meals must be served in three shifts.

I arrived at lunch-time, not by design but because the bus service is so infrequent – for which reason the students do not consider themselves privileged. From Key West I bore a letter to one of the academic staff (let's call him Juan) who received me with palpably mixed feelings. As his cousin's friend I was affectionately welcomed, as a foreign contact I made him jittery. Even in a Cuba that is fast changing, institutional xenophobia endures.

Awkwardly, Juan explained that before entering any building, or meeting any of the staff or students, I must be vetted as an 'international visitor'. He hurried me to the relevant office, past buildings all crying out for paint and minor repairs, but we found the door locked – '*Hora de comer*,' said a notice. Even more awkwardly, poor Juan asked me to wait nearby for the registrar while he took his turn in the canteen. When I had been 'approved' we could talk in his faculty's staff-room.

I sat under a ceiba tree and reflected that a country vilified for so long, in the world from which I come, has every excuse for official xenophobia, for suspecting any foreigner of being a counter-revolutionary snooper. We in the generally unsympathetic West have created this situation; xenophobia doesn't come naturally to the laid-back, warm-hearted Cubans. Sometimes I regretted having approached the island as I approach every country, being an anonymous stranger, wanting only to enjoy the company of whomever I chance to meet. In Cuba's case, I might have been wise to acquire 'references' from those of the Revolution's distinguished foreign friends who are also my friends.

Punctually at 2.00 p.m. the registrar returned, an elderly white woman, hair dyed auburn, tight-lipped and narrow-eyed. She viewed me with acid suspicion. Why should a *tourist* be interested in a *university*? The implication was that tourists should stay on their beach reservations enjoying Operation Three Ss. But now all is in flux and the bureaucrats are not always sure of their ground, having been told that tourists, however deplorably independent, are an important economic resource. Reluctantly, and very slowly, the registrar computerised my passport and visa details, then handed me a long form to be filled in – which task I could have completed while she was computing. (The questions included, 'How many years have you been at your present occupation?' I wrote, '65'.) Finally a junior clerk took my 'entry permit' to some apparently distant office for the registrar's signature to be rubber-stamped and counter-signed. Meanwhile Juan was sitting under the ceiba, picking his teeth with a matchstick.

In a large, high-ceilinged, airy staff-room, where the bookshelves were sadly uncrowded, Juan introduced me to a few of his colleagues, and several students, and for two hours a bland discussion of Eng. Lit. was enjoyed by all.

Towards sunset the university bus put me down opposite Santa Clara's colossal, ungainly Coppelia palace and I was tempted – but the evening queues stretched out of sight, around the corner. Moments later, near Parque Vidal, capitalism reared its ugly head in the shape of a giant plastic ice cream cone advertising one of those Nestlé pavement fridges I'd first noticed in Havana – inscribed 'Why wait when you can have it NOW?' It enraged me to see Nestlé targeting Coppelia, for forty years the Cubans' source of affordable, wholesome ice cream. However, these mobile fridges accept only convertible pesos for their much inferior product and are therefore unlikely to shorten Coppelia's queues in the immediate future. But their presence crudely illustrates the divisive power of Cuba's dual currency.

Back at No. 374 it was packing-up time; I would be on the road before dawn. My plan to walk across the Sierra del Escambray to Trinidad appalled the family – in those mountains there was nowhere to sleep and nothing to eat! I soothed them as best I could and they looked pleased (though sceptical) when I spoke of returning to Santa Clara in October 2007.

Chapter 10

I set out for Manicaragua in darkness yet already Santa Clara was awake and noisy: shod hooves raising sparks from the cobbles, pedestrians and cyclists exchanging shouted greetings, favourite son tunes emanating from bicitaxis' transistors.

Beyond a straggling, semi-moribund industrial zone I watched the sun rise above those low, bare hills mentioned by Ché. From numerous *bohios*, scattered across arid slopes, immaculately uniformed children were descending to the road where horse-buses or bicitaxis awaited them. The tall, buxom senior girls looked decidedly nubile in their navy-blue mini-skirts and pale blue blouses. The boys wore scarlet shorts, white shirts, scarlet neckerchiefs. Several fathers and mothers came pedalling towards me with a small child (or two) on the home-made carrier and cross-bar seats.

A night of heavy rain had brought perfect trekking weather: high bright clouds, intermittent sunshine, a strong following breeze. The wide grassy verge spared my feet and all became greener as the road climbed gradually through cattle ranches and canefields. No more than a dozen vehicles disturbed my twenty-mile walk. Each of the few villages had its primary school (named after some local hero of the Revolution) and its whitewashed health centre displaying lists of dates for the next round of children's inoculations and adults' AIDS-education sessions. CDR leaders make sure everyone attends.

At noon I ate a tin of sardines and watched pairs of oxen ploughing at the base of forested hills. Then suddenly the Escambray were quite close, a dusky blue unbroken wall, by Cuban standards real mountains – Pico San Juan reaches three thousand seven hundred and sixty-two feet.

At 5.15 I trudged wearily into Manicaragua; it was a long time since I'd carried a loaded rucksack so far. This smallish market town is unlikely ever to find itself on the tourist trail and I didn't look for a *casa particulare*. There was however a shabby two-storey hotel and, rather to my surprise, the friendly young man at Reception offered a single room for NP40. An equally friendly young woman led me upstairs and pointed out the communal bathroom. The hotel served no meals but there was a pizza stall around the next corner and the *organoponico* market would open at 7.00 a.m.

Ten minutes later the mulatta manageress arrived, overweight and breathless, looking flustered and embarrassed. It was all a mistake – she pressed those NP40 into my hand. This was a 'Cubans only' hotel, the nearest tourist hotel was Hanabanilla, twenty miles away – or I could return to Santa Clara. Behind her stood a small, slight, scowling man, grey-haired and xenophobic, wearing a track-suit and baseball cap. Stepping forward, he demanded to see my passport, checked the visa, said I must stay at the Hanabanilla. A taxi was about to leave, CP10 the fare, I must hurry – he gestured impatiently towards my half-unpacked rucksack. The manageress gave me a quick sympathetic look, then disappeared. My captor (as I thought of him) escorted me across the road to an antique Chrysler already packed with hotel workers who had been shopping in Manicaragua. When ordered to make room for me a slim young waitress seemed quite pleased to find herself on the lap of a handsome young waiter.

In the 1970s a small inoffensive dam created a reservoir some eighteen miles long, embedded in lush green forested mountains and curiously shaped; on the map it looks like an emperor poodle with an erection. It is now known as Lake Hanabanilla and the road ends at the hotel, a crass building on a bluff above the water. Although listed as a tourist hotel the management seemed unaware of foreigners' expectations. In my diary I noted, 'no bedside lights, erratic plumbing, grumpy staff, vile expensive food in a pretentious restaurant. I'm reliably informed the four hundred rooms are all booked up, mainly by Cubans, for the hot season. At present there are about forty here, all rowdy young convertible-peso-rich people whose competing transistors create a discordancy around the swimming-pool below my balcony.'

Then I met Miranda, a thirty-year-old from St Lucia who had just completed her medical training in Havana, all expenses paid by the Cuban government. She had an agreeably bouncy four-year-old daughter, a razor sharp mind and no inhibitions about analysing race relations in Cuba, a subject rarely discussed by the Cubans themselves. I shall have more to say about her views in the next chapter.

Miranda was one of my two reasons for not returning to Manicaragua next morning. The other was Lake Hanabanilla, its deep clear water almost cold in January, its surrounding mountains exhilaratingly beautiful. My fellow-guests were horrified to see me plunging into the 'dirty' lake – in their view a form of attempted suicide by hypothermia. Some looked affronted when I condemned their heated pool, reeking of chlorine and full of everybody's pee – as filthy and unrefreshing. In between swims, Miranda and I walked and talked in the woods while Rina played in the hotel crèche.

A ferry sometimes operates between the dam and Jibacoa, twelve miles down the lake on the Manicaragua-Trinidad road, but for lack of fuel this ten-person motor launch was currently inactive. Instead, a three-hour downhill walk took me to the main Cienfuegos-Manicaragua road. When I crossed the dam before sunrise a colourless mist veiled Lake Hanabanilla and as the road wriggled around hills too steep for cultivation the rising sun showed their bushiness flecked with red and yellow blossoms. Dwarf palms studded narrow valleys where horses grazed on nothing much. Then isolated *bohios* appeared and distant shouts seemed to emphasise the silence as men guided humped oxen to the scattered fields where their ploughs awaited them. A joyous content filled me in this hidden little corner of 'undeveloped' Cuba but too soon a sharp bend revealed the plain below. There old tobacco fields and new eucalyptus plantations surrounded the town of Ciro Redondo with its incongruously urban apartment blocks and obtrusive munitions factory.

From the junction I walked on hoping for a lift but the few passing vehicles were overcrowded. My plan was to get well away from Manicaragua before nightfall, into the Escambray's foothills, and there to find a secluded camp-site. For another two hours I plodded on, now feeling the lack of breakfast but reluctant to deplete my rations; such luxuries as sardines and olives can't be replaced in small *tiendas*.

Near the little town of Espejo a kind old man, thin and round-shouldered with bright blue eyes in a chestnut-brown face, beckoned me on to his mule-cart. He was taking two churns of milk to the market and in Manicaragua would accept no pesos.

Half an hour and two large pizzas later I was on the town's outskirts, relieved to have escaped the attention of the baseball-capped xenophobe. The road dipped to cross a trickling stream, then gently climbed around low hills – promising camping territory. But soon heavy blue-black clouds began to gather – *not* promising weather for the tentless. As I prepared for an unpleasant night, the Fates offered shelter: an abandoned *bohio* some way above the road with no other dwelling in sight. Climbing the steep path, I realised that I was very tired. It seemed this home had long been abandoned: its thatched roof was in shreds, its latrine collapsed. Happily the wide verandah had a sound tin roof (odd that nobody had appropriated it) and I was unrolling my flea-bag when a shout startled me. A young man was hurrying up the path, carrying a kid with a broken leg. For a moment he stood staring silently at me, understandably flummoxed. Then he became assertive in an amiable way and twenty minutes later (the rain by then torrential) I was the wet guest of the nearest CDR president.

My hostess, Maribel, and her family were non-bureaucratic and flexible. They didn't ask to see my passport and visa, were curious about but not suspicious of an Irishwoman's Cuban journey. Of course they all disapproved of my walking to Trinidad, but for humanitarian rather than political reasons. Maribel spoke broken but graphic English. 'You has small pesos no problem, I has able get free car for Trinidad.'

I explained that the issue was not pesos but my liking for walking alone over mountain ranges. At this point one could see Maribel diagnosing a nut-case, possibly senile but harmless. Next morning she sent me on my way with three hard-boiled eggs, five homegrown tomatoes and a chit to her colleague in Jibacoa asking him to shelter me for the night. She ordered me not to go beyond Jibacoa: I *must* stay with Carlos. An unnecessary stricture given that day's gradients; twelve miles was quite enough.

Another wet night had made for another almost cloudless sky with a coolish breeze. The badly broken road curved around wooded slopes, then dived into deep clefts – briefly climbed – dived again – each descent testing my brake muscles. I sauntered, often stopping to gaze over the jumble of hills on my left, separated by shallow irregular valleys, all green and glistening after the rain. Beyond those hills rose a phalanx of forested mountains, their crests irregular.

Near Herradura a barn-like coffee factory appeared – the region's only industry, a simple enterprise where beans are dried and packed. This village was a recruiting centre for the 'bandits' (Castro-speak) or 'patriots' (Eisenhower-speak) who fought on in these mountains until 1966, the terrain helping local militia to set up deadly ambushes while evading capture. The Escambray conflict, small scale but embittering, dragged on only because of lavish US air-drops: weaponry and food and medical supplies.

Jibacoa, an agreeably ramshackle little town, swarmed with pigs and poultry but in mid-afternoon people were absent. Eventually a trio of youths, astonished by my arrival on their baseball field, led me to Carlos's house (breeze block, 1970s), then hung around to observe my reception. A tall, muscular, light-skinned mulatto was sitting at the living-room table dealing with documents. He read Maribel's chit with comically raised eyebrows, then removed his spectacles to study me silently before summoning Rafael, his grown-up English-speaking son who shook my hand before translating. 'My father says you are not a tourist, not living like that. Why in Cuba did you not drive car? Every city have cars for tourist hire.' Carlos did want to see my passport and visa. Then his wife Carmen, black and plump, came bustling in, asked to see Maribel's chit, told her husband to relax, invited me to sit and have a cup of coffee. Whereupon the three youths, who had been listening from the doorway, returned to their baseball practice.

Sipping my coffee, I hypocritically admired the family dog, of a repulsive breed seen occasionally in Havana – completely hairless, looking more porcine than canine. I certainly wouldn't want to live with one yet Hoalla's engaging ways soon won me over. He was named, Rafael informed me, after some famous baseball player.

In many Cuban schools the English language is poorly taught and Rafael apologised for his limited vocabulary, then put it to good use while explaining the importance of his job as the Public Hygiene officer in the polyclinic. Preventative health-care underlies Cuba's impressive medical statistics. You don't ignore people until they're sick, you teach them how to stay healthy for as long as possible.

Carmen, a primary school teacher, spoke of her concern about the spread of STDs around tourist areas (Trinidad, for instance) where young girls, craving the things convertible pesos can buy, forget their sex education and are easy prey. At that Carlos frowned, muttered angrily and abruptly changed the conversation. Given tourism's current importance, any criticism of its negative side-effects could, I suppose, be seen as counter-revolutionary.

One hears rumours about CDR members having exceptional access to luxuries but neither of my sample households showed evidence of this. Supper was cooked on wood stoves and the breakfast coffee brewed on small electric rings such as we used in Ireland during the Second World War. In both homes the evening meal was identical: rice, beans, pork fat and a tomato salad.

Despite my protestations Rafael insisted on vacating his bed and sleeping on two large sacks stuffed with palm fronds and inscribed in English 'Vietnamese Broken White Rice'.

The most blissful and most gruelling stage of this mini-trek (a not unusual combination) took me from Jibacoa to Topes de Collantes. Two faded notices marked fourteen percent gradients, a third warned: Pendientes y Curvas Peligrosas.

For much of the way, sub-tropical forest pressed close to the road. The fungi were multi-shaped and multi-coloured – some massive three-storey growths, some tiny fragile spots of crimson or orange. Six-foot-high ferns drooped gracefully, their fronds inhabited by busy blue-black beetles. Instead of the previous day's breeze, a strong wind tossed the trees, swaying their curtains of tangled lianas, and a few detached epiphytes lay on the road – grotesquely beautiful bundles. Occasional shafts of sunlight gilded patches of lichen, their sudden glow amidst the green shadows seeming almost artificial. Two cars overtook me, and a van that coughed loudly as it tackled the gradients. All three drivers offered a lift and seemed worried as well as baffled by my preference for walking.

As I gained altitude the many unfamiliar trees were gradually mixed with, then replaced by, tall spindly pines; here the wind changed its tune to that distinctively mournful conifer music. When I found myself, unexpectedly, on a wide level shoulder, the trees thinned and below me lay vast expanses of summits and linking ridges – the very heart of Sierra del Escambray.

Then – a severe shock. Standing still, I could feel rage pushing up my blood-pressure. A mile or so ahead, on Topes de Collantes' highest ridge, loomed a monstrous edifice of incomparable ugliness. Perhaps to do with hydroelectricity? Or a factory? Or a high-security jail? That mile was 'as the crow flies'. Where the road dipped, before a final climb, the edifice disappeared. An hour later, around a sharp bend, its ten storeys loomed above the road, approached by scores of wide steps, stretching the whole length of that dominant ridge. It presented a curiously blank façade despite rows of small, square, close-together windows. Nothing indicated that this is the Kurhotel, built by Batista in 1936 as a luxury TB sanatorium and given spa hotel status when the Revolution had eradicated the disease. In Trinidad I borrowed an *Eyewitness Guide* and was diverted to find this Batista souvenir, which had so raised my blood-pressure, described as an 'anti-stress centre'.

From Topes de Collantes one can hike on approved paths through a national park covering more than a hundred square miles: guides are for hire in a little-used 'Visitors Facility'. Topes was my first and worst experience of a Cuban tourist zone, a harrowing example of 'development desecration'. The Kurhotel's three rivals occupy forested slopes linked by concreted roads, all the gradients so severe that stairways replace footpaths. At 5.30 p.m. one hotel was closed, another only half-built, the third almost full of Germans and Italians newly arrived in five coaches. My large, well-appointed, motel-type room, opening directly off a courtyard studded with flower-beds, seemed like good value for CP37 (buffet breakfast included) until I realised that its insatiable mosquitoes were undeterred by screening.

Next morning I overheard an elderly heavily-bearded German growling that Cubans can make even scrambled eggs unpalatable. His young Italian partner (English their common language) alleged that this was because Cuban hotels use Chinese powdered eggs. While helping myself to a third course I slipped three hard-boiled eggs and three triangles of processed cheese into my shoulder-bag: fuel for the twelve miles to Trinidad.

Repelled by those concrete stairways, I took a forest path to the road and soon a two-inch thorn, strong as steel and sharp as a needle, had penetrated my sandal's thick sole and my right foot. (Every misfortune strikes my right foot; its companion has survived unscathed throughout seven decades of equally hard wear.) I let the blood flow for a moment, before applying antiseptic ointment and a plaster. Later, at a wayside bar near Trinidad, where I sat with one sole visible, the barman drew my attention to another, shorter thorn. Very observant of him, I thought and typically Cuban to care about the welfare of a passing stranger. I last met this particular hazard in Tanzania where such thorns are the cyclist's bugbear.

Below the hotels, *bohios* mingle with traces of military occupation; Topes was a Rebel Army base during the Escambray campaign. Since then an Institute of Mountain Agronomy has been built, and its staff live in the scattered holiday villas of the pre-Revolutionary rich.

After a few switchbacking miles I was suddenly overlooking a calm sea glittering under a cloudless sky, two thousand one hundred feet below. Here the Escambray's wall rises abruptly from a narrow plain – narrow when seen from above, yet wide enough to have abundantly enriched a colony of cane-planters. On their southern slopes these mountains are treeless, having been clear-felled during the nineteenth century to fuel giant sugar mills. Until motor roads were built in the 1950s Trinidad depended mainly on sea-transport, supplemented by mule-trains. The clear air allowed me to see the indented coastline – a pirates' delight – for many miles to east and west.

During the descent a geological freak fascinated me – many tall, slim outcrops of silver rock, their tops symmetrically serrated as though a giant had bitten off mouthfuls. Isolated cacti flaunted flaming flowers, a yard long, and down on the plain towering stands of bamboo swayed and squeaked in the wind. Here grazed cattle, goats and sheep, on drought-stricken pastures with prickly pear hedges. At first I mistook the sheep for goats; they wore short dark brown fleeces and long silky blonde cravats.

Over the last two miles, on the Cienfuegos-Trinidad road, half a dozen vehicles felt like heavy traffic. Crossing the sluggish Rio Guaurabo, I thought of Diego Velasquez sailing upstream in December 1513 to found Cuba's third settlement. Hereabouts a hideous example of 'public art' welcomes visitors to 'Trinidad a World Treasure'. Then an odd sound intrigued me, a prolonged wheezing, moaning whistle – coming from an 1890's steam engine, drawing two carriages at five miles per hour and emitting a spectacular column of thick black smoke that half-filled the sky for ten minutes and smelt of my childhood.

Trinidad is over-supplied with *casa particulares* and touts compete on the outskirts. A youth offered to lead me to his mother's casa – 'Very near with all comfort!' Firmly I showed him the address I was seeking and cheerfully he said, 'I lead you, if no place you come my house'. In the wrong street he rang a doorbell and quickly muttered something to the old woman who hesitantly peered out. 'She has no room,' he declared. 'You come now my casa.' Angrily pointing to the street name I told him to get lost and went on my way feeling guilty about that anger. Toutish tricks are distasteful but one should make allowances . . .

I soon found the correct address but Candida's friend was at a wedding in Cienfuegos. Her neighbour directed me to a nearby alternative where the welcome was warm but the accommodation cramped: a windowless cell, a dim electric bulb, two single beds, no writing space. Camilla, my hostess, was understandably neurotic about payment; she had been twice cheated by back-packers who stayed a few nights – then vanished before dawn. My arrival without convertible pesos made her fidget until I'd been to the *Cambio*.

Camilla was a fortyish creole with an elderly mulatto husband. Their twelve-year-old daughter, Ana, was not on good terms with Mamma but could easily enlist Pappa's sympathy and support by bursting into tears. Such details were easily observed because I had to write at the dining-table. An adult nephew, mildly mentally handicapped and an orphan, occupied the cell beside mine and Camilla was more patient with him than with Ana. He spent hours being happily excited by the two TV sets (both on simultaneously) in the spacious front room and guests were rightly expected to take him in their stride. Within a few days a gossipy neighbour had informed me that he wasn't really an orphan. His parents had abandoned him, as an obviously defective infant, when they joined the Mariel exodus. But his Aunt Camilla chose to conceal that shameful fact.

That evening my fellow-guests were three repulsive young Swedish men, carrying ludicrous amounts of luggage for a fortnight in Cuba, with bellies flopping over their belts and an unpleasant way of exchanging significant gestures whenever Ana passed by – she pointedly ignoring them.

From my diary:

> In over-rated Trinidad foreigners seem to outnumber natives. Coach-loads arrive almost hourly: Dutch, Swedish, French, Italian, German, Canadian – even a few daring *yanquis*. In the Plaza Mayor, hub of tourist gawping, an ancient little man, wearing a huge sombrero, sits all day on a bony mangey donkey with a notice fixed between its ears: PHOTOS fifty cents. So far that sums up Trinidad for me. There's no charge for shots of the Plaza's two larger-than-life bronze greyhounds on plinths. (Perhaps commemorating those Taino-hunting Irish hounds?) But of course this 'unspoiled example of a Spanish colonial town' is visually delightful around daybreak – the tourists still dormant . . . By European standards it's newish, most buildings dating from the 1820s to '30s. The cobbled streets (sacrosanct since it was declared a World Heritage Site in 1988) are the oldest feature. Out of thirty thousand Trinitarios, six thousand or so populate what's lavishly sign-posted as 'The Historic Centre'. Unusually, many of the original families still live in these pastel-washed houses; some have arched, unglazed windows – almost as big as the doors – with radiating wooden slats in place of shutters. No two buildings alike: endless variety of detail – turned wood or decorated iron grilles, much fanciful plaster moulding, terracotta tiles covering roof-beams – but none of Old Havana's porticos or vestibules. The narrow streets and laneways (horse traffic only) are quite steep where the town climbs a hill and one glimpses the sapphire sea glittering between red-tiled roofs. The opulent mansions are now museums and a convent houses the Museum of the Fight Against Bandits. Much knowledge and skill has been devoted to Trinidad's preservation – but it's *too* restored, for my taste. This was my 'dutiful tourist' day: I 'did' Palacio Brunet (1808, stunningly beautiful), the Palacio Cantero, the Bandit Museum and the unexciting Holy Trinity Church (1892). Tomorrow I'll see where the other twenty-four thousand Trinitarios live.

Those cantankerous instant-reactions were soon forgotten as Trinidad revealed its less obvious charms. Many of the other twenty-four thousand live in a noisy, colourful district no more than ten minutes walk from the quiet colonial splendours. Here the simple brick shacks, each on it own little plot, look like DIY jobs – government-subsidised, immediately after the Revolution, when Cuba's housing shortage was, as it had long been, at crisis point. (Even now it's close to that point.) The humpy, broken laneways – litter entangled in weeds along the verges – would challenge a four by four; after a rainy night the potholes were serving as toddlers' paddling-pools and cyclists were wheeling their machines. The residents, mostly black, were jolly and animated and much given to spontaneous music-making but rather shy of the 'lost' foreigner. Guides do not lead their flocks in this direction. Four youths, riding bareback, recklessly raced young horses, seemingly only half-broken, up and down the wider streets – to the shouted disapproval of their elders.

Further on, towards the coast, I found Raimundo's Uncle Gustavo in one of several 1970s apartment blocks, built at a respectful distance from the Historic Centre. Like his nephew, Gustavo was very tall, very black, very kind and very articulate. He had been warned that one day 'a peculiar Irish traveller' would arrive on his threshold. Removing an indignant dachshund from a cane rocking-chair he invited me to sit and asked with a twinkle, 'Why are you so peculiar?' That was a good beginning.

Half an hour later we were discussing a topic still delicate in Cuba. Personally Gustavo was not complaining; he had reached the top of his academic ladder and experienced no difficulties on the way up. But the Special Period's destabilising effects on race relations bothered him. 'We're short of supportive relatives in the US. The *Centro de Antropologia* in Havana reported recently that thirty to forty per cent of whites receive regular remittances but only five to ten per cent of blacks.' Even worse, Gustavo had observed the foreign investors' racism reinfecting Cuba's whites. 'Look at the tourist coaches, how many guides or even drivers are black? Go to the tourist hotels, how many staff are black?' When the first foreign investors arrived, agreements were made to safeguard Cuba's anti-discrimination laws but the foreigners went their own way. Gustavo admitted, 'I'm naïve, I was shocked, I didn't know Europeans were still like that. I've lived in the US but I've never visited Europe. There's a bit of *déjà vu* around – some of the worst racists are Spanish investors! People tell me it's getting better since Guitart Hotels S.A. had their contract cancelled. When administering the Habana Libre Hotel – I suppose Cuba's most famous – they sacked eight hundred black employees! Said their sort of customer would prefer white or light-skinned mixed race. But our *Foreign Investment Act* of 1995 says Cuban laws apply to foreigners' employees. The Cuban Confederation of Workers took action against Guitart and won. Raul Castro stayed on their side, saying any establishment discriminating against blacks must be closed, whether or not it's a joint venture. The Parque Central Hotel also had to sack all its racist management or have its contract voided. El Commandate has always been an extreme anti-racist. I'm his age, I grew up watching how the Revolution worked for blacks, mulattos and the poorest whites.'

I quoted the comments of a 'black foreign student' (Miranda, as we walked in the Hanabanilla woods). 'My friend believes the Special Period killed the Revolution. The government pretended it was possible to compromise with capitalism, to have "regulated" outside investors. That was dishonest, she argues. Those people can't really be "regulated", they come with strings and once they're in they pull them.'

'It's a point of view,' said Gustavo. 'But what I've just told you partly disproves it. How long is this young man in Cuba?'

'Actually a young woman – five years in Cuba – and she herself has noticed racism increasing in all sorts of little ways. She arrived uncritical, now she has doubts, thinks maybe the Revolution should have gone more slowly, getting rid of Batista's gangs at once but letting ordinary counter-revolutionaries feel there was space for them.'

Gustavo smiled wryly. 'It's the age-group, my grandson talks like that – a clever fellow, starting university. He and his *compañeros* are fiercely anti-Communist, which doesn't have to mean counter-revolutionary. That might confuse some people but by now you must be used to our paradoxes. Those kids don't understand how things were in '59. Aside from Batista's gangs, nobody was "hunted out". The Revolution didn't want to lose the educated class – *needed* them! And the *barbudos* didn't yet seem like Communists though there were rumours about Raul and Ché. People jeer that Fidel didn't reform the real Cuba, had to tailor a demographically different country to fit his ideology. That's a favourite *Yanqui* line. Stuff about expelling all the "intelligent democrats", clearing the way to bully the morons who couldn't afford to leave! It's neurotic, denying that most of us backed the Revolution. Remember Playa Giron? Where were the thousands supposed to rise up all over the island to join the "liberating invaders"? They were in the CIA's imagination!'

Gustavo broke off to brew another pot of coffee, then continued. 'I'm sorry your young friend has felt discrimination – could it be more than racism in her case? I suppose she's at ELAM?' (Escuela Latinoamericana de Medicina, opened in 1999.)

I nodded. 'So she's lucky,' said Gustavo. 'One of thousands trained for free, only having to promise to work in their own countries among the poor. A Fidel pet project, and some youngsters don't approve of spending so much on foreigners. I've heard about their resentment showing. Cuban racism is still around – Raul and others admit we should have more mulattos and blacks as Party and government leaders. Legislation can only gradually dilute racism. Think of the time-scale – many of our oldest citizens are the grandchildren of slaves, men and women who were seen as commodities, not human beings. I'm one such. A few decades of legal equality can't always compensate for centuries of desperate poverty and ignorance. Certain families aren't able to benefit from equal opportunities – and they don't come more equal than we have them in Cuba! I'm not talking only about blacks, we've mulatto and *campesiño* families in the same sort of trap. When the Revolution threw them a lifeline they couldn't reach it – which I'm told makes Fidel very sad, in his old age.'

My host escorted me back to the Historic Centre where he had an afternoon appointment. We rode in a high four-wheeled carriage with a tasselled canopy, drawn by a well-groomed chestnut mare. I was invited to supper on the following evening to meet Gustavo's son and daughter-in-law – and possibly the 'clever fellow', depending on transport from Santa Clara.

Studying my inadequate map (nothing detailed is available), I wondered if it would be possible to trek 'off-road' through the eastern Escambray to Sancti Spiritus. At dawn I set out to do a recce, taking a long, steep street past two-hundred-year-old dwellings, their thick walls and handsome shutters designed for coolness. Near this hilltop several mulattos were milking the family cow while minute piglets squeaked with excitement on being released from their shed. Here, as throughout the town, most homes had one or two bird-cages hanging from the façade at head-height. For generations the Trinitarios have been fixated on their song-birds – black, swallow-sized, with white-flecked wings. In many streets, between January and June, scores compete in singing competitions; public appraisal determines the winners, judged by the frequency, duration and intensity of their trill. Champions are worth their weight in pesos; Gustavo knew several men who had paid three or four months' salary for an outstanding diva.

On the wide, flat summit of this limestone hill stands a solitary neglected little church, Trinidad's oldest (1740), now permanently locked. An un-usual three-arch bell tower was added in 1812 and the bells remain in place though long since silent. On my return journey a few endearing juvenile *jineteros* were hanging around with a pony, offering to pose as mini-cowboys for the unpackaged tourists who get this far. One enterprising lad, seeing I had no camera, offered to teach me how to pronounce Ermita de Nuestra Senora de la Candelaria de la Popa for fifty centavos – which sounded like a bargain.

Again, perfect walking weather: half cloudy, a strong cool breeze off the nearby turquoise sea. Ahead lay low hills, one almost concealing a motel, another – much the highest – defaced by a gigantic radio mast; but it might give me some idea of the lie of the land towards Sancti Spiritus. A gravely path climbed around slopes where coarse yellowish grass surrounded huge lumps of limestone. Half way up I saw two men in the distance, perhaps fifty yards apart, creeping slowly through low bushes, bent in two, then suddenly lying down, completely disappearing – then moments later leaping up, gesturing wildly and yelling. Drawing closer, I passed two occupied bird-cages hanging on bushes and the *centavo* began to drop. Sure enough, this erratic behaviour had an avian explanation; it was an attempt to capture birds without injuring them. The men hurried to the path, curious about me, then earnestly explained that singers needed to be taken for a walk at least three times a week, hung on bushes providing their favourite leaves, so that they themselves could pluck them from the twigs, and left alone for some time to commune with relatives and friends. Unless treated thus, their trilling deteriorated.

This hilltop, protected by its gradient, has escaped becoming a 'Viewing Point', complete with coach park and 'amenities'. In truth the view is heart-stopping. Suddenly one is overlooking the whole length of the Valley of the Sugar Mills, previously hidden, and beyond rise the Escambray's many royal blue ridges – subtly changing colour that morning as the high clouds slowly shifted. For a time I sat with my back to the radio mast, pretending it didn't exist, then I had to circumvent its fenced base to suss out the terrain to the east.

My footsteps alerted a border collie (sort of) bitch, who jumped a wooden gate to greet the intruder, then rolled over to have her tummy tickled. The solitary unarmed guard seemed equally pleased to have this break in the monotony of his twelve-hour shift and vigorously shook my hand. He spoke basic English and was yet another of those strikingly handsome Amharic types – though what struck me as an Amharic type could be the result of Taino genes.

As Jorge led me around the fence I saw why this mast looked so shiny new: it was a replacement for one knocked flat by Hurricane Dennis. Only when you see a prone mast, extending halfway down a mountainside, and then have to clamber through its complex innards, do you realise a) how gigantic these things are and b) how mighty is a minor hurricane.

Jorge fetched his powerful binoculars so that I could view some of the buildings on the valley floor. It was a friendly gesture, with no hint of peso-seeking. Several palatial haciendas have been restored – no wonder the slaves burnt so many canefields up and down this valley, eventually reducing their owners to bankruptcy and leaving the way clear for US corporations to move in.

I accepted Jorge's invitation to drink coffee in the guard's hut, then changed my mind on seeing that he had no cooking appliance, only a thermos of coffee to last him all day. When consulted about trekking to Sancti Spiritus he said there was no continuous track. I would have to follow the motor road – not a pleasing prospect.

Back in the Historic bit I refuelled on the terrace of a little bar in a narrow street near Parque Cespedes; there Trinitarios and unpackaged tourists gather, leaving the Plaza Mayor to the coachloads. Only four tables were occupied, one by one of the Swedes from my *casa* (who pretended not to notice my arrival) and two black schoolgirls – early teens, breasts budding, both conspicuously underclad and perhaps soon to be unclad.

An angry shout and a shrill yelp made me look up from my diary to see a burly, shaven-headed young man dragging one girl away, gripping her by the forearm and shouting abuse over his shoulder at the Swede. The other girl then stood up to go, looking rattled, but her 'patron' persuaded her to stay, stroking her silky bare shoulders and nuzzling her hair. I was about to leave when a slim mulatta emerged from the bar – fortyish, formally dressed in a grey pleated skirt and ruby-red shirt-blouse, carrying a worn leather briefcase and a camera. Few Cubans then used cameras, yet she didn't look like a tourist.

Approaching my table, Beatriz asked in English if she might sit with me and introduced herself as a Cienfuegos doctor, a founder member of a small NGO dedicated to pressurising the police into enforcing the laws against child prostitution. *Sotto voce* she requested, 'Please may I photo you like you're my friend? Two or three quick shots – for my report.' I nodded and played my part, smirking as I posed, holding up beer glass and notebook, the Swede and his acquisition in the immediate background but indifferent to the camera. Beatriz was in a rush just then but we met later, by which time she had detected that the burly young man was, as I'd guessed, the girl's brother.

'Why,' I asked, 'do you have to pressurise the police? And how come these foreigners are so *blatant*? They surely know they're breaking the law – but those questions must be related.'

'Yes,' said Beatriz, 'closely related. It seems cruel our reputation as almost AIDS-free attracts certain men. It's like a punishment for being good! What about Ireland, you also have problems?'

My knowledge of Ireland's problems in this area is limited, but a reference to our drugs/prostitution link apparently cheered Beatriz, obliquely, by making Cuba seem not so bad after all.

In *Pleasure Island* Rosalie Schwartz reviews the situation:

Another galling fact of [post-Soviet] life is increased prostitution, mostly amateurs who trade sexual favours for a restaurant meal, an evening in a nightclub, a shopping spree, or a weekend at a beach resort. Although foreign men arrive every day to be with Cuban women, the practice has little in common with Cuba's pre-revolutionary institutionalised sex shows and brothels. Nor does the market begin to compare in scope or intent with the chartered flights of men who buy their tickets for 'sex without guilt' in Asia and Africa. Nevertheless, purchased sex is troublesome for a government that has spent decades inculcating the values of nonexploitation of fellow humans and gender parity. After the government legalised the possession of dollars [in 1993], prostitution acquired a structure, that is, networks among those selling sex and procurers (taxi drivers, bartenders) . . . Clearly, Castro confronts a conflict. His country needs hard currency. Tourism is flourishing and is more profitable than sugar. Travellers from capitalist countries do generate expectations among Cubans, but the government cannot risk the internal upheavals that unavoidably diminish the number of visitors. It must be flexible to avoid negative publicity and disaffection but strict to sustain socialist ideals.

Evidently many police officers are being 'flexible' while crusaders like Beatriz are being 'strict'. Her loyalty to *el comandante* was unmistakable when we discussed 'internationalism', and she obviously saw her boldly independent NGO as a tool for the defence of the Revolution's integrity.

That evening I tentatively quizzed Gustavo and family about the government's attitude to NGOs – was it true some were discouraged?

Damian replied; he was a career bureaucrat notably less open-minded than his father. 'Cuba needs no small groups here and there. All citizens have their own big groups, *with power*. And with independence, not always doing what Party says. It's true some groups, NGOs, are discouraged, like you say, or suppressed if CIA gives them money and gifts.'

I would have liked to follow that scent but Gustavo said, 'For outsiders, even if they love Cuba, it's hard to understand our Communist Party. It can't suggest or enforce legislation – doesn't that surprise you? It can't nominate candidates for municipal, provincial or national assemblies. It doesn't *administer* the state. The people have maximum administrative authority.'

When I asked, 'Who nominates candidates?' Gustavo looked at his mulatto son (of a Canadian mother) and said, 'Damian has it all in his official head.'

Damian was being a New Man, slicing cucumber for the salad while his wife, Lucia, steamed rice. He finished his task before answering my question in such detail that his explanations belong to a later chapter.

Lucia placed the rice-steamer on the table as I asked, 'How long are election campaigns?'

Everyone looked shocked. 'We don't have them!' said Gustavo. 'Here is not the US – no cash needed! Now eat some food. You like Hatuey to drink?'

As we helped ourselves to rice, salad and stewed chicken Camillo the dachshund caused a diversion by hurling himself towards a window, barking shrilly. Gustavo chuckled. 'A turkey buzzard flew by – he hates them!'

When I quoted Fidel on the dangerous defects of Western 'democracy' Damian became perceptibly more genial, then offered me a lift to Cienfuegos on the morrow. His 1953 Chrysler, parked nearby, was astonishing – it had received so much t.l.c. it looked brand new. On *ad hoc* journeys one goes where the flow of chance contacts takes one and Gustavo had scribbled a note of introduction to his old Cienfuegos friend, Alberto, another retired academic well qualified to lecture me on crime and punishment in Cuba.

Chapter 11

When Damian met me by the bus station, as arranged, he was on foot. Trinidad's petrol ration had been delayed en route; the broken-down tanker was miles away awaiting a spare part. The search had begun for a sufficiently skilled blacksmith. Damian advised me to hitch-hike.

The Special Period's transport problem produced a new 'citizens' force', men and women wearing mustard uniforms with 'TRANSPORTE' arm-bands. (I thought of them as 'the Mustards'.) Standing at suburban junctions they ask hitch-hikers who wants to go where, stop vehicles which might not otherwise stop, organise queues when necessary and determine how many can safely board each vehicle. Drivers genuinely expect no payment and the Mustards' services are also free in theory though some seek a peso or two. Outside tourist-conscious Trinidad, NP3 were firmly demanded of me – hardly excessive for a forty-mile lift in a Second World War military jeep with no windows, no discernible springs and a patched canvas roof.

Quite often we stopped to let people off and take on replacements but there were never more than six on board this four-seater vehicle: a reasonable load, by Cuban standards. Everyone had to hug their luggage – my rucksack by far the most awkward item, two hens in a nylon sack the noisiest. Our youthful soldier driver sought advice from his passengers about vegetable growing. Cuba's army is expected to feed itself and devotes as much time to digging as to target practice.

For some twenty miles this ill-maintained road, built in 1952, runs level between the Escambray's forested flanks and a flat shore piled with hurri-cane debris. Then it swings inland, crossing slopes of dense green scrub with occasional inhabited areas where palms draw attention to mud-coloured *bohíos*. There was little movement; a few horses grazed, being deticked by egrets, a few oxen ploughed, a few carts were being loaded with machete-cut cane. Three narrow deep-set rivers were spanned by drearily utilitarian bridges; it's sad that modern technology has killed bridge-building as an art.

Eight miles from Cienfuegos our driver apologetically ejected me, with a big smile and an affectionate handshake. Traffic was sparse (perhaps extra-sparse because of Trinidad's problem?) and the dusty cacti hedges offered no shade. It made sense to walk on, despite the 10.00 a.m. heat.

Quarter of an hour later a rice-loaded lorry, its passenger seats surprisingly empty, stopped voluntarily to pick me up and was going all the way. Its grey-haired, vivacious mulatto driver (Carlos) associated Ireland with Christians killing each other and thought Cuba fortunate to have no such conflicts. After we had parted, as I was strolling towards the central Parque Martí, the lorry pulled up beside me: my purse had been jolted out of my pocket. It held more than CP100 – a small fortune, for Carlos. Yet he had turned his vehicle – not easy in the centre – to follow me. Had I been put down near a bar he could never have found me and his virtue would have been rewarded. In Cuba one doesn't take lost property to the police.

Cienfuegos is the only Cuban city founded by French settlers, migrants from Louisiana attracted by a safe, capacious harbour with a fertile, virgin hinterland. Led by Lieutenant-Colonel Louis Clouet (Rtd), they were a dogged lot. In the very year of Cienfuegos's foundation (1819) a hurricane destroyed most of the new structures and their replacements were repeatedly ravaged: in 1825, 1832, 1837. On 10 June 1832 Lieutenant Governor Manuel de Mediavilla reported to Havana: 'This newly reborn port that was recovering in its agriculture, the certain base of prosperity and the principal source of its happiness, has for the foreseeable future returned virtually back to its primitive condition . . . '

Hurricanes destroyed everything: growing crops, domestic animals and poultry, all the coffee, sugar and tobacco packed in warehouses ready for export, the flimsy homes of the poor and their few possessions. Wagon trails and railways became impassable. The coastal merchant ships, until recently more important than roads, were smashed to bits. Sugar mills suffered massive damage. Salt water killed vegetation over huge areas and rendered wells and streams, cisterns and vats undrinkable – sources of cholera. Yet Madrid was consistently unsympathetic and anyway too distant to provide emergency aid, even had the monarch been so inclined.

One notorious royal decision highlights imperial greed. News of the October 1844 hurricane took two months to reach Spain; meanwhile, the Havana authorities had decided to alleviate extreme hardship by suspending import duties on essential goods coming from the US – food, clothing, tools, building materials. But the royal exchequer mattered more than destitute Cubans. On 29 December word came from Madrid:

I have given the Queen a full account of the contents of the letters of Your Excellency . . . in which you describe the hurricane experienced on

October 4–5. The measures of October 7 in which absolute exemption
from duties is given . . . have not met with the approval of Her Majesty.
She thereby orders a return of all things to the state in which they were
found prior to the aforementioned hurricane.

Her Majesty's callousness surprised few Cubans and fed the island's
embryonic nationalism.

In 2005 UNESCO nominated Cienfuego a World Heritage Site and I
found the centre in transition. All Parque Martí's splendid buildings –
mostly former *palacios* – had been recently restored yet mere yards away
stately mansions were literally falling apart; pedestrian-protecting nets
'roofed' the pavements. Further out, the old residential districts were
pleasing in a predictable way: wide, straight, tree-lined streets and dignified
colonial homes in shrub-filled gardens, their charm somewhat diminished
by the proximity of affordable apartment blocks for the masses.

Taking Gustavo's advice, I looked for lodgings on the Punta Gorda, a
two-mile-long tapering peninsula appropriated a century ago by Cienfuegos's richest merchants. (One guide book, getting its categories mixed,
describes it as 'the aristocratic quarter of the city'.) A stylish boulevard, the
Paseo del Prado, leads to a half-mile Malecón where small boys sit on the
wall trying to net miniscule fish. Here a row of early twentieth-century
villas, art nouveau-flavoured, overlook the wide Bay of Jagua.

Then one is in a peculiar neighbourhood, its lay-out more Miami than
Cuba. Four hotels and a restaurant face an open-plan settlement of gaily
painted wooden houses, also early twentieth-century and slightly Potem-
kinish; that freshly painted look surely has to do with Punta Gorda being
Cienfuegos's tourist hub. Here too are a convertible-peso pharmacy, a
tourist office (never open during my visit), a petrol station (rarely open),
and a new free-standing *tienda* (open ten to five with two hours off for
lunch). The luxury hotels are offensively 'gated' and as for the restaurant –
one stands still and blinks incredulously. It's what happened when a sugar
merchant of incalculable wealth imported the Italian architect Alfredo
Colli and teams of artists and craftsmen (including thirty Moroccans) and
told them he wanted a two-storey home suggesting Granada's Alhambra,
with three towers of strongly contrasting designs and as many Venetian,
Gothic and Moorish motifs as could be applied inside and out, leaving no
square inch undecorated. The Palacio de Valle is sufficiently o.t.t. to have
reached the realm of entertainment. It took four years to build (1913–17)
but its owner, Acisclo del Valle Blanco, reckoned it was worth waiting for.

Cienfuegos is among Cuba's most polluted cities and on the far side of the lake-like bay (its outlet to the Caribbean Sea invisible) distant chimney stacks emit fumes perceptible even in Parque Martí – making one question UNESCO's accolade. Also on that shore is the aborted Juragua nuclear plant, begun in the late 1970s with Soviet aid and designed to provide twelve per cent of Cuba's electricity from 1993. Seen as one of the Revolution's most important industrial projects, it was employing one thousand two hundred workers – many highly skilled – when it 'became dormant' in 1992. Its Director, Isaac Edilio Alayon, then requested an International Atomic Energy Agency inspection and Juragua was duly declared 'safe' (or as safe as such plants ever are). Nevertheless, the Bush I administration, spurred on by Senator Connie Mack of Florida, tried to panic the general public about Juragua's threat to the whole US eastern seaboard. This was standing reality on its head. In fact Cuba would be at risk, for meteorological reasons, should Florida's defective Crystal River reactor one day run out of control.

Behind the 'Miami' area, one is back in normal streets of detached, unpainted houses in small gardens. (Very short streets: here the peninsula is less than a mile wide.) Soon I had found a *casa particulare* and been introduced by Nancy and Juan to their three dogs and two cats. The family's milking nanny was tethered on wasteland across the road. While brewing my initiatory demitasse of coffee, Nancy fulminated against the Spanish-Cuban consortium rumoured to be planning another hotel on that wasteland – 'eight storeys, blocking our sky'. This little house had one uncomfortable eccentricity: all the windows were kept tightly shut, twenty-four hours a day, in an attempt to deter Punta Gorda's rampant mosquitoes. My room was oven-like, by reluctant choice; it lacked a fan and I couldn't tolerate the raucous Soviet-era air-conditioning.

Punta Gorda's semi-rural hinterland illustrates layers of Cuban social history. On expanses of common land, yellow-brown in February, livestock mingle: pony-sized horses, wandering sheep, tethered goats, countless poultry. Rough tracks lead to once-magnificent mansions, now occupied by several families, with weeds and cacti sprouting from cracked walls. Not far off, modest affluence is suggested by new DIY homes, some only half-finished but already lived in. Footpaths winding through tall bushes lead to primitive shacks proving poverty. Even the remotest of these enjoy electricity, but not piped water. Their inhabitants, though adequately clad and well-groomed, are the sort of people Fidel had in mind when he spoke, at the 2003 Pedagogy Conference in Havana, about the 'many very poor white families who migrated from rural areas to the cities'.

The sad thing is to observe how poverty, associated with a lack of knowledge, tends to reproduce itself. Other sectors, mostly from very humble backgrounds, but with better living and working conditions, were able to take advantage of study possibilities created by the revolution, and now make up the bulk of university graduates, who likewise tend to reproduce their improved social conditions derived from education.

Punta Gorda's sky is dominated by the unlovely arc-lights of the 5 September stadium. This gigantic sports complex, complete with a psychology clinic for sportspersons, was internationally admired in the 1970s. Inevitably the Special Period took its toll and now the place looks as run-down as the nearby apartment blocks – which doesn't diminish the attendance at every game.

I had been told I must take baseball seriously, as the Cuban equivalent of hurling in Ireland or cricket in England, a sport that is more than a sport, an activity that permeates and expresses the national soul . . . Indeed, the numbers of boys who practise on Cuba's streets (rarely with bats, often using homemade balls and worn-out gloves) did remind me of Irish juvenile hurlers in times past, before our car-infestation. On a Sunday morning I dutifully checked at the stadium but no game was scheduled. Instead, I joined half a dozen small boys who were watching adults practising in a nearby field. Close to our vantage point a goat was tethered – a randy billy, with distinguished horns, who sucked frequently and frenziedly at his agitated penis to the boys' chortling delight.

For want of a mentor, this practice game merely baffled me. When one man crouched on the ground wearing a mask and body armour while another stood close beside him, wielding a bat, I couldn't decide whether the latter was the former's opponent or was attempting to defend him from balls thrown with lethal force. At intervals, for no reason apparent to me, certain men sprinted around the field as though pursued by a tiger – then suddenly stopped, at no particular point, to loud applause . . . There was an acute shortage of gear: everything had to be shared. The metal bats shocked me; when hearing of baseball bats being used by our street gangs to beat each other up, I had vaguely visualised something wooden and blunt.

Soon I moved on, to admire Parque Martí's eclectic range of buildings and monuments. In 1902, to celebrate the Republic's delusional birth, Cienfuego's workers' corporation commissioned Cuba's only triumphal arch. In 1906 José Martí was placed on his marble, lion-guarded pedestal. A smaller version of Havana's Capitolio, the Palacio del Ayuntaiento, contrasts with the arcaded and perfectly proportioned Teatro Tomas Terry commemorating a ruthless slave-trader, sugar-factory owner and mayor of Cienfuegos. The Palacio Ferreris (early 1900s), with its blue mosaic cupola, fanciful balconies and ornate wrought-iron spiral staircase, is another example of sugar wealth in action.

At right angles to the theatre is the small cathedral (neo-classical façade, two asymmetrical towers, agreeably simple interior needing some repairs). In the porch numerous faded photographs and posters recall the Papal state visit in 1998 – a P.R. triumph for both host and guest. Although this new alliance took some people aback (and infuriated Florida's hard-liners) its base was obvious: a shared anti-consumerism. Pope John Paul could have delivered Fidel's 1995 speech to the Social Development conference in Copenhagen:

> It must be stressed in today's world, a world which prefers to eat money, wear money and bathe in money, that there is something more valuable than money: people's souls, people's hearts, people's honour.

By 9.45 a thousand or so worshippers (I made a rough estimate during the sermon) had assembled. In the south transept a smiling teenage band (two girls, two boys) played their guitar, tres, claves and bongo with all the verve expected of Cubans and most people happily swayed along. The drummer was one of the few blacks present. This preponderantly elderly white congregation had a scattering of middle-aged couples and several rows of adolescents and children. An ancient, bald, invalid priest, with sunken cheeks, sat in his wheel-chair to one side of the high altar, being earnestly addressed by a portly, silver-haired, dark-suited man with a self-important expression. Two beribboned girls, in frilly dresses, aged five or six, were hanging about on the altar looking expectant. When the tall, broad-shouldered celebrant appeared in his green chasuble they rushed to greet him and he affectionately hugged and kissed them before leading them by the hands into the sacristy. (At that point, in twenty-first-century Ireland, hairs might have prickled on the backs of some necks.)

Punctually at 10.00 the pre-Mass procession emerged from behind the altar, led by three teenage girls in low-slung blue jeans and tank-tops that showed lots of midriff despite the porch's prominent strictures about apparel. (Beggars can't be choosers and Cuba's Roman Catholic church is well behind in the popularity ratings.) The teenagers walked abreast, slowly, followed by the celebrant holding one little girl by the hand and two tall thin youths in white surplices, swinging censers. Meanwhile many worshippers were accompanying a children's choir in rousing hymns. Back on the altar, the celebrant led the other little girl to a nursery-size armchair opposite the wheel-chair, but in a position of equal honour – and there she sat, alone and motionless, for the next hour, looking rather complacent. I tried, but failed, to imagine Zea in this role.

The teenage girls led the credo and read the epistle and gospel confidently and clearly. At the consecration, when the invalid was wheeled to the low altar table, he steadily held the chalice aloft while uttering the magic words in a quavering voice. Afterwards, many old women queued on the altar to kiss his ring. At the exit the priest chatted with his departing flock, absent-mindedly patting the little girls' heads while they gazed up at him adoringly, stroking his brocade chasuble at thigh-level. I'm not hinting at anything undesirable; all this simply showed how innocently remote Cuba is from a world traumatised by child-abusing priests and parsons, too often shielded by senior churchmen.

In Cuba small girls hitch-hike solo, not always at points supervised by Mustards, everyone assuming they will be safe hopping into a car with one unknown male. And obviously they are safe or this custom would not have taken root, Cuban parents being no less protective than others. In Havana I met a New Zealander who insisted that Cuba must have its quota of child molesters – hidden, for 'image-protection' reasons – whereas our media provide maximum publicity, thus triggering neurotic fears. I agreed with him about the neurotic fears, palpable now in some countries and dreadfully destructive of wholesome social relationships. But I felt he was missing the point that Castroism has protected Cuba's population from the moral degradation promoted by Capitalism Rampant – admittedly at the cost of certain fundamental human rights.

'Human Rights' (denial of) is the anti-Castroists' biggest stick. Obviously it's a real stick, but how big is it? Two separate though linked issues confuse this debate: a relentless, multi-faceted US effort to destabilise Cuba, and the West's predisposition to be deceived by men like Armando Valladares.

The Valladares case, spanning decades, clearly illustrates how those issues converge. In 1960 this twenty-three-year-old former Batista police officer was convicted of three terrorist bombings and sentenced to thirty years in jail. During the 1970s many prominent Europeans campaigned for his release, presenting him as a tragic, talented victim of Communism, a hero who was managing to smuggle poetry out with the laundry. On his release in 1982 he settled in Spain and wrote *Against All Hope*, widely read and lavishly praised – especially in the US and Britain. ('A magnificent tribute to the human spirit' – *Sunday Telegraph*. 'A quiet account of remarkable bravery' – the *Economist*.) In his introduction Valladares assures us that he was imprisoned 'solely for having espoused and expressed principles distinct from those of the regime of Fidel Castro'. (Sabotaging public buildings is of course an increasingly popular way of 'espousing principles'.) The English translation blurb describes the author as 'a law student, poet, sculptor and painter' – just the sort of young man Batista recruited to his police force. It also claims that he 'suffered torture, starvation and lack of medical care which left him paralysed'. Writing in 1984, Valladares asserted, 'Today, at this very moment, hundreds of political prisoners are naked, sleeping on the floors of cells whose windows and doors have been sealed. They never see the light of day, or for that matter artificial light'. Around the same date, US legal teams and Amnesty International delegations were inspecting Cuban prisons. They found 'no widespread complaints from common prisoners about their treatment in the prisons'; and 'no evidence to substantiate accusations of torture'. They did however find many buildings in dire need of refurbishment and they recommended some quite drastic changes in the administration. On both counts the Attorney General's office, in charge of all Cuban prisons, reacted positively to their criticisms.

In October 1982, Valladares flew directly from prison to Paris. His supporters and their attendant journalists assembled at the airport to welcome him and were astonished to see a hale and hearty 'hero' descending the aeroplane steps, his 'paralysis' having been cured en route. The usual suspects funded his subsequent European lecture tour. Then, having obtained US citizenship (a quickie job), he was appointed to represent the US at Geneva as a member of the subsequently discredited UN Human Rights Commission. At that point a disillusioned and embarrassed Regis Debray commented, 'The man wasn't a poet, the poet wasn't paralysed, and the Cuban is now a US citizen'. Debray, a French writer, had acted as Ché's main link with Fidel during the Bolivian venture.

Vice President George Bush nominated Valladares as 'an American hero' in October 1988 and a few months later the departing President Reagan honoured him with the Presidential Medal. Thus reinforced, Valladares forgot both human rights and international law. On 31 August 1994 he joined in the demand for a military blockade of Cuba and asserted the Florida hardliners' right 'to launch military attacks from US soil' against his homeland.

In 1994, when Special Period deprivations were at their worst, the US Interests Section in Havana sent an interesting report to the Secretary of

State, the CIA and the Immigration and Naturalization Service:

> In the processing of visa applications for refugees, there are still few
> solid cases. Most of those who file applications do so not out of real fear
> of persecution, but because of the deterioration of the economic situa-
> tion. Particularly difficult for USINT and INS officials are the cases
> presented by human rights activists. Although we have done everything
> possible to work with the human rights organisations over which we
> have the greatest control, to identify those activists who are truly perse-
> cuted by the government, the human rights cases represent the least
> solid category within the refugee program. In recent months, accusa-
> tions have persisted of fraudulent applications made by activists and the
> sale of letters of support from [foreign] human rights leaders. Due to the
> lack of verifiable documentary evidence, generally USINT officials have
> considered human rights cases the most susceptible to fraud.

From Parque Martí I took a horse-bus back to Punta Gorda, where Gustavo's
friend, Alberto, was expecting me for a late lunch. As I approached his
home he overtook me, an eighty-two-year-old pedalling vigorously through
the afternoon heat with his toddler great-grand-nephew on a crossbar
seat – rather a grand seat, intricately carved and painted sky blue. The
toddler's mamma, Clara, a marine biologist/ecologist allergic to mass
tourism, was sitting on the verandah sewing a shirt for little Tomas. This
substantial family home (c.1890s) was now divided into three flats and
surrounded by 'development'.

While Tomas was being fed Alberto and I relaxed in a spacious patio
shaded by vines and presided over by a badly chipped marble statue of
Minerva. 'My grandfather stole her, on an ox-cart, in 1897,' said Alberto.
'From a sugar-magnate's garden – he was pioneering "redistribution", he
would have made a good *fidelista*!'

I already felt sufficiently at ease to protest, 'But Fidel never *looted*!'

Alberto chuckled. 'True, he only "redistributed" – why we live in one-
third of my grandfather's home.'

Had Gustavo not told me Alberto's age I would have guessed 'late
sixties'. He had a thick grey thatch above keen grey-green eyes in a face so
long and bony I thought 'El Greco!' His grand-niece was a tall, willowy
mulatta, her exuberant African hair and stern Spanish features adding up
to great beauty. (Mulattas seem less inclined than blacks to hair-straighten:
somebody must have written a thesis on that.) Clara spoke no English,

Alberto's fluency dated back to his Harvard days in the early 1950s.

Lunch consisted of rice, chicken, salad; for those without convertible pesos, menus are constrained. As we ate Clara raged against the new hotel at the peninsula's end, not because of its obtrusive ugliness but because it has much reduced the locals' fishing area – locals who fish in earnest for protein.

This was a one-bicycle family; after the wash-up Clara lifted Tomas into his seat (no nonsense about harness or helmet) and pedalled off to her mother's distant flat. By then, on my host's suggestion, I was busily taking shorthand notes.

For thirty-five years Alberto had been involved in the evolution of Cuba's justice system, a long, hard struggle (not yet over) to reconcile what the Revolution inherited with what the Revolution needed for its day-to-day protection and functioning. We tend to overlook this aspect of 'revolution'. Obvious upheavals hold the attention: nationalisation, redistribution of land, the launching of island-wide educational, medical and housing programmes to benefit the majority. But nothing can work without a coherent, generally acceptable, body of laws. Of course Cuba's enemies scorn the Revolution's criminal justice system – without bothering to study it, as Alberto angrily remarked. 'We're always being charged with violating international standards – ironical, when ours is probably Latin America's most efficient and fairest system. It's certainly unique – has to be, for two reasons. One: to defend our independence from the *yanquis'* non-stop *active* antagonism. Two: to help with the promotion of social justice. Our early "people's courts" didn't always work too well – some did "violate international standards"! Then the whole legal apparatus was taken apart and redesigned.'

Like many of his generation, Alberto could not 'think positive' about the Special Period. Rhetorically he asked, 'When the Soviet collapse caused so much hardship, why did so many go on supporting an apparent failure? Every day, Radio Marti sent loud messages about exiles rushing to the rescue if we rebelled against Fidel. Instead, we listened to his call to think and plan and work together to get through the crisis – its length unpredictable. The first major economy was reducing the armed forces from three hundred thousand in '89 to fifty-five thousand in '97. Isn't that remarkable? Not an expanding army, because deprived people might rebel, but a shrunken army told to grow food!' Alberto paused, suddenly looking sad. 'Now, I'm not so sure . . . The austerity of the Special Period was unifying. Today's young are challenged by that divisive two-tier currency. You've seen the damage for yourself, every foreigner notices. Inequality is back – maybe never really went away but for decades we *fought* it. Now its got to look like a built-in part of the structure. Some believe the Revolution can and will protect its foundations. I don't see that. I see corporate waves eroding the base of our socialist cliff. Clara disagrees, says I don't have enough faith in the young's pride in Cuba's independence. I'd like to be wrong!' When the mosquitoes drove us indoors at sunset Alberto wrote an introductory letter to his friend Félix, an Angolan war veteran living near Jagua, from where I planned to trek to the Bay of Pigs. He advised me to take the 8.00 a.m. ferry – which meant joining the queue at 7.00 a.m. *latest* . . .

In darkness I set off for the ferry berth and, on the Paseo del Prado, asked directions of the only person in sight, an elderly man carrying a pair of spurs and a machete. '*El barca?*' – he wasn't sure but if I walked with him he'd find out. We continued under the arcade and at a street corner met a black woman, carrying a besom over her shoulder, who gave precise but complicated directions. (Cienfuego's port is vast.) I had to follow a long, unlit street, then turn this way and that – and the berth was unmarked, hard to find. My escort looked worried and was volunteering to guide me when a small lorry appeared. He stopped it with a shout, ran after it, enlisted the driver's help – willingly given. At the ferry berth this young mulatto left his cab to assist me with my backpack and pointed out the obscure entrance. The Cubans are very couth, as a young friend of mine logically described nice new neighbours hours after learning the meaning of 'uncouth'.

By 7.30 all the backless concrete benches in the waiting area were occupied. The ferry, invisible beyond a ramshackle shed, could only be boarded when someone unlocked a wire-mesh gate giving access to a narrow walkway. At 9.00 the gate remained locked but my companions cheerfully assured me we'd soon be sailing. By 10.00 most people looked less cheerful and by 11.00 many were restive. At 11.20 a uniformed official announced 'No fuel'. He pointed to the problem, an antique tanker-barge immobilised halfway across the bay. If the ferry couldn't sail by 4.00 p.m. a truck-bus would take us to Jagua the long way round: twenty-five miles instead of six. Cuba's oil reserves are kept for emergency vehicles, priority being given to ambulances, then fire-engines, then police vehicles – an interesting order. Tourist buses (to Clara's indignation) have a separate reserve supply organised by private enterprise with the government's reluctant blessing.

I decided to try again the next morning and spent the rest of the day touring Cienfuegos's renowned cemeteries. One, a National Monument, dates from the 1830s and is densely populated by larger than life angels. The other (1926) is park-like, its 'gate lodge' a replica of the Parthenon, its neo-classical tombs including a monument to the 5 September Martyrs. These young men died in 1957 when local revolutionaries joined the Rebel Army in an unsuccessful attempt to capture Cienfuegos's important naval barracks.

Back in Punta Gorda, hunger pangs reminded me of a missed breakfast. In a newish but grotty restaurant, where waves were splashing through open windows on to grey plastic tiles, I was the only customer. Five waitresses, sitting chatting around a central table, at first ignored my beckoning. When I loudly demanded a beer one sour-puss strolled over, grunted in response to my greeting, then indicated a wall notice. Alcohol must not be consumed on the premises. Five minutes later she sauntered back with the menu and before I could order rejoined her *compañeros*, took out a pocket-mirror and comb, did some hair-fixing, applied lipstick (a scarce commodity) and pretended to forget me. This team wore neat orange-and-blue uniforms. Two of them were playing chess which somehow added a surreal note to the episode.

The menu listed only two fish dishes (both 'off') and paella. The watery paella, when served half an hour later, was accompanied by a small saucer of chopped white cabbage (the 'salad') and an even smaller saucer of shrimps in batter – by far my least edible Cuban meal and expensive at CP8.

On my dissatisfied way out I encountered Louise, Nancy's niece, with whom I'd talked briefly the day before. She had heard I was in the restaurant and wanted to talk more. We sat outside in the starlight on a wooden deck-bar, extending over the water, where family groups were enjoying Hatueys and Tukolas. When I wondered why alcohol was forbidden within Louise laughed rather nastily and said, 'Ask *el comandante!*'

It seemed Nancy had been commenting on my pro-Revolutionary stance and Louise felt this needed correcting. *El comandante* having lost his grip, any Cuban could say what they thought to any foreigner without fear. 'You can write my name in your book, it's OK, Amnesty is watching, I won't go to prison because I think he's no more powerful. The Special Period finished him. People my age saw he couldn't run Cuba without help. I was eleven in '92 and I was hungry, for three years or more. His independent Cuba is a lie. We must be dependent. Soviets, Americans, I don't care. We need help or we're hungry. Or like now, people stand two, three hours on the road hoping for transport that isn't there. In other countries people don't stand for hours doing nothing. They spend time making money, then have fun spending it – never *doing nothing*!'

I asked, 'Would you like to move to Miami where some Cubans make lots of money?'

Louise's eyes flashed: large dark eyes in a small sallow face. 'Cuba is my country! I love Cuba! I won't ever be "an exile" – what's that? A person *not* loving their country! Soon no more blockade, many more tourists and Cuba can be OK – you agree?'

'No,' I replied. 'I disagree. The Cuba you love is a child of the Revolution, handicapped but legitimate. Would you have loved the Cuba your great-grandparents grew up in?'

'That,' snapped Louise, 'is a stupid question!' She peered then at my watch and said she must go, she had promised to babysit for her sister. Her farewell lacked the normal Cuban warmth and her outburst had been so very unusual that for a wild moment I speculated – '*agent provocateur?*'

As though anxious to make amends, the rusty little ferry left twenty minutes early next morning. A strong wind made the bay choppy and most passengers huddled within a canvas 'tent' while I sat, amongst the bicycles, waving at the racing skiffs that skimmed past on their regular morning outing, some crewed by girls.

Throughout this six-mile, hour-long voyage (fare: NP2) the narrow exit to the sea is hidden by a long islet, at first seeming to merge with the green ridge of the bay's southern shore. We paused at three other bushy islets for men equipped with buckets and sacks to jump on to wobbly jetties. At the second stop a young black man boarded and I made room for him beside me on a coil of rope. 'Thank you missus – missus is right? You Canada? I like we talk! I have getting English for work with tourists. I get good English, I get good work, much peso!'

Not a promising beginning, yet Fausto proved to be good company. Realising that I wasn't a *bona fide* tourist, he let it become obvious that he viewed that species as sub-humans to be used for profit. 'Fair enough,' I thought, 'the exploited having a go at exploiting.'

Soon after entering the channel, which links the bay to the ocean and was little wider than the Thames at Westminster, one is underwhelmed by the squat, seventeenth-century Castillo de Jagua just visible above Perche, a fishing village that seems about to slip off its steep slope into the water.

This anti-pirate Castillo was Cuba's third most important fortress in the eighteenth century and is now ineffectually being put to use as an Historic Monument.

From the landing-stage I set out to look for illegal lodgings; because of visiting Félix my trek would begin on the morrow. Perche's natives were wary of the aged back-packer who was trying to tempt someone to break the law, but eventually someone did – a young white woman, Maria, after a long confab with an elderly mulatto. If I didn't mind sharing a bed with a four-year-old I could stay for one night only: lodging and supper CP15.

This three-room home was lapped by water; one could – and my host did – fish from the verandah. Beneath it ducks quacked and splashed and elsewhere a litter of six-weeks-old puppies gambolled, their lurcher mother growling if the strange-smelling visitor approached. Off the kitchen, a fully furnished *banyo* had been added when piped water was promised. Then the authorities ran out of pipes so the loo had to be flushed with sea water and Maria was still fetching well-water from the hill-top.

Beyond Perche's packed little dwellings and rough pathways a motor road led to a 1960s high-rise town, created around industries hard hit by the Special Period. At once I was reminded of Siberia's 1970s BAM towns, memorials to over-ambitious planners in distant offices. But here the apartment blocks were in better condition and the residents healthier.

Félix, however, was not healthy – he had been rushed to hospital the day before. His distraught wife, having read Alberto's letter, clearly felt obliged to offer coffee but equally clearly felt relieved when I declined with effusive thanks.

I wandered then in search of beer to drown my disappointment; I'd been looking forward to talking with an Angolan veteran. Had this town prospered, it could have been a tolerable place to live: wide streets, grassy embankments, ample playgrounds, a capacious stadium, a theatre-cum-cinema and no through-traffic (even when there was traffic) because Jagua is at the end of the road. But the Special Period had left it dejected. I could find no open bar, café, restaurant, nor any 'private enterprise' pavement snacks. However I persisted, as one does when beer-hunting, and eventually a *tienda* appeared, its fridge half-full of Buccaneros. In that little shop the pace of commerce was pleasing. A young black woman, trying to decide which scent to buy with her precious CP5, conferred at length with the mulatto saleswoman. Seven little bottles were sniffed by both and compared and sniffed again while two amused young black men and I waited patiently. Here too the counter display-case showed single wrapped sweets priced individually (CP 0.50), and mini-lollipops (CP 0.10) and mini-chocolate bars (CP 0.15). I bought one of each, to enable me to condemn their poisonously poor quality.

Avoiding the road, I returned to Perche a long way round, on dusty laneways linking *bohios* and crossing grazing spaces where the cows wore bells and underfed horses and mules reinforced the dejected aura.

Supper was served in the neat, clean living-room: a whole fish just out of the channel, fried in batter, a large bowl of plain white rice and a cabbage, tomato and cucumber salad. All cooking was done on two small electric rings.

In the sweltering little bedroom (fans are a luxury) a high shelf of gimmicky toys – presents from Miami – served as ornaments rather than playthings. A slatted blind admitted both mosquitoes and some unfamiliar winged insect which whizzed round and round the dim ceiling bulb. The predictable crisis came soon after I had retired; naturally, four-year-old Marita objected to sharing her bed with a total stranger. As this was the household's only bed I proposed moving to the cooler verandah but the family insisted on sleeping in rocking-chairs.

The coastal track to Playa Giron begins at Luz, a small town eight miles from Perche on a dreary tarred road. The sea was invisible beyond a uniform expanse of dense, drab bush, man-high; on the other side lay empty parched fields. Those who blanket describe Cuba as 'a beautiful island' are being too kind. Where it's beautiful it's very beautiful and its unspoiled beaches are soothing. But sea, sand and palm trees, while nice to be with, don't really challenge one's store of superlatives. And many regions, away from the sierras and the coast, are unexciting.

I had walked scarcely a mile when a farm lorry stopped and two teenage girls made room for me in a cab smelling strongly of pigs. My trekking plan alarmed the elderly black driver; at Luz he borrowed my dictionary to look up 'dehydration' – what I would die of between Luz and Playa Giron. Seeming touchingly worried, he embraced me at the junction where the track began. Cubans are generous with spontaneous embraces.

By 7.30 I was happily on my way, the dawn golden over a slightly choppy sea, the silence broken only by the husky grating of wavelets playing with pebbles on a flat, stony shore. Inland, as far as the eye could see, that monotonous bush prevailed. (Why no palms in this region?) Two hours later I paused to eat raisins and drink water – a rationed amount, I could refill my bottles only at Venero Feo, the one village en route. Already the sun felt aggressive and I was beginning to wonder if three days of this monotony would be two days too many. But one doesn't turn back, at least not voluntarily.

At 11.00-ish came the sound of trotting hoof-beats; I was being pursued by a policeman, mounted on a diminutive mule borrowed from his brother when the lorry driver had reported a dotty old foreigner risking dehydration. With the aid of my map it was explained that Playa Giron could not be approached from the coast. A military zone intervened and swamps made its circumvention impossible – to find water I would have to return to Venero Feo and might well die of thirst on the way. Had this track been more beautiful and/or more exciting I would have grumbled. In the circumstances I was quite content to ride back to Luz, the charming young policeman carrying my rucksack.

Four vehicles took me over the sixty-odd zig-zagging miles to Playa Giron. A high truck cab to Abreus; a normally overcrowded bus to Macagua; the back of an open truck (the best bit) to Babiney – and finally a battered and perilously overcrowded bus that swayed sickeningly on the badly broken road through the swamps surrounding Playa Giron.

The first and longest stage, to Abreus, crossed level, apparently uninhabited country where several new banana and mango plantations had replaced canefields. Some patches of cane remained and we passed lines of laden ox-carts, often in the charge of grandparents who were simultaneously toddler-caring. On a few ranches cowboys were lassoeing calves for branding: is Cuba the last country where genuine cowboys operate? In between the new plantations it bothered me to see many square miles of equally fertile land lying idle, while Cuba imports so much of its food and thousands are unemployed or underemployed. Remembering how effectively the *barbudos* organised millions of workers during the 1960s, I wondered what would happen if the present government applied such measures to a generation not fired by Revolutionary zeal . . .

At sunset all five of Playa Giron's *casa particulares* were full – or so they claimed . . . I deduced the proprietors were repelled by my appearance; one never sees a scruffy Cuban. Happily the tourist accommodation was congenial – three hundred (mostly unoccupied) *cabañas* widely scattered across the grassy shore where Cuba's army and the invading exiles killed one another in 1961. Each cabin comprises sitting-room, double bedroom and *banyo* with ample hot and cold water, enabling me to launder those offensively scruffy garments. By then even my linen money-belt had its own distinctive stink.

One could write a whole book about the Bay of Pigs invasion and many specialists, working in various fields, have done just that. I'll therefore confine myself to a quote from *The Rough Guide to Cuba* which gives an admirably succinct account of this seminal event.

On April 15, 1961, US planes disguised with Cuban markings and piloted by exiles bombed Cuban airfields but caused more panic than actual damage, although seven people were killed. The intention had been to incapacitate the small Cuban airforce so that the invading troops would be free from aerial bombardment, but Castro had cannily moved most of the Cuban bombers away from the airfields and camouflaged them. Two days later Brigade 2506, as the exile invasion force was known, landed at Playa Giron. The brigade had been led to believe that the air attacks had been successful and were not prepared for what was in store . . . The unexpected Cuban aerial attacks caused much damage and confusion; two freighters were destroyed and the rest of the fleet fled, leaving 1,300 troops trapped on Playa Giron and Playa Larga. During the night of April 17–18 the Cuban government forces renewed attacks on the brigade . . . Several B-26 bombers, two manned by US pilots flew over the Bay of Pigs from Nicaragua in an attempt to weaken the Cuban army and clear the way for the landing of supplies needed by the stranded brigade. Most of the bombers were shot down and the supplies never arrived. Castro's army was victorious having captured 1,180 prisoners who were eventually traded for medical and other supplies from the US.

Without its recently acquired historical significance, Playa Giron would never have made it on to the tourist trail. All around stretch mangrove (and other) swamps and the post-Invasion village, a mile or so inland, is a dusty straggle of detached one-storey houses replacing a wretched charcoal-burners' settlement. (The motor road came after the Invasion.) Along the shore an ugly defensive wall, constructed to deter future invasions, completely blocks the *cabañas*' view of the sea. Nearby, tattered little notices nailed to fences warn – in a whisper, as it were – 'Military Zone'. The locals, ignoring these, take short cuts across the forbidden territory.

In the other direction, I enjoyed a three-hour shore-walk, setting out as a crimson sun rose behind a fretwork of palm fronds, confirming the validity of all those Caribbean postcards. At intervals a low wooded headland or a mound of hurricane litter forced me on to a narrow cul-de-sac road – ending where the track to Luz begins. Off this people-free coast nude swimming was feasible, the water deep, clear and only slightly too warm. On my way back fellow-guests were splashing in a chemically polluted pool and I asked myself yet again, 'Why have people become so estranged from – or afraid of – the natural world?'

Developers were then making strenuous efforts 'to enhance Playa Giron's image' but the hotel kitchen was not playing its part; *casa particulare* would never serve such a meagre and disgusting breakfast.

I now learned that different provinces have different currency regulations. In a *tienda* opposite the hotel (one of a row of brand-new 'facilities') a saleswoman refused my CP100 note and a domineering security man requested 'evidence of identity'. Returning from my *cabaña* with the documents, I watched another woman, called from a back room, inscribing all my passport and visa details in a massive ledger which I then had to sign, twice, before spending CP3 on two bottles of Buccanero. This can't be the best way to enhance a resort's image.

The Invasion Museum is reason enough to visit Playa Giron. Its intelligent lay-out and choice of exhibits are inspired (praise not earned by every Cuban museum) and its lucid introduction to the background fills an obvious need. By now 'the Bay of Pigs' means nothing to most people – and indeed, seen against the twentieth-century's bloody backdrop, it was a minor affray. More people have been killed during football riots and political rallies, as one Australian tourist peevishly pointed out. Her guide tried to explain that the death toll wasn't the issue but by then she and her group were impatiently edging their way towards the exit. In fact this attack so strengthened the Revolution that its CIA organisers did good for Cuba.

My guardian angel was on duty that day. In the hotel bar I *chanced* to meet a British Embassy official who *chanced* to mention, during a general discussion on visas, the importance of one's return ticket – in relation to consular problems with British sailors who have entered Cuba illegally via Key West. That was a close shave; I had been planning to renew my visa in Bayamo but had left my return ticket in No. 403. Without those chance remarks, I would have arrived in Bayamo by slow train and needed at once to return to Havana by fast tourist bus to avoid the US$50-fine for each over-stay day.

It's unlike me not to eat a meal I've paid for, but Playa Giron's hotel breakfast would not have compensated for wasted cool hours. Before dawn I was on the road to Havana, planning to hitch-hike when over-heated.

During a four-hour walk, close by the deep, calm, pellucid waters of the Bay of Pigs, I counted one hundred and sixty-one roadside obelisks honouring those killed in defence of the Bay. These crude concrete monuments, not tended by anyone, seemed forlorn against their background of mangroves. Several breaks in this mangrove barrier gave access to the sandless limestone shore, where broken diving-boards and collapsed picnic huts – provided for snorkellers – recalled Hurricane Michelle. In 2001 an eighteen-foot wave devastated this coast, sweeping away hundreds of thatched huts, never rebuilt. The whole region had been evacuated the day before and these *cenagueros* (swamp people) now endure over-crowded conditions in Playa Giron and continue to burn mangrove charcoal. Before Michelle, this strip of coast was striving for a slice of the tourism cake. Outside its one small restaurant, closed at 8.00 a.m., I watched three turkey vultures, ungainly when grounded, squabbling over the scattered contents of garbage bins. A white-haired mulatta, hanging laundry on the restaurant balcony, invited me to rest and wait for a lift; but I wasn't yet overheated.

No vehicle disturbed the peace until 10.45, when I was about to swim. I hesitated, then decided it would be rash to decline a lift all the way to Havana.

Eugenio was an outspoken young army officer-cum-agronomist driving a strange-sounding Lada, its back seat packed with tall potted plants, blocking the rear view. He stopped to pick up another passenger – luckily a slim youth – at Playa Larga, a bigger town than Playa Giron but not more exciting. Here the road turns inland to cross the vast Zapata swamp and National Park – still teeming, said Eugenio, with iguana, mongoose, wild boar and a treasure trove of rare birds including the Cuban pygmy owl. He often spent days there, alone, but unfortunately foreigners had to hire a guide. We joined the *autopista* near Australia, Fidel's headquarters during the invasion.

Beyond a citrus plantation, covering many square miles, the land again looked underused. Eugenio was uninhibited in his criticism of incompetent direction from above, leading to abrupt changes of plan, incompatible adjacent projects, and bad advice (or none) for farmers when they receive seeds to grow unfamiliar crops.

Even on this *autopista* the traffic merely trickled and Eugenio picked up six village-to-village hitchers, one so bulky I had to sit with an arm around his shoulders. These hundred miles traverse what must surely be Cuba's most boring landscape: flat and colourless (at least in February), its few towns misleadingly named Buena Vista, La Esperanza, Nueva Paz.

Being unexpectedly back in Havana felt odd, the streets so bustling and noisy compared to where I had been – and nowhere else even approached Centro's extreme dilapidation. But it was good to be hugged again by Candida and Pedro. Just as I arrived a downpour started though no rain is expected in February. And last April, Candida complained, when it should have rained every day, not a drop fell.

Chapter 12

In Havana University's Museo Montaine Antropologico I learned that 'Huracan' is a Taino word, the name of a deity who had to be regularly placated by music, song and dance. In Spanish the word soon became 'huracane' and by the late seventeenth century 'hurricane' was the accepted English form. Uncannily, meteorologists' TV images of hurricanes closely resemble the Tainos' rock engravings of Huracan.

During his 1494 voyage, Columbus recorded the first known European confrontation with a hurricane and found himself unnerved by the New World's tropical excesses; even the toughest conquistadors suspected malevolent spirits at work or were cowed by an implicit divine threat. Fr Bartolomé de las Casas didn't try to soothe them but characteristically identified the sixteenth century's unusually frequent hurricanes as God's punishment for cruelty to Indians – who themselves blamed the new-comers for an exceptionally violent 1511 hurricane.

Geography makes Cuba peculiarly vulnerable to tropical storms. Its seven hundred and fifty-mile east/west axis, stretching along the New World's middle latitude, blocks the path followed by most hurricanes on their way from the Caribbean to the Gulf of Mexico. Powerful gales combine with low barometric pressure to lift mountains of water from the ocean basin and these gain height and momentum while moving towards land across shallow coastal waters. A liquid mountain can be fifty miles wide and, over flat terrain, its crests may penetrate up to forty-five miles inland. Hurricanes making landfall near estuaries commonly drive rivers backwards, causing catastrophic flooding. Heavy continuous rain invariably follows the quieting of the gale, provoking massive mud slides and more flash floods in the sierras and leaving the plains water-logged for weeks.

After the 1509 hurricane a pioneer colonist, Gonzalo Fernandez de Oviedo, could scarcely believe his eyes:

Innumerable huge and thick trees were fully uprooted, their exposed roots as high as the loftiest branches of some of them; others broken into pieces from top to bottom . . . It is something to marvel to see some of them so distant from the site where they matured and with their upturned roots, some upon the others, in such a way locked together and piled and interweaved, that it appears to be by design, a work in which the devil has taken part.

Exactly a century later Virginia-bound William Strachey, who had known many turbulent seas, lost his coherency:

A dreadful storm and hideous, swelling and roaring as it were by fits, at length did beat all light from Heaven; which like a hell of darkness, turned black upon us, so much the more fuller of horror as in such cases horror and fear use to overrun the troubled and overmastered senses of all. What shall I say? Winds and seas were as mad as fury and rage could make them.

Strachey's vessel had been driven on to the Bermudas and his survivor's tale is believed to have inspired *The Tempest*. (See Scene 1, Act I – 'The sky, it seems, would pour down stinking pitch, / But that the sea, mounting to the welkin's cheek, / Dashes the fire out.')

The Havana archives list sixty-nine major 'hits' between 1494 and 1850 (severe storms not included). A hurricane's effects precluded exaggeration; the most articulate found their vocabularies inadequate. Everyone emphasised noise. In 1772 Alexander Hamilton wrote to his father:

It seemed as if a total dissolution of Nature was taking place. The roaring of the sea and wind, the prodigious glare of almost perpetual lightning, the crash of the falling houses and the ear-piercing shrieks of the distressed were sufficient to strike astonishment into Angels.

Eight years later the Reverend George Wildon Bridges marvelled:

The sea seemed mingled with the clouds and to the distance of half a mile, waves carried and fixed vessels of no ordinary size, leaving them the providential means of sheltering the houseless inhabitants . . . The midnight horrors of the scene were to be viewed as the last convulsions of an expiring world . . . The scattered remains of houses whose tenants were dead or dying – the maddening search for wives and children who were lost, the terrific howling of the frightened Negroes as it mingled with the whistling wind . . .

In 1888 an anonymous journalist reported:

The horrible whistling of the wind sounded like the prolonged moaning of all of humanity . . . The frightful crash of buildings collapsing, the

clash of doors and windows and of zinc sliding, and tiles and a thousand
other objects that whirled through the air crashing against one another
. . . And in the midst of all this despair, the screams and ayes that
seconded the horrific noises made it sound that the way was being
opened to reach the throne of Eternity.

In 1910 a five-day hurricane, one of the longest ever recorded, hit Pinar
del Rio. In 1926, at 10.45 a.m., winds above a hundred and fifty miles per
hour reached Havana, killing more than six hundred and leaving tens of
thousands badly injured. 'Fishing boats floated down streets like deserted
gondolas, dead cows dropped on rooftops and houses flew overhead like
birds.' In 1932 twenty-five-foot waves washed away the entire fishing village
of Santa Cruz del Sur, drowning all but five hundred of its three thousand
or so inhabitants. In 1944 winds approaching two hundred miles per hour
were recorded in Havana.

Until Louis A. Perez produced his riveting *Winds of Change*, historians
paid strangely little attention to hurricanes, despite their influence on
Cuba's economic, social and political development. Several times during
the Wars of Independence (1868–98) 'hits' intervened. On 30 September
1873 de Cespedes' diary laments 'this horrific hurricane's' disruption of
his transport and communications. Later, at a crucial stage in the final
campaign, a hurricane helped the Cuban Liberation Army by entirely
ruining the tobacco crop (including seeds) west of Havana. Ricardo Del-
gardo then informed the army planner, 'These poor tobacco farmers find
themselves today in the most desperate situation. They have nothing to
do, nothing to eat, and would give themselves with a song in their heart if
they could come over and join our ranks.' General Maceo acted on this
information and two months later triumphantly led his augmented troops
into Pinar del Rio.

In Oriente the 1890s hurricanes had no such compensatory outcome.
Around Baracoa the 1894 'hit' totally destroyed every banana plantation
and when all those small farmers went into production again, on borrowed
money, an 1899 hit reduced them to bankruptcy. The United Fruit Company (of ill repute throughout Latin America) then bought all their
lands – an enormous area – and planted it to cane, thus worsening Cuba's
sugar-dependency.

Every district, and each generation, has its own memories of terror and
heroism, of tragedy, turmoil and triumph. Louis Perez comments on the
extent to which 'hits' helped to forge a Cuban identity. All classes shared in

the fear and grief and, to varying extents, in the subsequent hardship. To survive, and then to pick up the pieces (often literally), everyone had to cooperate: black, white and mulatto, young and old, rural and urban, rich and poor, the illiterate and the scholarly. Thus hurricanes had bonding-power, making Cubans feel justifiably proud of their communal resilience. (There was one exceptional group; after each hit bands of slaves fled to the mountains, though not as many as one might have expected. Most were too debilitated for such adventures.)

By now meteorologists and modern communications have raised strong protective barriers between Huracan and the general public. Yet in 2005 more than three thousand died, the majority in the US, the world's most technologically advanced country. During that record-breaking season fourteen hurricanes (plus twelve severe tropical storms) raged across the Caribbean Sea and the Gulf of Mexico. Unusually, only two hit Cuba hard: Dennis and Wilma. In July the former twice made landfall in Central Cuba, wrecking more than a hundred and twenty thousand homes, killing sixteen people and felling Trinidad's radio mast. In preparation for Dennis the local authorities evacuated 1.5 million human beings and four hundred and seventy five thousand animals. (The unfortunate citizens of New Orleans, it will be remembered, were told to make their own evacuation plans in preparation for August's Katrina, though twenty-five per cent of the threatened population lived below the poverty line and twenty per cent of families were carless.) When Wilma hit Cuba in late October more than six hundred thousand people had been evacuated. Ten days of non-stop torrential rain flooded eleven of the fourteen provinces but no lives were lost. Nor were any lost in 2001, in Cuba's most destructive hurricane since 1944. Or in 2004, when another 1.5 million (more than one-tenth of the population) were moved before Ivan demolished twenty thousand homes.

After Flora hit Oriente, in 1963, a week-long deluge swept away eleven thousand homes and killed more than a thousand *campesiños* though one hundred and seventy-five thousand had been evacuated. Fidel then said, 'The hurricane has done its thing, now it is time for us to do ours.' At present, Cuba is being held up to the world as a model. 'The Cuban way could easily be applied to other countries with similar economic conditions and even in countries with greater resources that do not manage to protect their populations as well as Cuba does' – so says the UN International Secretariat for Disaster Reduction. 'The Cuban government's zero-risk attitude and awareness raising programmes are leading the way in the Caribbean' – so says the International Federation of the Red Cross.

Awareness raising begins in primary school where children are taught how to prepare calmly for a hit and how to play their part when it comes. All residents of endangered areas know where to find the nearest group shelters, holding stocks of water, food and medical supplies. Health workers keep lists of those most at risk: the handicapped, the elderly, pregnant women. Each municipal authority is obliged to identify buildings or homes with structural defects and organise evacuations accordingly. Public warnings are issued five days before a probable hit; two days later evacuations begin and well-trained rescue teams go on stand-by. Annually, at the end of May, the whole country participates for a few days in Mete-Oro, a hurricane simulation exercise. And all this 'disaster reduction' is achieved despite a petrol drought.

When Cuba is loudly praised by international organisations some people protest in righteous tones that only a dictator could organise such speedy mass-evacuations. Democracies can't save lives by pushing individuals around, every citizen must be left free to choose how to react. These mean-minded inanities (and they are numerous) perhaps helped to inspire an Oxfam America report:

> Cuba has a strong, well-organised civil defence, an early warning system, well-equipped rescue teams, emergency stockpiles and other resources. Such tangible assets are impressive, but if they were the only deter-mining factor, then other wealthier countries such as the US would have lower disaster death tolls. Cuba's significant intangible assets include community mobilization, solidarity, clear political commitment to safeguard human life and a population educated in the necessary action to be taken . . . The single most important thing about disaster response in Cuba is that the people cooperate en masse.

All night the downpour that had welcomed me back to Havana continued, water cascading off No. 403's roof to swirl and gurgle in the patio. Next day the *habaneros* were depressed and I was energised by a low dark grey sky, a strong cool wind, ten-foot waves crashing over the Malecón and long showers that sent disillusioned tourists scuttling for shelter. On the Prado I overheard one Englishwoman exclaiming, 'It's like being at home!' A plaintive cry; not for this had she spent good money leaving England in February.

The Immigration Section of the Department of Internal Security (open 9.00 a.m.–3.00 p.m.) is a brisk ninety minutes walk from No. 403. At 10.30 I joined a very long queue only to be told I must return next morning because that queue was the day's quota. No special office caters for tourists; they must merge with the multitude. I then discovered that cash is not acceptable. One has to buy special visa stamps at a particular guichet in a particular (distant) bank and get a signed and sealed statement from another guichet guaranteeing that you, personally, have bought those stamps. Yet Cuba's London consulate can deliver a visa in *seven minutes*!

In the bank I queued for more than an hour; as customers accumulated, three of the eight guichets closed. There were however easy chairs and sofas scattered between the pillars, leading me to suspect 'a joint venture'; the ascetic Revolution, left to itself, would never authorise such sybaritism. One's time of arrival seemed irrelevant; a gorgeously uniformed six-foot-six security officer decided who would go to which guichet when. The etiquette for my second queue, to acquire the guarantee, required me to stand – beside an empty chair – for what felt like another hour.

Next stop – Cuba's Central Post Office, by way of an experiment undertaken without much hope. In this enormous building I entrusted a fat envelope to the only person in sight, an amiable middle-aged black woman sitting behind glass at a bare desk. (Her isolation suggested a basis for my lack of hope.) When I asked 'How much?' she frowned anxiously, then made a soothing sound and disappeared with the envelope. Returning six minutes later she said, 'CP0.85' – which, given the letter's weight, seemed absurd. The four stamps eventually found at the back of a drawer celebrated 'Gatos Domesticos' – a mother carrying her kitten – which would delight the Trio should this letter ever arrive. Carefully the clerk licked each stamp and took pains to place them symmetrically in the four corners, giving the impression that this was not an everyday task. Then that anxious frown reappeared: the stamps were not sticking. Another soothing sound and off she went on a nine-minute search for glue. Clearly she was committed to my envelope's welfare. Having delicately applied the glue, she pounded each stamp with a fist, looking resolute. As I counted out the centavos in small coins, to get rid of a surplus, the stamps took anti-glue action – curled up at the edges. Distraught, my friend (as I now thought of her) removed them, produced a new set, applied glue only. She then used eloquent sign language to convey her theory that saliva and glue are chemically incompatible. That letter arrived in Italy seven weeks later.

On the Malecón little fish were being flung across the road and seaweed was piled below my favourite bar's steps and spray drenched me as I drank and wrote. The longer this wind blows, the higher the waves build up in the Straits of Florida.

Are the Cubans neurotic about slight temperature variations? That day I saw many dogs wearing coats, not the sort of tailored canine jackets fashionable in Kensington/Chelsea but improvised garments: men's under-pants, children's T-shirts, women's tights and, memorably, two oversize bras encasing an extra-long dachshund. My woolly white terrier friend on San Rafael, for whom I had felt pity in November as he panted through the noon heat, was now guarding his doorstep swaddled in towelling tied on with a string. No wonder so many concerned *habaneros* were stopping me in the street, sympathetically exclaiming '*Frio!*' – then being astonished, on feeling my bare arms, to find me not '*frio*'.

My visa contretemps left Candida guilt-stricken. She had provided me with the essential document, signed by us both, to prove my place of residence but had assumed I would know about the stamps. And she'd got the timing wrong, the office opens at 8.00, not 9.00. I hugged her to wipe out all that guilt. We in the reserved West should make more use of hugging.

Next morning, to be sure of a place in that day's queue, I set off when the streets were empty of all but cats. Havana's energy-saving street lighting is adequate but, given the hazardous state of Centro's pavements, one has to move cautiously before dawn. As I watched my step, a mild electric shock was administered to my scalp. Looking up, I saw an illegal cable suspended between a pole and a ground-floor flat at just the height to shock your average Cuban (not a very tall person). The cable was still in place on my next visit to Havana.

No less startling was a hazard on a busy footpath where someone had covered a deep hole with the top (or bottom) of a tar barrel. This had been knocked off-centre so that it presented the equivalent of a sharp rusty knife to the shins of oncoming pedestrians. Anyone watching out for dangling cables would certainly have been gashed.

Twenty-eight stood ahead of me outside Immigration's one-storey pre-fab buildings on a ridge unprotected from Atlantic gales. Soon even I was *frio* – chilled through, hands and feet numb. All morning the sun tried to shine but the clouds won. Wistfully I remembered the bank's easy chairs and wondered why Internal Security took asceticism to such an extreme, not even providing wooden benches for people (many of them elderly) who had to stand for four or five hours – four hours and twenty minutes in my case.

The monotony was broken only by two litters of tiny frolicking kittens and, as time passed it became clear that their entertaining presence was no accident. These were not feral families; at a little distance, watching them, sat two teenage girls with cardboard cartons. All ten kittens were tame and very tempting and several in the queue gradually gave way to temptation – an interesting process to observe, winning ways overcoming practical considerations. Two couples disagreed, loudly and at length, about their household's need for another animal. In both cases victory went to the tempted. I wondered if this solution to the 'good homes' problem would work in Ireland – but then, we don't have five-hour alfresco queues.

When the office opened, twenty minutes late, the queue exceeded one hundred and fifty (we counted to amuse ourselves). Only two women were on duty, each in a little doorless office minimally furnished – camp chairs on either side of a table hardly big enough to hold a computer. A sharp-tongued man, wearing an Internal Security peaked cap, monitored us, opening a gateway at intervals to admit eight and, should a ninth try to slip in, banishing him/her to the end of the queue. When my turn came, the rest of the octet registered changes of addresses or relatives visiting from abroad, applied for tourist taxi licences or permits required to receive parcels from the US. Such matters are time-consuming but, after all that stamina-testing, my visa-renewal procedure took less than ten minutes.

Some Cubans insist that the Bay of Pigs invasion pushed the depressive and alcoholic Ernest Hemingway over the edge, that he shot himself three months later because it seemed he could never return to Finca La Vigia, his beloved home for twenty-one years. Everywhere nostalgia is a tourist asset and the Havana authorities have restored this villa at a cost of more than 2.5 million. Here, too, the embargo operated. The Boston-based Hemingway Preservation Society wished to donate but were informed, 'Any contribution would violate trade sanctions by boosting tourism'. Then a compromise allowed Boston's enthusiasts to help conserve and catalogue the bulky archives found in the villa's mouldy cellar.

Cuba's tourist bosses have recently given a tincture of romance even to the Batista era. In the celebrated art deco Hotel Nacional, opened in 1930 on a high bluff above the Malecón, I was startled to be offered a tour of 'the suites where Al Capone and Meyer Lansky lived'. This trend worries me in the first decade of the twenty-first century when real, live Mafia types abound in our financial, corporate and political worlds – some of their schemes making the Cosa Nostra look like tyros.

In 1929 another art deco spectacular arose near the Presidential Palace at a cost of one million dollars. This was Edificio Bacardi, a new head-quarters for the rum company, built of pink granite and coral limestone with terracotta tiles around the windows and the Bacardi symbol (a bat) perched on the pyramidal roof. On 9 January 1959, when *el comandante* led his victorious guerrillas into Havana, they saw something astounding. High above the street, extending the full length of this dominant building, hung a banner saying 'GRATIAS, FIDEL'. For all their business acumen, the Bacardi tribe had misjudged Fidel and helped in a small way to fund his army, believing that its main aim was to get rid of Batista – an aim then shared by most Cubans, rich or poor. Who could take seriously all those impractical promises made to the masses? When the young rebels came to power they would surely behave like sensible politicians, providing only enough marginal reforms to placate their followers while they secured for themselves lucrative positions in the new government.

One Bacardi manoeuvre had been thwarted in mid-December. When the dictator's defeat seemed assured, he received a visit from Earl Smith, the US ambassador, who instructed him to put in place a junta, to begin to organise elections – and then to leave, for good. Smith had already chosen the junta and Pepin Bosch was a senior member. However, Batista ignored his would-be boss and no junta impeded the Rebel Army's swift take-over.

On 7 January a group of businessmen, including Pepin Bosch and Daniel Bacardi, met in Havana and sent an urgent message to President Eisenhower pleading for immediate US recognition of the new regime 'because this government appears far better than anything we had dared hope for'. So influential were these men that the State Department granted diplomatic recognition that very day.

Fidel kept his promise to organise a calm transition to reform by appointing former Judge Manuel Urrutia as President and José Miro-Cardona (once his professor at Havana's Law School) as Prime Minister. This interim cabinet contained only three guerrillas (rtd) but Fidel appointed himself as Commander-in-Chief of the Rebel Armed Forces.

Then the Revolution's glory was tarnished by the execution of four hundred of Batista's most loyal and brutal SIM military police – 'Special Service' torturers. Their trials in Havana's sports stadium were shown live on TV with vengeful crowds demanding instant executions and Ché signed more than fifty death sentences. In Santiago Fidel's brother Raul supervised the machine-gunning of seventy-one soldiers. When international outrage flared – the US pouring petrol on its flames – Fidel angrily pointed out, 'We are not executing innocent people or political opponents. We are executing murderers . . . Revolutionary justice is not based on legal precepts, but on moral conviction.'

In his biography of Fidel, Leycester Coltman, former British ambassador to Havana, comments:

> Most Cubans accepted and indeed welcomed Castro's position. It increased their sense of liberation. He was liberating them not only from the tyranny of Batista, but from the tyranny of a legal system which had rules and codes and procedures, but did not deliver justice. Under the old system money, influence and clever lawyers would enable a man to get away with murder while the poor found no redress. For years the American mafia had run huge gambling and prostitution rackets, in collaboration with corrupt Cuban police officers, and had enjoyed impunity from the law. Most Cubans had more confidence in Fidel's moral conviction.

When Fidel first visited the US in April 1959 President Eisenhower hardly noticed – he had a golf date to keep. Cuba's Revolution left him unbothered; perhaps it was veering too far left but when the Guatemalan government did likewise in 1954 it had been easy to get rid of Jacobo Arbenz: one crisp Presidential order to the CIA and regime change was effected.

During a three-hour meeting with Vice-President Nixon Fidel and his team of economic advisors – including Felipe Pazos, president of Cuba's National Bank – discussed and disagreed about land reform. Fidel, as he had expected, found himself in a minority of one though his plan to limit private ownership to four hundred hectares (about one thousand acres) seemed not unreasonable. When the Land Reform law came into force in June, the US sent a note of protest, fulminating about the compensation offered. It was based on the landowners' own assessments of value, as recorded on their tax forms over the years – an impeccably correct legal procedure. This hoisting of the super-rich on their own petard must have tickled Fidel's sense of humour while sparing Cuba's coffers – almost emptied by Batista and his entourage before they fled.

In July 1960 Law 851 led to the nationalisation of the Bacardi Company's Cuban assets, by then only a tiny fraction of their wealth. Eventually most foreign companies (Mexican, Canadian, British, Swiss, French) accepted that Castroism had arrived to stay and took whatever was on offer, always calculated on the basis of taxes previously paid. To this day, however, the Bacardis and the US government have refused compensation on Cuba's terms.

A fortnight before the Bay of Pigs invasion, Bacardi donated a small ship to the Miami exiles' Christian Democrat Movement and she promptly set sail for Cuba with José Ignacio Rasco on board – the CIA's choice to lead the hoped-for puppet government. Two and a half years later, when a Kennedy/Castro rapprochement seemed a possibility in the week before President Kennedy's death, Adlai Stevenson resentfully noted that 'the CIA is still in charge of everything to do with Cuba'.

Soon after the Brigade 2506 debacle, Pepin Bosch began to organise a second invasion, more carefully planned. According to Alvaro Vargas Llosa, the Cuban American National Foundation (CANF) spokesman, Bosch was determined 'to gather a group of exceptional people, prominent men of the Cuban republic, and subject them to a referendum in order to create a world representative body of exiles who would be mandated to carry out actions in favour of the freedom of Cuba'. A National Security Council (NSC) memo, dated 28 May 1963, reveals that Washington knew of this plan.

By the beginning of 1964 Pepin Bosch had found five 'exceptional people' to lead the Miami-based Cuban Representation in Exile (RECE its Spanish acronym). The CIA provided its main funding but Vargas Llosa records that 'Bacardi gave the organisation $10,000 per month and paid each of the five leaders $600 per month' – even then not lavish sums, by Bacardi standards. Soon RECE ranked amongst the Western hemisphere's most deadly terrorist groups and Luis Posada Carriles (who was still making global headlines in 2006) held a dual position as its chief planner and a CIA 'special operative'. In 1985 US Congressional investigators obtained an FBI document exposing CIA funding for a RECE sabotage attack on a Cuban ship in the Mexican port of Vera Cruz. Other revelations came in 1998, with the release of a report on Congressional probings into President Kennedy's death and concurrent CIA plans to assassinate certain foreign political leaders, Fidel being first on the list. The letter attached to this report merits quotation in full:

The White House
Washington
June 15, 1964

MEMORANDUM FOR MR BUNDY
Subject: Assassination of Castro

1. Attached is a memorandum from the CIA describing a plot to assassinate Castro, which would involve US elements of the Mafia and which would be financed by Pepin Bosch.

2. John Crimmins is looking into the matter. He is planning to talk to Alexis Johnson about it and feels that it should be discussed in a Special Group meeting. John's own inclination is that the government of the United States cannot knowingly permit any criminal US involvement in this kind of thing and should go all out to stop the plot. This would involve putting the FBI on the case of the American criminal elements involved and intervening with Bosch.

I have not yet thought this through and respectfully withhold judgement.   Gordon Chase

McGeorge Bundy, the Special National Security Assistant to President Johnson (and formerly to President Kennedy), was responsible for the administration's relations with the CIA.

The eight-point memo passed by the CIA to their director, Richard Helms, noted that Pepin Bosch had offered $100,000 of the $150,000 demanded by the Mafia and their Cuban-American underworld links for 'taking out' Fidel, his brother Raul and Ché. (A bargain, some might have thought – only fifty thousand dollars each!)

Richard Helms, whose wealth had been considerably diminished by Fidel's nationalisations, ended his report on the plot:

Note: It is requested that this agency be informed of any action contemplated in regard to the persons mentioned in this report before such action is initiated.

Who knows why such action never was initiated? Possibly because the CIA failed to co-ordinate the four hundred or so counter-revolutionary cells then vying for their support.

Pepin Bosch was active on many fronts. After the nationalisation of Cuba's oil refineries he resolved to bomb them, throwing the island into the chaos of darkness. In the ensuing anarchy, Castro's victims would surely rise up against Communism. This bombing was to be launched from Costa Rica, that favourite CIA base for covert activities. As Pepin Bosch's second-hand B-26 lacked rockets, he visited Venezuela's arms bazaar, found it temporarily out of rockets and hurried to Brazil where the dictatorship presented him with a pair of left-overs from a dodgy consignment. Back in Costa Rica, Nature intervened. Weather delayed the bombing run, some alert journalist investigated the mysterious B-26 with the uncommunicative pilot – and then spotted an international 'celeb' (as Pepin Bosch would now be known) lurking nearby. When the *New York*

Times published a photograph of the plane, with a questioning caption, the Costa Rican government made haste to avert a major scandal by confiscating this embarrassing Bacardi possession.

Castroism's twenty-first-century harshness towards US-funded and trained subversives is rooted in Cuba's exposure to terrorism before its security services acquired the know-how to outwit CIA agents and RECE saboteurs. William Blum reviews the 1960s in *Killing Hope*, a book described by John Stockwell, a former CIA officer, as 'the single most useful summary of CIA history'.

Throughout the decade, Cuba was subjected to countless sea and air commando raids by exiles, at times accompanied by their CIA supervisors, inflicting damage upon oil refineries, chemical plants and railroad bridges, cane fields, sugar mills and sugar warehouses; infiltrating spies, saboteurs and assassins . . . anything to damage the Cuban economy, promote dissatisfaction, or make the revolution look bad . . . taking the lives of Cuban militia members and others in the process . . . organising pirate attacks on Cuban fishing boats and merchant ships . . . The commando raids were combined with a total US trade and credit embargo so unyielding that when Cuba was hit by a hurricane in October 1963 and Casa Cuba, a New York social club, raised a large quantity of clothing for relief, the US refused to grant it an export licence on the grounds that such shipment was 'contrary to the national interest' . . .

By 1970 so many commandos had been capture or killed in Cuba that the CIA/Bacardi/RECE alliance decided to operate elsewhere and William Blum records that 'During the next decade more than a hundred serious "incidents" took place in the US . . . including at least one murder.'

In 1976 the CIA's new director, George H. Bush, organised the more extreme exile gangs into a coalition known as CORU and chose Orlando Bosch to lead them. This Bosch (a paediatrician, unrelated to Pepin) had until recently been advisor to General Pinochet's infamous secret police (DINA). In 1968 he had been convicted of sabotaging a Polish cargo boat in Miami harbour, a peccadillo the future President George H. Bush didn't hold against him. On 14 October 1976, not long after starting his new CORU job, Orlando Bosch and his RECE colleague Luis Posada Carriles were arrested by the Venezuelan police and charged with dynamiting a Cubana Airlines plane.

Posada Carriles had been planted in Venezuela by the CIA to 'advise' the Venezuelan security forces who so appreciated his advice that they made him Commissioner of their political police. Following his arrest in Caracas the CIA's terrorist tactics were partially exposed and Washington felt painful national and international pressures. It seemed Castroism's defeat would require another strategy: less direct action, more political manoeuvering. In Varga Llosa's words, 'RECE wedded itself to rum and politics again, and Bacardi was put in charge once again of almost all the bills.'

During the early 1980s RECE was replaced by a far more coherent and economically powerful alliance, the Cuban American National Foundation (CANF), skilfully constructed by a few RECE terrorists (rtd), several Bacardi directors and major shareholders, and enough experienced CIA operatives to give the others a new glow of confidence. Soon, surely, Cuba would be *free*!

From its inception, CANF was involved in President Reagan's secret NSC Directive No. 77 ('Project Democracy' – Oliver North, Irangate and so on.) The Foundation, studded with names respected in the best circles, served as a useful conduit for the National Endowment for Democracy's (NED's) funding of the Contras. Several high-ranking Bacardi executives were 'Associates' of CANF, providing sheaves of strings to be pulled and dollars beyond reckoning.

As part of Project Democracy, the setting up of Radio Marti was approved in 1983, though many in the US Congress opposed it, foreseeing that it would boomerang. Its most enthusiastic backer was Charles Wick, director of the US Information Agency (USIA), the main US generator of mis-information. Richard Allen of the NSC described it as 'CANF's first important act in collaboration with the US government'.

After the establishment of the 'Bacardi Chair' at the University of Miami in 1986, notable visiting academics, linked to both the Company and CANF, regularly lectured on such themes as 'The History of Cuba' and 'Understanding Cuban Culture'. Among them was Jaime Suchlicki, author of *Cuba from Columbus to Castro and Beyond*. He is misinformative about the post-Soviet Cuban economy, the poor state of the health service, the US invasion of Grenada, the US embargo and the Castro brothers' alleged involvement with the drugs trade. Oddly enough, he nowhere mentions CANF. However, this well-written history is worth reading for the insights it gives into the formation of the CANF-style mind-set during pre-Revolution generations.

As the Soviet Union lay on its deathbed Washington's NED was working overtime to ensure that all former members of the Soviet bloc would toe the line exactly where it was being drawn by the Unholy Trinity (the World Bank, the International Monetary Fund and the World Trade Organi-zation). CANF's richest leaders, including a strong Bacardi component, were predictably involved in this enterprise. Soon two NED directors, the Republican politicians Robert Graham and Connie Mack, were accompanying a CANF pressure group to Moscow, to discuss with senior government officials the desirability of quickly turning Cuba adrift. As a reward, New Russians would receive preferential economic treatment in the US – especially in Florida. Who could spurn such a reward? Certainly not any of the New Russians then being seduced by the Unholy Trinity.

Early in 1990 Jorge Mas Canosa, CANF's chairman, issued a document for the eyes of his fellow-directors only. It 'laid out the tactical elements which will be implemented prior to the expected collapse of the [Cuban] communist government'. Read in conjunction with the State Department's 'Commission for Assistance to a Free Cuba', Mas Canosa's blueprint is chilling. It ends:

> Organise a task force to systematise and strengthen working relations established with the State Department with the aim of jointly devising and developing new international policies which respond to the present situation . . . Nothing nor no one will make us falter. We do not wish it but if blood has to flow, it will flow.

Before noon on 25 December 1991, hours after the birth of the New Russia's, a CANF delegation met Foreign Affairs Minister, Andrei Kozyrev. Everyone was happy. As Varga Llosa has recorded:

> The minister promised to put an end to subsidies and change the relationship with Cuba to one based on strictly commercial lines . . . to speed up the withdrawal of troops and to vote against Cuba in Geneva . . . That was when the glasses were raised to toast a free Cuba. Because in a way that morning sealed Castro's fate. That was when the halting of economic aid to Castro was announced to the world . . . There was nothing secret about the discussion. We raised a toast in front of the TV cameras with Bacardi rum. The box and bottle stood out in the middle of the table, the name of the rum displayed for all to see.

As we now know, that toast was premature.

The 1990s saw three Cuban-Americans elected to the US Congress: in New Jersey Robert Menendez, in Florida Ileana Ros-Lehtinen and Lincoln Diaz-Balart (a nephew of Fidel's first wife, Mirta Diaz Balart). To increase the Special Period's hardships by penalising any company trading with Cuba, the Cuban Democracy Act of 1992 (aka the Torricelli Act) was sponsored by a Democrat from New Jersey where many Cuban exiles had settled. Robert Torricelli and his fellow-lobbyists received generous funding from the Bacardi family, as did CANF's pressure group in Washington which modelled itself, very successfully, on the American-Israel Public Affairs Committee.

When President Clinton partially lifted the embargo on Vietnam in 1994, CANF feared he might do likewise for Cuba. Sounding more than slightly mad, they called for a nation-wide 'Great Patriotic Strike' to hit factories, shops, offices. They demanded the revocation of 'the agreement with the old Soviet Union, made during the Cuban Missile Crisis in 1962 and in which the US undertook not to invade Cuba'. Frantically they called on President Clinton to accept their 'preparations for military action against Fidel Castro's government'. In support of this strike call, Xiomara Lindner, political advisor to the president of Bacardi Imports, provided a fleet of buses to take a thousand or so Miami protesters to Washington where they stood outside the White House brandishing banners accusing Clinton of 'communism'. Bacardi (by then Bacardi-Martini) must have had some hidden reason for encouraging these rabid subversives.

By 1995 it had become apparent that Torricelli was not working, that Fidel was in no danger of being lynched by starving mobs. Instead, Cuba's economy was being revived by transfusions of hard currency from the tourist trade. And so the Bacardis opened their purses yet again to grease the wheels of the Cuban Liberty and Democratic Solidarity Act (aka the Helms-Burton Act). This was designed to intimidate investors from Europe, Japan, Latin America, Canada; its designers were sensitive to the fact that, come the new 'democratic' free-market Cuba, all those foreign investors would get in the way of US and Cuban-American entrepreneurs.

CANF invited Jesse Helms to Miami in April 1995 while he was seeking support for his Bill. A local newspaper, *Diaros Los Americas*, reported:

> Lunch was taken in an atmosphere of true patriotism, attended by many of the most representative and distinguished Cuban exile groups. Pepe Hernandez, CANF president, gave a speech heard with rapt attention. Next up to speak was Rodolfo A. Ruiz, president of Bacardi Imports, who eloquently addressed the audience expressing the feelings of all those present that it was imperative to see a free Cuba. Senator Helms stepped on to the platform to outline his thoughts. He had always been a dedicated fighter on behalf of the freedom of all peoples, on this occasion by presenting a Bill that would worsen the economy for the oppressive Havana regime.

The *Baltimore Sun* noted: 'Bacardi executives joined Jorge Mas Canosa, who heads CANF, in sponsoring a fund-raising lunch for Mr Helms which grossed more than seventy-five thousand dollars.'

Miami's *El Nuevo Herald* noted: 'The Bill contains measures that will benefit businesses such as Bacardi and the Fanjul family of sugar magnates. This is normal given the tradition that exists in the US of lobbying in Congress on behalf of private interests. In this case, however, criticisms are raised due to its openly stated political aims.'

The *Miami Herald* noted that 'on the Hill' the Helms-Burton proposals were known as 'the Bacardi Bill' and Wayne Smith referred to it as 'the Bacardi Claims Act'. Juan Prado, advisor to the chairman of Bacardi's Miami board of directors, made no attempt to deflect such criticisms. Bluntly he stated – 'Bacardi would be a prime beneficiary if the Helms Bill became law'.

El Nuevo Herald commented: 'Although Bacardi's headquarters are in Bermuda, its US subsidiaries or any one of the around five hundred family members who have become citizens of our country could benefit from this Act and lodge claims in the courts.'

What Jesse Helms described as his 'Adios, Fidel Bill' had been designed as an 'enhanced' anti-Castroism missile. But then, like many such weapons, it caused unexpected collateral damage. The Unholy Trinity and kindred institutions didn't appreciate being threatened with US sanctions if they eased Cuba's economic discomfort in any way. The EU's rage was white-hot – how *dare* the US try to bully other countries into obeying its laws! Helms-Burton violated the general principles of international law! Canada also took umbrage, quoting the case of Ian Delaney, Sherritt's CEO, who was forbidden to enter the US because his company had set up a joint venture in Havana. It seemed the State Department's Bacardi-driven lawyers, beavering away in their Washington offices, had lost sight of reality; everyone united to condemn the Helms-Burtons Act which stays on the statute books but has been used gingerly. However, the relevant financial institutions have remained cautious and the Cuban government must still pay abnormally high interest rates to private lenders.

Chapter 13

Undaunted by previous experience, I booked a seat on the twice-weekly Havana-Bayamo train service (alleged dep. 7.25 p.m.). The only alternatives were hitch-hiking, which could take several days, or a Viazul coach.

At 8.50 p.m. we passengers were loosed on to the ill-lit platform and confusion immediately set in; even by daylight the faint print on my ticket, giving coach, compartment and seat numbers, was well nigh illegible. When I opened a coach door at random its inner panel fell off, blocking my way. Clambering over it, I groped down a corridor by a glimmer of platform light and found an empty compartment where I was still alone at 9.45. The engine then made eerie noises, setting it apart from any other engine I've known, and moved off at a slow walking speed. All this seemed too good to be true; silence and darkness blessed my coach, whatever its number: I could stretch out and sleep, at least until the first stop.

Some time later three chain-smoking adults and a fretful toddler woke me. Unsurprised, I sat up, eyelids drooping, and tried to determine from the voices how many of each sex were present; for moments the toddler was so fretful I thought s/he (?) was two toddlers. Soon the adults (two male, one female) were furiously quarrelling and exhaling rum fumes. Cubans tend to shout, even when not arguing, possibly because conversations must often compete with insanely amplified music coming from several different directions. This row, inexplicably, quieted the toddler.

An hour or so later, when the last cigarettes had been stamped on the floor and everyone except me was asleep, all hell broke loose nearby. A conductress was on the prowl, checking everyone's seating. In Havana, where conflicting views were held about the numbering of twelve unmarked coaches, many passengers had settled wherever they could find space and now resented being moved.

Oddly enough, my companions were correctly placed – very clever of them, I thought. Now the combination of her own dying torch and my faintly inked ticket challenged our conductress. Only when one of the men lent his cigarette-lighter could she see that mine was seat three in compartment B in coach six – three coaches away. She then recruited this same man to lead me through total darkness. He wore my rucksack, I carried my shoulder-bag and used my umbrella to steady myself: hereabouts the train was behaving like a small boat on a stormy sea. One is accustomed to the bits between coaches moving beneath one's feet – that's unalarming. In this case however there were no bits: one had to leap from coach to coach. As we moved slowly along the corridor of the second coach I felt the floor giving beneath my feet and momentarily I panicked. (Readers of some of my previous books – e.g., Laos, Siberia – will understand why.) However, the sinking floor sensation happened repeatedly and was just another of the Bayamo service's idiosyncrasies and not immediately threatening – though one day those rotting boards may well claim victims.

In coach number 6 my guide used his cigarette-lighter to peer at labels, then roused a man comfortably curled up on two seats – his and mine, apparently. Without complaint, he shifted his position as I thanked my guide; until then, he and I had exchanged not a word. With rucksack on lap, because I couldn't see where to store it, I leant back in my seat and received a small but painful scalp wound; it oozed enough blood to matt my hair. Where a headrest had been three sharp metal spikes protruded. My bag contained one tin of Buccanero, for emergencies. I now felt its time had come and quickly drank it – a mistake . . .

In due course those 355 ml. sought the exit and by the light of a full moon, newly emerged from dispersing clouds, I located the *banyo* – seemingly occupied. Having waited a reasonable time I tried the door again, pushing hard. It swung open to reveal a vacuum: below was Mother Earth. At a certain point one ceases to believe in the reality of what's happening – it must all be an illusion – yet somehow one has to go along with it. But for the moon, I would have stepped forward to my death – not exactly a premature death but an unpleasant and rather silly way to go. The door bore a prominent notice – DANGER! DO NOT OPEN! – but some more drastic deterrent is required in an unlit train that habitually travels by night. Opposite the *banyo* was the coach exit, its steps conveniently missing so that one could pee, more or less accurately, on to the track. But only more or less: such situations provoke penis envy.

The *banyo* at the other end of number 6, visited during the day, had no door – or loo or washbasin, though their sites were obvious. Here one had to relieve one's bladder and bowels in full view of passers-by. The latter activity was performed as close as possible to the walls – a much used space, halfway through our twenty-hour journey.

We covered the first two hundred and fifty miles in eleven and a half hours including a long stop in Santa Clara, while a passenger train and two freight trains passed on their way to Havana. Then, speeding up, we achieved fifty miles in one and a half hours. After that I lost interest in our progress and concentrated on my awakening companions. All five were going to a conference at Bayamo University and their company made the travail of moving to coach 6 seem worthwhile. Four spoke English – 'necessary for our research'. Academic salaries left them with no choice but to take this un-believable train, one-third the price of the cheapest bus. My tourist ticket cost CP25.50, they paid the equivalent of CP1.50.

Moribund sugar-mills, their stacks visible from afar, punctuated these hundreds of miles of flatness. Some were inscribed 'MADE IN PERU: 1978'. My commenting on the job losses brought a sharp response from Aleida, leader of the academics. All those workers had been retrained, given new jobs. When I asked what sort of jobs my tone perhaps suggested scepticism and the Professor snapped, 'In factories and municipalities'. It would have been too provocative to wonder how those institutions suddenly came to need thousands of extra workers.

Aleida seemed to distrust the foreign writer. Her four male colleagues would, I intuited, have talked more freely but she, their senior in age and status, retained firm control of our exchanges. Sometimes my companions spoke English for my benefit, sometimes they argued in Spanish about Bush, Guantanamo Bay, tourism – and then one sensed the men's hesitancy when disagreements arose. Rather than assert themselves, they exchanged furtively supportive glances. It was of course a coincidence that the professor happened to be white – a thin, tense, humourless little woman – while her much more outgoing juniors were mulattos and a black.

From Bayamo's station a ten-minute walk took me to Miranda's rather luxurious *casa particulare* where my hostess exclaimed, '*Desde Havana el tren! Muy dificil!*' '*Si,*' I agreed, '*pero muy interesante!*'

Later, writing my diary, I recalled a stimulating debate at Key West's literary seminar: to what (if any) extent is it permissible for travel writers to embellish or exaggerate incidents – even to enhance narratives with fiction if that makes for a 'better read'? Our divergence of opinion was decisively age-related. The oldies – Peter Matthiessen, Barry Lopez and myself – were adamantly opposed to any element of fiction and only grudgingly tolerant of embellishments and exaggerations. I think it was Barry Lopez who noted that travel writers have a duty of accuracy. By being strictly factual they can make a small but not insignificant contribution to future generations' knowledge of how things were, in countries A, B or C, when they went that way. Someone mentioned Afghanistan as an example. The version of that country's culture and history currently being promoted is counter-balanced or contradicted by such travel writers as Mountstuart Elphinstone, Robert Warburton, George Robertson, Robert Byron, Ella Maillart, Peter Mayne, Eric Newby, Peter Levi (and myself). Incidentally, Peter Levi's perception seems even more painfully keen now than it was when he wrote in 1971: 'As a political entity Afghanistan is nothing but a chewed bone left over on the plate between Imperial Russia and British India.'

All of which leads up to a solemn declaration. I can assure my readers that the foregoing pages give a true and faithful account of the condition of Cuba's Havana-Bayamo rail service in the year 2006 AD.

How does the chemistry work, between people and places? Some find Bayamo 'dull', yet within hours it had captivated me – a quiet little city with a strong persona. In 1975, when Oriente province was divided, it became the capital of the new province of Granma but its significance has nothing to do with that 'promotion'. As the second (1513) of Velazquez's seven settlements, and the starting point of the Ten Years War (1868), and one of the starting points of the Revolution (1953), it is proudly and palpably history-soaked. My hostess, Miranda, disapproved of the few townsfolk who foolishly aspired to compete with Trinidad as a foreign exchange earner. She abhorred the prospect of thousands of coach passengers swarming through her territory. 'It's nicer,' she said, 'if people come with their independence – nicer for us and for them!' I couldn't have put it better myself.

Since the seventeenth century Bayamo has been one of Cuba's most prosperous towns, its wealth based on the usual mix of cattle, cane, rare timbers and large scale smuggling. For some two hundred years pirates visited regularly, despite the city being some forty-five miles inland, and in 1604 a French contingent killed the bishop. Prosperity was displayed in many fine buildings, of which few remain; Céspedes torched most of the town in January 1869, rather than surrender it to the Spaniards from whom he had captured it three months previously.

Carlos Manuel de Céspedes (rich planter, flowery poet, canny lawyer) also sacrificed his own son to the cause of liberty. The Spaniards held Oscar hostage and, when his father rejected a peace deal on their terms, they shot him, as threatened. In reply to the threat, Céspedes had declaimed, 'Oscar is not my only son. I am father to all the Cubans who have died to liberate their homeland'. He is therefore known as 'Padre de la Patria' though in fact he was less concerned about independence than about getting rid of Spanish rule. I was taken aback, during our train conversation, to realise that my well-read companions knew nothing about

Céspedes's annexationist tendencies. Silly of me to be surprised: in most (all?) countries, history's sails are trimmed to the prevailing wind.

The 1869 fire spared the town centre, and Céspedes's home survived. (Could the rebels have engineered this? Many were Céspedes's freed slaves, armed with machetes and a few guns.) Now Casa Natal Céspedes is a museum, the finest building overlooking the Plaza de Armas, its ground floor eighteenth century, the top floor an 1833 addition. The curator has contrived a credible copy of a colonial sugar magnate's residence with Cuban Medallón-style and nineteenth-century Spanish rococo furniture mingling beneath ornate chandeliers in high-ceilinged airy rooms. After Céspedes's death (in a skirmish with Spanish soldiers) in 1874, Oscar's infant son, another Carlos Miguel, inherited both the casa and those annexationist genes.

All vehicles, motor and equine, are excluded not only from the Plaza de Armas (aka Parque Céspedes) but from the narrow surrounding streets of single-storey, brightly-washed terraced homes. This tranquil park, bounded on four sides by mature trees, is paved with glossy pinkish marble. A bust of Perucho Figuerado, who fought in the front line during the Battle of Bayamo in the Ten Years War and composed 'La Bayamesa', has the words of Cuba's national anthem (since 1940) engraved on its plinth:

> To battle, run, people of Bayamo
> Let your country proudly observe you
> Fear not a glorious death
> For to die for your country is to live.
> To live in chains is to live in insult and drowning shame.
> Listen to the bugle calling you
> To arms, brave ones, run!

Dominating the park from atop a heavy granite column is a larger-than-life bronze 'Padre de la Patria'. Both this statue and the bust in his *casa natal* depict a remarkably handsome man without humour or warmth: but that could be the sculptor's fault.

Just around the corner, on the cobbled Plaza del Himno, is another survivor of the fire, Bayamo's most treasured possession, the sixteenth-century Iglesia de Santisimo Salvador, partly damaged in 1869, subsequently neglected but recently well restored. Here an unusual mural above the high altar unites religious and political themes: Bayamo's parish priest is blessing the rebels' flag on 8 November 1868. At that same service 'La Bayamesa' was first sung, by a women's choir. The flag itself, sewn by

Cespedes's wife, is on display in a very beautiful side-chapel, Capilla de la Dolorosa; its Mudejar-style ceiling, dating from 1740, remained miraculously (some say) untouched by flames.

Old Bayamo's long commercial street, General Garcia, had just been repaved with golden-brown stone slabs and showed ominous symptoms of 'joint ventures' – workmen converting dignified old buildings into snazzy *tiendas* and restaurants. This street takes one to Parque Ñico Lopéz, formerly the grounds of the military barracks.

Ñico Lopéz was a black printer from Havana, one of the youthful Fidel's closest friends and a founder member of the Movement, as Fidel's pre-Moncada following was known. On 26 July 1953 he and twenty-seven other young men attacked Bayamo's barracks while Fidel and his chrysalides guerrillas were attacking Moncada barracks. The plan was to stymie Batista reinforcements for Santiago. But even the best trained cavalry horses are scared by the unexpected and so many dark shapes silently swarming over the barrack's walls provoked much loud whinnying. Several of the rebels were immediately shot dead and are commemorated in the park. Ñico himself escaped, joined the Moncada exiles in Mexico in 1955, and in 1956 sailed back to Cuba aboard the *Granma*. When she was wrecked on the Cuban coast, he was among those killed by the Rural Guard. The few survivors, including Fidel and Ché, went on to form the nucleus of the Rebel Army.

In this secluded and well-tended little park, divided into sections by flights of marble steps, one suddenly feels close to the birth of the Revolution – much more so than around Santiago's Moncada barracks. Groups of *abuelos* were relaxing under the palms, reading *Granma* or playing chess. Finding the museum locked I made enquiries, then got into conversation with two octogenarians; both had learned basic English while training Rhodesian guerrillas in the late 1970s and had been encouraged, back home, to maintain their acquaintance with the language. To my astonishment, I set off an explosive argument by referring to Lopéz as the man who introduced Ché to Fidel. One *abuelo* furiously contradicted me, insisting that Raul had introduced them. His friend took my side (not that I had any strong feelings on the matter) and as they continued their argument in Spanish I marvelled at the passion aroused by this detail. Later I discovered that Raul was in fact responsible for that momentous introduction – but Ché first heard of Fidel through Lopéz, then asked Raul to introduce them. So in a sense both grandads were right. To my disappointment, neither was willing to reminisce about their posting abroad.

Velazquez's settlement was built on a highish curving cliff-top overlooking the Rio Bayamo, a site close to Parque Cespedes but now occupied by *bohios* and a few shaky-looking two-storey dwellings. When I went that way at sunrise, pigs and poultry were foraging along the grassy cliff edge and the shallow river was hidden by a dense mass of water-lilies – a serious environmental deterioration, complained Miranda. No more fish . . . She disbelieved in the municipality's plan to organise a clearance; they were spending too much on repaving General Garcia.

New Bayamo comes suddenly into view, most of it developed after the birth of Granma province. Here are the standard model four-storey apartment blocks, enormous schools, hospitals and municipal offices, sports grounds, playgrounds, a theatre, a cultural centre and dual-carriageways with thriving shrubs down their spines.

Beyond a suburb of substantial villas, a long walk took me to the almost-rural lakeside Parque Granma whence the Sierra Maestra, only rarely glimpsed in the city, is magnificently visible. Here grass grows high around tamarind and wild cotton trees, and an expansive children's park is fully furnished. The longer I spent in Cuba the more clearly I saw *concern for children* as one of Castroism's most significant features.

Returning by a different route, I passed under an incongruous motorway on stilts where squealing pigs were up for auction, arriving on bicycle carriers ingeniously adapted for the purpose. The bidding was brisk, men leading their purchases away on ropes. Pig manure is a precious fertiliser and two women carrying buckets and shovels were angrily disputing ownership of the various deposits. In New Bayamo other forms of litter were not being removed: evidently the historic centre keeps most street-sweepers fully occupied.

Even in February Bayamo is *hot* hot and by noon I was flagging and dehydrated. Wearily I plodded along a dual-carriageway, longing for a *tienda*. (Britain and Ireland, sharing a lurch into excessive drinking as a hobby, have much to learn from Cuba. Castroism has made drunkenness socially unacceptable and alcohol quite an elusive commodity – easily done, when a government is not in thrall to corporate interests.) I was about to take a horse-bus towards the centre when, outside the Astro bus terminus, a delivery man appeared carrying two crates of Hatuey. Following him into a bare little yard, behind a high blank wall, I saw five rickety round tables shaded by torn umbrellas. There was no counter, no shelving: one fetched Hatuey (only) from a small window in the bus station's rear wall. The young barman hesitated to serve a tourist: I should have been elsewhere, drinking Buccanero or Kristal. But he was a kind – and honest – young man who broke the law for this exhausted *abuela* and declined my proffered convertible peso, insisting on the correct Hatuey price: NP18.

The only other customer, a stocky white man in his mid-thirties, had observed my arrival with interest. On his way to fetch another Hatuey he paused to look down at my open note-book and asked, '*Pais?*'

'*Irlanda!* My lovely country for reading! And you my first *irlandesa* to meet! Wilde, Shaw, Joyce – all translated I read! I am artist, painter, many pictures – and ten the inspiration by *Ulysses*! But *Finnegan's Wake* makes too much problems for me . . . You have time to talk, we sit together?'

I was very happy to talk provided my companion did not expect me to solve his *Finnegan's Wake* problems.

Nelson had learned his English working on the fringes of Santiago's tourist industry and might be described as a 'dissident'. 'My parents named me for honouring Nelson Mandela, a better leader than ours. For his Africans he made many friends with big strong rich foreign companies. In South Africa everybody can buy everything they want in their own shops – not *tiendas*.'

It felt strange – almost shocking, yet reassuring – to hear a Cuban in Cuba referring to someone as 'a better leader' than Fidel. Then I wondered by whom (Radio Marti?) Nelson had been misinformed about the average South African's purchasing power.

Both Nelson's grandfathers had been imprisoned for a year or so in the early 1930s when they opposed Machado's régime. His father, a Communist Party official, had retired a few years previously. Likewise his urologist mother, though she had immediately volunteered to work on in Venezuela where she was earning no more than her keep. The 1998 Papal visit had caused a family rift. Nelson became deeply emotionally involved, deciding that only Roman Catholicism could save Cuba and the world. His parents were not amused when he condemned Revolutionary Cuba as 'a country of materialists' where Catholicism has been 'made dirty' by 'pagan superstitions'. He brushed aside my comment that his 72-year-old mother, working for nothing in some comfortless Venezuelan hilltown, could hardly be described as 'materialistic'.

Nelson was married to a young woman gainfully employed in a tourist hotel. He wanted five children, she wanted two at most and none until she had saved up enough 'to give them everything'. Nelson frowned at me and said, 'That's materialism!' I agreed, but pointed out that it was generated not by the Revolution but by its enemy, consumerism. Nelson thought for a moment, looking puzzled and worried: he was a very mixed-up young man. Then he fetched two more beers, refusing in a macho way to allow me to pay, and confessed that he was thinking about a divorce which would make him sad and guilty because the Catholic Church forbids divorce. However, it is also pro-babies – perhaps five babies would cancel out the divorce? What did I think? I suggested his seeking advice elsewhere, Roman Catholic moral theology being *ultra vires* for me.

Moments later the barman shouted a warning: the Santiago service was filling up. Nelson hugged me, thriftily poured the rest of his beer into my half-empty glass and rushed away. On his advice I spent the rest of the day in the Casa de la Trova where the most celebrated local group, La Familia, were playing – and where my impression of Bayamo as Cuba's friendliest city was reinforced.

My plan for the morrow was to try to get an eight-mile lift on the Bayamo-Manzanillo highway, then walk into the Sierra Maestra on a minor cul-de-sac road, via the little town of Bartolome Maso.

The packed truck-bus would accept no pesos, because I had to stand on its steps, clinging to a bar. From this vantage point I had a good view of expansive ranches, their arched and crested hacienda gateways still in place though rusted, their cattle in prime condition despite desiccated pastures.

Where my trek began the landscape was hilly and partially wooded and the Sierra Maestra loomed seductively, its creased ridges now discernible. For miles this narrow, broken road was accompanied by a clear green river in which *campesiños* laundered and ducks swam. The humidity was punishing; I became a Niagara of sweat and needed frequent rests. Here *bohíos* were scattered on open slopes, their livestock numerous: pigs, sheep, horses – no cattle. At noon I collapsed under a ceiba tree and for two hours read *The Fertile Prison*, Mario Mencia's account of Fidel's educational time in jail – foreshadowing those 'universities' that were to evolve in Northern Ireland's jails. Meanwhile I was being persecuted by tiny ferocious red ants. How can creatures *so* tiny contain a weapon able to cause such pain?

By 4.30 the scene had changed: cane fields surrounded me and the road was shadeless. An hour later I arrived in the straggling village of San Antonio de Baja, fifteen miles from my starting point and five miles from my destination. Five miles too many: heat exhaustion had defeated me. Unhopefully I roamed around asking, '*Tienda?*' But of course there was none. Then my roaming bore fruit. As I was leaving the village, in search of a secluded camp-site, an anxious looking young mulatta pursued me. 'You need food? Where you sleep? Come my house!' Alicia was a school teacher, living with her parents in a large roadside *bohío*. There was, unfortunately, a spare bed: her brother lay in Bayamo hospital with a fractured spine having fallen off an ox-cart piled high with cane. Both parents worked in Bartolomé Maso's *ingenio* – her mother as an accountant – and they farmed in a small way: three pigs, twenty sheep, uncounted poultry and four hectares of cane.

Over supper (the usual menu) Alicia translated her father's childhood recollections of three of Fidel's *compañeros* being hunted after the Moncada barracks attack, then finding refuge in this village. Alicia's maternal grand-father had been associated with the Bayamo barracks attack, as a provider of weapons.

I soon realised that this was another amiable and paradoxical CDR intervention – the foreigner in the village being kept under surveillance, judged harmless, then cared for though the caring involved breaking a law which the CDR was formed to ensure was not broken. A fascinating paradox, with its nice balance between the letter and the spirit . . . The Revolution genuinely fostered humanitarianism and it's reassuring to know that in places like San Antonio de Baja bureaucracy does not Rule OK.

Alicia assumed my destination to be Villa Santo Domingo, a small tourist centre deep in the Sierra Maestra, at the end of the road. From there groups are guided, at a price, to Turquino's summit and/or Conan-dancia de la Plata, Fidel's Rebel headquarters. I didn't reveal my plan to get off the road long before reaching Santo Domingo and coming to officialdom's attention. It irritated me to have to skulk when I only wanted to be alone in the mountains for a few days, possibly finding my way down to the coastal road where I had trekked with Rachel and the Trio, possibly emerging somewhere else. Exactly where didn't matter.

Next morning I lost the cool hours, so determined was my hostess to strengthen me with an omelette and so long did it take to find eggs 'laid wild'. By the time we said '*Adios*', at 8.45, I should have been out of cane-land at the beginning of the climb to coolness.

The sugar mill's survival explains Bartolomé Maso's air of well-being. It is what I incoherently think of as 'a big little town', a place with a friendly intimate feel though its long streets of single-storey tiled houses, in untidy sub-tropical gardens, cover a wide area.

Here came another delay. Tinned rations were essential for the days ahead but the *tienda* (a metal shipping-container) functioned only from

1.00 to 3.00. When the restaurant opened at noon I 'did a camel' and in this large, dingy, welcoming establishment ate well for NP37: a mountain of rice and beans, at least half a pound of tender *lean* roast pork, a hill of sweet potatoes and a mega-salad of tomatoes and crisp lettuce. (That last was a rare treat; Cubans are not keen on their greens despite the urgings of generations of health educators.)

All this over-filled my hump and, having bought six tins of Brazilian tinned beef, the digestive process required me to lie under a fig tree on the town's edge, watching a misfortunate horse scratching an open shoulder wound against the next tree. Beside me a hen was dealing with a hunk of coconut while across the road her week-old brood sought tasty morsels in horse manure. When a turkey vulture came gliding into view, just above the tree tops, Mother squawked a warning and hustled the chicks into a lean-to shed where a cow was tethered with her new-born calf. I had been told that these birds are valuable scavengers, not killers, but Mother Hen thought otherwise.

At 2.30 I went on my sweaty way, the gradient ever more severe, the panorama on my right ever wider and grander – crowded green foothills sloping down to a distant hazy plain. On my left irregular deforested slopes were separated by stony gullies: no *bohios*, no fields, no paths. One vehicle overtook me, an open lorry, newly painted and carrying a score of Turquino-bound Dutch. It stopped to offer a lift and my 'No thanks' caused comic bewilderment.

Where an earth track branched off I hesitated before noticing a small hand-carved arrow pointing to 'Campismo'. Around the next mountain came a surprise – a steep, brief descent to a few concrete dwellings and a polyclinic. This hamlet was still visible when at last I saw a faint path on a wide grassy slope. It led diagonally to a perfect camp-site (level, not stony) on a ridge top overlooking a wooded ravine containing a few palm-thatched *bohios*. Happily I unpacked my flea-bag and used it as a stool while diary-writing. The young man who soon ascended from the *bohios* hurried past me looking scared, not returning my greeting. As he traversed the slope I admired the grace of his speedy loping.

Forty minutes later a motor-bike's snarl ravaged the silence, then stopped. A figure appeared, hastening directly towards me, ignoring the path, and without any exchange of words I was captured by a brown-uniformed forest ranger wearing a hostile expression. Of course he was only doing his duty, though he might have done it more pleasantly. It seems we really were lucky in November, perhaps because of the Trio's disarming presence.

I did not enjoy my four-mile pillion ride to the *campismo* at the end of that earth track. I suspected Grumpy's accelerating around sharp bends was calculated to raise my fear-level (already high) and it displeased me to have to hold him in such a close embrace. As tourist resorts go, the *campismo* was innocuous, a score of thatched *cabañas* dotted around the sides of a bowl-valley with an alfresco restaurant overlooking many mountainous miles. Grumpy dumped me outside the reception office, then seemed disproportionately angry on hearing that Germans had occupied every *cabaña*. Much acrimonious debate followed; I wanted to sleep out, Grumpy insisted that I must register and sleep under a roof. He and the staff were not on good terms and as the light faded their quarrel widened to take in other topics. Finally I was led to a staff *cabañas*, the tariff reduced from CP26 to CP9 because it lacked TV, telephone, fan, bedside light, running water. When I tried to switch on the broken *banyo* light it gave me the worst electric shock of my life – for an instant I imagined, 'Heart attack!' But I appreciated this *cabañas*'s isolation: it stood near a forested mountainside not too steep to be investigated at dawn, before Grumpy or his equivalent came on duty. Cuba's tourist controls can be quite stressful when one isn't of an age to enjoy Cowboys and Injuns.

At Bayamo's Casa de la Trova a retired history teacher, whose English dated from the 1940s, had propounded his theory that the Sierra Maestra is short of transmontane paths not only because of the range's awkward configurations. Until comparatively recently, he said, most goods travelled from port to port; shipping cargoes from Santiago to Manzanillo or vice versa was both simpler and cheaper than driving mule-trains across the Sierra Maestra. Hence Cuba never needed the system of traders' tracks I had used in Nepal, Ethiopia, the Karakoram, the Andes, Laos – where the mountains are so much more formidable but water transport is not an option.

During the next three and a half days I was repeatedly baffled – but enjoyably so – by 'awkward configurations'. Escaping from Campismo Popular was the easy bit. Directly behind my *cabaña* the dawn light revealed concrete steps built into a one-hundred-foot cliff, giving access to a natural swimming pool in a sluggish river. This 'amenity' seemed little used by the Campismo guests; vegetation was taking over. Upstream from the pool secure stepping stones led to a distinct path – With One Bound I Was Free!

Any stranger focused on a particular destination would find these mountains frustrating. Several times, over the next few days, I had to retrace my steps: when an apparently purposeful path ended on a cliff-edge and I realised its only users were wood-cutters; or when the way was blocked by a creeper-entangled fallen tree, an obstacle I might have tackled ten years ago but not now with aged bones to be considered. As I had pre-calculated, water was no problem; a delicious stream ran through every ravine. The humidity was testing but the sun rarely touched me. Amidst these dense, damp forests I was moving through a green twilight, emerging at intervals on to open terraced slopes where two or three families cultivated coffee, their crop flourishing in the nearby shade. My CDR apprehension was not justified; the astounded *campesiños* were of course curious but never interventionist. I got no whiff of the suspicion and hostility encountered by the exhausted *Granma* survivors who struggled into the Sierra Maestra in December 1956. Soon they were reunited with other survivors and recruited four locals, bringing the platoon up to twenty by the end of the month.

At that date no government had provided the Sierra Maestra farmers with either protection or social services and most families, though they might have been occupying their homesteads for over a century, were regarded as squatters by the big landowners who claimed the right to evict them without warning. Many were in more or less permanent conflict with the authorities and therefore disinclined to help Batista's rebel-hunting Rural Guard. However, in early 1957 they were not yet ripe for revolution. Volunteers from the cities joined the Rebels in far greater numbers and Ché found the *campesiños*' apathy depressing. Fidel patiently set about overcoming it, emphasising that the Revolution would not only redistribute land but provided education and medical care for all. He also took a genuine interest in personal problems and listened to individual's opinions, a new experience for peasants so accustomed to being abused and humiliated. Moreover, the Rebels paid for food and other assistance, in contrast to the Rural Guard and National Army who helped themselves to whatever they fancied and sometimes requisitioned precious pack-mules. Fidel's execution of Chicho Osorio, a peculiarly vicious *mayorale* (land agent), also helped the Rebel cause. Usually the *mayorale* was a region's most detested man.

The family who sheltered me on Night One consisted of a thirty-ish couple, two small boys who soon overcame their shyness and invited me to play baseball, and a grandfather, Angel, who initiated me into the art of palm thatching. Unusually, they allowed me to sleep on the verandah, perhaps judging it kindest to give in to the whim of a daft foreigner who didn't know where she was going.

A new *bohio* was being built nearby, on the edge of the forest, to house Angel's younger son and his bride. It was to be three-roomed, all wood, earthen-floored, palm-thatched; the bamboo rafters were already in place. One tends to equate palm thatching with putting up a tent but in fact, as Angel demonstrated, preparing the fronds is labour-intensive. First you must find those of exactly the right quality and length and let them wither naturally in the sun before spreading them on wooden slats under a roof of other fronds and saturating them with water (in Angel's case hauled up from the bottom of a ravine on a fearsomely steep path). Three soakings are needed, leaving a day between the fronds drying out (*not* in the sun) and being resaturated. During this process unsuitable fronds are detected, those that might be responsible for future leaks. It's cheering to know that in a few places people retain the skills, and have access to the necessary materials, to build themselves a sound new home – for free.

The Sierra Maestra is famous for its shortage of zig-zag paths, despite such very steep slopes. Each day I came to a few dodgy stretches, some with unnerving drops into ravines – though given so much vegetation one wouldn't fall all the way. The main hazard is the friability of the soil in places – loose and dry, without boulders or roots to bind a path together. This makes for difficult ascents and terrifying descents, best accomplished on one's bottom. During the second afternoon I had my self-esteem restored by a *campesiño* who was doing the same thing, sitting on a wooden tray evidently designed for the purpose. I was then crawling up, clinging to shrubs, and on seeing me he grabbed a branch to halt his descent and expressed extreme concern. Where was I going to? Coming from? And why? My idiotic replies didn't reassure him and he went on his way – having offered me his toboggan – looking so worried that I feared he might contact a park ranger.

Some of the vegetation, varying with altitude, was unfamiliar: aggressive-looking bromeliads brandishing swords and spears, acres of blue-green thorny thickets, exuberant fountains of ferns, orchids large and small (given as one reason for guides being mandatory), and numerous, bizarre, contorted plants stirring memories of fairytale illustrations. As in Laotian forests (of which these reminded me) the bird-life was tantalising: flashes of red, blue, white, green, chestnut, only glimpsed through the obscuring foliage. In November the ornithological scene had disappointed us – but then, the chatter of tiny tongues does not facilitate bird-watching.

At most I walked six hours a day, slowly, and spent the other hours enjoying my immediate surroundings and chewing raisins while saluting the Rebel Army's energy. One exceptional journalist, Enrique Meneses, writing for *Paris Match*, spent four months with the guerrillas (other journalists gave up after four days or less) and reported that Fidel changed camp almost daily, leading his men up and down these gruelling gradients for at least twelve hours with occasional stops if they came to a *bohio* offering coffee. Whenever food was accepted (this happened rarely) the host received a hundred-peso gift.

Everybody around the few *bohios* I passed was friendly and invited me to rest but the usual gestures of welcome – water, coffee, homemade snacks – were absent. (I recall the same unavailability of refreshments at odd hours in rural Cameroon, far from all motor roads, where strangers are a novelty.) All these homes were earthen-floored and without running water but each had electricity. This is in telling contrast to the situation in many African countries where ginormous corporate-sponsored pylons span hundreds of miles of remote territory while beneath them thousands of homes are still lit by rags soaked in kerosene. There's no profit for generating companies in the wattage used by hut-dwellers.

These mountains are not camper-friendly (the Rebels used hammocks) and Night Two was sensationally uncomfortable. Having seen no *bohio* since noon I walked too far, hoping to reach one, then had to make my bed across a precipitous path where the law of gravity precluded sound sleep. My own fault: stupidly I had climbed out of a ravine where I could have slept soundly on the stream's level bank. Then the sun set and I dared not descend in darkness. However, the night noises almost made up for my perpetual motion. By day only bird calls break the silence, by night one becomes aware of a bustling population – croaks, hisses, grunts, wauls, squeaks, whines (some insect other than mosquitoes) and much rustling through the dead leaves. Of course nothing alarming: Cuba's fauna is benign, the ants and mosquitoes merely tiresome.

In the summer of 1958 Batista, emboldened by the failure of a badly organised general strike, announced a major assault on the Sierra Maestra. Against Fidel's three hundred or so guerrillas, General Eulogio Cantillo deployed ten thousand US-armed troops. By then there were quite a few foreign journalists around and a watching world could scarcely credit the news from Cuba. Cantillo's thousands were not winning quickly . . . Time passed and they were not winning slowly . . . Could it be Fidel was right when he insisted 'the people are with us'? Those ten thousand came from 'the people' and, if not yet 'with' the Rebels, they were unenthusiastic about opposing them. Especially on a battleground where the 'enemy' had had time to become intimate with every ridge, precipice, track, river and ravine. Cantillo's ill-trained men had never been required to operate on such demanding terrain.

On Day Three I was close to this battleground and, looking up at two of the highest crests, I wondered which one prompted Fidel's Thermopylae remark. Hereabouts a small band of hand-picked sharp-shooters, concealed on a crest, killed hundreds of troops as they clambered up these slopes, their heavy arms more of a hindrance than a help. No Rebel could ever be targeted amidst the trees, no conscript could hope to reach the crest alive. Thermopylae with knobs on . . .

In July 1958 two hundred and twenty soldiers were trapped in a ravine and disarmed. Fidel then asked Ché (an excellent chef) to prepare lunch for them while he was making arrangements to hand them over to the Red Cross – with maximum publicity. Another battalion, surrounded and captured in August, received the same treatment. Fidel then wrote to General Cantillo (one of several letters):

> . . . After all, we are your compatriots, not your enemies . . . Perhaps when the offensive is over, if we are still alive, I will write to you again to clarify my thinking, and to tell you what I think you, we and the army can do for the benefit of Cuba.

The Comandante also wrote to a battalion commander whose men had been put in Red Cross care:

> It would have been hard to imagine when we were together at university, that one day we would be fighting against each other, even though we perhaps do not even have different feelings about our country . . . I have often wondered about you and the comrades who studied with you. I said to myself: 'Where are they? Have they been arrested in one of the many conspiracies?' What a surprise to learn that you are here! And although the circumstances are difficult, I shall always be glad to hear from you. I write these lines on the spur of the moment, without asking you for anything, only to greet you and to wish you, very sincerely, good luck. All your men will be treated with the greatest respect and consideration. The officers will be permitted to keep their weapons.

Those who talked and wrote of 'Cuba's civil war' were missing the point. Civil wars have a different flavour.

By the end of Cantillo's eleven-week campaign it was clear that Batista would soon be replaced. His army was falling apart, many getting the

Thermopylae message and refusing to fight on, many others simply deser-
ting. The prospect of Rebels in government – even as part of a coalition –
horrified the head of the Caribbean desk at the US State Department. When
reminded that most people regarded Batista as a son of a bitch, he achieved
immortality of a sort by exclaiming – 'At least he's our son of a bitch!'

On Day Three I twice came upon vestigial ruins, bombed *bohios* and
outbuildings on ledges where coffee was still being cultivated. Throughout
Batista's offensive, bombing was not confined to the Rebels' real or imagined
positions. *Campesiños'* homes were attacked with equal ferocity, whether or
not particular families supported Fidel. (There's nothing new about NATO's
brutality in Afghanistan.) These bombers and bombs had been provided
by the US with the sickeningly hypocritical proviso that they would be used
'only in external defence' – shades of Britain's sales of armaments to
Indonesia and elsewhere. When in need of refuelling and rearming the
Cuban Air Force was made welcome at Guantanamo Bay naval base.
However, the US anti-Batista lobby was gaining strength and in response
to its pressure Lyman Kirkpatrick, the CIA's inspector-general, feebly
protested to Cuba's Minister of Defence about 'the extreme nature' of
BRAC's favourite tortures. (When is torture not extreme?) Hugh Thomas
has described BRAC as Batista's 'anti-Communist bureau which was
practically a branch of the CIA'. More effective than Kirkpatrick was the
US refusal to replenish Batista's armoury, though the British soon hastened
to his rescue with the sale, in September 1958, of seventeen Sea Fury
aircraft and fifteen Comet tanks. One of Batista's best buddies, the General
Manager in Cuba of the Shell Oil Company, promoted this deal and we
hardly need to be told (by Leycester Coltman) – 'The motives for the
contract at the British end were commercial rather than political.' Before
this deal was concluded Fidel telegraphed Harold Macmillan, the British
prime minister, begging him to stop the sale because those weapons would
be used against innocent civilians. His communication was ignored.

On the morning of Day Three I had to think about where I was, in
relation to any road. I had made provision for a three/four-day trek and my
rations were dwindling. The Sierra Maestra paths demanded lots of raisins
and those utterly repulsive tins of Brazilian beef contained more cereal than
protein. I intuited that I had been going around in circles and wasn't very
far (thirty miles?) from my starting point – which proved to be the case.

At noon I washed in a stream, lunched sparsely off those dwindling
raisins and considered my options. Here two routes converged: the easier,
narrow path went downstream through dense vegetation, the other was a

wide boulder stairway. Then I noticed horse-droppings on the stairway, quite fresh, suggesting a *bohio* not too far away.

An hour later – above the stairway, close to a ridgetop – the path ran level across a bare, red-brown cliff-face for some fifty yards. I was nearly over when the earth began to crumble beneath my feet – and here a falling body would hit boulders rather than bushes. That was a nightmare moment. I completely lost my nerve and when I put a hand on the cliff to steady myself it too crumbled. I should then have hastened forward (safe ground lay scarcely five yards ahead!) but in panic I froze, leaning on my umbrella which of course sent more of the cliff gently dribbling down. At that I regained my nerve and proceeded, the path continuing to crumble in my wake. Back on safe ground something unusual because man-made caught my eye: a sign (white paint on wood) hanging from a branch. It said: PELIGRO DE MUERTE, pointing to the cliff. Where the stairway ended I had taken the wrong path.

Resting on a mossy fallen tree-trunk, I remembered that potentially far more dangerous moment when terror immobilised me on a cliff-face high above the Indus river in the Karakoram while a six-year-old Rachel, unaware of my panic, trotted confidently ahead. An odd phenomenon, panic. Its paralysing illogic cancels out one's instinct of self-preservation, supposedly our strongest instinct though I've never believed that. The sane and normal reaction to a shifting cliff-face is to get off it, fast – not to stand around poking it with an umbrella.

Soon after 4.00 I prudently accepted an invitation to stay in one of three *bohios* on a flat ridgetop scattered with boulders almost as big as the dwellings. From here – my highest point – I was overlooking a mass of lower ridges and beyond them glittered the sea. So these were the very mountains I had gazed at, longingly, during our coastal trek. As happens in close-packed ranges, Turquino was now too near to be visible. The sea was scarcely ten miles away, as the turkey vulture flies, but a four-day trek, said my host, with no reliable source of food on the way. Andres was an elderly muleteer whose four sturdy pack-mules carried coffee to the motor road for onward transport. By sheer chance (that guardian angel again!) I had come to the start of a track – rather than a path – leading directly to the village of Santo Domingo.

As Andres and I walked back to the *bohio* from the mules' paddock two little boys pointed to me, burst into giggles and for this discourtesy were sternly reprimanded by their grandfather. It was easy to forgive them; tobogganing down long slopes without a toboggan had left my bottom on public display. That evening I sadly discarded a shredded garment of much sentimental value, bought in Sarajevo in 2000.

Andres made unusual efforts to help me over the language barrier; in Angola he had had years of multilingual experience. His four-roomed *bohio* accommodated himself and his wife Dora, their only son and his wife and the grandsons who continued to find me vastly amusing though they stifled their giggles when *abuelo* was around. A table and four chairs, all homemade, furnished the kitchen-living-room. On one plank wall hung several unidentifiable antique tools, three machetes, various bits of mule harness and a picture of the Sacred Heart – that same picture seen in many Irish homes until very recently. Above the nineteenth-century iron woodstove hung dented and chipped enamel mugs and jugs, and dented but shiny clean pots and pans, and a green plastic sieve looking incongruously 'modern'.

Dora was a vigorous septuagenarian able to carry loads of firewood I could hardly lift off the ground. She and Andres argued about my sleeping space, he being inclined to humour me, she definite that I must have the boys' single iron bed in the smallest room. At bedtime Andres pointed to the ceiling – palm fronds visible between the rafters – and said not to worry about nocturnal noises; the cat had kittened up there.

No number of mewing kittens could have disturbed me after that night on the path. In fact I overslept: the sun was up before me. Then, setting off, I observed Dora retrieving those smelly trousers I had furtively thrust under a boulder. No doubt her beloved Chico (who looked like a cross between a poodle and a mastiff) had sniffed them out.

The downward track had some slow difficult stages, large loose stones on steep slopes which reminded me of the extraordinary agility of mules. (As if I could ever forget!) Otherwise this was a comparatively easy seven-hour descent. Now I was impatiently looking forward to Islazul's tourist restaurant. I had eaten sparingly with the *campesiños*; no one I saw in the Sierra Maestra looked underfed but neither of those *bohios* had a surplus and rice served to a guest would mean someone going short.

The temperature rose horribly during the final hour. Villa Santo Domingo consists of twenty simple *cabañas* tucked away amidst tall trees, a restaurant/bar roofed but not walled and a tacky little souvenir shop with a despondent air – all of necessity on the right bank of the Rio Yara, this valley being almost a ravine. At 3.30 the receptionist explained that no food could be served before 6.00 p.m. And the *tienda* (a tiny hut) didn't sell food. At 6.00 the menu was limited to pasta smothered in ersatz chemical-flavoured tomato sauce containing something minced. But just then my only concern was quantity and to the waiter's astonishment I ate two *cenas*.

According to the leaflet beside my bed: 'Adventures are interesting, exciting and important facts that come our way and mark our lives forever. Santo Domingo Villa, from Islazul Granma, is where you can find your best adventure.'

One adventure takes tourists around Turquino to Las Cuevas on the coast. When the Villa's English-speaking manager assured me that I could follow this trail solo, because I had no ambition to climb Turquino, I did a private deal with a friendly waiter. He had access to surplus cooked pasta and, thus provisioned, I set off before sunrise.

The Turquino National Park's official border was no mere pole across the road but a two-storey wooden structure from which emerged a smiling, charming, stunningly handsome Park Guardian in a pea-green uniform. The manager had misinformed me. No walker was allowed beyond this barrier without a guide. (Had I been forty years younger, and had that Guardian been the guide, I might have said 'Yes please!') Motorists could drive on guideless to the end of the road, from where one path ascends Turquino and another descends to Las Cuevas. But throughout the park unguided walkers are *verboten*.

Señor Handsome, who spoke English on a par with my Spanish, seemed to understand, as few do, my wish to be alone with the mountains. (The manager had probably mistaken that wish for parsimony; guides are expensive.) On my map Señor Handsome pointed to the low ranges west of Havana – many footpaths, no guides required. Thanking him, I turned back towards Bartolomé Maso, toying with the notion of returning to that mule track and spending another few days (pasta-fuelled) going around in different circles. Then Señor Handsome (telepathy?) called me back. Gesturing towards the relevant area, beyond the Yara, he conveyed, with a kindly twinkle, his awareness that already I had been illegally going solo – an offence not to be repeated. The Sierra Maestra *campesiños* may be deprived of mobile phones but news gets around.

As promised by Fidel in 1957, the spread-out village of Santo Domingo has its school and its polyclinic and I paused to watch scores of cheerful pupils gathered around Martí's bust chanting a vow to emulate Ché. Their seniors go to a weekly boarding school in Bartolomé Maso.

The fifteen-mile San Domingo-Bartolomé Maso concrete road (one of Fidel's pet projects) was completed in 1981 and may well qualify for the

Guinness Book of Records. Many gradients' surfaces have to be deeply grooved, lest vehicles might fall off what can feel more like a cliff-face than a road. Despite being in reasonably good condition, I had to pause every thirty yards or so on the first ascent from Santo Domingo's ugly bridge. (This replaces a graceful wooden footbridge, its photograph now decorating the Villa bar.) On several descents my brake-muscles ached and I envied those locals who sat on plank trays, with four tiny wheels, and scooted past me at life-threatening speeds. In this exceptional terrain their lightweight trays, easily carried up the next ascent, are more energy-saving than bicycles.

The large, shapeless village of Providencia marks the halfway stage and has grown since finding itself on a motor-road – though not enough to support a *tienda*. Below the village, on the valley floor, I sat under a mango tree near a weedy stream too polluted for drinking and lessened my load of pasta (much more palatable on its own). These fifteen miles are almost entirely shadeless, following the contours of foothills long since deforested, and one sweats accordingly. When my water ran out I remembered the Campismo Popular bar, not far off the road, but fortunately resisted that temptation. I therefore arrived in Bartolomé Maso at 2.20, as a truck-bus was beginning to fill up for Bayamo. It also carried livestock: small kids – beautifully marked and distraught – stoically silent adolescent pigs, multi-coloured cockerels tucked under arms, a duck and drake gagged and bound in a bucket.

Rapid movement by public transport is uncommon in contemporary Cuba but that was my lucky day. By 4.30 I was in the Astro bus terminus booking the last seat on the overnight service to Havana. As it lacked air-conditioning or perceptible ventilation I streamed sweat for fourteen almost sleepless hours – then immediately transferred to the 9.00 a.m. Havana-Pinar del Rio service. Apparently Astro and Viazul were no longer rivals; the former had passed me over to the latter and all my fellow-passengers were Viñales-bound: German, English, Scandinavian, Canadian, Italian. Pinar del Rio, I was to discover, is not on the tourist industry's agenda for promotion.

Chapter 14

Beyond Havana's ailing industrial estates, which have leached out into Pinar del Rio province, the landscape is flat, deforested and intensively farmed. To the north rise the Cordillera Guaniguanico, my new playground, a long line of low blue hills running parallel to the *autopista*.

One has to struggle to imagine how this region must have looked in the nineteenth century when it was eulogised as 'the Garden of Cuba'. Those eulogists were numerous; European and North American travellers found Cuba – so conveniently placed on the main Caribbean/Gulf of Mexico sea lanes – an attractive détour and quite a few stayed much longer than planned. A list of their books, in English alone, needs several pages – fat volumes explicitly entitled *Letters from the Havana During the Year 1820 Containing an Account of the Present State of the Island of Cuba* (London 1821), *Letters Written in the Interior of Cuba* (Boston 1828), *The Island of Cuba: Its Resources, Progress and Prospects* (London 1853) – and so on. During the first half of the century, when coffee was as important as (in this region more important than) sugar, the *cafetales* stimulated much purple prose. In 1844 John Wurdemann wrote:

> Imagine more than three hundred acres of land planted in regular squares with evenly pruned shrubs . . . intersected by broad alleys of palms, oranges, mangoes and other beautiful trees; the interstices between which are planted with lemons, pomegranates, cape-jessamines, tube-rose, lilies and various other gaudy and fragrant flowers . . . And when some of the flowers have given place to the ripened fruit; and the golden orange, the yellow mangoe, the lime, the lemon, the luscious caimito, the sugared zapote; the mellow alligator pear, the custard-apple and the rose-apple, giving to the palate the flavour of otto of roses; – when all these hang on the trees in oppressive abundance, and the ground is also covered with the over-ripe, the owner of a coffee estate might safely challenge the world for a fairer garden . . . The cultivator also plants his grounds in maize and plantains, which he sells to sugar estates; and yams, yucca, sweet potatoes and rice, which yields well on the uplands, for his own consumption.

Between 1792 and 1796 the world price of coffee had doubled and the number of *cafetales* increased from two in 1774 to two thousand and sixty-seven in 1827. For years the three hundred thousand coffee trees on the Carlota estate yielded an annual harvest worth more than one hundred thousand US dollars. A *cafetale* cost much less to establish and run than an *ingenio*; less land was needed, and fewer slaves and livestock, and simpler buildings and machinery. Thus coffee enabled a minority of creoles, some starting with few resources, to enjoy a patrician lifestyle on tastefully landscaped garden-farms providing an agreeable setting for 'cool and shady mansions . . . floored with marble, furnished with rich deep-hued Indian woods' each surrounded by 'its village of thatched huts laid out in a perfect square'. Levi Marrero noted that *cafetales* were designed as 'centres of civilisation and gracious living for their owners and invited guests'.

In mid-century three factors contributed to sugar's conquest of coffee: shifts in the international market, new technologies making cane the more profitable crop and the damage done by two major hurricanes, 4/5 October 1844 and 10/11 October 1846. (By then the custom of naming hurricanes after the saint's day on which they began was well established; these were San Francisco de Asis and San Francisco de Borja.) All the tall trees essential to protect young coffee bushes were snapped in two or torn up by the roots and replacements would take decades to mature. The more resilient *ingenios*, though equally devastated, usually recovered within a season or so. Estimates of slave hurricane casualties are imprecise, the injury or death of such creatures being commonly included with loss of cattle and other 'damage to property'.

Sugar's victory spelt disaster for the *cafetale* slaves. Most resident owners were comparatively humane, usually providing adequate food and some basic medical care, as one looks after valuable sick animals. *Cafetale* slaves lived in soundly constructed huts, en famille, and were allowed to grow vegetables for their own sustenance, and to rear poultry and pigs, and sell any surplus. They worked no more than ten hours a day and quite a few were able to save enough money, from the sale of livestock, to pay for a replacement and thus become 'a free person of colour'.

In contrast, on the fast-expanding *ingenios* slaves were crammed into fortified wooden barracks, some built 'to contain one thousand negroes'. Many owners lived in Havana or New York, ignoring the methods used by *administradores* to produce maximum profits. During the same period, many Irish peasants were also being exploited by absentee landlords. As the numbers of imported slaves increased, their working conditions and accommodation deteriorated and tensions heightened. Not surprisingly, the sale or lease to *ingenios* of 'pampered' *cafetale* slaves provoked more frequent and desperate rebellions. The same Dr John Wurdemann quoted above, a visitor from the US, reported on how 'people of colour' were punished after the 1843 rebellion when the authorities suspected an island-wide conspiracy. Accused men

> . . . were subjected to the lash to extort confessions . . . A thousand lashes were in many cases inflicted on a single Negro; a great number died under this continued torture, and still more from spasms, and gangrene of wounds.

In the 1850s a British merchant, Jacob Omnium, echoed many other shocked observers of the *ingenios*:

> On every estate (I scarcely hope to be believed when I state the fact) every slave was worked under the whip eighteen hours out of the twenty-four, and, in the boiling houses, from 5 a.m. to 6 p.m., and from 11 a.m. to midnight . . . The sound of the hellish lash was incessant; indeed, was necessary to keep the overtasked wretches awake.

Another Englishman, Robert Baird, commented that between 1845 and 1850:

> . . . the price of slaves rose greatly; and such was the demand occasioned by the increase of sugar cultivation, that slaves formerly considered so old, infirm and superannuated as to be exempted from working were again put to work; and some were drafted from the lighter work of the coffee plantations . . . and these consequences arose solely from the fact that the slavers were unable to supply the demand with sufficient rapidity, being prevented by the vigilance of the British and French cruising squadrons.

British ships had been regularly patrolling Cuba's coasts since the early nineteenth century when, for diverse reasons, Britain was leading the anti-slavery campaign. These patrols sought to enforce the new law against slave-trading, as distinct from slave-owning, and were so successful that smuggled Africans became ever more expensive. The Creoles sullenly resented what they regarded as Madrid's subservience to London and this boosted 'annexationism'. As Domingo del Monte, a prominent planter, pointed out in 1838, 'The USA has since its founding enjoyed the greatest political liberty, and they still have slaves'.

The *autopista*'s twelve-foot-high roadside hoardings announced the local presence of various agricultural organisations and agencies: UBPC, CCS, ANAP, CPA, INRA. INRA is the Daddy of them all, the National Institute for Agrarian Reform which in 1959 and 1963 redistributed twelve thousand estates. (In 1958 seventy per cent of agricultural land was still owned by eight per cent of the population – if one may include in Cuba's population those US citizens and corporations who were among the largest landowners.) The government converted forty-four per cent of all ranching and arable land to state farms on which former seasonal workers were permanently employed at a fixed wage. Small farmers retained possession of their land and the number of such farms increased from forty-five thousand to one hundred and sixty thousand. *Campesiños* may sell land only to the government (a safety device against the emergence of new large estates) but they may present or bequeath it to relatives.

In September 1993, when the Special Period was biting hard, the Basic Units of Cooperative Production (UBPCs) were formed to increase food production by replacing inefficient state farms with energetic co-ops. Hitherto the state had controlled seventy-five per cent of the agricultural economy. Now, under Decree-Law 142, the UBPCs gained the permanent right to use land (of course rent free) and to enjoy outright ownership of their produce. Each UBPC elected its own leader, managed its own bank account and was free to link wages and productivity. However, the state continues to demand quotas and fix prices. ANAP, the National Association of Small Producers, negotiates with the government about policies and prices. I never did find out what CCS and CPA do.

Pinar del Rio province, despite its fertility and nearness to Havana, lay undeveloped until the early eighteenth century when an influx of Canary Islanders first planted tobacco. (Cuba's widespread development began even later; in 1774 the population was 172,000 (or so) and only in the 1840s did it reach one million.) To this day tobacco remains Pinar's main crop; from here come the world's most illustrious cigars. However, the factories moved to Havana in the late nineteenth century and ever since the provincial capital, founded in 1669, has been a backwater.

At 11.00 a.m. the half-dozen *jineteros* awaiting the Viazul coach rushed towards me. Firmly I explained that I had friends to stay with and did not want a taxi or a porter to carry my rucksack. They gave me a few sullen stares, and muttered amongst themselves, but hassled no more.

Pinar's broken streets and pavements and paint-starved buildings reminded me of Centro Habana without the buzz – but with the stench of blocked drains and rotting garbage. The centre's neo-classical buildings affirm lost prosperity, their Corinthian or Ionic columns austerely plain or lavishly decorated with bas-reliefs. The most striking edifice, on a corner of the arcaded Calle Martí, is the Palacio de Guasch – 1909, a late addition. This might be described as a souvenir of Dr Guasch's travels. A wealthy globe-trotter, he acquired a taste for Gothic spires, Moorish arches, Baroque twirls, menacing dragons and other mythical monsters. The locals are very proud of this Palacio; I wondered what had been lost to clear its site.

A long walk took me to one of those dreary suburbs created when Castroism took on Cuba's housing shortage. My Key West letter of intro-duction to Aida and Garcia was unnecessary; they had been warned. English-speakers both, and recently retired, they lived on minute pensions irregularly augmented by their only emigré relative, not himself well-off. I knew how much he worried about their being doomed to a lonely old age. They had no children, were not *fidelistas* and had been badly shaken when some of their dissident friends were jailed.

Only Aida was at home when I arrived – a tall, handsome, silver-haired woman evidently in poor health. Garcia was out working on their vegetable plot. This couple belonged to one of the categories most vulnerable to Special Period privations: unlinked to tourism with few incoming dollars and too many middle-class inhibitions to learn how to wheel and deal effectively.

No doubt my exhaustion was obvious; after the ritual demitasse of coffee Aida suggested a siesta and I slept for three hours.

Next, a shopping expedition, my least favourite occupation but now essential (trousers). Luckily an equine bus, rare in Pinar's suburbs, soon overtook me; the other fifteen passengers were returning from some outlying market. Both mules looked over-worked and underfed; the Trio would have been outraged.

Calle Martí was crowded – with linking, chattering strollers, not with shoppers. Many wide windows displayed only a few pairs of shoes, or one length of fading curtain material, or a few saucepans, or two bras and a pair of briefs. In Sloane Street this use of space sends a certain would-be subtle signal, in Calle Martí the signal is different. Numerous young men were wearing brand new shoes – totally unsuitable, heavy brogues – which meant a supply had recently arrived; new imports are ipso facto coveted. Perhaps, I thought, this also explained the many skin-tight T-shirts, seeming several sizes too small. Aida later confirmed that the sloppy model is no longer trendy and the latest fashion much prized because it emphasises well-developed biceps and torsos. In one *tienda* baseball caps were marked CP11.50 to CP14.80 and an Adidas track-suit CP66. All garment departments catered for the Cubans' addiction to vibrant colours which somehow don't look garish when worn by them. I had to settle for a pair of khaki trousers (male): it was that or scarlet slacks with orange and blue vertical stripes. I didn't waste time seeking a new watch-strap; even in Havana such a luxury proved unobtainable. But a cobbler to mend my disintegrating sandal was spotted down a side street, sitting on his doorstep fixing a high-heeled slipper. A ten-minute job cost NP5.

Most guide-books ignore Pinar's stark two-towered Catedral de San Rosendo, standing in a bare yard surrounded by high railings. Happening upon it, I surveyed the porch notice-board; most eye-catching was an announcement that at 7.00 p.m. that very evening a meeting would be held to promote the beatification of Felix Varela. Interesting – beatification is a long step on the way to canonisation and a Cuban saint could be seen, by some, as boosting the counter-revolutionary cause. It was then 6.30 and, finding the inner door locked, I strolled nearby for twenty minutes.

In 1998, when Pope John Paul II described Felix Varela as 'the foundation stone of Cuban national identity', he wasn't greatly exaggerating. But the irony is that John Paul II might well have censured this brave Creole priest, a lecturer in philosophy and constitutional law at Havana's San Carlos seminary and one of a small clerical team who imported the Enlightenment to his homeland. As a member of Cuba's 1820 delegation to the Cortes in Madrid, he argued (without any support) that for the island's well-being slavery must be abolished completely and soon. (It was abolished sixty-six years later.) In 1823, after liberalism's collapse in Spain, Varela was exiled to the US where he published a newspaper, *El Habanero*, advocating Cuban independence. Although this had to be smuggled into Cuba, and distributed secretly, its message became so popular, especially among the young, that the Spanish authorities despatched a fortunately inexpert assassin to New York. Three years later Varela withdrew from direct political activity but his campaigning had already supplied a yeast to help the dough of nationalism rise faster.

At 6.50 I joined the score or so (mostly men) awaiting admission to the cathedral. On my approach, everyone fell silent; had they been dogs, one could have seen their hackles rising. In response to my amiable 'Buenas tardes!' a young man wearing a track-suit stepped forward. 'You want Mass? Not now, Domingo.' When I expressed interest in their Varela meeting an older man snapped something decisive and the young man said, 'Not for public, no enter now' – and turned away. I retreated, feeling ridiculously at a disadvantage and slightly angry. A large notice in a church porch does not suggest a private gathering.

Back with my friends, Garcia said he could have told me I wouldn't be admitted to any such meeting. That led to talk of the Varela Project – nothing to do with canonisation, everything to do with régime change. The project's aim had been to collect at least ten thousand signatures for a petition seeking a nation-wide referendum on multi-party democracy, respect for free association and free speech, an amnesty for dissident prisoners and more scope for private businesses. By now it was a dead duck within Cuba (shot down by constitutional lawyers) but its carcass was still being displayed and arousing sympathy on the international 'Transition to Democracy' scene.

I had just observed Garcia filling buckets from a Heath Robinson tangle of roadside pipes and Aida was unhappily apologetic about their lack of running water; it therefore seemed a good idea for the guest to move on next day. But no, my host and hostess looked genuinely dismayed, said I must stay at least three nights if I could put up with the discomfort. Several of their friends, who had signed the Varela Project petition, would like to talk with me, one in particular was an expert on its rise and fall. Thus tempted, I stayed – with the proviso that I, personally, would haul all the water I needed from the pavement pipes.

The next two days disquieted me not a little. Aida and Garcia and their friends were educated, thoughtful citizens, not rabid counter-revolutionaries but people who realised, when the Special Period set in, that Cubans needed, collectively, to reconsider the island's future, to debate various alternatives to the 'revolutionary socialism' of the previous three decades, not necessarily rejecting socialism per se but devising modifications to the 'Revolutionary' brand. The little group I met (seven in all) recognised that in 1959 radical action was inevitable, there was no room then for compromises. Now, however, unavoidable compromises were being made, willy-nilly – with more to come – yet they and their kind didn't feel free to contribute what they could to the restructuring process.

In 1997 a prominent quartet of would-be reformers emerged, led by Vladimiro Roca, a government advisor on foreign investment whose father had helped to found Cuba's pre-Revolutionary Communist Party. The others were Marta Beatriz Roque, an economist, Felix Bonne Carcasses, an engineer and Rene Gomez Manzano, a lawyer. Together they published a constructively critical analysis of the government's economic policy, a sober work, not written in a counter-revolutionary key. Yet in 1999 they were jailed, having been found guilty of inciting sedition and undermining Cuba's economy. Roca did about half of his four years and while inside became a convert to Catholicism. The others were soon released because of pressures applied by the Vatican, Mexico and Canada. If the quartet were not counter-revolutionaries when jailed, they certainly were on their release. All four then collaborated with Cuban-American hard-liners such as Ileana Ros-Lehtinen and Lincoln Diaz-Balart. And they were soon recruited by the US Interests Section for use in a campaign to encourage 'non-violent actions of destabilisation'.

When I asked what form such actions took I was given four examples from Pinar, three of which seemed to me not very 'destabilising'. However, were such endeavours coordinated and sustained one can't estimate the likely island-wide effect.

Firstly: financial and other support was given to a press agency describing itself as the 'Union of Independent Cuban Journalists and Writers'.

Secondly: a bond was forged between Pinar's Centre for Trade Union Studies and a Cuban-American Electrical Power Plants Trade Union in Miami.

Thirdly: Pinar acquired an 'independent library', the Interest Section chief (US ambassador by another name) arriving in person to deliver cartons of books to a dissident's home.

Fourthly: (and here I could smell danger) – the shortage of medicines and medical equipment, mainly caused by the US blockade, left an opening for the Interests Section to subsidise 'independent' pharmacies and basic clinics, often in the homes of dissident doctors who in two cases had gained US visas as rewards for co-operation. Through the 'independent' press agency this 'humanitarian aid' was widely publicised, internationally. Radio Marti regularly announced the opening of new clinics and pharmacies and centres where people might obtain treatment for a specific complaint such as asthma. Pinar's Union of Young Democrats of Cuba, egged on by two Miami hard-liners, Frank Hernandez Trujillo and Enrique Blanco, opened a pharmacy where medicines were handed out by a young man who knew as much about pharmacology – Garcia complained – as a dog about a holiday. Martha Beatriz Roque vigorously supported this medical project and claimed to have received enough money from Miami to equip two new clinics. The 'independent' Medical Association of Cuba depended on the Miami Medical Team Foundation, one of whose members, Dr Manuel Alzugaray Perez, was a friend of Otto Reich. In 1988 – Garcia recalled – Reich, as US ambassador in Caracas, organised the early release of the terrorist Orlando Bosch from his Venezuelan jail. In 2002, when Bush II appointed Reich his Special Envoy for Latin America, he at once set about securing government funding for Dr Alzugaray's counter-revolutionary projects.

In May of that year, as ex-President Jimmy Carter was on his way to Havana, the Varela petition, with 11,000 signatures, was handed in to the National Assembly. Days later, on Cuban TV, Carter praised the Varela initiative and Fidel – certainly embarrassed and probably enraged – started the legal scrutiny of the constitution that would kill it. According to the 1976 constitution, a ten thousand bloc of voters had the right to propose new legislation – but not to demand a referendum. The constitutional lawyers soon made this distinction clear. Anti-Castro legal eagles conceded that those lawyers did not have to distort the letter of the constitution to thwart the petition. Under Article 75, only the National Assembly may call a referendum and there is a crucial difference between an initiative to pass a new law and an initiative to amend the constitution – the pre-requisite for a multi-party election.

Despite Castroism's domestic victory over Varela the government's twitchiness persisted and less than a year later seventy-five dissidents – Roca among them – were arrested. For this Aida, Garcia and their friends, all signatories of the petition, laid much of the blame on Special Interests and their Cuban-American allies. Garcia lamented that Washington's attempt to impose 'democracy', US-style, on Cuba was leaving no space for 'democracy', Cuban-style, to grow. Those non-*fidelista* members of the intelligentsia I met in Pinar (and elsewhere) are genuine patriots in rather an old-fashioned, uncomplicated way that reminded me of my father. They value their country's independence, are proud of its having survived the Special Period and resent the Commission for Assistance to a Free Cuba. Aida spoke of the government's catastrophic failure to distinguish between patriotic dissidents, like the people in that room, and US puppets.

Cuba's leaders have not forgotten that in 1964 the CIA engineered the overthrow of Guyana's Cheddi Jagan government and initiated twenty years of extreme violence in Brazil. Also in the 1960s, they organised two military coups in three years in opposition to Ecuador's non-compliant elected governments. Similar manoeuvres triumphed in Indonesia, Guatamala, Chile. In the mid-1970s it was Portugal's turn; with CIA help the leftwing military government that had overthrown Salazar's dictatorship was replaced. When Ronald Reagan visited Pope John Paul II in June 1982 they colluded to put Solidarity in charge of Poland. A generation later, in 2001, Senator Jesse Helms proposed spending a hundred million dollars 'to duplicate in Cuba the success in Poland of the CIA, NED and the Vatican'.

On 20 May 2002 Bush II presented his 'Initiative for a New Cuba', based on 'increased and direct assistance to help build Cuban civil society leading to a new government'. A year later USAID boasted of spending six million dollars 'to promote a peaceful transition to democracy in Cuba'. The salient features of that transition had been made plain in the US Congress in 1998: the privatisation of agriculture, industry and education and 'the complete restructuring of the social security system'. The USAID website specifies seven uses for those six million dollars: 1) Solidarity with human rights activists; 2) dissemination of the work of independent journalists; 3) development of independent NGOs; 4) promoting workers' rights; 5) outreach to the Cuban people; 6) planning for future assistance to a transition government; 7) evaluation of the program.

Realpolitik is now, more than ever, synonymous with double standards, as Robert Cooper made plain in the *Observer* on 7 April 2002:

> The challenge to the postmodern world is to get used to the idea of double standards. When dealing with more old-fashioned kinds of states outside the postmodern continent of Europe, we need to revert to the rougher methods of an earlier era – force, pre-emptive attack, deception, whatever is necessary to deal with those who still live in the nineteenth-century world of every state for itself.

Robert Cooper is a senior British diplomat, was head of the Defence and Overseas Secretariat in Tony Blair's cabinet and then the prime minister's Special Representative for Afghanistan 2001–2. No doubt in that nineteenth-century state it gratified him to observe all the methods he prescribes being used to slaughter uncounted Afghan non-combatant men, women and children.

The Guantanamo Bay prison camp is, naturally, the Cubans' favourite example of double standards. Why is it OK for the US to kidnap and hold men captive for years on end, without charge, in defiance of both US and international law, and not OK for the Cuban government to imprison, after due process, citizens found guilty of collaborating with the foreign planners of régime change?

I suggested that certain collaborators may be too dumb to realise that on every continent Capitalism Rampant uses 'the spreading of democracy' and 'the defence of human rights' to disguise their real designs. That excuse was unpopular. One woman crisply observed, 'Even dumb Cubans have memories. We all know about those designs.' Garcia added realistically, 'And some Cubans like them, if they themselves can make a profit.'

Curiously, throughout all our long and intense conversations, Fidel's name was never mentioned. Although everyone criticised aspects of 'the government' or 'the Revolution', there were no excoriations of 'the dictator' or 'the tyrant'. I longed to ask, 'What do you make of Fidel as a *person*?' But such bluntness would have been a serious *faux pas*. The cross-currents were complex, many remarks delicately nuanced. I was with disillusioned people who still appreciated the self-respecting Cuba that Fidel had made possible. At that point *el comandante* would insist on a correction, arguing that the Cubans themselves, when at last given a chance, had made it possible. But his leadership gave them their chance and one has to wonder about the durability of Castroism's immaterial achievements.

That last evening in Pinar I wrote: 'Yes, all Cubans should of course be free to agitate for *change*, to protest against the Revolution's errors and inflexibility and to argue for constitutional adjustments. But *regime change*, as planned in detail by Washington, is something else: a take-over of a sovereign state by interests indifferent to the welfare of most citizens.'

Walking away from Pinar city, towards the Cordillera Guaniguanic, those wavy blue ridges along the horizon seemed puny substitutes for the Sierra Maestra. But in due course they would pleasantly surprise me.

Tobacco harvesting was not quite over and I watched top leaves being tenderly gathered in red earth fields. This labour is not amenable to mechanisation and many *vagueros* (tobacco farmers) are reputed to talk encouragingly to their plants. Gauze netting covered several fields, protecting the wrapper leaves from too much sun: those must be more pliable than the rest. I ventured off the road to peer into one of the tall, windowless *casas de tabaco*, thatched barns crudely constructed of wood but precisely aligned east to west for consistent exposure to sunlight. These might have been built by the earliest *vagueros*; the twentieth century – never mind the twenty-first – has left no mark here. Objects made of metal, or any synthetic material, must never be allowed anywhere near these precious drying leaves; sewn together in batches, they hang from long horizontal poles for about two months before being packed in wooden chests and stored for three fermenting months. Then, after grading, they go to Cuba's various factories to be carefully moistened and fermented for another two months.

Again they are dried, packed in bales wrapped in palm bark and left to mature for four years before being rolled into the sort of cigars not many people can afford to smoke.

Pinar del Rio planters whose land had been redistributed tried to achieve comparable crops in the US, Honduras, Nicaragua and Santo Domingo. Their total failure proved that this region is uniquely suited to growing the world's finest tobacco. In 1717 the colonial government established a monopoly and all tobacco had to be sold to Spain. Now the state is the sole manufacturer and distributor of cigars but individual *vagueros* are allowed to own seventeen-acre plots.

Both tobacco-growing and cigar-rolling are presumably immune to corruption, but I wondered to what extent it has effected 'distribution'. On Pinar's outskirts one of a new rash of wayside hoardings warned: 'Through corruption we can destroy ourselves and it would be our fault – Fidel.' According to Aida, twenty-eight thousand students had recently been re-cruited, all over Cuba, to combat corruption. In Cienfuegos and Pinar I saw some of those youngsters, always moving in pairs, wearing black T-shirts saying 'Social Worker' (a trifle bland, given their duties) and looking rather self-important as well they might. Some supervised petrol stations and reported that approximately fifty per cent of sales went unrecorded, were 'on the black'. Economics students, sent to audit state companies, found many cooked books and much evidence of deft pilfering on a daily basis. Garcia looked up his file of *Granma* cuttings and informed me that in 2003, during the last anti-corruption campaign, the police had found five hundred and twenty-five clandestine factories, three hundred and fifteen disguised warehouses and one hundred and eight-one illegal workshops. A government economist, having read this report, noted: 'With our crisis, and in view of wage levels, little can be done to stop embezzlement and corruption.'

To some Cubans of my generation the need for this Student Inspector Brigade marked another phase in the waning of Castroism's moral code. In Aida's view, those Oldies were talking nonsense because not all who operated 'dishonestly' (most Cubans) were corrupt counter-revolutionaries. Why – she demanded – should factories be clandestine, warehouses dis-guised and workshops illegal? Cubans were just using their energy and ability to create private sector opportunities. Garcia added that you can't produce a highly educated population and then expect people not to use their brains when their families are hungry. A strong point, I thought.

A three-hour walk – dull apart from the tobacco interest – took me through populous countryside on a squalidly littered minor road. My abrupt transition from one end of Cuba to the other spotlit the 'two Cubas' image: the allegedly more Caribbean-flavoured Oriente and the more (let it be said in a whisper) US-flavoured Occidente. In 1859 Anthony Trollope foresaw Havana becoming 'as much American as New Orleans'. Being ignorant of the rest of the Caribbean, I wouldn't know myself about Oriente's flavour but Pinar del Rio's country dwellers are noticeably less outgoing than the Sierra Madre *campesiños*. They also seem less racially mixed and their fellow-Cubans tend to depict them as backward, slow-thinking, bucolic. However, tobacco farming requires immense skill and slow-thinking doesn't mean unintelligent – or I hope it doesn't. (My own thoughts move at snail's pace, hence literary festivals and suchlike unnerve me; I think of the appropriate thing to say ten minutes after it would have been appropriate.)

At noonish I turned on to an four-mile earth track leading towards the base of the sierra and ending at a small hotel – tree-surrounded, standing on the shore of a reservoir created around 1990 and stretching to the horizon. Aida and Garcia were responsible for my living, during the next two days, in a style to which I am not accustomed. They had arranged for me to meet Oscar, another of their 'dissident' friends, in this secluded spot where three multi-course meals were included in the daily tariff – the most delicious food to come my way in Cuba. As I was to be on very short commons for the subsequent three days, this reinforced my faith in the camel system.

The lodging was less satisfactory because of the lake's proximity on three sides (one couldn't think of it as a reservoir). At breakfast-time clouds of mosquitoes dined voraciously before retiring for the day; rarely have I been so comprehensively bitten from ears to toes. By night their whine sounded like a CIA torture tool. My bedroom had one glass wall, net curtained, giving on to a wide balcony with a memorable view of the shimmering lake, the wooded plain and the looming mountains – now looking much less puny. The bed linen and three soft towels were brand new yet there was neither table nor chair, bedside light nor fan. The four bedrooms shared two large bathrooms without loo paper or soap, and the taps yielded a mere trickle. Figuring out those bathroom locks reminded me of the Rubic cube. When the doors closed they locked automatically and could be opened only from the other side which meant going through someone else's room. If the someone else did likewise with their other door at about the same time that bathroom became inaccessible until Management intervened, using a corkscrew in mysterious ways. There were no keys involved. The solution was to leave both doors permanently ajar which didn't bother me but the Dutch couple next door seemed shy about doing bathroom deeds behind unlocked doors.

Oscar arrived at sunset; a sprightly black octogenarian, he had hitch-hiked from his nearby home-town, then hired a *vaguero*'s horse and cart to take him up the track. We sat on my balcony, using pillows instead of chairs, ineffectually blowing clouds of cigar smoke towards clouds of mosquitoes and drinking rum and coke – a detestable mix but Oscar had generously arrived with the bottles.

I soon realised why my companion had been keen to talk with me. Researching Cuba's esoteric involvements in Africa was his hobby and he enjoyed publicising this aspect of the Revolution – little understood within Cuba, he asserted, and often misunderstood elsewhere. He himself first experienced Africa in Guinea-Bissau in 1969, three years into Cuba's 'intervention' and he spoke with reverential affection of Amilcar Cabral whom he knew well. 'A very, very clever guerrilla leader. An inspiring organiser – and wise, with integrity. Even Americans, when they met him, were impressed. He told us he wanted his country non-aligned, we weren't helping that tiny place to add it to the Soviet bloc. What's to be remembered, please, is something important. The Soviets didn't put us into our twenty-five-year cooperation with Guinea-Bissau, it started with Ché's African journey. The Soviets had weapons there since 1962 but no personnel. All those backward tribes couldn't use the arms until we came to teach them.'

Oscar failed to conceal his personal hurt and anger at Guinea-Bissau's later disloyalty. As the Special Period put an end (almost) to Cuban aid, the government, turning West, sought to delete their long relationship with the country which had been midwife to Guinea-Bissau's birth – helping the guerrillas to defeat the Portuguese, then training the army, founding the medical school and providing half the state's doctors. On the departure of Cuba's main military and civilian missions, a small medical team was left behind, funded by WHO and a Dutch NGO, with a meagre input from Havana. As the Portuguese began to reassert themselves many of the local doctors set up in private practice, including some who had been trained in Cuba at no cost to themselves. Oscar proudly reported that the remaining Cuban doctors, by then living on the skin of an onion, continued to treat the majority for free, an idiosyncrasy deeply resented by the private practitioners.

Between November 1975 and March 1976 more than thirty thousand Cuban soldiers went to Angola accompanied by two hundred doctors, in-cluding Oscar. His description of the post-colonial scene echoed stories I had heard in 1993 from Portuguese settled in South Africa. The retreating colonists stripped Angola of everything needed to run the administration and the economy – and of skilled personnel. By the end of 1976, one thousand four hundred Cuban experts – additions to the military and medical teams – were replacing some of the departed technicians at no cost to the Angolans.

Oscar regarded the CIA reaction to Angola's civil war as 'predictable'. They hired the press agency Black, Manafort, Stone and Kelly to 'sell' the right-wing UNITA and its leader, Jonas Savimbi, to the American public. Then, in cahoots with various European secret services, a high-powered psy-ops campaign was launched, inundating Reuters, AP, UPI and over two hundred radio stations with lurid stories about the Cuban troops' burning of villages, destruction of crops, mutilation of prisoners, raping of women, slaughtering of babies . . . 'Of course there was some raping,' said Oscar, 'but not much because the punishment was painful. The rest was lies.'

According to Roger Faligot, a French political analyst with a particular interest in secret services, this campaign (since exposed and condemned by a US Senate investigation) 'was successful in that a large number of intellectuals, "independents", "neutrals" and other noteworthies collabo-rated . . . many ignorant of the manipulation in which they played a part.'

Soon 'other sorts of Cubans' (Oscar's phrase) came on the scene. With the approval of the State Department and NSC, Black & Co. devised a working partnership between UNITA and CANF to frustrate the 1976 Clark Amendment, whereby the US Congress outlawed military support for either side in the Angolan Civil war. After the Amendment's repeal in July 1985 heavy arms worth hundreds of millions of dollars were rushed to UNITA. On Savimbi's arrival in Washington six months later he received a tumultuous welcome and CANF made a public announcement:

> Our ties with Jonas Savimbi and UNITA, his visit to the US and the material aid he is currently receiving from this country show the success of CANF's efforts in properly educating and informing US public opinion.

In April 1988 a group of CANF council members visited UNITA-held territory in Angola and signed a joint declaration. Point 5 promised: 'UNITA is committed to providing its determined efforts to assist the Cuban people until liberty and democracy are restored in their country.'

Come the '90s, no one who mattered seemed to notice the UN's repeated condemnations of UNITA's barbarities. Black & Co. continued to earn fat fees as they strove to keep the Savimbi image shining brightly through the African gloom. UNITA continued to be supported by the US and (less obviously) the EU. Oscar was fascinated to hear that my son-in-law then spent time in Angola attempting to alleviate the sufferings of the displaced – misfortunates born into a country where for so long diamonds, oil and iron have caused blood to flow fast and frequently.

During dinner we talked of things non-Cuban, though only the jolly mulatta waitress was present – a *habanera*, working so far from home because she had fallen in love with a *vaguero's* son. She sat on the edge of the next table as we ate, chatting non-stop, an amiable demonstration of democracy I had also noticed in the Hanabanilla and Playa Giron hotels. Taking Oscar as a sympathetic *abuelo* figure, she confided that her parents disapproved of her beloved because he couldn't (or wouldn't?) move to Havana – where she could earn far more, being a personable young woman, in any of the big tourist hotels. Afterwards Oscar told me he encouraged her to put love before convertible pesos. Being unable to follow their rapid conversation I was relating to Carlota, an enchanting half-grown tabby who could be heard raucously demanding breakfast before dawn and who frisked all day amongst the ceiling-high potted shrubs in the lobby-cum-restaurant. Her play was vigorous yet gentle; she kept her claws sheathed and her love-bites were nicely judged not quite to draw blood.

Next day, between swims in the too-warm lake, Oscar talked Africa non-stop. The oddest feature of Cuba's involvement on that continent was its seamless cloak of secrecy. The outlines of the internationalists' contribution to the defeat of South Africa's army had to be revealed – but not the details. Most Westerners know little or nothing about Cuba's missions, military and civilian, in Benin, Ethiopia, Cape Verde, Guinea, Mozambique, Sao Tome, Tanzania, the Congo. Were I a betting woman I'd wager a hundred pounds on ninety-nine per cent of my readers never before having heard of Cuba's crucially important role in Guinea-Bissau. And during the relevant decades uninvolved Cubans were no better informed. The internationalists, on returning home, followed their leaders' example and kept mum about their endeavours and achievements – which in itself was an unusual achievement, given the numbers involved. In the areas of health, education and construction, tens of thousands of Cuban experts – far outnumbering their military colleagues – worked for years in punishing environments.

'We were there to help free people,' said Oscar, 'not to make profit or propaganda for Cuba. All volunteers – able to choose if the salary stayed in the bank for our return or went every month to families. For the Africa bonus officers got US$30 a month and the rest US$20. Our food, except fruit, came from home – no luxuries, rice, beans, oil, coffee, sugar. Not the way Western aid workers live – big salaries, big hardship pay, fine houses, free vehicles and cheap drink! We lived same as Africans, all losing weight even if we didn't get parasite diseases, and Washington called our missions "Cuba's adventurism"!'

Towards sunset a bicitaxi collected Oscar and as we were saying *adios* he gave me a slip of paper and said, 'This book you must read, it tells everything honestly. Everything publicly known today, but there's more to come.' That was a very precise note, even giving the ISBN of Piero Gleijeses's *Conflicting Missions*. I bought it on my way home, in a Miami bookshop, and it is, as they say, unputdownable. Possibly Oscar provided the author with some of his information.

Chapter 15

No doubt my subconscious organised the next few days during which I saw not one human being. I didn't deliberately get lost but nor did I seek the most direct mountain path to Viñales, a small town half-an-hour's drive from Pinar. By noon on the first day I was in uninhabited territory though I didn't yet realise its extent. The area was without dwellings but not pristine; pre-Special Period it had been partially deforested and a few of my tracks were loggers'. These would have taken me more directly to peopled places but I was tempted by pathlets diving into densely wooded narrow valleys – untouched by loggers – and by mysterious stone cul-de-sac stairways leading to high precipices from which I gazed over apparently infinite expanses of ridges and ravines and summits.

I've said that Cubans are Cuba's main attraction yet this solitary interlude felt blissful. Perhaps I was an anchoress in a previous incarnation; I do need to be alone with a country to complete the bonding process. Barry Lopez understands this:

> My guess would be that someone someday will trace the roots of modern human loneliness to a loss of intimacy with a place, to our many breaks with the physical Earth. We are not out there much anymore. Even when we are, we often move too quickly to take things in. A member of the group who insists on lingering is "holding everyone else up" . . . The practice I strive for when I travel is to meet the land as if it were a person. To encounter it as if it were as deep in its meaning as human personality. I wait for it to speak.

Day One, the toughest stage, took me to an altitude at which the midday sun was endurable and the breeze cool. Juana (she with the boy-friend problem) had kindly provided an early breakfast and at sunrise I was crossing the pine-clad ridge above the lake. After a steep descent, through thick mixed forest, I forded a slightly murky stream before climbing diagonally across rough pastureland where grazed a few sheep, goats, horses. Then suddenly a small oval valley lay far below, completely enclosed, intensively cultivated, a cluster of *bohios* at one end – the last dwellings on my route. Soon after the path vanished on the edge of a recently ploughed field so precipitous that no tractor could ever have violated its rich red-brown soil.

Garcia told me that when the oil ran out the oxen-wise farmers in such mountainous regions were much in demand as agricultural instructors.

Retracing my steps, I found a little-used level pathlet winding through jungle; here two hands were needed to cope with the dangling creepers. That led to another world, an open golden-grassed plateau marked by an extraordinary phenomenon, a track some two yards wide, made of massive slabs and boulders of smooth brownish rock. Yet *not* 'made' but embedded in the earth, matching the low outcrops visible all around between bottle-brush pines and an abundance of flowering shrubs: pink, yellow, blue. Until sunset I followed this track wondering if just possibly, over many generations, the feet of indigenous tribes had defined it?

I then gathered a mattress of pine branches; even by the most Spartan standards all this uneven rockiness threatened sleep-deprivation. During 'supper' (sardines and bread buns) the temperature dropped pleasantly and before slipping into my thin flea-bag I donned all my garments: three T-shirts, two pairs of trousers.

An important part of the bonding-with-a-country process is sleeping out, feeling united with the totality of a place, sensing its nocturnal activities. Also, it helps to get our own planet's worries in perspective if the stars are allowed to do their hypnotic thing. Rationally regarded, that twinkling universe reduces all human concerns to insignificance. But at 4.10, when I awoke shivering, my discomfort became of immense significance. One thinks of dew as something gentle and rather poetical. Given time, it isn't – and now I was very damp. I considered walking on in the dark (no moon) but even by daylight that rock-track demanded caution.

Three miserable hours later I was on my way and soon lamenting my camera's recent breakdown. Although not a keen photographer, having no talent in that direction, I craved pictures where the track became strangely beautiful beyond verbal description. Erosion has wondrously sculpted all these rocks and now, underfoot, there was something else – eerily symmetrical designs. Imagine smooth expanses of pale grey and pale yellow rock, extending for miles, decorated with squares and triangles and oblongs and exact figures of eight – all drawn in brown, as though by someone using a broad-tipped marker, and in size quite uniform, from about six to twelve inches square. What force of nature could have produced such patterns? Again my mind went back to those indigenous tribes – but no! – too fanciful.

Next came long stretches where the boulders' colouring was almost equally astounding: marbled blue and silver, green and pink – bright, shining colours. These rocks were friable and on steep inclines the many little slivers – some transparent – made the track slippy.

When there are no fellow humans around one's mind rambles off in odd directions. Thinking about how close we all are, in time, to our primitive ancestors, I wondered if in some individuals certain genes skip thousands of generations – then reappear. Can one miss out on a whole evolutionary stage? My own gatherer gene is notably assertive: I'll happily spend many hours gathering watercress, wild garlic, blueberries, wild strawberries, mushrooms, blackberries, crab-apples, sloes, chestnuts. Yet I feel no impulse to grow anything, despite having a fertile acre or so on which enough could be grown to feed several families. This does suggest a missing gene, the one that enabled my ancestors to evolve from being wandering hunter-gatherers to being settled cultivators. And that lack may have a contemporary manifestation in my failure to keep up with our present evolutionary stage. My genes reject car ownership, TV, washing-machines, cell phones, computers, iPods and other such complex inno-vations. Were I a species rather than an individual I'd be doomed to extinction as a creature unable to adapt to its changing environment.

By mid-afternoon I could see, in the distance, my track ascending to the crest of a treeless, grassy ridge. Half an hour later it became a boulder stairway before ending – just like that. I stood on the brink of a deep inaccessible ravine, directly below me lay an almost sheer pine-covered mountainside.

At the foot of the stairway I should have taken a narrow pathlet which now led me across a level saddle to a lightly forested mountain where woodpeckers were busy. Descending to the meeting of three paths, at a stream crossing, I erected a 'tent' of pine branches to ensure a dew-free sleep. But of course the mosquitoes came to dinner; most streams have adjacent pools of stagnant water.

Next morning I chose the stream-side path. It climbed briefly, before winding for hours from mountain to mountain through cool forest – a few pines, mostly a tangle of unfamiliar trees and shrubs. Sometimes ground-creepers formed trip-wires and vine-swathes hung at face level and the birds – rarely visible – were numerous and melodious. Then came an open plain where a sandy track showed – not recent – traces of equine traffic. No trees remained, only hundreds of stumps and occasional charcoal-burning residues amidst low, red-leaved bushes, slender saplings and tall clumps of delicately tinted flowers – ideal bird-watching territory. Of the half-dozen species on view I could identify only hawks, woodpeckers and finches. I mistook the cartacuba for the zunzuncito – the smallest bird in the world, weighing one-fourteenth of an ounce. As cartacubas make wrens look burly this was an understandable error. Several of these exquisites flashed by me and at noon, when I had been sitting motionless beside a bush for some moments, one perched a mere yard from my face. I could see its eyes glinting, its long needle-like beak, its emerald back and crimson throat. That made my day.

The sandy track continued for miles across gently undulating deforested territory, brightened all the way by those glorious wild flowers and cooled by a steady breeze. In every direction long ridges and rounded summits stretched to far horizons.

At 5.15 I paused beside a small isolated hill, hereabouts a geological aberration. Near its base huge slabs of grey rock protruded and beneath one such shelf the sandy level ground looked like a comfort zone. I hesitated; my supplies were running low and it might be more prudent to walk on until dusk. But looking ahead I could discern no raw material for a 'tent' and that site was very tempting . . .

While eating my last tin of sardines I noticed dark clouds massing to the west – rain clouds? So perhaps I had been wise to give in to temptation.

Any Cuban could have told me that strong winds accompany blue-black clouds and unluckily this quasi-cave faced the wrong way. For an hour around midnight a gale drove heavy rain into my refuge. Then the clouds were swept away, the stars twinkled again and I deeply regretted not having an emergency flask of warming rum.

Day Four permitted no loitering; all those multi-course meals had done me well but now my hump felt empty. For eleven hours I walked with occasional five-minute pauses. An alarmingly reduced water supply made me grateful for that rain storm; it had left deep puddles on the track, slightly muddy but otherwise pure. Although not yet *suffering* from thirst I soon would be. When a mini-snake darted across the track – about a foot long, whip-thin, jet black – I hoped it augured well, like meeting a black cat.

At 1.20 the sand track joined a tractor-wide loggers' earth road, forming a T-junction. Should I turn left or right? Where was the nearest *bohío/* water? As this track – crudely bulldozed through the landscape – bore no signs of regular traffic it would probably be safer to go west, towards Viñales, instead of gambling on a nearer *bohío*.

During the next three hours I found myself listening anxiously for sounds of human habitation – playing children, barking dogs, crowing cocks. But the silence remained unbroken on this wide plateau, so long deforested that secondary growth flourished: scrawny trees, thick scrub. I met two families of feral pigs, the large sows wearing stiff crests of carroty hair, the tiny furry red-brown piglets reminding me of their Andean cousins. For an astonished moment they stood and stared, before fleeing into the bushes.

By mid-afternoon I knew I had a parasite problem; the itchiness earlier attributed to mosquito bites came from something very much worse – of which more anon.

At 4.00-ish my track could be seen turning left to climb a ridge and forty minutes later I was overlooking the extraordinary Viñales Valley, at which point I drank my last few mouthfuls of water. The descent took me to a hamlet on the edge of a motor-road, but I didn't ask for *agua*; my mind was veering towards Buccaneros – many Buccaneros. Beside a milestone saying 'Vinales: 10 km.' I sat waiting for a lift and soon a school bus illegally picked me up, the driver refusing any payment.

Viñales is a congenial small town, farm-based, founded in 1607. Its two tourist hotels are discreetly invisible from the centre where I was immediately captured by an elderly white woman waving a scrap of cardboard inscribed: 'BLANCA $20'. Blanca assured me her home was just around the corner. She lied. Around a corner, yes – but at the end of a mile-long street of single-storey *casas*. If uncaptured, I would have chosen one of the several main street lodgings. As we walked – Blanca wheeling a rattling bicycle – oxen were ambling back from the fields to their stables behind the houses and children were shoo-ing hens to their coops and next door to Blanca's home (which didn't display the logo) excited porcine noises greeted the filling of troughs.

In a stuffy room almost filled by two single beds I stripped quickly to inspect my tortured body and colonised garments. The invaders were bigger than human fleas but smaller than bedbugs: dark brown, hard-shelled, shiny, fast-moving – though easier to catch than fleas. They had fed chiefly off my buttocks, crotch, thighs and armpits with a few experimental forays elsewhere. Their bites were spectacular: crimson welts ten times their own size, extremely painful – throbbing that evening – and of an incomparable itchiness. The itch persisted for a week and as time passed the bites oozed a nasty goo; then the painfulness became soreness. A fortnight later, at home in Ireland, I was still suffering enough to crave sympathy from those of my intimates who could decently be invited to view my buttocks and adjacent areas. Presumably these insects normally reside in my quasi-cave, feeding off small mammals. Despite my long walk, I did not sleep well that night or for several nights to come.

As the missing logo indicated, Blanca and her large, lumbering mulatto husband were skiving. Together, looking slightly tense, they requested me to sign an obviously phoney register which neither the immigration officer not the tax inspector was ever going to see. I pretended not to notice though I should have haggled about those CP20, the tariff for first-class accommodation. My room didn't even have an interior light switch; at bedtime I had to cross the hallway. The bathroom lacked towel, soap, mirror, loo seat, shower curtain – and the shower was no more than a sporadic drip. Apart from that last, such 'lacks' don't bother me but when a daughter appeared, speaking basic English, it seemed kind to warn her that some fussy foreigners, if charged the top rate for this accommodation, might complain to officialdom. She took my warning with a light laugh; maybe her parents had 'an arrangement' . . .

Although the *mogote*-studded Viñales Valley attracts so many tourists, the town itself seems indifferent to Cuba's new industry. There was not a souvenir shop to be seen, or an open-air café featuring 'traditional' music, or a tourist office or taxi rank. The long pine-lined main street, of red-tiled, one-storey, porticoed houses with deep verandahs, is being officially preserved as a classic example of a colonial agricultural settlement. As some guide-books complain, there is 'nothing to do' in Viñales. This suited me: I needed a 'do nothing' day and dawdled around enjoying the nearby *mogotes* and noticing an unusual concentration on the Miami Five; all over the town their photographs and protesting posters were prominently displayed. Also, with the assistance of a small boy I found the beginning of the track to La Palma: this halves the road distance, making for an easy day's walk.

Being again in a supervised area, my track plan was thwarted in the first hamlet en route. A panting middle-aged woman pursued me. Where was my guide? No guide? She frowned and sighed and patted my shoulder sympathetically before turning me around: I must follow the motor-road or hire a guide. In the Viñales Valley – she consoled me – there is much for tourists to do. Everyone likes to visit the village where healing waters are sold, and the caves where runaway slaves used to hide, and the under-ground lakes where the fish are blind – and so on. At one of the hotels I could hire a guide. Thanking her for her advice, I took a short-cut to the main road, through tobacco fields.

The wide Viñales Valley and its numerous side-valleys (of which I was now being deprived) are populous and prosperous, the red soil fertile, the *mogotes* improbable – Nature at its most eccentric. 'Mogote' means 'haystack': an ill-chosen simile, lacking respect and dignity. Many of these freestanding, conical limestone outcrops rise to a thousand feet and one fantasises about their having been separately transported to this flatness from some sierra's foothills. In fact their formation is estimated to have begun one hundred and sixty million years ago. All are domed and sheer-sided and vividly green, supporting an immense variety of trees, shrubs, lianas, mosses, epiphytes, ferns. This specialised environment wildly excites a whole range of 'experts'. Here are more than twenty species of endemic flora, the cork palm grows nowhere else and *Chondropomete* is found only at a certain altitude on a few *mogotes*. This snail has long, fluorescent orange eyestalks visible by night from a considerable distance and a unique self-defence mechanism; extruding a length of elastic glue, it hangs beneath rocky shelves. (As I scratched, I wondered if my invaders are also something special, endemic to that sandy plateau.) Thrice I sat at a *mogote*'s base, gazing up in awe at its dense variety of vegetation, exhibited on so small a space.

Now hitch-hiking was inevitable; Cuba's least hot months (January and February) were over and I couldn't walk eighteen miles on that shadeless tarred road. At a junction ten miles from La Palma, I joined several would-be passengers in a collapsing bus-stop shelter surrounded by acres of tobacco, malanga, yuca, sweet potatoes. One man spoke English – Raul, a high school teacher on his way home to La Palma. Within half an hour two young men had jumped aboard a horse-cart going towards Viñales, then a young woman got a ride on a motor-bike. When an ambulance appeared Raul waved and shouted and pursued it, then vigorously beckoned me. We were in luck, the driver was his cousin and the ambulance was off-duty having just delivered a patient to Pinar del Rios's cardiac unit. Proudly Raul showed off the paramedical equipment which reminded me of the control room of a nuclear power station. According to the statistics, patients rarely die in Cuban ambulances, whatever their fate on arrival. Raul remarked that if the government has to choose, because of the US blockade, between the health service and public transport, he regards spending hours by the roadside as a lesser evil. An admirable attitude, yet it worried me. Using the blockade to explain all Cuba's difficulties is a thought-stopper. Cubans need to be asking, 'What else has gone wrong?'

La Palma – about the same size as Viñales but off the tourist trail – has no hotel or *casa particulares*. As a leading citizen known to everybody (many his past pupils), Raul set about breaking the law on my behalf with the assistance of a young army officer who recommended a certain *casa* on condition I paid in national pesos; were the family noticed spending convertible pesos they could be in trouble. The more I saw of the dual currency system the more it exasperated me.

As we walked through dreary streets to a pleasantly rural suburb, Raul gave me some disappointing advice. I had hoped to find a track from La Palma into the Sierra Rosario but – 'only with a guide . . . ' Raul, himself an enthusiastic hiker and amateur botanist, recommended instead a three-day walk from Bahia Honda to the little town of Los Arroyos a few miles from San Cristobal. He knew those mountains well, it was a clear path and if I kept well away from Soroa, where ecotourism was being developed, I should escape observation.

Outside the four-room *casa non-particulare*, Raul paused to 'explain' the family: a white octogenarian *abuelo* who had been senile for some years, his much younger mulatto wife, their two sons, a daughter-in-law and a grandson. The older son, Juan, worked in an agricultural co-op; his wife, Odelia, was a vet. Jorge, aged twenty, was jobless and a bit of a problem; Raul left the problem undefined.

My arrival bewildered everyone but recovery was rapid. Raul didn't linger: he had to attend what he described as 'a local democracy' meeting.

Behind the living-room, with its TV set and floor of polished cement, a small dark kitchen held a large fridge (Soviet made, long since defunct, now a cupboard), a homemade tin wood-stove and a chipped sink. Everything looked dingy, rusty, cracked, dented – but spotlessly clean. As in Jagua, the fully furnished bathroom was waterless. The verandah served as a fifth room where *abuelo* sat in his rocking chair, dribbling slightly and wearing a vague, sad smile while his wife chopped vegetables and sifted rice, keeping one eye on the year-old who had just begun to walk and was often held up to kiss his grandfather. As the family went to and fro everyone (including the problematic Jorge) paused to greet *abuelo*, to check that he was sitting comfortably, to dry his chin, to ask if he needed a drink – or just to stroke his forehead. This was a poor household in material terms but otherwise rich.

At sunset Odelia summoned me to eat in the kitchen at a little table under which sat a hopeful black and white cat very like my own beloved Francis; he stimulated a rare pang of homesickness. Soon his hopes were fulfilled: the boniness of the fish course defeated me. But the rice and chicken wing and green tomato salad were delicious.

Jorge didn't seem to resent being ousted from his room, a lean-to shed off the kitchen, its camp bed beneath an unshuttered window. Outside, within arm's length, a magnificent fighting-cock occupied a spacious cage and crowed aggressively from 12.50 a.m. but the tick bites were keeping me awake anyway. They bled that evening, surely a positive development – poison being eliminated.

The next day's heavily overcast sky made it possible to walk the twenty-four miles to Playa La Mulata on an equine earth-track beside a traffic-free road. This was a subtly tinted landscape of palm-filled hollows and goat-supporting hillocks, new-ploughed tobacco fields, coffee groves, orange orchards and paddy-fields. From these last rose swarms of daytime mosquitoes – and whoever said mosquitoes don't go for moving objects was wrong. That day's most durable memory is of a pearly grey sky above the navy blue Sierra Rosario above sloping expanses of orange ploughland.

In the little town of Playa La Mulata the vibes were rather disagreeable. Why do I say that? What right does one have to judge a place on fifteen minutes acquaintanceship? But that's too wide a debate for here and now. Let's just say that at 5.40 p.m. on 7 March those residents of La Mulata I chanced to meet didn't like me. (And come to think of it, why should they?)

A signpost directed me to the only *casa particulare* (two kilometres) and to a simple cliff-top motel (three kilometres) – the latter, alas! forbidden to foreigners. Mentally I congratulated the authorities who had reserved for Cubans this superb coastal stretch, undefiled by developers. But Pedro, the son of the *casa particulare*, later pointed out that jagged rocky shorelines do not appeal to tourists. Beautiful they may be, but not economically viable. That phrase caught my attention and I discovered that Pedro, through a cousin in New Jersey, was doing a business management correspondence course.

Outside this substantial tiled farmhouse, its six rooms high-ceilinged and bright, a flock of noisy turkeys gubble-gubble-gubbled under lime and mango trees while beside the verandah a sow nursed ten two-day-old bonhams. In the dining room and front parlour china cabinets were filled with cut-glass brought back from 'reward' trips to Czechoslovakia and gay tiles patterned the floors. Marta, a tabby cat, rarely left her cushioned chair in the parlour where a nylon rice sack draped the TV, even when Roberto and Angelica were sitting in front of the set, listening attentively.

Pedro explained. TV images greatly agitated Marta whose first litter was imminent. Her owners had diagnosed ultra-sensitivity to unnatural movements and lighting effects. Pedro, smiling indulgently at his parents, diagnosed premature senility.

The register revealed that I was the first guest in over three months. Hence the low tariff: CP19 for B&B, the breakfast a sustaining three-course meal served at 6.30 to convenience me.

An alarming weather forecast (*cloudless!*) made an early start essential though Pedro reckoned I'd easily get a lift to Bahia Honda. Luckily I couldn't foresee that he was wrong; throughout that gruelling day hope sprang eternal. A few school buses overtook me but one should use them only in crises. None of the four truck-buses would stop; youths were clinging to the cab roofs.

Swayed by Pedro's optimism I'd skimped on water and by 11.00 needed to approach a *bohio* with my empty bottle. Yes, the surly young woman would fill it at the communal well – for CP3!

In a rare patch of shade I read for two midday hours, an odd little book by a sociologist, Aurelio Alonso Tejada, entitled *Church and Politics in Revolutionary Cuba* – the theme fascinating, the translation execrable. For example:

> Even though the Methodist text is still a criticising document and coincides in aspects that have been mentioned and emphasised on the same way by the Catholic message in the moral aspect, the Methodists do not pretend to outline an alternative project, either they grant the dialogue the role to broaden with the exile the social individual.

(Not recommended reading when it's 98°F in the shade.)

I struggled on beneath my umbrella which gives minimal protection in such temperatures. By now the terrain was more hilly: on my right recently deforested slopes, dusty and naked, on my left flat scrubby land. Then for a few miles my view was restricted on both sides by a reforestation scheme, high brown embankments dotted with junior palms, their fronds dull and apathetic. Next came a hill, still pine-clothed, where charcoal-burners were at work. From this crest the sea suddenly took over, its glittering blue immensity making the coastal strip below seem curiously insubstantial.

My least enjoyable Cuban hike ended at a bus-stop where a faded sign said Bahia Honda: five kilometres. When a packed bus arrived many more squeezed aboard and I wondered how often ribs are fractured on Cuba's public vehicles.

In an enormous town centre *tienda*, TRD Caribe, I stocked up for my

final treklet, then took a mule-bus to Motel Punta de Piedra. As Bahia
Honda has no tourist accommodation foreigners are accepted, though not
encouraged, in this motel two miles north of the town near the start of my
mountain path. That night I was the only foreign guest, the rest being
young Cuban labourers working on Soroa's development.

By dawnlight I was off, feeling rather tense, keen to get away from Bahia
Honda's outlying *bohios* before the residents had rubbed the sleep from
their eyes. A red-earth track climbed between royal palms and tall banana
plants, passing several *bohios* entwined by pink and white convolvulus.
Puzzled *campesiños* stared at me but none asked awkward questions. I ignored
them, as is not my wont, and tried to look purposeful and authoritative,
like a person on some important mission. (Botanical? Ornithological?
Entomological? The Sierra Rosario attracts all sort of experts.) By noon I
could relax: no habitations were visible.

Cuba's sierras don't lack variety: my three treklets took me into very
different worlds. Here were conical hills separated by narrowish valleys,
their vegetation so dense it seems impenetrable when seen from above, yet
all these little paths are much used and well defined. However, Raul had
not warned me about the plural; he had spoken of 'a clear path' and left
me with the impression one couldn't go astray. In fact, at the many
junctions, nothing pointed the way to Los Arroyos. And now I couldn't
afford to get lost; there was a plane to be caught, the sort that refunds
nothing if you miss it. In such circumstances their sense of direction helps
most people but not me; maybe hunter-gatherers didn't need this sense as
they wandered from cave to cave.

At 5.00-ish goats bleating in the distance led me to a long grassy ledge
near a summit. Amidst the *bohios* stood a neat little thatched polyclinic; it
really is true that Castroism brought health care to everyone. To camp so
early seemed unwise but where was the next level space? Then an elderly
woman noticed me, looked scared, called the doctor. He appeared in his
underpants with soap suds in his hair; he had spent the day touring his
district on foot – the paths were too steep for a riding-mule. A handsome
young black, Sofiel towered over the stocky locals. Anxiously I asked if this
was the path to Los Arroyos – it was. Sofiel's English improved as he
relaxed and stopped worrying about grammar but I don't think he ever
quite understood why an *abuela* was on the loose in these mountains.

In the *bohio* where Sofiel lodged his host – a blue-eyed, white-haired
coffee-farmer – grudgingly agreed that there was no alternative to shel-

tering me for the night. Later he softened and wanted his guest to know that he had served for three years in Angola and without Cuban help South Africa's apartheid régime would still be in power. (2006 was the thirtieth anniversary of the Cuban troops' first deployment to Angola, an event officially celebrated. Therefore many veterans felt free to refer proudly to their own contribution, about which they had kept silent for so long.)

At sunrise I was dismayed to hear an argument about a compulsory guide for the tourist. Sofiel sided with me, I'm not sure why. The dynamics between the elderly farmer and the young doctor were interesting, Sofiel's role in the community and his academic/urban background being finely balanced against seniority and CDR authoritarianism. When Sofiel won I went happily on my way as the eastern sky blazed, sheets of fiery cloud glowing through the treetops.

The descent from that ledge was tricky and one couldn't toboggan – too many tree roots and boulders. It led to a wider than usual valley where the shallow San Cristobal river had to be forded. Beyond, the way was un-mistakable: no more junctions and instead of going straight up and down the path zig-zagged humanely. As on the previous day, clouds half-filled the sky.

I met four solo *campesiños*, all men, and felt liberated enough to greet them cheerfully. Two muttered nervous responses while hastening past me, two stopped to satisfy their curiosity and one insisted on presenting me with a banana leaf package containing fried malanga, the homemade local equivalent of potato crisps.

By 6.30 I was beginning to dread a penitential sloping camp-site amidst dense vegetation of the thorny sort. Then the last of the light showed a tiny isolated *bohio* perched on stilts and occupied by a young black family, the father a provider of palm fronds ready for thatching. A three-year-old daughter shrieked in terror as I emerged from the bushes and initially her parents seemed almost hostile; but when I sought permission to sleep on the porch (some three feet by six) they offered the living-room floor.

Here were disturbing family vibes: a bullying husband, a cowed wife and child. I pretended to be asleep in a corner long before I was. There-after, itch and hunger pangs woke me repeatedly; it had seemed tactless to gorge on expensive delicacies (sardines, bread, chocolate) when there wasn't enough to share – perhaps a silly inhibition.

Day Three started with breakfast, once beyond sight of that hut. Soon after a riverside hamlet appeared, far below me, and ahead lay new terrain, the hills grassy, only dotted with dwarf palms. Therefore no shade . . . But a strong wind was blowing off the sea, pushing comforting clouds inland. I assumed such open hillsides – though broken by occasional bush-filled gullies – would be easy to negotiate. Not so: within an hour my distinct path had become a maze of pathlets, looking from a distance like a tangle of brown rope thrown on the green slopes. Twice I followed the least indistinct pathlet only to find it petering out in a gully. For over an hour I was flummoxed and in mid-afternoon mightily relieved to see one wide track going directly down to the Bahia Honda-San Cristobal motor road – never far from my route though now visible for the first time. Given my time constraint it seemed sensible to descend here. Thus I came to the road some fifteen miles from San Cristobal and ten miles short of Los Arroyos.

Where paths from opposite mountainsides met the road I joined five men and three women sitting on massive tree-root 'stools'. Some had been waiting since morning and one couple were prepared to go either way; they could do their business equally easily in Bahia Honda or San Cristobal. When a huge ancient open truck approached – less than half full – everyone cheered except me. How to get safely on board? This Soviet monster lacked a movable back, or steps, and its rusty, thin, wobbly metal sides were so high one could barely see the passengers' heads. My practiced companions scrambled up, using the colossal wheels as ladders while grasping a length of wire rope. Those already in situ shouted encouragingly and helped to haul them aboard. Eventually warnings about no other vehicle appearing overcame my solicitude for old bones. Up I went and two strong men heaved me over the loose, sharp side.

Whatever cargo this truck normally carried was oily and leaked; the floor resembled a black ice-rink and several women complained at length about their ruined clothes. Six people climbed off at Los Arroyos, nine climbed on. As we lurched slowly over potholes, I was just tall enough to be able to appreciate the panorama on our left – ranks of bleakly magnificent rock ridges, utterly unlike the mountains nearer the coast. When the wind became a gale a silver veil was drawn over those ridges and moments later rain drenched us and my shivering companions wailed and cursed. But the deluge was brief. Soon the distant plain came into view, its expanse gold-tinged in the evening light. San Cristobal's industrial outskirts looked, from afar, more important than the centre. Yet the middle-aged man who had moved to stand beside me, to practise his English, lamented the city's joblessness. Cuba's new industry wasn't helping, no tourist ever visited, the hotel was not for foreigners. But I could try my luck – he scribbled the address on my notebook cover – they might admit a stranded *abuela*.

When we stopped in a previously prosperous suburb two strong knights picked me up and delivered me over the side, like a sack, into the truck-driver's muscular arms. As my rucksack was being handed down a youth who had registered my accommodation problem shyly offered to help me find a *casa particulare*. Sergei was no *jinetero* (a species endemic to tourist zones) but a typically kind Cuban who lived in this suburb and hoped one of his neighbours might shelter me. A false hope: we knocked on three doors and three householders understandably declined to break the law by entertaining an inexplicable old woman wearing a battered and by now oil-stained rucksack. I then had to dissuade Sergei from guiding me to the hotel, far away in the centre.

San Cristobal (as big as Pinar del Rio) became notorious for a few weeks in 1962 as a Soviet nuclear base but is ignored by all my guidebooks and by the numerous Cuba-related volumes in my library. Unquestionably, this is Cuba's dreariest city; its dependence on heavy industry made it extra-vulnerable during the Special Period and now it feels and looks like a shunned place. If we may revert to vibes, San Cristobal's are . . . peculiar.

A sprawling three-storey building, on a corner of a colonnaded resi-dential street, had been the hotel but was now the city's Social Services' cultural centre. Outside the entrance fizzed an excited crowd; a morale-boosting visit from a famous Havana band had been organised for San Cristobal's Social Services workers and their families. This was explained by a sympathetic young black woman as I stood wearily leaning on the receptionist's desk. Looking around, I saw a half-collapsed sofa in a corner of the foyer – could I sleep on that? The young woman smiled, nodded, said 'OK.' At that moment a middle-aged white man appeared and was not sympathetic. Taking in the situation, he said 'No!', then tongue-lashed my ally before literally pushing me out on to the pavement. There he beckoned to an elderly black man with a hang-dog expression and a slight limp and ordered him to lead me to a lodging-house.

For a mile or so I followed José (a gentle character, clearly afraid of Señor Nasty) along broken pavements made malodorous by blocked sewers. The lodging-house proved to be a caravanserai where *campesiños* tethered horses and mules outside rooms forming three sides of a large courtyard. The proprietress, a frizzy dyed blonde, snapped 'No room!' and scowled at me. José pleaded for floor-space in her own quarters: he knew I was equipped to sleep anywhere. In reply she slammed the door. On his own

initiative José then tried three other *casas* – scattered, we were walking for half an hour. Obviously Señor Nasty had no power to order anyone to shelter me; José was on the same mission as Sergei. By now it was dark, San Cristobal's minor streets are unlit and the pavements' defects presented a real hazard. Back at the non-hotel Señor Nasty abused my guide for his 'failure', then ordered us to try again in another *barrio*. Whereupon I rebelled, sat on the steps and said, truthfully, that I was too tired to walk one more metre. At that José borrowed a bicycle from a by-stander and pedalled away into blackness.

By the light of a solitary tall street lamp I observed the passing traffic. One cyclist was transporting a large child on his carrier and the woman balanced on his handle-bars embraced a bucket. A pair of oxen were drawing a long creaking cart piled high with planks. Another cyclist pulled a wooden trailer containing two smallish pigs. Overhead, dozens of bats swooped swiftly. At ground level dozens of mosquitoes went for the Irish option – delicious new blood! Then two taxis (1950s vintage) delivered the Havana band plus Orestes, my saviour.

Orestes (small, slim, fortyish) was a senior provincial official and his presence at once subdued Señor Nasty. He spoke fluent English and asked, 'What's your problem?'

'I don't have one,' I replied. 'All I need is space to lie down, not a room with a bed. Someone else has the problem.'

Orestes laughed. 'But here we have a room with a bed, not a tourists' room but an OK place. And you're no tourist, they don't come here!'

Señor Nasty sulked in the background as Orestes led me up three flights of rickety stairs to an ill-lit canteen providing subsidised meals and Hatuey at NP10 per bottle. My host urged me to eat but I was too tired, craved only Hatuey. Over two bottles it transpired that Orestes came from Barracoa, where his wife and sons lived, and for eight months he hadn't been home 'because of our transport problems'. It impressed me that a senior official accepted, sadly but resignedly, his share of the Cuban people's hardship regime.

Orestes showed me to my room, one of many leading off a high gallery overlooking an enormous quadrangle/patio in which the *habaneros* were testing their sound equipment. This room's door was off its hinges, the walls didn't meet the sagging ceiling, all the electric fittings had been removed and both single-bed mattresses were blood- and semen-stained. It was a hot night so Orestes now called upon that Cuban ingenuity and adaptability of which Fidel so often boasts. A youth hurried in with a fan lacking a plug and

I watched in horror as he attached it to naked wires protruding from the wall. I hadn't seen such a contraption since my last visit to India some thirty years previously. Its noise resembled a grinding snore; occasionally it faltered, as though pausing to regain energy, then ground on relentlessly. I considered silencing it by pulling on the frayed flex but feared electrocution. Then, as the over-amplified band began its first number I realised how useful that fan would be, as a toothache is useful in conjunction with gout. Sleep was impossible until the party ended at 4.30 a.m.

At sunrise I could find no one to unlock a door – until, exploring beyond the patio, I almost fell over José, asleep on a pile of old carpets with a key around his neck.

Now San Cristobal's drab streets were enlivened by colourful groups of chattering, laughing schoolchildren, as well turned out here as elsewhere, the seniors wearing heavy satchels – some beautiful, woven of palm-fibre. I passed two schools, most teachers arriving on bicycles. At the *autopista* junction two women and two men were already waiting on the north side (for Havana) and several more on the south side (for Pinar). One woman grumbled about the Mustards being late because of that Social Services party . . .

From here the old nuclear weapons site was visible and it occurred to me (only half in jest) that perhaps San Cristobal has never quite recovered from that traumatic episode. But how valid is the general perception that all of humanity was then at risk? I reckoned (aged thirty-one, politically ignorant) that the superpower leaders were playing silly buggers. Now, reading and comparing Robert F. Kennedy's *Thirteen Days* and Carlos Lechuga's *In the Eye of the Storm*, 'silly buggers' seems to sum it up. Some US generals did yearn to press the button but neither Nikita Khrushchev nor John F. Kennedy was insane enough to go over the edge. Then, as now, it suited MIC (the military-industrial-complex against which Eisenhower famously warned his compatriots) to keep irrational fears on the boil. The self-authorised nuclear powers have never even pretended to abide by the Non-Proliferation Treaty. No wonder rational people everywhere are enraged by the illogic of Iran and North Korea being forbidden nuclear weapons while others 'enhance' their arsenals. What gives the present nuclear powers the right to a deterrent others may not acquire? Had Hans Blix discovered nukes ready to go, would Iraq have been invaded in March 2003?

My east-bound group numbered sixteen by the time two Mustards arrived with their STOP signs, tin whistles and pouches for pesos. I always enjoyed watching them at work, a fine example of crisis management.

Here NP3 was their reward for securing an *automovil* lift; truck passengers didn't have to pay but usually dropped a few centavos into the pouch. That morning most *automovils* were tourist-driven, therefore not stopped. Having been an early arrival did not entitle me to a seat in the first two *automovils* because our Mustard, an efficient elderly mulatto, had established that I wasn't in a hurry; men with important appointments in the city got those seats. A crowded Havana-bound farm truck was stopped, then condemned as unsuitable for the foreigner; even at a distance it reeked of pig manure. Senor Mustard urged me to wait for the next *automovil* and looked annoyed when I climbed aboard, far preferring a slow open truck to enclosure in a speeding car.

Two young women with infants on their laps squatted in corners; everyone else stood. Near me, leaning against the cab, a stressed-looking old man held a squirming, half-grown trussed pig between his legs. Three women were cherishing cartons of agitatedly cheeping chicks. Two young men were cherishing nylon sacks, each containing an indignantly crowing fighting cock. When one broke loose pandemonium preceded his capture. He was of an unattractive breed, his underparts featherless, all naked scarlet skin. Having once attended a cock-fight, in Ecuador, it shocks me that this barbarism persists in Fidel's Cuba.

Where the truck dropped me off, near the National Aquarium in Miramar, I had a two-hour walk to No. 403. The pace of change along the Malecón upset me. Granted, restoration was urgently needed – but not demolition. A quirkily handsome building had given way to a Fiat car showroom, its façade plastic-tiled. Other buildings, under the arcade, were being converted to tourist-bait shops while makeshift cafeterias had sprouted on recently cleared sites. All this within one month, since my visa visit. The Malecón buildings are not as old as they seem (mere centenarians) and as demolition proceeds, and one compares them with Old Havana's semi-ruins, they look much less soundly constructed. According to a too-credible rumour, various US fast-food chains had already made 'informal arrangements' to acquire certain Malecón properties in an unblockaded Cuba.

As I crossed Parque Central next morning (the eve of my departure) it seemed some sort of serious trouble was brewing. Civil dissension surfacing? Gang warfare breaking out? Or could those men be drunk or on drugs? But that would be very unCuban . . . I sat and watched the two large groups frenziedly arguing – loud hoarse shouts, aggressive gestures of a strange nature, faces distorted by passionate emotions. I feared at any moment to witness grievous bodily harm – yet none of the many passers-by paid the slightest attention to these extraordinary confrontations. Eventually the centavo dropped. All this emotional turmoil was to do with an international baseball game and the men's alarmingly violent gestures were no more than demonstrations of what some player should or should not have done.

Relieved, I went on my way to say 'adios' to friends in Old Havana, then found a *jinetero* keeping pace with me. 'You want cigars? Twenty-five Juliets, CP30 – in shop much bigger price. Real export cigars, no fake!'

I hesitated; cigars were on that day's shopping list. In fact CP30 was the exact *tienda* price but should I not let someone outside the tourist economy have those convertible pesos? Or would that be a counter-revolutionary encouragement of corruption? Should I sternly refuse to buy stolen goods? As the youth stood by a wide arched entrance, saying no more, his pleading expression decided me; his demeanour was diffident rather than slick. When I nodded he led me into a splendid falling-asunder mansion smelling of rotten wood. Within his third-floor flat all was neat and clean, as usual. His parents greeted me politely and offered coffee while he was unroping a large worn suitcase packed with cigars – many in the 'US$75 for five' category. Then he realised that here were no Juliets and I wanted nothing bigger. Gesturing towards a chair he said, 'Small moment you wait!' Out on the staircase he whistled piercingly and within a very small moment his brother appeared, carrying over his shoulder a sack of cigars, including Juliets. Then, to my dismay, I discovered that my purse held only CP10 – very embarrassing! My apology was elaborate, followed by a promise to do a deal on my return to Cuba in 2007 for the fortieth anniversary of Ché's execution. But CP30, eighteen months hence, was of no interest; that promise, though genuine, must have sounded unconvincingly glib. The young man thrust a box of Juliets into my hands and said, 'CP10 OK, give now please!'

As I stood irresolute, looking down at the box's pretty picture, Mother intervened. 'Is OK, CP10 – is all profit! Is hard to sell cigars another way, CP30 is right price, CP10 is best than no price!' Seeing her point, I handed over the note and departed with my stolen goods feeling immoral. Halfway down the staircase Mother overtook me, registering anxiety; I must conceal the box in my shoulder-bag, not let it be seen on the street as I left this building.

And that is the sad story of how a normally respectable *abuela* became a corrupt counter-Revolutionary.

Chapter 16

All the way to the airport my unlicenced taxi driver (by now an old friend) was listening tensely to a radio commentary on the Cuba versus Dominican Republic game. Once he became perilously over-excited and didn't notice a red light – which around Havana matters less than elsewhere. Evidently Cuba was losing, thereby traumatising a large percentage of the male population. In the airport's uncrowded outer concourse all eyes were on the overhead TV sets and at intervals viewers yelled or moaned or buried their faces in their hands.

The Air Jamaica desk was deserted; my 20.50 departure had been postponed to 23.45, arriving Kingston 1.15. A quick mental sum suggested a plane borrowed from some Aviation Museum: in one and a half hours you could almost sail the distance. Then I thought positive. My flight to Miami was scheduled for 14.50 next day and a pre-midnight landing would have involved an expensive hotel room, passengers being forbidden to sleep overnight at the airport. Arriving at 1.15 on my departure date I would not be overnighting . . .

Choosing a café table giving a wide view of the surrounding countryside, I slid a Buccanero out of my shoulder-bag; the airport price was unforgettable, CP2.50 for a one-convertible peso tin. Had I foreseen a five-hour wait that tin would not have been alone. At the next table three beautiful mulattos, surrounded by sierras of luggage, were joined by a policeman friend come to see them off; he too had brought his Buccanero from Outside. Immediately he lit a cigarette, defying the ubiquitous NO SMOKING signs, and in his protective presence several others quickly lit up. Watching the Caracas-bound mulattos moving to a check-in desk I noticed how light was their bulky luggage. Doubtless they were in the import business.

My waiting hours were profitably spent, reading a slim vol. found in the famous Plaza de Armas book market – Fidel's *Main Report to the 2nd Congress of the Communist Party of Cuba*. This 1980 speech, far from being obsolete, is essential reading for an understanding of the strengths and weaknesses of twenty-first-century Cuba. The anonymous translator was competent and I wondered why most of the expensive translations recently published by the Instituto Cubano del Libro are so atrociously mangled.

Twenty-four passengers underloaded our two hundred and sixty-seater plane. The only Cubans aboard – Lina and José, a middle-aged couple – were en route to a conference on the new Latin America/Caribbean economic union. Lina vomited frequently and the Japanese youth beside me wanted to do likewise but used some esoteric mind-over-matter technique to control his turbulent guts. This required him to let his body go limp and keep his eyes shut and isolate himself mentally from the rest of the world. The other twenty passengers were young Chinese doctors who had spent two weeks studying Cuban AIDS-control. José suspected they'd been wasting their time; what works on a small island with an efficient health service was unlikely to work in the New China.

At Manley airport the well-organised Chinese were swiftly processed in bulk and disappeared on a special coach. Air Jamaica then partially redeemed itself by providing free bunk beds in a windowless cell for those who had no hotel booked. At 2.00 a.m. our plan to share a taxi to Kingston, ten miles away, and there seek cheap lodgings, was quashed by a security officer.

In a maladorous airport workers' cafeteria my breakfast was filling but not tasty: yam, yucca, sweet potatoes and a kidney stew that made me feel like a dog chewing a tennis ball. It was depressing to be back in the globalised disposable world where a giant bin awaited my plate and cutlery. Most customers dumped part of their meal.

Then off by bus for a three-hour glimpse of Kingston. Billboards lined the road, branded foods competing garishly, and insurance companies, banks, digital cameras and cell phones proclaiming their superiority. Some agencies (those puzzled me) offered a Midas service: 'We help You to be AS RICH as You Want to be!' The culture shock was severe, after months of billboards quoting only the lofty thoughts of José Martí, Fidel, Ché & Co. Meanwhile, studying my fellow-passengers, I saw people poorly clad in dirty frayed garments and worn-out shoes, slumped in their seats looking not very healthy. But the Cubans would envy them their regular, affordable and not overcrowded bus service.

Downtown Kingston was sweltering (82°F), scruffy, thronged, colourful, raucous, grossly littered, reeking of urine (an olfactory experience sharper than Centro's defective drains) and with an unpleasant buzz: aggressiveness jangled. Bargaining in the open-air markets often brought out hostility between buyers and sellers, highlighting the benefits of fixed prices clearly marked, leaving no scope for 'free-market' hassles. The variety and quantity of available goods made Cuba seem seriously deprived, in consumerist terms. By any other standard, Jamaica seems the deprived country.

Kingston's motor traffic unnerved me; speeding cars rounded corners in the city centre as though on a race track. I had two very narrow escapes. Every few hundred yards giant billboards urged drivers to slow down – an obvious waste of public funds.

On the return bus journey a young woman – an Air Jamaica employee – deplored Kingston's murder rate. When I opined that Jamaica urgently needs a Fidel the young woman looked shocked and exclaimed, 'But he's a *Communist!*'

When the first wave of 'refugees' surged to Miami (and, in lesser numbers, to other US destinations) the Revolution's durability was unthinkable – seemed impossible. As counter-revolutionaries, backed by the US, they looked forward to an early return. Between January 1959 and October 1962 more than two hundred thousand emigrated; thirty-one per cent were technicians, managers, professionals, thirty-three per cent business-men and bureaucrats – the classes trained to run a country and economy. According to Cuba's 1953 census, fifty-two per cent of their generation had less than a fourth-grade education, but only four per cent of the émigrés (usually loyal family retainers) came from that layer.

It's futile to speculate but sometimes hard not to . . . *If* the US had accepted Cuba's Revolution, taken the compensation on offer to corporations and individuals, established normal trading relationships with the new regime but otherwise left the island to its own devices, Cuban socialism could have developed in its own non-aligned way, independent of the USSR. Moscow was not lusting to acquire a Caribbean property. Granted, Raul Castro and Ché were keen on the Soviet model of Marxism but Fidel did not declare Cuba to be a Socialist state until the very eve of the 1961 Bay of Pigs invasion when it became clear that the Revolution had to get off the Cold War fence.

My host-family in Miami were comparatively recent émigrés and allergic to hard-liners. Merci and Eber claimed to have migrated in 1993 not because they felt politically 'repressed' but because they were hungry and unwilling to expose their small sons to Special Period hardships which then seemed likely to continue indefinitely. Being sensible people, they were sceptical about the 'American way of life' as assiduously promoted by

Radio Marti and had never pictured themselves living in luxury in Miami. In fact their flat was more cramped, and very much more expensive to run, than the Centro flat where I had been entertained by Eber's mother. And the unutterable dreariness of their Miami suburb – pavements almost pedestrian-free, fast motor traffic incessant – felt humanly impoverished in contrast to Centro's crowded streets and vibrant squalor. The chronic homesickness to which they both admitted was not assuaged by living in the US's most Cuban/Latin American city where the Spanish language prevails over English. In fact that had made the readjustment harder – a 'so near and yet so far' feeling. And the implied requirement to be (or seem) anti-Castro upset them. 'We weren't against Fidel,' Merci insisted, 'only against hunger!' In 1994 they had considered moving elsewhere and rearing the boys simply as 'Americans' – delete 'Cuban'. But given their limited resources that would have been too risky; Miami's exile network had soon placed Eber in a steady job, ill-paid but secure. And Merci had found work, when the children were old enough, as the daily help of fabulously rich Cuban-Americans who employed three other servants. Her bus rides were long and expensive and her wages low but the perks were good: as-new cast-offs, that could be sold on another exile network, and high quality left-over foods – thrown in the trash can by most US house-holders. The boys also worked at weekends, washing-up in a Cuban restaurant, and were doing reasonably well at school and so far expending all their adolescent energy on baseball and netball. 'They're good guys,' said Eber proudly. Merci added, 'They know we left Cuba for them, as family. But they're real Americans, not interested in Cuba. That's OK, we wouldn't want them feeling political.'

This couple were themselves completely apolitical, too concerned with day-to-day survival to bother about the role of the Cuban Mafia in Florida, or the fate of Cuba post-Fidel, or the disadvantages of living in a non-socialist state. 'We're OK,' said Merci, 'so long as we stay healthy. Here it gets real bad if you're sick.'

Strolling the stereotypical streets I was conscious of being an oddity because on foot. Numerous attorneys' offices advertised their ability to solve tax/immigration/work permit/marital/property transfer. Numerous churches (Inc.) advertised – mostly in Spanish – their ability to save your soul/bring the Lord Jesus Christ into your home/protect your children from alcohol/rescue the unborn. Numerous car-stickers proclaimed (usually under the Stars and Stripes) – 'I'm proud to be American!' – 'God Bless America!' – 'One Nation under God!' – 'God Protects America!' There has to be some dis-ease at the root of all this vocal godliness. It's inconceivable that any European nation's citizens would thus affirm their patriotism. Other stickers warned, 'Iraq now, Cuba next!' Those are provided by CANF and at first their popularity alarmed me because a recent poll had showed some twenty-five per cent of Miami Cubans eager to go home. Then I reassured myself: as the original Cuban population ages, so the hardliners' influence is weakening.

My friends' flat was in a low-rise, run-down residential district well supplied with family-owned Cuban cafeterias where hand-written menus, propped on the counter, listed homemade dishes. In several I drank cups of excellent coffee à la Cuba but my experimental admission that I'd just spent a few months enjoying their homeland aroused hostility rather than interest.

On Merci's advice I took a free ride on the elevated metromover and had to admit that much of Miami's cityscape is quite beautiful in its excessive way. A fifty-five storey edifice of polished granite – then on Brickell Avenue the Southeast Financial Centre, seeming from afar like a piece of captured sky – and in every direction a surreal blending and contrasting and competing of soaring precipices and improbable curves and daring angles – all hectic innovations, outgrowths of the post-war boom.

Back at ground level my search for a watch-strap took me through a bazaar-like quarter of small boutiques, carpet-shops and jewellers' heavily defended stores. In one of the latter a white-haired Russian émigré decently volunteered to mend my strap instead of selling me a new one.

When Merci's employer, Vicente Mazaparra, learned of my existence he telephoned to offer hospitality; he did a little writing himself, I'd be very welcome to stay, we could talk books. My declining this kind invitation seemed to take him aback. Then he suggested dinner next evening and so I found myself in an architectural hybrid, an Old Havana palacio crossed with a Vedado villa.

In the Mazaparras' enclave mansions stood on wide green lawns surrounded by palms and pines and a planned variety of shrubs, some always in bloom. Elsewhere in Miami the grass was then brown and such well-watered expanses seemed an insensitive flaunting of wealth (green grass robbed of its innocence). High, wrought-iron gates were reinforced by cunning electronic gadgets, not crudely obvious but lethal (Vicente boasted) to intruders. The well-swept streets – not a cigar stump in sight – were tranquil, free of through traffic. Tall trees almost concealed forty-storey condominiums rising in the distance beyond a canal spanned by dainty arched foot-bridges. All these mansions (no two alike) had distinctively Cuban house names.

A distant black servant (security-officer-cum-butler) pressed some button to open the gate, then advanced, smiling, to escort me up a short driveway, past a graceful sparkling fountain incorporating Aphrodite. In a circular glass porch Vicente hugged me; the fact that hugging strangers had survived the move to Miami pleasantly surprised me. A moment later Flora appeared, as beautiful as her husband was handsome. More hugging and kissing before we moved through an amazing space – high ceiling, Moorish arches, mosaic floor, a white marble staircase with glowing mahogany banisters, illuminated by a stained glass triptych showing treasure galleons in Havana harbour. Slim marble columns framed a patio where ferns rioted and climbing orange trees wove tendrils around the balustrade of an upper gallery. There we sat in cane rocking-chairs (a nice link with the common man) – and what would I like to drink? A Mojito or Cuba Libre? Gin, whisky, brandy, vodka, wine? 'A Buccanero, please.' Vicente looked startled, then summoned the butler. Were there any Buccaneros in the servants' quarters? Happily there were . . .

Vicente's parents had left Havana within weeks of the Bearded Ones' arrival in January 1959. Flora too was Miami-born; her parents took fright in October 1958 as the Rebel Army moved closer and they visualised machete-armed mobs swarming into Miramar and beheading the rich.

'That was a bit silly!' laughed Flora. 'They weren't Batista's friends, they needn't have rushed away without their valuable stuff.'

Vicente emphasised that he had nothing against those left behind, he was only against Castro whose brigands has so terrorised the population into submission. 'Our people are OK,' he explained earnestly. 'Like in all Communist countries they're victims of tyranny. Once he's gone, they'll recover fast. It's happening already, Communism is dead in Cuba, same as elsewhere. In China now they're only pretending.'

'That's why Bush should lift the embargo this minute,' said Flora. 'Anyway most Americans never wanted it. It's been helping Castro for forty-four years, a lid hiding all his mistakes. Lift it and let's see what's underneath!'

The Mazaparras disdained Miami's CIA-aligned hard-liners; an unfortunate phenomenon, long since irrelevant. They themselves were quietly confident that a 'democratic' Cuba was nigh. 'That guy's had Parkinsons for years!' (This was three and a half months before Fidel's operation.) Not that they would want to leave Miami; their prosperity was deeply rooted in Florida's soil. But it would be fun to have a holiday home on the island and to extend their numerous interests southwards. Vicente readily acknowledged that the Revolution had bred an uncommonly well-educated population, a great resource for incoming investors. In a liberated Cuba the educational system would of course need drastic modification to purge future generations of the Communist infection and give them an appreciation of 'market mechanisms'. Flora quoted one Frank Nero, leader of the Beacon Council, a public-private consortium of four hundred Miami-Dade County businesses. According to Mr Nero, Cuba's shortage of pretty well everything meant that 'US construction firms are going to be very much in demand post-embargo'.

Complacently, Vicente foretold that soon Cuba would be where it was in the 1950s – richer than any Latin American country, richer even than Italy! Mildly I recalled that most Cubans were then ill-educated, malnourished and unmedicated. My companions seemed not to hear. I noted their assumption that Cuba's diaspora was entitled to take over the running of the island post-Fidel and would be welcomed home by a population most of whom were born since the Revolution. If you can only see a population longing to escape from a tyrant it's logical to assume that those who have always opposed the tyrant will be greeted with shouts of grateful joy.

The wide glass-roofed corridor to the loo had polychrome tiled wainscoting enlivened by dramatic bull-fighting moments and scenes from Don Quixote. In the dining-room – its square columns also tiled – a marble-topped console table supported a four-foot Virgin of Regla surrounded by porcelain and cut-glass. On one wall hung a large rococo-framed Sacred Heart, facing three life-size nudes by a celebrated Havana artist who has exhibited in New York's Museum of Modern Art but whose name escapes me (as all names do nowadays, unless written down on the spot). We sat close together at one end of a long mahogany table, its fourteen chairs mock-Chippendale, and enjoyed a meaty minestrone, red snapper, deep-fried pork steak stuffed with ham and cheese, fruit salad and/or ice-cream. Our table talk was of books and the environment. Vicente mentioned the possibility of completing the Cienfuegos nuclear power plant by way of celebrating Cuba's 'liberation' and my reaction caused Flora – a veteran anti-nuclear power campaigner – to become overexcited. Suddenly she had identified me as the author of *Race to the Finish?* (published in the US as *Nuclear Stakes*) and we happily ganged up against Vicente, an ardent advocate for the revival of the US's nuclear power industry.

Back in the patio, now softly lit by ingenious copper lantern-chandeliers, my curiosity was piqued by the Mazaparras' being so well-informed about recent 'human rights abuses' in Cuba, of which I had heard rumours en route. According to Vicente there had been a new surge of Actos de Repudio, 'acts of repudiation' involving mobs who harass the homes and persons of alleged counter-revolutionaries. He gave me a list of names and dates produced by his computer and coinciding with those rumours whispered to me in various places.

In January Juan Carlos Gonzales Leiva, President of the Cuba Human Rights Foundation, had for several days been put under house arrest by a mob who prevented his family from entering their home, played music to torture level on the pavement and cut off his electricity, water and telephone.

On 21 January a similar mob invaded the home of Juan Francisco Sigler Amaya, a member of the Alternative Option Independent Movement. Two of his brothers had been in jail since the March 2003 mass arrest of dissidents.

On 3 February Dr Pedro Arturo Hernandez Cabrero, President of the Commission for Attention to Health had had his home searched and numerous books, letters, photographs and a radio confiscated.

On 16 February Marta Beatriz Roque Cabello (released from jail in July 2004), was confined to her home for several hours while members of a Rapid Response Brigade shouted insults, played loud music and prevented anyone from entering or leaving the house.

On 31 January Guillermo Farinas, who described himself as 'an independent journalist' began a hunger-strike to obtain access to the internet for all Cubans. About him, Vicente commented, 'Remember what people said after Communism died in the Soviet Union? They said the fax machine killed it! And Castro knows the internet could do the same for Cuba!'

I agreed that all those cases were deplorable – and, I believed, had been accurately reported. But when the State Department openly admits that it funds dissidents, is it surprising that some *fidelistas* get very angry and behave very badly? As my Pinar friends had pointed out, Cubans who should be sitting down together, arguing constructively about Cuba's future, are pushed by US interference into destructive and embittering confrontations.

Vicente's riposte was a quote from John Bolton who had stated, when Under Secretary of State for Arms Control and International Security, 'We believe that Cuba has at least a limited offensive biological warfare research and development effort. Cuba has provided dual-use biotechnology to other rogue states.'

Flora then asked, 'Do you know that Cuba is listed in Washington as a "state sponsor of terrorism"? That's why we must intervene to help the dissidents. It wouldn't be right to leave them to fight alone!'

In my 'thank you' letter to the Mazaparras, written from Ireland, I quoted Wayne S. Smith, Chief of the US Special Interests Section from 1979-82 and a vigorous anti-blockade activist:

> When the US says its objective is to bring down the Cuban government, and then says that one of its means of accomplishing that is by providing funds to Cuban dissidents, it in effect places them in the position of being the paid agents of a foreign power seeking to overthrow their own. Inevitably, that severely limits their effectiveness.

Although the Mazaparras were so credulous about so many of Washington's absurdities ('rogue state', 'sponsor of terrorism', etc.) they did rage against Bush II's 2004 curtailing of émigré-island exchanges – reducing gift parcels, cash remittances and family visits. Indignantly Flora protested, 'That's punishing ordinary people, not the Party members who've never suffered a shortage of anything!'

Weeks later I was informed by Washington's Bureau of Western Hemisphere Affairs that the remittances restriction applied only to private individuals. 'NGOs wishing to provide financial support to civil society or religious organisations or members of such groups can apply for a specific license from OFAC to do so.' Such NGOs are mentioned in Caleb McCarry's 2006 report as valuable conduits for funding dissidents.

I was taking my leave, at midnight, when Flora decided that I must meet Paula and her parents. Despite the late hour she rang them and immediately I was invited to lunch next day. I sensed that as a protégé of the Mazaparras I would be welcomed into many local homes.

'This family will give you another angle on the Revolution,' said Vicente, doubtless hoping for a conversion. 'They're Mariel people, escaped in 1980.'

As was comically obvious, the black chauffeur found my working-class destination very puzzling. He himself was an interesting character, a fourth-generation family retainer, a preacher in his parish church and a vituperative counter-revolutionary.

In retrospect, the Mariel exodus is easily explained. A decade of increasing prosperity ended abruptly when plant diseases and bad weather wrecked the 1979 cane and tobacco crops. Belts had to be tightened while suspicions grew that too many Cuban pesos were being spent on Central American interventions. Also, the island had recently been exposed to a different way of life. In November 1978 Fidel decided, for multiple reasons, to allow Cuban-American families to visit their relatives (a freedom later limited by Washington) and restrictions on Cubans travelling abroad were eased, though never abolished. More than one hundred thousand Cuban-Americans flew into José Martí airport in 1979, injecting millions of dollars into the Cuban economy. They bore gifts of consumer durables, and circulated US magazines aglow with seductive advertisements, and showed photographs of their sleek new cars, parked outside brightly-painted homes surrounded by shiny swings and slides. Not all those photographs were genuine but that didn't lessen their unsettling effect.

Mariel's dramatic genesis made a big international story – drew journalists who for years had been ignoring Cuba – and the story besmirched Castroism. When ten thousand besieged the Peruvian embassy in Miramar, claiming political asylum, a Cuban soldier on security duty was killed and the crowd's unprecedented defiance of the Revolution brought out the worst in an angry Fidel. Echoing him, *Granma* denigrated the would-be migrants in disgraceful language – 'criminals, lumpen, anti-social elements, loafers and parasites – never subject to political persecution, in no need of the sacred right of diplomatic asylum – scum lured by consumerism to betray their fatherland.'

After much unpleasant confusion, an agreement was reached. Cubans who wished to leave could do so if someone sailed from Florida to fetch them. Relatives or friends then organised the six-month boat-lift, hundreds of small vessels arriving in Mariel harbour, not far from Havana, where the government opened special offices to ensure an orderly, documented departure. It also staged, for the benefit of foreign journalists, a singularly nasty series of jeering anti-migrant demos, calculated to prove that most Cubans despised those disloyal to the Revolution.

Between April and October 1980 some 125,000 disillusioned or discontented Cubans sailed away. This stirred false hopes in Washington; the administration seemed to hear the rumble of crumbling foundations. Superficially it did look bad, so many wanting out when Fidel and President Carter agreed to make the exodus feasible. (A move, on Carter's part, that contributed to his defeat by Reagan at the end of the year. Fidel had released several thousand would-be-émigrés from prisons and detention centres; six years later nearly two thousand were housed in Atlanta's state jail.) Yet, 125,000 migrants, out of a population of nine million or so, was no more remarkable than the average annual migration from Latin American countries to the Land of (for some) Plenty.

The Gomez family (Eugenio and Marisol and their daughter Paula) lived a few miles from the Mazaparras on a much less opulent though pleasant enough boulevard bisected by a line of tall pines. When they migrated their two sons were newly graduated as construction engineers and Paula, aged eighteen, had just left school, keen to become a journalist. Because the engineers had quickly found well-paid jobs their parents lived in a two-storey clapboard house with a compact flower-bright garden and a small swimming-pool. We lunched on the verandah, attended by two bossy Siamese cats and a neurotic miniature poodle. Paula's husband had been drowned in 2002 ('too much rum, then snorkelling') and, being childless, she moved back to the parental home. But soon she'd be leaving again, with an unprepossessing local politician (pudgy, balding, self-important) who joined us after lunch.

Eugenio had recently retired from his factory foreman job; Marisol was still working part-time as secretary to a CANF lobbyist. Eugenio spoke of 1958 when the Gomez and their two little boys were contentedly living in Marianao, lamenting Batista's corrupt tyranny but not often discommoded by it. At first the Revolution had felt acceptable but after the Missile Crisis of 1962 they began to resent its 'bullying'. Living as they did in a close-knit community on the fringes of affluent Miramar, and conditioned to aspire to a US lifestyle, they were uninterested in the working-class and thus insulated against Revolutionary fervour. By 1963 Fidel's radical reforms had obliterated their small family business, inherited from Eugenio's father, and 'redistributed' half their six-roomed house. Castroism attacked their material and emotional security, reduced them from being an in-dependent family, earning an honest living through hard work, to being, in Paula's words, 'the frightened slaves of Marxism'. Such families, then a significant minority of the urban population, detested the ruthless regi-mentation inseparable from the Revolution's extraordinary achievements. 'We had everything to lose,' said Marisol, 'and nothing to gain.'

I ventured to ask, 'Didn't your sons gain? Could they have gone to university under the old régime?'

Marisol shrugged, hesitated – left it to Paula. 'Maybe not,' said she, 'but with their energy our business could have grown to give them good jobs. The Communists killed individuals' initiative, took away every Cuban's independence, tried to turn us all into zombies like the Russians.'

On the bus to José Martí Park, to meet Merci and Eber, I wondered if Paula knew that the CIA was a main employer of the 1959–60 émigré influx. It might have been tactless to raise that subject in the presence of a local politician who boasted of powerful business connections in Brazil and Columbia. (Boasts which didn't quite ring true.)

In *Miami* Joan Didion recorded:

> . . . the CIA's JM/WAVE station on the University of Miami campus was by 1962 the largest CIA installation, outside Langley, in the world, and one of the largest employers in the state of Florida. There were said to have been at JM/WAVE headquarters between three hundred and four hundred case officers from the CIA's clandestine services branch. Each case officer was said to have run between four and ten Cuban 'principal agents', who were referred to in code as 'amots'. Each principal agent was said to have run in turn between ten and thirty 'regular agents', again mainly exiles. The arithmetic here is impressive. Even the minimum figures, three hundred case officers each running four principal agents who in turn ran ten regular agents, yield twelve thousand regular agents, each of whom might be presumed to have contacts of his own. There were, all operating under the JM/WAVE umbrella, flotillas of small boats. There were mother ships, disguised as merchant vessels . . . There were hundreds of pieces of Miami real estate, residential bungalows maintained as safe houses, waterfront properties maintained as safe harbours. There were, besides the phantom 'Zenith Technological Services' that was JM/WAVE headquarters itself, fifty-four other front businesses, providing employment and cover for various services required by JM/WAVE operations. There were CIA boat shops. There were CIA gun shops. There were CIA travel agencies, there were CIA real estate agencies and there were CIA detective agencies.

The inspiration for all this activity was a gentleman by the name of Fidel Castro Ruz. Overkill? But then it turned out to be underkill . . .

At a Cuban restaurant near José Martí Park Merci and Eber joined me for a farewell meal, a 'thank you' for their hospitality. Soon they were reminiscing about their struggle to survive during the Special Period. Almost everyone lost weight, even some high government officials – but not all senior army officers . . . Eber insisted that the most gruesome of the teeming urban myths spawned by those years was not a myth. From personal experience he could confirm that just occasionally livers were removed from fresh corpses in hospital mortuaries and sold as 'pig's' livers. 'But only from accident corpses, not anyone diseased.' Merci furiously reproved her husband for shocking their foreign guest – and during the meat course! To soothe her I explained that I wasn't as shocked as she might think I should be. Very rarely, in remote places, I have been really hungry, to the point of exhaustion. And a really hungry purchaser of a providentially supplied pig's liver wouldn't quibble about that trade description. I forbore to enquire about the precise nature of Eber's 'personal experience'.

After a certain number of neat rums and most of a bottle of Californian wine (Merci merely sipped) Eber revealed that what is generally known as the 'the Ochoa case' (though thirteen others were directly involved) had made his family's migration easier.

'We didn't have to feel too much guilty about betraying the Revolution,' said Eber. 'We felt like it was dying,' added Merci.

No one in Cuba would speak to me about Fidel's insistence on executing one of his closest *compañeros*, and three other Pillars of State, after they had confessed to multiple misdeeds, which had brought shame on the Revolution but had not caused any deaths. In a few one-to-one situations, when I had dared to mention 'Ochoa' the reaction hurried me on to another topic.

Division General Arnaldo Ochoa, commander-designate of the Western Army, Hero of the Republic of Cuba, had joined the Sierra Maestra guerrillas as an eighteen-year-old, stood at Fidel's side (literally) at the Bay of Pigs, gone on to distinguish himself in most of Cuba's internationalist military campaigns and led the victorious troops in the crucial battle for Cuito Cuanavale in Angola. Among his closest friends were the twin brothers, General Patricio de la Guardia, head of the Special Forces in Angola, and Colonel Tony de la Guardia, head of the Convertible Currency (MC) Department in the Interior Ministry. The MC was a blockade-busting unit which ran trading companies (their Cuban origin concealed) in Panama's free-trade zone and brought much hard currency to Havana's treasury through innovative commercial enterprises. Colonel Tony also laundered smuggled ivory and diamonds in MC's Havana office before exporting them to Panama, to be swapped for weapons to arm the Cuban troops in Angola. General Ochoa regularly imported sugar to Luanda, sold it on the black, then illegally bought those diamonds and ivory to equip (and sometimes to feed) his men. Between them, Graham Greene and John Le Carre couldn't make it up.

Eventually innovation was stretched too far – the MC allowed Columbian drug-dealers to use a military airstrip near Varadero for the transshipment of cocaine to Florida. Colonel Tony demanded a fee of $1,000 per kilo, not all of which went to the government's coffers. From this evolved the scandal described by Richard Gott as 'the Revolution's most serious internal crisis in thirty years'. All the accused pleaded guilty. Yet many people, at home and abroad, scorned Fidel's argument that only the deaths of Ochoa, Tony de la Guardia and two others could prevent that stain of corruption from spreading all over the island.

Several foreign statesmen and 'famous names', including Fidel's old friend Gabriel Garcia Marquez, pleaded for leniency. The Pope instructed his Nuncio to seek a meeting and to emphasise that to commute the death sentences would enhance Cuba's image. During a two-hour discussion Fidel explained that, contrary to popular belief, his powers were limited; it wasn't for him to reverse the unanimous decision of the Council of State. The Nuncio retorted that El Chef had enough moral authority to persuade the Council to think again. Fidel then conceded that his moral authority did exceed his formal authority under the Constitution – but in fact he himself agreed with the sentences.

The interwoven Angola-Havana-Panama-Varadera-Havana-Angola plots and sub-plots and counter-plots are brilliantly unpicked and objectively analysed by both Leycester Coltman and Richard Gott. The non-*fidelista* Marifeli Perez-Stable deals with the episode more briefly and clumsily, under-exposing Ochoa's wheeler-dealer career and thus presenting a partial account. The *fidelista* Isaac Saney skims over the whole crisis in two sentences, sounding uncomfortable and defensive. The chapter covering the Ochoa case in Castro's *My Life* (the seven hundred and twenty-four-page result of two hundred hours of interviewing) shows Fidel at his most verbosely evasive and clarifies nothing.

Who knew what – and *when* – about MC's three-year involvement with drug-dealers? In Leycester Coltman's view (not all would agree) –

Castro's attitude to drug-trafficking was pragmatic rather than moralistic. His concern was to avoid giving the Americans a weapon to use against him. Normally confident that nothing moved in Cuba without his knowledge, he was genuinely shocked to discover that de la Guardia's men had been flouting his orders . . .

The hardline Cuban-Americans rejoiced. 'Told you so! He's always been in the drug shit!' More rational anti-Castroites refused to jump to conclusions; Fidel's integrity was widely recognised, even by many of his enemies. A spokesman for Miami's Drug Enforcement Agency, John Fernandez, (quoted in *Time*, 10 July 1989), stressed that 'There is no reason to believe that Fidel Castro or people in the presidential palace were in sympathy with the smugglers'.

For three decades the Revolution had been presenting itself as the medicine needed to purge Cuba of centuries of corruption. Richard Gott writes:

> Another senior general, José Ramon Fenandez . . . minister of education in 1989 . . . expressed his shock at the revelations. In his eyes it was unimaginable that Cuba could condone drug smuggling. It was also dismaying for old revolutionaries like him to have had revealed to them the scale of corruption and personal enrichment that appeared from the Ochoa affair to be endemic . . .

To this day speculation persists about *motive* . . . Had Fidel seen Ochoa, the de la Guardias and their group as capable of clearing the way for Cuban versions of *perestroika* and *glasnost*?

Merci remembered hearing about Ochoa's approval of the Gorby reforms which Fidel abhorred. (In 1988 he saw exactly what was happening as Capitalism Rampant invaded the collapsing Soviet Union.) Said Eber, 'Folks outside – and some inside – swear those four were killed to keep *el chef* in power. Looks to me he killed them to save the Revolution from capitalism. I hated those killings, round the world it made Cuba look bad. They showed Ochoa was right, we needed change. When we saw it not coming we left.' As he reached for the rum bottle Merci restrained him and firmly announced that we must move, the bus journey home would take an hour. Before curling up on my sofa-bed (I had stymied the boys' being ejected from their room) I packed my rucksack in readiness for an early flight to Italy via Gatwick.

Chapter 17

On 1 August 2006 I was at home in Ireland. Early that morning I switched on the World Service and heard jubilant cheering and chanting, car horns honking, toy bugles blowing, rattles clattering, raucous singing, whoops of glee. Vaguely I assumed the end of some big football match.

The BBC reporter who explained this tumult couldn't quite suppress his disgust. Thousands of Miami Cubans were thronging the streets of Little Havana celebrating the previous evening's announcement that Fidel was undergoing emergency surgery and had temporarily handed power to his brother Raul, his designated successor since 1959. Momentarily, I felt physically nauseated, as did millions who saw this spectacle on television. Even my detailed knowledge of the hard-liners' vicious activities had not prepared me for such a public display of hatred. The cheering and flag-waving and dancing in the streets continued all night and into the next day, causing traffic gridlock. All age groups participated. Some wore T-shirts emblazoned with the skull and crossbones, the skull bearded . . . Many believed Fidel was already dead, the rest were confident he couldn't possibly recover.

The news itself was sad but unsurprising, the Miami reaction shocking and unCuban. Immediately after J.F. Kennedy's death, when Fidel and the French journalist, Jean Daniel, were listening together to broadcasts from Dallas, a radio reporter talked excitedly of Jackie Kennedy's blood-stained stockings and Fidel was angered. 'What sort of mind is this? There is a difference in our civilisations after all. Are you like this in Europe? For us Latin Americans, death is a sacred matter. Not only does it mark the close of hostilities, it also imposes decency, dignity, respect . . . '

Juanita, Fidel's younger émigré sister, hadn't spoken to either Fidel or Raul for forty years. Now she unexpectedly went public. 'These demonstrations were unnecessary. They don't offer the world a good image of our cause, our country and the exile community as a whole. I don't hate anybody and I'm taking the first step by talking about it and expressing concern over the future of Cuba. The hate exists on both sides. It's time we stop the hate and start to love one another.' While Fidel was addressing the General Assembly of the UN in October 1979, Juanita had denounced him on a US radio station as 'a brutal despot'. But hearing of his illness she belatedly realised that family ties should prevail over political disagreements.

USA Today reported – 'Many Cubans on the island thought the Miami celebrations were in poor taste. A Havana waitress who wouldn't give her name said, "We aren't going to celebrate someone's illness".'

On 30 July, the eve of Fidel's collapse, Phillip Hart had a full-page article in the *Sunday Telegraph*, its lead-in eerily serendipitous: 'As his eightieth birthday looms, Cuba is at long last breaking one of its biggest taboos – discussing the prospect of El Comandante's death and what happens next.' Phillip Hart got off to a confidence-shaking start by naming Bayamo as 'the scene of an attack that he led on an army barracks on July 26, 1953'. There followed lots of nonsense (oft repeated during the months ahead) about 'keeping the succession in the family'. And the free cataract operations provided in Cuba for thousands of penniless Latin American peasants were described as 'a lucrative business for the regime'.

Carlos Valegciaga, Fidel's secretary, read his letter to the nation on TV on the evening of 31 July. Having reviewed his recent hectic journeys to and fro across Latin America the octogenarian admitted:

Days and nights of continuous work with hardly any sleep, have caused my health, which has withstood all tests, to fall victim to extreme stress and to be ruined. An acute intestinal crisis with sustained bleeding has obliged me to undergo a complicated surgical operation. All the details of this health accident can be seen in X-rays, endoscopies and filmed material. The operation will force me to take several weeks of rest, away from my responsibilities and duties.

As our country is threatened in circumstances like this by the government of the United States, I have made the following decision:

1. I delegate in a provisional manner my functions as first secretary of the Central Committee of the Communist Party of Cuba to the second secretary, comrade Raul Castro Ruz.

2. I delegate in a provisional manner my functions as Commander in Chief of the heroic Revolutionary Armed Forces to the same comrade, Army Gen. Raul Castro Ruz.

3. I delegate in a provisional manner my functions as president of the Council of State and of the government of the Republic of Cuba to the first vice president, comrade Raul Castro Ruz.

4. I delegate in a provisional manner my functions as the main driving force behind the National and International Program of Public

Health to Politburo member and Public Health Minister, comrade José Ramon Balaguer Cabrera.

5. I delegate in a provisional manner my functions as the main driving force behind the National and International Education Program to comrades José Ramon Machado Ventura and Esteban Lazo Hernandez, members of the Politburo.

6. I delegate in a provisional manner my functions as the main driving force behind the National Program of the Energy Revolution in Cuba and cooperation with other countries in this field to comrade Carlos Lage Davila, member of the Politburo and secretary of the Executive Committee of the Council of Ministers.

The relevant funds for these programs – health, education and energy – should continue to be assigned and prioritised, as I have been doing personally, by comrades Carlos Lage Davila, Secretary of the Executive Committee of the Council of Ministers; Francisco Soberon Valdes, Minister President of the Central Bank of Cuba; and Felipe Perez Roque, Foreign Relations Minister, who have accompanied me in these duties and should constitute a committee for this purpose.

From the international media came a spate of speculative 'What Next?' articles and interviews, mostly based on the assumption that Fidel had been running a one-man dictatorship until 31 July and therefore chaos was to be expected when he died. On 2 August a BBC reporter sounded surprised – 'On the streets of Havana there has been a remarkable sense of calm, almost nonchalance, in the face of the dramatic news. People have been going to work as normal. Shops remain open. Cinemas are full.' On the same date the US Coast Guard also sounded surprised – 'We are on alert but so far have seen no sign of mass migration from the island.'

Amos Rojas, of the Florida Department of Law Enforcement, addressed those who were talking of joining Cuba's dissidents, the moment Fidel's death was announced, to resist 'the remnants of the regime'. 'Don't attempt to leave,' said Mr Rojas. 'If there's a problem on the island the Coast Guard will blockade it and we're not going to let people go from here.'

For the *Independent* (3 August), David Usborne reported, 'A common theme of all the Cuban exile groups is that whatever plan the regime might have for engineering a seamless succession to brother Raul . . . cannot be allowed to happen.'

John Harris, who had recently been in Havana making a 'Newsnight' film on Cuba's health service, wrote on the *Guardian* website: (1 August)

Gazing into the post-Castro future, few would deny the imperative for fair elections and press freedom . . . There is, however, one caveat: anyone who would let loose a free market hurricane and sweep away Castro's public services would be in deep, deep trouble.

On 2 August Ricardo Alarcon, President of the National Assembly, described Miami's street parties as 'vomit-provoking acts led by mercenaries and terrorists'.

On the same date Senator Robert Bennett, after a meeting with Bush II, quoted one of his President's more profound comments – 'I think all of us can say we had no idea this was coming. We'll have to wait and see.'

A defence official explained that because of tropical storm Chris (a teenaged hurricane) navy ships were not yet moving closer to Cuba. But a large number of vessels, from destroyers to frigates, were in range and ready to respond if the situation changed. Next morning the Houses's three Cuban-American members, Ileana Ros-Lehtinen and the brothers Mario and Lincoln Diaz-Balart, met with the National Security Council before flying to Miami.

Rupert Cornwell, then the *Independent*'s man in Washington, wrote (3 August):

Eastern Europe cast off Communism in 1989, and two years later the Soviet Union collapsed . . . but somehow Cuba avoided this fate. Separately, repression and human rights abuses are somehow easier to overlook in a sub-tropical setting than in the frozen wastes of Siberia.

As though Cuba's jailing of dissidents were analogous to Stalin's death-camps! Rupert Cornwell concluded:

Washington will have a crucial role in ensuring an orderly return of the exiles, and disabusing them of the notion that power in a post-Castro Cuba is their birthright.

For the *Sunday Herald* (6 August) Elizabeth Mistry interviewed Caleb McCarry 'whose job description includes overseeing the post-Castro scenario on the island'. His mention of British government support surprised the journalist. In November 2005 he had met Lord Triesman of Tottenham, the Foreign Office minister responsible for Latin America and the Caribbean, and found him 'very receptive. An undemocratic Cuba is a destabilising force in the region and we believe a democratic Cuba could once again be part of the international system. Britain shares a common goal of seeing Cuba become a democracy and shares our message that all democracies should be working together to support democracy in Cuba.' This contradicted the Foreign and Commonwealth office's stated position which prefers 'constructive engagement rather than isolation'. Accordingly Robert Miller, director of the Cuba Solidarity Campaign, submitted a request under the UK Freedom of Information Act 'to determine the breadth and content of the discussion between our government and Caleb McCarry'. Yet again the Act didn't work. Robert Miller told the *Sunday Herald*, 'Over two hundred MPs have signed an early day motion criticising the Commission for Assistance to a Free Cuba and I think the British people should be asking why our government is talking to a guy whose sole remit is régime change in another country.' The F.C.O. refused to respond to the *Sunday Herald's* enquiries about Lord Triesman's meeting with McCarry.

On Sunday 6 August, in Havana Cathedral, Cardinal Jaime Ortega led the congregation in prayers that 'God accompany President Fidel Castro in his illness and illuminate those who have provisionally received the responsibilities of government'. Across the Straits, in Little Havana's Peter and Paul Catholic church, an usher said, 'We pray for Cuba and Cubans but not for its leader. The church asks us to pray even for our enemies but I don't do it.'

People asked me, 'Are you going back now to see the changes?' Very few seemed to know that change had been happening for more than a decade – since the early '90s when Carlos Lage was chosen as (in effect) prime minister. For years Fidel had been shrewdly grooming a team (in our terms a Cabinet) of able and widely experienced younger men who would now be running the country under Raul. I saw no reason to change my plans. Instead, I began to keep a sporadic 'Cuba Diary' as scraps of news and comment came to my attention.

14 August. Yesterday Fidel celebrated his eightieth birthday. (Actually his seventy-ninth but more of that anon.) Cuban TV showed him talking and laughing with Raul and his young (comparatively) friend Hugo Chavez, the Venzualan president who has long regarded Fidel as his mentor. He looked remarkably well, almost frisky in his red, white and blue Adidas jacket – which scandalised me. Good socialists don't buy Adidas. His birthday message said: 'I feel very happy. For all those who care about my health, I promise to fight for it. To say the stability has improved considerably is not to tell a lie. To say that the period of recovery will be short and there is now no risk would be absolutely incorrect. I suggest you be optimistic and at the same time always prepared to receive bad news. The country is running well and will continue to do so.'

Those words told us that *el comandante* was facing involuntary permanent retirement with his usual courage.

An editorial in today's *Independent* warns Bush II against the émigré pitfall – something I've been thinking about since the Little Havana street parties. Before reducing Iraq to anarchy the US invaders took advice from Iraqi émigrés, a coterie with their own agenda led by the convicted swindler Ahmed Chalabi. CANF cheered that illegal invasion and at once printed their 'Iraq Today, Tomorrow Cuba!' stickers. Caleb McCarry repeatedly talks of the need 'to ensure that the Castro regime's succession strategy does not succeed'. In a world where the Western version of democracy (multi-party elections) frequently prolongs or causes bloody mayhem (Nigeria, Afghanistan, Georgia, Kenya, Pakistan, Zimbabwe, Nepal and etc.) there is something peculiarly perverse about seeking to upscuttle a régime that has devised an orderly 'succession strategy'. As the *Independent* notes, 'The views of Little Havana are highly unlikely to represent the wishes of the majority in Cuba where Mr Castro . . . still seems a popular figure.'

4 October. Today it came to my attention that Oswaldo Paya, founder of the Christian Liberation Movement and organiser of the Varela Project, congratulated Pedro Carmona in an open letter when it seemed Carmona had ousted the *democratically elected* President Hugo Chavez in a US-backed coup in 2004. The EU awarded Paya the 2003 Sacharov Human Rights prize and in December 2005 he was invited to London to attend a Foreign Office conference on human rights. Very sensibly, Havana denied him an exit visa. Would Washington allow a US citizen to travel to a foreign capital to encourage 'régime change'?

In February 2004 the Mississippi Consortium for International Development engaged Oswaldo Paya to co-ordinate several courses to 'develop leadership' for the soon-to-be-free (they hoped) Cuba. The MCID operates in several countries where the US wages ideological warfare: Angola, Nigeria, South Africa, Romania, Russia, Kyrgyzstan, the Ukraine. In Iraq this institution secured a five million dollar-contract for guiding the University of Mosul as it 'developed leadership' for Iraq and the Middle East generally. Two MCID representatives, travelling as tourists under the names Careen Bishop and Patricia Jernigan, have been visiting Cuba since 2002.

Ramon Humberto Colas Castillo, whose name I first heard in Pinar del Rio, was employed by Special Interests to set up 'independent libraries' in Cuban cities – his reward a job in Mississippi as a MCID researcher. In October 2005, when McCarry organised an important meeting in Madrid, Colas was there and had a long private discussion with Adolfo Franco, husband of Ileana Ros-Lehtinen and then director of USAID's Latin America and Caribbean Department. To a House of Representatives Foreign Relations sub-committee Franco gave evidence that within less than three years twenty million dollars of USAID money had been diverted, via Miami, to support Cuba's 'dissident groups'. In Havana I was shown a photograph of Franco presenting Jaime Suchlicki with a USAID cheque (eight feet wide) for US$ 1,045,000 to finance 'a transition project' in Cuba.

24 October. Some light relief (sort of) in today's post. Miami's public school system has banned a children's book about travel to Cuba because so many parents complained that it shows pictures of schoolchildren smiling and therefore portrays an 'idealised' and 'overly-favourable' vision of the island. The American Civil Liberties Union has filed a lawsuit against the Miami-Dade County School Board, claiming that the ban violates the First Amendment. *Vamos a Cuba* was first noticed by hard-liners after a child brought it home and her father, who describes himself as 'a former political prisoner', flew into a rage. Funny ol' place, Miami. I never saw a group of Cuban schoolchildren who were *not* smiling.

15 November. The amount spent on bribing journalists by the US government's Cuba Transmissions Office proves the importance of a steady flow of misinformation. The *Miami Herald*'s publisher recently resigned when it was discovered (through the US Freedom of Information Act) that two of the paper's most virulently anti-Castro journalists, Pablo Alfonso and Wilfredo Cancio, had been paid, since 2001, US$175,000 and US$150,000 respectively, as 'retainers'. The publisher, Jesus Diaz Jr, talked of 'violating the sacred confidence between journalists and the public'. He added that the nine journalists who accepted payments would not be disciplined because 'our policies prohibiting such behaviour may have been ambiguously communicated, inconsistently applied and widely misunderstood over many years in the newsroom'. The journalists concerned also worked for Radio Marti and TV Marti, described by many British reporters as 'the Cubans' source of objective news from outside'.

17 April 2007. In yesterday's *Guardian* Duncan Campbell reported:
Barclays Bank has told the London branches of two Cuban organisations (Havana International Bank and Cubancan) to take their accounts elsewhere in what is seen as the latest example of pressure exerted by the US on British companies to enforce its embargo of the island.

When challenged by the *Guardian* Barclays replied:
We operate in a number of jurisdictions around the world and that requires careful monitoring to ensure compliance with different regulations.

Last year the Union Bank of Switzerland and Credit Suisse closed all accounts with Cuban connections, indirectly referring to Cuba as 'one of the sensitive countries'. In July 2006 the US Treasury Department added the Netherlands Caribbean Bank (an ING joint venture with two Cuban state-owned enterprises) to their list of companies with which US companies and private citizens are forbidden to do business. Early this year, the Austrian bank that sounds like a pantomime character – BAWAG – closed more than a hundred Cuban accounts citing 'US sanctions'. An infuriated Foreign Minister, Ursula Plassnik, then informed Parliament that she had started administrative proceedings against BAWAG for breaking EU rules against applying anti-Cuban sanctions on European soil. Showing the sort of independence unknown in a Britain eviscerated by the 'special relationship', she proclaimed, 'US law is not applicable in Austria . . . We are not the 51st of the US states'. In reaction to Barclays' compliance, Colin Burgon MP observed, 'Those who prattle on about national sovereignty and losing rights to Brussels are strangely quiet on the fact that the US is passing legislation which dictates policy in the UK'.

12 May. It's interesting that despite all Washington's efforts to isolate Havana, Cuba now has diplomatic relations with one hundred and eighty-one of the one hundred and ninety-two nations in the UN General Assembly where rejection of the US blockade is almost unanimous. Also, Cuba has been elected to 'chair' the 118-member

Nonaligned Movement, recently returned from the near-dead in response to US plans for 'full-spectrum dominance'.

29 June. My personal favourite, among the heroes of the Revolution, died on 18 June, aged seventy-seven. Vilma Espin was Raul's ex-wife; they met in 1958 when she – a MIT student and daughter of a senior Bacardi executive – exchanged her palatial Santiago home for a guer-rilla camp in the Sierra Maestra. They fought side by side in the mountains, married in Havana in January 1959 and in due course had four children. In their very different ways, each became a pillar of the Revolution – Vilma much the stronger. Most obits refer to her as 'Cuba's unofficial first lady' which description, with its connotation of 'a first gentleman' in charge, would certainly displease her.

While still a bride, in November 1959, Vilma led a delegation to a congress of Latin American women in Chile and on their return Fidel asked her to found the Federation of Cuban Women (FMC). Under its aegis, more than nineteen thousand women who were household ser-vants in 1959 received special schooling to equip them for alternative jobs. The FMC played a crucially important part in the setting up of Cuba's novel rural education and public health systems.

As one of Cuba's most powerful leaders, Vilma drew up the 1975 Family Code which gave women equal rights and gave many men a nasty shock. They were now obliged, by law, to do their fair share of childcare and housework. Such laws never take instant effect but if the legislators are not merely posing they do gradually remould attitudes. I noticed a surprising number of young and not-so-young husbands being more domesticated than one would expect given their *machismo* inheritance.

Writing in *The Nation* (28 June) a Havana journalist, Rosa Miriam Elizalde, remembers interviewing Vilma in the early '90s when prosti-tution was seeping back on to the streets as tourism expanded. Said Vilma: 'Don't forget that *jineteras* are not mere prostitutes. They are *our* prostitutes and we must not demonise them, because we run the risk of attacking the victim instead of attacking the wrong.'

Rosa pays tribute to Vilma as – ' . . . the first person to talk to our people about gender equality and, specifically, about the rights of homosexuals and trans-sexuals to a full life, swimming against the tide of the sort of Victorian Marxism which in our country blended with a native plague of machismo that caused much suffering to quite a few.'

About eighty-five per cent of women belong to the FMC, making it one of Cuba's most influential institutions, and when the government declared a day of national mourning many thousands of both sexes streamed through the Karl Marx theatre in Havana to pay homage to Vilma.

9 July. This is Operation Miracle's third anniversary. The WHO estimates that curable blindness handicaps at least thirty-seven million throughout the Majority World. With this figure in mind, Fidel visited Havana's Ramon Pando Ferrer Opthomological Institute, on 9 July 2004, and proposed 'Operation Miracle' to its director, Dr Marcelino Rio Torres. When *el comandante* could evade the bureaucracy, things moved fast in Cuba. Within a year fourteen thousand had benefited from free eye surgery and by now sight has been restored to almost seven hundred thousand from all over Latin America and the Caribbean. Thirty-eight opthomological clinics, staffed by more than six hundred Cubans, have been established in Bolivia, Ecuador, Guatemala, Haiti, Honduras, Nicaragua, Mali, and Panama. In all, throughout the Majority World, some forty-two thousand Cubans (doctors, nurses, teachers, agronomists, engineers) are at work.

Recently, Felipe Perez explained to a group of bemused Minority Worlders, 'We don't hand out what is surplus to us, what we do is share what we have.' This prompts cynics to ask, 'But what would all those well-qualified Cubans be doing at home? Given an over-educated population and limited job opportunities on the island, doesn't Cuba need to have them occupied abroad? Isn't all this internationalist humanitarianism a safety valve?'

Those cynics have a point – but they're missing another point, to do with the Revolutionary ethos. Well-qualified Cubans don't have to work for a pittance in remote regions. They could defect and earn comparatively big bucks, as of course a few do. But astonishingly few . . . And what about the forty-seven thousand (to date) young foreigners who have graduated for free from Cuban universities?

Last month Dr Carlos Dupuy Nunez, leader of the Henry Reeve Brigade, spent three weeks touring England. In response to the 2005 earthquake, he and two thousand four hundred volunteers spent seven months working in Azad Kashmir. Most aid agencies moved out after two months or less. Within six days of the quake, eighty-six doctors were on the scene; within weeks the Brigade had set up thirty-two fully equipped field hospitals.

One interviewer asked Carlos, 'Why does such a small country send so many doctors abroad? And why to Pakistan, to help a country that's a main US ally in the "war on terror"?'

Carlos replied, 'It's not for glory, it's not for material wealth, but for solidarity. Our health system is based on internationalist principles. When I first applied to medical college I got a form asking "Do you feel able to give your services for free to any people in the world?" I said "Yes". When you grow up in this kind of society, you feel like that.'

Those keen to profit from ill-health don't know how to cope with Castroist humanitarianism. The various brigades' existence and effectiveness can't be denied and they are among the Revolution's most admirable achievements. Some even argue (a dodgy argument!) that they cancel out the injustices inflicted on jailed 'dissidents' who have tried to change the anti-capitalist régime that makes such endeavours possible.

Writing in the *Tablet* (2 September 2006), Paraguay-based Margaret Hebblethwaite (the ex-nun widow of the ex-Jesuit Peter Hebblethwaite) reflected on the thirty-five-year dictatorship of the recently deceased Alfredo Stroessner. She continued:

'And what about the other long-running dictator, Fidel Castro, who has also been in the news for reasons of health? It seems strange to someone in Paraguay to hear him described as a dictator, for his dictatorship is of a different class. In most Paraguayans' perception, Cuba is the country that most holds out a helping hand. Our doctors in Santa Maria are Cubans, on two-year contracts, because no Paraguayan doctor wants to live in such an economic backwater. Our blind people and cataract sufferers are flown to Cuba for free eye operations. Our bright young school leavers are given scholarships to study medicine in Cuba. If any country has put its money where its mouth is, it is Castro's Cuba . . . When Castro came to Paraguay for President Nicanor's inauguration, he received the biggest round of applause as the various presidential cars unloaded their occupants (closely followed by Hugo Chavez of Venezuela – the other icon of resistance to the US). Castro later addressed a crowd in a football stadium and spoke for three hours solid. Even that did not put people off. Those who were there said he was impressive.'

Here we see the tap-root of US anti-Castroism. Forget 'Communism'. The threat to Capitalism Rampant comes from Castroism's *proof* that a non-capitalist régime can significantly reduce Majority World suffering. To free-marketeers the accumulation of personal wealth – material wealth – is the valid primary goal of every sensible person. Castroism preaches and practices concern for the poor, whose numbers increase in proportion to the free-marketeers' global successes. It's a new idea, this holding out of helping hands – an ethical/spiritual rather than a political revolution, a mind-set remote from Kremlin doctrines. And its potential, as a global influence, terrifies all rampant capitalism and drives the US species to frenzy.

A few weeks ago Fidel pointed out that Cuba could train seventy-five thousand doctors for the price of Britain's new Tridents – seven point two billion dollars. It's good to know he's still doing his sums!

31 July. The first anniversary of what one must now think of as Fidel's retirement. And the Revolution goes peacefully on its way.

Companies and financial institutions accused of 'associating' with Cuba have now been listed on the US Securities and Exchange Commission's website to enable investors to avoid business links with 'state sponsors of terrorism'. (One doesn't know whether to laugh or swear – *Cuba* as a sponsor of terrorism!) The Institute of International Bankers has protested that 'This action has been taken without prior public notice or consultation with reporting companies and other interested persons'. European tycoons are complaining that nine out of ten banks won't open accounts for companies operating in Cuba. Yet increasing trade with many countries – especially Venezuela, China and Spain – are vitiating the blockade; last year the Cuban economy recorded a ten per cent-growth rate. Now US pressures are affecting individuals more than the state; when a Cuban children's theatre group was invited to a drama festival in Buenos Aires the Argentinean government refused them visas. When a Miami-based consortium bought Spain's Pullman-tour cruising company two hundred and twenty Havana workers were sacked. US-owned hotels around the world have sacked their Cuban musicians. Specialist US computer programs and equipment are being denied to blind Cubans – and so on and on . . .

13 August. This is Fidel's real eightieth birthday, as all readers of Leycester Coltman's biography are aware. Aged fourteen, Fidel was determined to move from the Jesuits' Dolores College in Santiago to their even more prestigious Belen College in Havana. He was a bright lad, academically ahead of his contemporaries, but no boy under fifteen was admitted. So Pappa acquired a new birth certificate and 'To avoid the embarrassment of acknowledging this fraud, Fidel spent the rest of his life claiming to be a year older than he really was'.

27 August. At last month's Havana conference on 'The Environment and Development' Cuba was given cause to purr. Achim Steiner, head of the UN Environment Program, said: 'Cuba has countered crippling energy shortages plaguing the island as recently as 2004 without giving up a long-term commitment to promoting environmentally friendly fuels. Electricity still depends too much on heavy polluting diesel generators but important steps have been taken toward developing wind and solar power with six hundred windmills now installed and plans for more. In terms of a short-term response, it is quite remarkable how Cuba, under its economic conditions, managed to solve a real energy crisis. My organisation wants to put a spotlight on these efforts.'

1 September. Granma boasts that the Reverend Nerva Cots is 'only the eighteenth in the world' – the eighteenth woman bishop and the first in the 'developing' world. Representatives of Afro-Cuban religions attended her Episcopal Church consecration. Caridad Diego, director of Cuba's Religious Affairs Office, said 'The government is proud we now have a woman bishop. I believe Communists and religious leaders share many ideals and we should work together for the good of humanity'. I remembered those words when a friend wrote on her Christmas card – 'Do you know Cuba has the worst record in the world for the persecution of Christians?' McCarry et al. at it again!

21 September. Bush II, addressing the UN General Assembly, has referred to Fidel's illness – 'The long rule of a cruel dictator is nearing its end. The Cuban people are ready for their freedom'. Felipe Perez Roque naturally led his delegation out of the chamber and later issued a statement: 'Bush is responsible for the murder of over six hundred thousand civilians in Iraq . . . He is a criminal and has no moral authority or credibility to judge any other country. Cuba condemns and rejects every letter of his infamous tirade.'

On 29 September I return to Havana, hoping to see all my old friends and track down a few new contacts, people with a particular interest in Cuba's 'transition period'. For that's what this decade is – and was, long before Fidel fell ill.

PART THREE

September–October 2007

Chapter 18

In my Gatwick departure lounge I sat beside Ben, an engaging young architect excited about his first visit to Havana, as a job-seeker rather than a tourist. It seemed the Architects' Council of Europe foresaw a replacement soon of 'Cuba's hardline regime', followed by 'immense opportunities for its members'. Ben quoted his ACE boss. 'We don't care what the Americans think. They tried to force the EU into a trade boycott and were told to get lost.' Ben reckoned members keen on conservation could work for UNESCO in Old Havana but – 'I'd prefer to help rebuild Cuba by regenerating infrastructure. In exchange Cubans can learn from us, travel to Britain when they're not shackled any more! They've three schools of architecture, turning out about five hundred a year, but they've never seen anything worthwhile going up.' With that last opinion I had to agree, but the phrase 'to help rebuild Cuba' grated. We've heard it too often in recent years from the bombers of Afghanistan and Iraq.

I had a folder of press-cuttings in my shoulder-bag, too precious to be entrusted to airline baggage-handlers, and I urged Ben to read the last few paragraphs of a Brian Wilson article. This former Foreign Office minister was the only member of the British government to maintain regular contact with Cuba between 1997 and 2005. In the *Guardian* (8 February 2007) he wrote:

No one in a senior government position in Britain has any first-hand knowledge either of Cuba or of the people who run it. Our influence is zero, because we have chosen to accept the Washington orthodoxy that regime change is just around the corner. Ostensibly, the justification for this position is concern about Cuba's record on human rights. When Margaret Beckett made her first major speech as foreign secretary on human rights it was, remarkably, Cuba that was given pride of place. Our glorious ally, Saudi Arabia, did not even merit a mention. Not only the Cubans are entitled to complain about this epic display of double standards. The British are too. The Americans' camp-followers on Cuba have never been prepared to acknowledge that a country which has lived under constant economic siege for almost half a century, and which has been subject to more foreign plots than any other might be entitled to define 'dissidents' in terms that do not match those of their persecutor . . . By recognising that regime change cannot be forced by external intervention, Britain could restore mutually respectful relationships with Cuba. There is still time. But if our sole objective is to destabilise the Cuban government and support American manoeuvres to replace it, there will be no point in even going to the funeral. Because nobody will speak to us, except the man from the CIA.

Replacing the cutting in my folder I unkindly remarked, 'British firms of architects may be less popular than the Canadians and the Spanish.'

By 2.00 p.m. we were approaching Havana, flying slightly out from the coast. The first change was seasonal – a landscape vividly green. The second change was equally predictable: that long, bare, dingy space where Rachel, the Trio and I had waited through the small hours was now a garishly commercialised concourse – we might have been in any international airport. And the taxis, all licensed and in good condition, were under traffic officer control with no bone-shaking free-lancers parked around the corner.

My middle-aged black driver, Gerardo, became chatty on hearing that this was my third visit. 'For you Cuba is good! For me too! From Ireland many come – another island, maybe we same sort?' I acknowledged a certain temperamental affinity, then ventured to ask, 'How is Fidel?'

Gerardo chuckled. 'He's OK, not dying the way the *Yanquis* want! He came on TV last week, with an interviewer for an hour, quick with his mind but thin and tired. He says a lot with his pen in *Granma*, still seeing what's wrong with the world. And next week we'll watch him talking with Chavez.'

Noticing Havana's shiny new buses I exclaimed in wonder. 'From China,' said Gerardo. 'Hundreds of them and the oil from Venezuela, 90,000 barrels a day, below half-price. We give 14,000 medical people to work free for Chavez – it makes the *Yanquis* mad! Radio Marti says in any country our brigade workers can go to the US embassy and get a free ticket to the US. And a work permit. And citizenship after a year. Then they get madder so few want to go!'

When we had said goodbye I turned into San Rafael, happy to be back but soon demoralised by the humid heat, incomparably worse than in November-March. Candida reminded me that it would be even hotter in Oriente – and hottest of all when I reached my ultimate destination, Playa Las Coloradas.

A saddening change was the permanent police presence (always a lone young officer) at a street corner close to No. 403. I had never before seen police keeping Centro under surveillance. Crime was rapidly increasing, warned Pedro. I shouldn't carry my passport with me, or much cash, and I should always wear my shoulder-bag around my neck.

Candida added, 'Last year we had two million tourists, mostly European and Canadian, spending one and a half *billion* dollars! But they also bring problems . . . '

Overnight the weather relented slightly and as a gusty wind delivered frequent heavy showers I revisited the former presidential palace, now the Museum of the Revolution. Here one is educated in such detail that my previous two visits had left many rooms unseen. As usual, groups of schoolchildren were imbibing history and neither they nor their teachers looked bored. English children may not know their Corn Laws from their Magna Carta but Cuba can't afford to neglect history; it nourishes the Revolution's roots.

The Wars of Independence had inglorious aspects, some creoles favouring annexation by the US, some mulattos distrustful of their white comrades-in-arms, many blacks – even after 1886 – not too keen on being counted as Cubans. Yet with hindsight one sees how much those struggles achieved. Gradually and painfully they created an emotional environment in which people were prepared to be forged – by Martí and then by Fidel – into a unified nation. (Did processes not dissimilar happen in Europe millennia ago, as disparate tribes fought over territory and resources?) By 1950 one of Martí's most important messages ('Being Cuban is more important than being white or black') had been dripping steadily on to the stone of prejudice for some sixty years.

Pre-1959 racism per se was not on Fidel's agenda. For obvious reasons the Rebel Army's leadership was mainly white, as was the first interim government which at once opened to all Cubans the previously segregated clubs, beaches, parks, theatres, hotels.

Ironically, Spain's exit in 1898, followed by the island's take-over as a US playground, had led to more rigidly enforced segregation than any previously experienced. In 1985 Martha Gellhorn revisited Cuba where she had lived as Ernest Hemingway's wife from 1939–44. After a forty-one year absence she observed:

I had never thought of Cubans as blacks, and could only remember

Juan, our pale mulatto chauffeur . . . A form of apartheid prevailed in central Havana, I don't know whether by edict or by landlords' decisions not to rent to blacks. Presumably they could not get work either, unless as servants . . . The mass of Cubans had no education and no sense of identity. Being Cuban meant being somebody else's underling, a subordinate people. I knew a few upperclass Cuban sportsmen; they spoke perfect English. Not in words, nor even in thought, but instinctively they were felt to be too superior to be Cubans . . . Now, through innumerable museums, Cubans are being shown their history, being told they have been here a long time: they are a nation and they can be proud to be Cubans.

This psychological transformation is arguably the Revolution's greatest triumph; it is easier to raise a people's material standard of living than to raise their morale. To many Rich Worlders it seems the Revolution nurtured self-respect in a paradoxical sort of way, not by encouraging Cubans to value themselves as individuals (our route to 'self-esteem') but by educating and organising them to co-operate for the general good, persuading and sometimes coercing them to obey government directives in order that they might enjoy a range of benefits denied to their ancestors. Even the *jineteros* and *jineteras*, officially and unjustly labelled 'counter-revolutionary parasites', have a non-obsequious way of going about their business rarely observed among their equivalents elsewhere.

That afternoon I searched through Havana's second-hand book market in Plaza de Armas for copies of the English translation of *Fidel and Religion*, subtitled 'Castro talks on Revolution and Religion with Frei Betto'. I wanted several copies, for distribution among my friends, this being, in my estimation, one of the single most important books written about Cuba since the Revolution. When first published in 1987 it became an instant bestseller in Cuba, where more than 200,000 copies were sold within a few days and 1.3 million within a few months – to a population of, then, some ten million. All over Latin America sales were comparable and soon editions had been published in the USSR, the GDR, Italy, Poland, Spain, Hungary, Czechoslovakia, Japan, Australia, Vietnam, Bulgaria, India – twenty-three countries in all, served by fifteen translations. In Santiago thousands queued to buy copies autographed by the Brazilian Dominican priest, Frei Betto. In Switzerland the Roman Catholic Church devoted an hour-long TV programme to debating the book. Harvey Cox, in his introduction, wonders why there was such worldwide interest and remarks, 'The loquacious Fidel's sermon, whatever else one may say about it, is keeping the folks in the pews awake'.

Shortly before leaving home I had read an advance copy of *My Life: Fidel Castro with Ignacio Ramonet*, based on a hundred hours of interviews spread over three years. *Fidel and Religion* is based on four long conversations – real conversations, not interviews; the Dominican scholar was on Fidel's spiritual wavelength. Ignacio Ramonet deals with twenty additional years, using a journalist's technique and being at times too hagiographical. *My Life*, though full of fascinating detail, fails to dig deep, stays on the political surface, doesn't alert us to the extraordinary nature of the Cuban experiment and its relevance to twenty-first century needs. Frei Betto's three hundred and seventeen pages take us to the place where Fidel's vision shines clear.

In the Cuban Book Institute, under the Plaza de Armas arcade, I made a new friend. Tall and thin, white-haired and sad-eyed, Donatilo wore threadbare jeans and a too-big bush-shirt that didn't suit his non-macho persona. We got into conversation about my failed quest for *Fidel and Religion*, then I had to explain myself and soon Donatilo was inviting me to his Miramar flat – 'Come to drink coffee, I offer no more for I live alone and don't cook.'

Donatilo's English was fluent; in 1959 he had been halfway through a Yale course when enthusiasm for the Revolution drew him home. 'I'm a maverick; as my family took off for Miami, I took off for Havana!' Later I learned that this maverick had resumed his academic career at Havana University, become an internationally recognised authority in his field and married a fellow-academic whose death, a few months previously, explained those sad eyes.

Next day even the *habaneros* were glistening with sweat and complaining about the humidity. It drastically reduced my walking range so I waited twenty-five minutes for a Chinese bus; the public transport improvement was relative. From the coast road many hurricane souvenirs were visible: smashed rowing boats flung far from their moorings, roofless sheds, ponds of scummy stagnant water, jumbles of driftwood to which householders had added garbage of interest to mangy, stray dogs.

For me Miramar – Havana's early twentieth-century development beyond the inconsequential Rio Almandares – was (almost) *terra incognita*. The seriously rich once occupied super-mansions on its wide tree-lined boulevards and Miami's influence is perceptible, as is the recent recovery of

Cuba's economy. Here be handsome embassies, and sleek speeding cars
with CD plates or corporate logos, and a disfiguring rash of brand new
multi-storey tourist hotels. My search for Donatilo's flat took me up and
down a few pleasant, narrowish avenues, linking the boulevards – the
residences smaller, flowering shrubs spilling over garden walls, dachshunds
and poodles with smart collars guarding flimsy gates.

Donatilo's ground-floor flat (two rooms, plus kitchenette and *banyo*)
overlooked a privately-owned *organoponico*, created and cultivated by Donatilo's daughter and son-in-law and two grandsons, who lived upstairs. I
had anticipated a tête-à-tête over coffee but the family invited me to join
them for supper. Julia and Felipe were both government officials – senior
civil servants, in our terms, a species not often encountered by chance in
Cuba. The boys were out at their ballet class, an acceptable interest for
your average Cuban lad.

Over *cervezas* and daiquiris Felipe guesstimated that in 1985, when
Fidel and Frei Betto so fruitfully conversed, the former was long-sightedly
preparing people for the emotional as well as economic shock of the
Special Period. Fidel, he believed, longed for the world to recognise that
Cuban Communism was a separate phenomenon, far removed from the
Soviet version.

Julia doubted that *el comandante* was all that long-sighted, Donatilo
agreed with his son-in-law and felt the book had helped Cubans by drawing
a clear ideological line between Havana and Moscow. All were agreed that
it had had a drip-drip effect in Latin America and contributed to the
region's new assertiveness.

Remembering those two hundred thousand who bought *Fidel and Religion*
as it came off the presses in 1987, I enquired about the present publishing
scene. Felipe's aunt had helped, pre-Special Period, to run Ediciones Vigia,
an illustrious publishing house which produced hand-made books in
limited editions of two hundred – for free – to be presented as academic
prizes. Youngsters keen to learn book-making used to queue up for ap-
prenticeship places. Now Ediciones Vigia must bow to market forces and
sell its books for convertible pesos to be able to afford recycled paper.

In 1989 more than four thousand titles (including schoolbooks) came off
the presses: a total of fifty-five million copies, yet supply could never satisfy
demand. By 1993 book production had fallen to 1959 levels and from the
Casa de la Americas came many wails and much gnashing of teeth. Yet now
I was again hearing good of the Special Period. Said Donatilo, 'Comecon
wasn't only an economic storehouse, it was a cultural muzzle. Being left on

our own was liberating and stimulating. Subsidising books as much as we did was unhealthy – depressed standards. Recently we've had a good crop of vigorous young writers, not expecting subsidies, just wanting to be left to write as they think. Having no cash for foreign authors is a problem but some present us with their rights – like Gunter Grass and Alice Walker.'

Ediciones José Martí, the main publishers of political writings, could only bring out twenty titles in 1993. By now its commercial reincarnation, allied with foreign publishers for co-editions of poetry and fiction, is thriving – though without any foreign distribution network. When I condemned the poor quality of its expensive translations Julia urged me to complain to the Minister of Culture; later I discovered that she worked in his department.

Bus routes only serve the edges of widespread Miramar and it's not bicitaxi territory; carless residents either hitch-hike or use car-owning friends as unlicenced taxis. Donatilo advised against hitch-hiking after dark. 'A few years ago, always safe – not any more.' Felipe telephoned a neighbour who drove me as far as the Malecón in a vintage Lada.

Next morning Candida lent me a detailed street plan of Necropolis de Colon's one hundred and thirty-seven acres. Among the world's largest cemeteries, it accommodates some two million dead Cubans, equal to Havana's present population. The Church authorities bought this farmland in the 1860s, planning to provide enough consecrated ground for at least one hundred and fifty years, then ran a competition won by a well-known Spanish architect, Calixto Aureliano de Loira y Cardosa. His inspiration was a Roman military camp – everything rigidly symmetrical – which no doubt appealed to the Roman Catholic hierarchy. The construction took fifteen years (1871–86: there were money problems) and Calixto never saw his design completed. Dying at the age of thirty-three, he became, as it were, a pioneer corpse.

I set out on foot but even at 7.00 a.m. the humidity was obliterating. A CP 0.50 bicitaxi ride left me opposite the main entrance half an hour before opening time. Sipping coffee on a café verandah I contemplated Faith, Hope and Charity in Carrara marble, decorating the massive triple-arched portal. This is described in guidebooks as 'neo-Gothic' though to my eyes it looks closer to neo-Romanesque.

Here, alone on the verandah, I was exposed to another of Cuba's sad recent changes: a child beggar, aged perhaps eight or nine, insistently pleading for 'one dollar, pleeeze!' He was well-fed, well-dressed, well-shod, well-groomed and on a weekday morning would certainly have been at school. Sternly I told him he should be ashamed of himself, this was not how José Martí, or Ché, or Fidel expected Cuban children to behave. That litany of 'role models' brought an interesting reaction. He blushed (he was a white child), stared at the ground for a moment, then ran away. I had seen several other little boys, equally sturdy and well-turned out, pestering tourists in *al fresco* cafeterias along the Malecón. Poor Fidel! It used to be one of his proudest boasts that there were no beggars in Cuba. Gloomily I reflected that those children represent the fraying edge of the Revolutionary ethos.

I 'collect' cemeteries (have done since childhood) and this necropolis is like no other. Disconcertingly, it seems part of the city – as might a recreational park – rather than the last resting place of two million. Avenida Colon bisects it, a tarred dual carriageway on which stands the octagonal three-tiered Capilla Central (1886). All the main 'streets' – many shaded by towering fig-trees and ceibas – are long and straight. The living are much in evidence – workers clipping shrubs, scrubbing monuments, sweeping streets – little groups strolling to or from family graves – cyclists, motor scooters, the occasional taxi. Two tourist coaches parked by the Capilla for their loads to admire its attractive cupola, very beautiful German stained glass and a Cuban artist's less pleasing fresco, above the altar, in which fallen angels look more congenial than the Christ who is packing them off to hell. These unfortunate tourists were only given time to photograph the nearby Falla Bronat pantheon before being rounded up by a guide with a whistle.

A combination of great wealth and Roman Catholic mythology is no guarantee of aesthetic satisfaction and many prominent tombs, statues, vaults and pantheons had the unintended consequence of making me want to giggle. Among the more austere memorials, at the end of Avenida Colon, is the Fuerzas Armadas Revolucionarias, housing scores of heroes of the Revolutionary Armed Forces including Celia Sanchez, Fidel's constant companion for twenty-two years. (Some say he has never fully recovered from her death in 1980.) Two pleasant soldiers were guarding these special bones and the young woman obligingly took photographs of me saluting the life-size bas-reliefs of Fidel and Ché on the monument's otherwise undecorated façade. Behind this pantheon lie the scores of *Granma* warriors slaughtered by Batista's Rural Guard at Alegria de Pio on 5 December 1956. Having paid my respects to them I took a dirt-track going towards the as-yet-unused wilderness at the southern end of the necropolis – whereupon the male soldier came hurrying after me, shouting agitatedly. I must turn back, stay on the *calles*, that area ahead was closed to the public. I could see no STOP sign or barrier and this bossiness irritated me; it seemed petty to try to exclude tourists from the untidy acres. However those soldiers, being on guard duty, were easily eluded.

Turning east, towards the Osario General (1886, one of the oldest constructions) I soon found another path into a semi-wilderness where the thorny *marabu* had been controlled but the grass grew long. Here were occasional simple, newish graves, adorned with bunches of dried flowers. Ahead loomed four ugly, incongruous concrete block edifices – enormous, doorless, with three floors, like open-sided car-parks. Before investigating, I looked around: there was no one in sight. Moments later I was walking along a narrow corridor surrounded by thousands of concrete boxes, about three feet square, untidily stacked from floor to ceiling, crudely inscribed in black paint with names and dates. Each bore a large 'X' chalked in white. Those close enough to be legible dated from the mid-1990s. Many lids were loose, several had fallen off, exposing jumbled skulls and bones – the spines of necessity broken. I was tempted by one femur which would have fitted neatly into my shoulder-bag and been a companion for the Tibetan thigh-bone bugle in my study. But sounds of an approaching funeral deterred me, thus averting a possible headline in *Granma*: 'Irish Author Jailed for Stealing Cuban Bones'. Nearby were two other half-built ossuaries. From all my friends I sought information about this 'not-for-tourists' corner of the necropolis. How had all those corpses been so quickly reduced to clean bones without, apparently, the use of fire? And why had they not been buried, given the amount of unused land available? But blank stares gagged my questioning. I seemed to have come upon a Cuban family secret.

Every half-hour from 8.00 a.m. an ancient flat-bottomed motor-boat, carrying a hundred or so standing passengers, crosses the bay from Old Havana's Muelle de Luz to Regla on the east coast. This ferry is the equivalent of a local bus yet the security checks in the rickety little embarkation shed recalled Heathrow. Inside the door a wand-wielding policeman checked each body – and not casually – though he did ignore the frantic bleeping provoked by my pocketful of coins. Then, at a long counter, every bag, box, bucket and sack was thoroughly searched by two young women in smart brown uniforms. This time-consuming routine must bewilder tourists uninformed about the notorious Regla ferry hi-jacking which had such momentous consequences in 2003.

On 1 April eleven men armed with a pistol and knives hijacked the day's first crossing. There were twenty-nine other passengers aboard including one child and four tourists: two Frenchwomen, two Swedish women. The gang-leader was, as we say in Ireland, 'known to the police', having appeared in fifteen criminal (non-political) court cases and been jailed four times. As the hijackers veered towards the open sea in a vessel designed for inland waters the authorities decided against an interception but as usual notified the US Coast Guard. Soon after, the hijackers talked ship-to-shore on the marine band radio and demanded – while holding knives to several of the hostages' throats – a fast boat to take them to Key West. If denied this request they would throw a few hostages overboard, beginning with the tourists.

At this stage (mid-morning) Fidel was informed – less than twenty-four hours after he had brought to a safe conclusion the hijacking, on 30 March, of an AN-24 plane carrying forty adults and six children from the Isle of Pines to Havana. That hijacker pretended to be armed with a hand-grenade, sham but realistic-looking, and negotiations were extremely convoluted, prolonged and tense. On 19 March, two hours before the invasion of Iraq began, another Isle of Youth-Havana flight had been hijacked by six men armed with knives who forced the pilot to fly to Key West. On the eve of the Regla hijack news broke that those six had been released on bail in Miami, where anti-Castro terrorists habitually enjoy 'soft landings'.

When the ferry's tank ran dry she stood more than twenty miles out and a ten-knots wind was raising a sea heavy enough to endanger her. The hijackers agreed to a tow and Fidel directed the Minister of the Interior and the border patrol chief to oversee the rescue from Mariel. Three boats and a tug were deployed. By the time the ferry had been moored to the pier with a line several yards long, Fidel was on the scene. The hijackers continued to demand a faster boat while keeping knives to the throats of several women. It was then midnight and Special Forces, intent on freeing the hostages, had replaced the Coast Guard. But Fidel ordered them to take no action lest lives be lost. Through a police cruiser's radio, he and his colleagues then tested the gang-leader's state of mind and concluded that he was a genuine hazard, unlike the solitary hijacker with the mock grenade. At intervals he held his pistol to a Frenchwoman's head, the safety clip off and the hammer cocked.

At dawn the gang leader sent one of his men to the pier to open negotiations which continued all day, the troops ever alert on the dockside. Then the Frenchwoman who had had the pistol to her head sent an almost imperceptible signal to an officer. By now the leader was showing signs of exhaustion and stress; as part of this psyops, all communication with him had been cut for more than an hour. As the two Frenchwomen suddenly jumped into the water, a hostage simultaneously grabbed and disarmed the leader, both men falling overboard as they wrestled. The pistol went off, but harmlessly. And near-tragedy became farce when everyone else – passengers and hijackers together – jumped ship. As the curtain fell on this bloodless drama, Fidel congratulated the Frenchwomen – 'Very brave, very daring!' Havana friends showed me film footage taken at Mariel during the final hours – harrowing shots of the little boy's terror and a stupefied look on one Swedish woman's face as she stood in a parody of an embrace with a long knife being held to her throat. But nothing justifies the execution of three of the hijackers nine days later.

The Regla trial and the thirty-seven trials of the seventy-five 'dissidents' arrested in March 2003 (not all were tried individually) came close together – close enough to thoroughly confuse the Vatican which described the hijackers as 'dissidents' rather than 'terrorists'. Many of Castroism's most distinguished friends (e.g., Noam Chomsky, Howard Zinn, Eduardo Galeano, José Saramago) also angrily condemned 'Cuba's recent violations of human rights' – referring to the three hijackers' summary executions on 11 April.

In Cienfuegos my legal friend Alberto (by no means an uncritical *fidelista*) had gone on the defensive about those death sentences. He recalled that Regla had followed on a spate of US-condoned aeroplane and boat hi-jackings, and other destabilising provocations. Therefore the government, a few weeks after the illegal and apparently successful 'régime change' in Iraq, was asking 'Which régime next . . . ?' All eleven Regla hijackers were convicted under the *Law against Acts of Terrorism* (December 2001), hastily passed by the National Assembly in reaction to 11 September and extending the death penalty to include armed hi-jackers.

I am only ninety-nine per cent anti-death penalty (after the Rwandan genocide it seemed to me appropriate) but I found Alberto's excuse wholly unacceptable. As was Fidel's feeble and disingenuous defence of the executions, wrapped up in his 2003 May Day speech. Even after forty-four years of active US antagonism, *el comandante* cannot have been gripped by a real fear of US invasion – although he was said to have been genuinely rattled on 25 April when Cuban diplomats were officially informed that Washington saw the numerous recent hijackings as 'a serious threat to the national security of the United States'. (Another through-the-looking-glass statement, since the US courts declined to prosecute those hijackers who landed safely in Florida, whatever the degree of violence used en route.)

As I was often reminded by *fidelistas*, the US per capita rate of executions far exceeds Cuba's and in the National Assembly the death penalty provokes angry debates. 'Soon it will go,' Alberto had assured me. 'Our Supreme Court President [Ruben Remigio-Ferro] argues nothing justifies it; it's against the Revolution's humanistic ethos.'

In the context of Cuban dissidents, the US Penal Code of 2001 makes interesting reading:

> An organisation is subject to foreign control if it solicits or accepts financial contributions, loans, or support of any kind, directly or indirectly, from, or is affiliated directly or indirectly with, a foreign government or a political subdivision thereof, or an agent, agency or instrumentality of a foreign government . . . Whoever prints, publishes, edits, issues, circulates, sells, distributes or publicly displays any written or printed matter advocating, advising, or teaching the duty, necessity, desirability, or propriety of overthrowing or destroying any government in the US is guilty of a crime.

The Cubans jailed in 2003 were guilty of such crimes. In reaction to the international outcry against their convictions Havana moved fast. On 24 June 2003 the Minister of Foreign Affairs, Felipe Perez Roque, launched a volume entitled *The Dissidents*. It had been put together in ten days and was based on sixty hours of interviews conducted by two well-known professional writers assisted by twenty-four researchers. The interviewees were twelve State Security agents who had infiltrated some of the groups from which the contentious convicts emerged. When the agents gave evidence in public their secret careers ended; most were not sorry to resume normal life and be reconciled with families who for years had been distressed by their apparent betrayal of the Revolution.

The Dissidents is valuable despite the high speed, high-tech manner of its production. It provides a verbal and pictorial record of the experiences of 'amateurs' (ordinary citizens from varying backgrounds) who because of chance contacts became spies for Cuba's Ministry of the Interior. All concerned seem to have been amateurish. The US Special Interests officials happily handed out open passes to any Cuban who presented him/herself as a counter-revolutionary. Thus equipped, such people could and did wander in and out of the Special Interests building, together with up to three companions, using its computers and snooping at will. One almost feels sorry for those obtuse US officials, so sure of the Revolution's unpopularity that any apparent counter-revolutionary was assumed to be genuine and made welcome not only in their offices but in their homes.

This Mickey Mouse scene in no way resembles the bad old commando days when many lives were lost and huge damage was done to Cuba's vital installations. As the spies infiltrated numerous small dissident groups they found ideological squabbles, jealousy about who gained what from the Special Interests hand-outs, fierce personality clashes and a rapid turn-over in memberships as coveted 'refugee' visas rewarded not very tangible achievements. Few projects with genuinely destabilising potential were uncovered. Going by the letter of the law, those subversives jailed in 2003 were undoubtedly guilty and needed restraint – but surely not imprison-ment? When I said as much to Alberto he argued rather implausibly that their sort could become a menace if used by McCarry's threatening 'Commission'.

In his launch speech, Felipe Perez asked, 'Will this book be known beyond the borders of Cuba? Will it enjoy the same front page coverage as the media campaigns waged against Cuba? We will have to wait and see if newspapers print reviews, if television networks come to seek the truth and interview the people who have revealed this truth.' As far as my observation goes, *The Dissidents* is virtually unknown outside Cuba. Yet in another political context it might have become a bestseller, given its extraordinary blend of 'human interest' and the tensions that go with spying – however amateurish. The narrative has a peculiarly Cuban flavour; it is light-years away from the noxious world of CIA/KGB activities. As Felipe Perez notes, 'This is not the story of a repressive regime that obtained confessions through torture . . . The Revolution has used the method of infiltrating the enemy; it has used intelligence, shrewdness, covert activity, but within certain limits . . . ' He also points out that Revolutionary Cuba is the real 'dissident', its counter-revolutionaries the conformists allied to 'savage capitalism', seeking 'to impose a single system on the world, a single way of living, a single model of conduct'.

I was crossing the Bay of Havana to visit Normando, a genuinely indepen-dent dissident to whom I had a letter of introduction from my Pinar friends. During that twelve-minute ferry ride early clouds glowed rose-pink and old-gold above the two fortresses – Castillo de Moro and Castillo de la Punta – massively guarding the deep channel linking bay to ocean. Here one fully appreciates Havana's contribution to Spain's empire-building. This wide, sheltered bay might have been custom-built to protect treasure fleets from well-armed pirates. Now an occasional cruise liner, defying the blockade, moors briefly at an Old Havana terminal near the Plaza de Armas while freighters regularly deliver cargoes of containers – some brightly painted and variously logo'd, seeming alien amidst the drab dilapidation of the docks.

Many of my fellow passengers were cyclists who pedalled away on the narrow wooden pier. Across the road stands a small, recently restored early nineteenth-century church dedicated to Nuestra Señora de la Virgen de Regla, who has a dual personality. She is also Yemaya, the Santería patroness of the sea and mother of all men. This statue arrived from Spain in a hermit's luggage in 1696 and fourteen years later was appointed patroness of Havana and of all Cuban fishermen; nobody knows its origin. Two black hands hold a fair, pink-cheeked Infant Jesus on the Virgin's lap and her shrine is surrounded by a bank of white and blue artificial flowers – Yemaya's colours. Each Santería *orisha* has his/her own combination of colours. (In West Africa's Yoruba religion *orishas* are spiritual messengers from Olofi/God.) I sat for a little time in the comparative coolness of this agreeably simple church, watching Yemaya's worshippers offering half a cigar, a banana, a bunch of blue and white wild flowers, a sprinkle of rum. Two old men came together, and three young men wearing dockers' uniforms, and a few women on their way to the market.

Regla is a compact, attractive, tranquil town, founded as a fishing port in 1687. It grew with the sugar industry; colossal warehouses dominate the shore south of the pier. Many freed slaves settled here and the Santería ambience is perceptible as one strolls on broken pavements through quiet pot-holed streets lined with paint-hungry eighteenth- or nineteenth-century houses, often handsomely tiled, not grand but suggesting a sufficiency. Some tourist dollars must percolate through from Havana, but not enough to trigger economic renewal. No householders were selling coffee or buns or ham-rolls from their doorways, no pizza stall catered for the long bus queue on a neglected plaza – its flowerbeds empty, its fountains dry and littered. The bus, when it came, was not Chinese. As Normando put it, 'Regla stays stuck in the Special Period'. The Municipal Museum, said to provide a particularly interesting exposition of Santería, was closed for repairs. Likewise the Liceo Artistico y Literario where Martí delivered one of his most famous and stirring speeches on Cuban in-dependence. However, the natives were friendly and cheerful. A lanky black youth went out of his way to guide me to Normando's home on a low hilltop where a ten-foot-high Lenin (a guru not often commemorated in Cuba) surveys the port from a rocky inset.

Normando lived alone in a newish two-roomed clapboard dwelling built on the site of a *bohío*; young banana plants formed a 'hedge' around two *organopónico* beds made of timbers salvaged from a derelict warehouse. We sat indoors, on either side of a revolving fan, and I mopped with an already sodden sweat-rag while Normando gave me news of our mutual friends in Pinar.

My host, I had been warned, liked an argument; with *fidelistas* he tended to excoriate Castroism's failures, with anti-*fidelistas* to praise its successes. His 'CV' was remarkable. The Revolution orphaned him – a mother killed by Batista's bombing of the Sierra Maestra in 1958 when he was a toddler, a father killed four years later during the Escambray 'civil war'. Grandparents reared him, the Revolution educated him, he grew up a loyal *fidelista*, graduated as a biochemist, then came to resent 'Sovietisation' and migrated. In the US he was employed for twelve years by a biotechnology company listed on the stock exchange and found it hard to take the influence of commercial pressures on his own and his colleagues' work. Post-Comecon, he chose to leave his secure job and return to experience the Special Period. 'I always believed in the Revolution,' he explained, 'and now we Cubans had got it back.' A Miami-born wife and twin sons were abandoned without, it seemed, too much heartache on Normando's part. In the mid-1980s he had heard about the discovery, by Havana's Finlay Institute, of an effective meningitis B vaccine – a world first. This breakthrough inspired the establishment in 1986 of the Centre for Bio-technology (CIGB) and Normando's homecoming coincided with the government's decision – at once reckless and shrewd – to invest vast amounts in those biotechnology industries generally presumed to be the preserve of Minority World scientists.

In 1994 the Centre for Molecular Immunology (CIM) was opened and quickly justified its existence. 'By 1999,' said Normando, 'we were exporting medical products to India, China, Russia, Latin America – over fifty countries. The First World of course locked us out – an alliance of US blockaders, pharmaceutical bullies and complicated drug protocols. Then Canadians came to the rescue, helped us develop international clinical trials for six products now selling all over North America and Europe. An English friend who often visits' [Professor Michael Levin, head of the Paediatric Unit, St Mary's Hospital, Paddington] 'says our doctors, scientists and laboratories are world-class in spite of a crashed economy.

This year Chinese oncologists are using CIM's Theracim Hr3. Two other CIM therapies are being manufactured in India and China under Cuban supervision. And guess what – the State Department has allowed one US company [Cancervax] 'to carry out clinical trials for the US market! Still the *Yanquis* can't focus on our advantage . . . it's not true you only get monkeys if you pay peanuts.'

Cuba's on-a-shoe-string successes (twenty-six discoveries, more than a hundred international patents granted) rile those who lavish billions of dollars on medical research with, proportionally, far less impressive results. According to Normando, this outcome should baffle nobody. 'In the First World, *accountants* decide whether or not new formulae are developed as medications.'

The dread word 'accountants' gave me an opening to moan about the calamitous role of that breed in the twenty-first-century publishing world where full-time professional editors ('not cost-effective') are threatened with extinction.

Suddenly Normando's mood changed and he spoke frankly as an unorthodox but committed son of the Revolution. To him the fateful spring of 2003 marked a turning point at which the government lost its compass. Jailing the dissidents, he believed, was a mistake, because their collaboration with a foreign power didn't really matter. 'They're a shoal of feeble no-goods, best ignored – rounding them up played the *Yanqui* game. Then we looked scared and they seemed influential. Which they weren't and could never be for one obvious reason. However we resent the way things are, we do not – repeat *not* – want to become again a US colony!'

I asked, 'Why d'you think they lost the compass?'

'Cason rattled them – *de facto* US ambassador but not keeping the diplomatic rules. He arrived in September '02 and personally, publicly, tried to organise dissidents. Didn't Rene and Luis show you their shots of him delivering books to Pinar's "independent library"? Everyone could see him in action, in his own residence he ran workshops for "independent journalists". When Perez Roque sent warnings about "breaches of diplomatic status" he ignored them, went on taunting Cuba. He even invited foreign journalists to meet him at sedition-stirring sessions in dissidents' homes. I guess our guys thought they'd look weak, at home and in Washington, if they let him get away with insulting his host government.'

'Then why not send him home? Wouldn't that have been wiser than jailing seventy-five who could be used as "prisoners of conscience"?'

Normando's gesture expressed impatience and some anger. 'Sure we should've packed him off and shown the media the evidence against the traitors shown in court. Governments like diplomats to keep the rules in public. We could've got international sympathy instead of being kicked up the backside. I don't know why our guys couldn't see that. I've heard rumours Fidel favoured the *persona non grata* route. If so, there's another example of him accepting collective decisions – something Cubans know about and outsiders refuse to believe! Since '59 it's been a war of nerves with the US. But keeping us twitchy is two-edged. Having to think so much about defence weakens us, having to be united against aggression strengthens us. Being always on guard against saboteurs, we've never had space for political-ideological open debate – the enemy could turn it into a weapon.'

After a lunch of cold roast pork and tomato salad Felix escorted me down to the ferry. On the way we paused to drink rum with a Santería friend of his who was also a librarian and had much to say about US-funded 'independent libraries'. These became a focus of controversy in the US after the mass-jailings. Allegedly, ten of the seventy-five were 'independent librarians', highlighted by the media as cultured literary folk muzzled by communists. However, the prestigious sixty-four thousand-strong American Library Association, which has long-term links with Cuba, thought otherwise.

Back in 2001 Rhonda L. Neugebauer (Bibliographer, Latin American Studies, University of California) led a delegation of librarians to Cuba where, since 1989, she has been regularly meeting colleagues and touring libraries. Subsequently she wrote a long paper for the 'Information for Social Change Journal' (No.13, Summer 2001). It concludes:

I must say a few words about the 'independent libraries'. I leave them for last because they are really a small group of people . . . who do not represent Cuban librarianship and do not deserve mention as part of its history. They are the brain-child of the US government, as is much of the anti-Castro opposition within Cuba. And this is admitted by State Dept officials as well as by the 'independent librarians' themselves. The supporters of these 'libraries' are using them to claim all sorts of things that go way beyond the scope of a book collection . . . If they are so 'repressed' why are their materials available for me to see? Why do they tell me what they are doing and from whom they receive funds? Why can an 'independent librarian' also be an 'independent journalist', phone and fax reports to Miami on a daily basis about 'repression' (that only they witnessed) and receive money from a foreign government f or their 'services'? We are able to give you first-hand reports on the activities of these groups because we visited them in their homes and saw their libraries . . . They told us themselves that they are using the front of an 'independent library' in order to call themselves opponents of Castro and receive monthly cheques from the US government! They are clear about what they are doing – although some claim to have actually circulated books – they know their purpose is merely to exist so that outsiders can claim there is opposition to Castro in Cuba . . . In Cuba I heard a lot of critical remarks about the government (from many sources) but the 'independent librarians' are not independent thinkers and we confirmed that they are not librarians . . . The real librarians in Cuba are aware of the misinformation that is being spread . . . and resent these attempts to put a human face on foreign intervention by using librarians and the rallying cry of 'intellectual freedom'.

As this 2001 report makes plain, 'dissidents' (though always under surveillance) were not harassed until James Cason took over at the US Interests Section.

In December 2003, eight months after the round-up, Nat Hentoff wrote an article in the *Village Voice* ('In Castro's Gulag – Librarians') deploring 'Castro's crackdown on Cuba's dissenters for the crime of advocating freedom of thought'. He criticised the American Library Associations' annual meeting in Toronto where 'Cuban independent librarians were denied a speaking place on the program while Castro's librarians were given the freedom to speak for nearly three hours'. A week later Nat Hentoff's contribution was entitled 'Criminalizing Librarians' with special reference to Victor Rolando Arroyo 'who directed an independent, private library before being sentenced to twenty-six years in prison and also belongs to the Independent Cuban Journalists and Writers Union'. In Pinar del Rio, Arroyo led all the US-funded groups including the Centre for Trade Union Studies which every Saturday ran lectures (thinly attended) on how to be a successful subversive. In his mother's home in the Jacinto district he met with Cason and his predecessor, Vicky Huddleston. He regularly misinformed the outside world that two million Cubans, out of eleven million, were dissidents. An extreme hard-liner, he urged Cason to suspend family remittances from the US and cancel all flights between Havana and Miami. The principal evidence against him was documentary, including receipts for funding that had come directly from CANF. Among Pinar's other counter-revolutionaries he was unpopular but tolerated because of his exceptionally close links to the US Interest Section. Nat Hentoff asks, 'Is Victor Arroyo a "Traitor to Cuba"?' The answer is 'Yes'.

Chapter 19

On 6 October I walked to the railway station between heavy showers, and got quite a shock; since my last journey to Santa Clara this service had been transformed. Punctually we departed in a conventionally comfortable train: open-plan, well-lit, unvandalised coaches, our tickets checked by a cheerful middle-aged conductress who dispensed complimentary salami rolls, bottles of Tukola and that morning's *Granma*. I didn't grumble, though I do prefer corridor trains; they allow more freedom of movement – and more bonding, in face-to-face carriages. My seat companion, a slim young woman clasping a large drum, slept all the way. Our conductress had suggested putting the drum in the luggage annex but evidently it was too precious to be deserted.

Granma's front page commemorated this being the thirty-first anniversary of the fatal bombing of a Cubana Airways plane taking seventy-three passengers to Havana. Another article outlined the latest injury inflicted by the blockade. Inside pages reported the many events being organised throughout Latin America for the Ché anniversary, Lula's fuzzy comments on privatisation, the misdeeds of DynCorp in Puerto Rica, plans for the conservation of historic monuments in Cienfuegos and the killing by US forces of Iraqi women and children. One page was devoted to brief theatre, ballet and book reviews, another to baseball, boxing and fencing prospects. The back page extolled, with reams of statistics, a co-operative building project being undertaken in Granma province as a tribute to Ché and Camilo Cienfuegas, his second-in-command during the Battle of Santa Clara. *Granma* does not strive to entertain.

It was good to be back in a city centre where human voices are the dominant sound and 'traffic noise' means hoof-beats. Surprisingly, no municipal contributions to the Ché 'event' were visible; I had been expecting banners, bunting and scrolls. Santa Clara's first commemoration was happening on 8 October, forty years after Ché's wounding and capture. On the 9th, the date of his execution, Acting-President Raul had to be M.C. in Havana. Five days later he would return to Santa Clara with President Hugo Chavez of Venezuela for the most solemn commemoration, to be attended by Ché's family. This I had discovered belatedly, after arranging to meet an important friend of a friend in Camaguey – someone I couldn't contact to try to change our appointment, and he would be travelling from elsewhere to meet me.

By 7.30 a.m. on 7 October the Plaza de la Revolucion was all action. Dozens of ebullient schoolchildren, directed by two adults, were neatly arranging thousands of dark blue plastic chairs on the concrete expanse overlooked by Ché's statue. Pathways were being vigorously swept with twig brooms. Teams of sound technicians were erecting pylon-like ampli-fiers that arrived in bits on trucks, their reconstruction reminding me of childhood struggles with Meccano. (I pre-date Lego.) This whole area, quite dejected on my first visit, had been spruced up: weeds gone, fountains splashing, grass clipped, flower-beds glowing, broken concrete steps mended, faded billboards renewed, though Ché's exhortations remained the same: *Hasta la victoria siempre.*

I turned towards the inconspicuous museum and mausoleum, closed for repainting during my last visit. At a nearby kiosk one exchanges one's bag for a ticket; here the tourist industry defers to Ché's principles and entry is free – as to a synagogue, church or mosque. The museum exhibits are standard: Ché's weapons, pipe, camera, binoculars, field-radio, beret, combat jacket, the asthmatic's inhaler he so desperately needed, the dental instruments he used in his camp clinics. Seeing his uniform, one realises he was a smaller man – less tall and broad – than one imagines him to have been. But what counts in this museum is the collection of enlarged family (and other) photographs illustrating Ché's transformation from beloved, pampered baby to defiant, emaciated guerrilla warrior. One notices his mother's large strong hands as she poses with her infant son in his long christening robe. The toddler, sucking two fingers, looks serious and determined. The schoolboy in short trousers sits on a car bonnet, the adolescent enjoys rugby, golf, basketball, the young man motorcycles the length of South America – by now a famous journey. A much-reproduced Sierra Maestra group photograph shows Celia smoking a cigarette, as do many other shots of Fidel's most significant friend. (She died in her fifties, of lung cancer, whereupon Fidel 'became convinced that the ultimate sacrifice I should make on behalf of public health in Cuba was to quit smoking. Teach by example.') My favourite in this collection shows Ché reclining on the ground in an African hut reading Goethe while cuddling a pup.

From the museum one enters the mausoleum, a shadowy cave-like chamber. Here Ché and seventeen other guerrillas occupy ossuary niches in the cliff wall. An eternal flame, lit by Fidel on 17 October 1997, flickers amidst boulders and greenery suggesting the jungle in which these *compañeros* fought and died. The atmosphere is reverential – and powerful. Those rare places where emotions, positive or negative, are palpably concentrated have always intrigued me. I've come upon them in Nepal, Coorg, Eastern Turkey, Northern Ireland, Rwanda, the Russian Far East but in Santa Clara, a mere decade after the entombment, this concentration was wholly unexpected. We have wandered on to contentious territory, the way ahead obscured by a cloud of unknowing. Politics, propaganda, the packaging of Ché as a 'celebrity' don't adequately explain the atmosphere, generated by an accumulation of individuals' responses to Ché's message. I left with a lump in my throat.

On the other side of the city, at the site of Ché's battle-winning train ambush, the wrecked wagons had recently been repainted – a bad idea, they looked much less authentic. The adjacent example of 'public art', a singularly ugly irregular conglomeration of long concrete slabs, was being dutifully photographed by Viazul tourists. Two Canadian matrons were registering outrage at the cost of the 'museum' wagon ticket. To feel a thrill at Blinidad one needs an intimate knowledge of Ché's military exploits.

At 6.00 a.m. the old moon lay in the arms of the new and, nearby, Venus shone lustrously in a starless sky. Seeing children on their way to school took me aback; I had expected this to be a Special Day in Santa Clara. Between Parque Vidal and the Plaza large cheerful crowds were gathering at each street junction, apparently awaiting leaders, and as the first sun rays touched Ché's bronze form I was approaching three skimpy barriers blocking the road – the sort a child could move. These were manned by a quartet of young toughs – evidently marshalls, though wearing no uniforms, badges or arm-bands. I walked ahead on the verge, ignoring the barriers, but was ordered to return and await their removal. Just then all those crowds I had passed earlier could be seen processing towards us, filling the long, wide street. I joined the vanguard, noticing that everyone carried a postcard-sized blue and green pass or ticket. When a marshall demanded mine I stared at him, nonplussed – then showed my passport. He shook his head: without a ticket I could not proceed. My first reaction was disbelief: there must be some misunderstanding. I stood silent, stunned and bewildered – then began to plead, expressing devotion to Ché, explaining that I had come all the way from Ireland for this occasion. The marshall shouted at me, rudely, making a dismissive gesture. At that a mixture of rage and disappointment brought me close to tears and for a wild moment I considered walking on, testing the marshalls' authority – which would have been stupid, inviting deportation. Instead I sloped off to try my luck elsewhere, with little hope of success though I knew the environs quite well and could think of three peripheral places where the Plaza merged into the surrounding fields. But of course each possibility was now being surveyed by a policeman – all three young, lightly armed, friendly and polite. They listened to me attentively, looked sympathetic, seemed genuinely to regret having to do their duty.

Back at the road-block, tension had gathered. For Cuba's tourist industry, this was a PR mini-disaster; pass-less Ché-worshippers, from four continents, were protesting against their exclusion from the Plaza. However, this wasn't an anti-foreigner rule; we were surrounded by furious pass-less Cubans who expressed their fury between themselves, not directing it at the marshalls. One young Australian woman sobbed as she begged for mercy; she spoke fluent Spanish and a Cuban friend stood beside her, giving useless support. She was writing her thesis on Ché's 'New Man' concept and had been saving up for two years to be in Santa Clara for 'the fortieth'. My own rage was refuelled by the marshalls' insolence as they glared contemptuously at us foreigners while yelling abuse at any argumentative Cuban.

Had we been allowed to remain at the original barrier site we could have seen a fraction of the ceremony (though not the 'stage', the enormous plinth on which Ché's statue stands) and heard the speeches led by Raul's panegyric. But now the bullies herded us far down the road and spitefully summoned three gigantic trucks from some nearby depot to block our view. Hatred flared then amidst the frustrated locals, reminding me of incidents during that long visa wait in Havana. Petty officials drunk on a little power bring out the worst in everybody. It was easy to imagine those marshalls harassing dissidents and greatly enjoying it. Later, Tania slyly observed that I perhaps needed this experience to blunt my scepticism about certain human rights violations.

With hindsight it was obvious that for this occasion I should have overcome my allergy to group-travel and joined fellow-members of the Cuba Solidarity Campaign in London. It's an uncomfortable fact that official Cuba can't cope with independent solo travellers – unlabelled individuals. As a member of a group that is expected, one is shown everything: schools, hospitals, factories, farms, laboratories – even prisons. The group can be indiscriminately labelled: teachers, musicians, brick-

layers, historians, doctors, chefs, cyclists, nurses, architects, artists, philosophers, organic farmers. All are welcome – if expected, their names filed
and their movements pre-arranged. The individual traveller is of course
also welcomed by the individual Cuban but excluded from all institutions.
Several teachers and doctors wanted me to see their workplaces but my
being unlabelled disqualified me from crossing those thresholds. This
rigidity feels unCuban, a too durable residue of the Soviet phase. Tania
saw it as 'a sharp weapon for our enemies. Cuban institutions have nothing
to hide. We're not and have never been like the Soviet Union. But this
stupid behaviour gives another impression'.

One of the high, wide billboards overlooking the Plaza de la Revolucion
said, 'Be more efficient every day, be better every day' – a Ché quote
obviously heeded by Santa Clara's municipal workers. At dawn on 9
October I had the Plaza to myself and, astoundingly, not even one Tukola
tin or scrap of paper littered this space where 45,000 people had assembled
twenty-four hours previously. An even greater gathering was to take place
five days hence yet the chairs had vanished and the sound system had
been dismantled.

I was on my way to Santa Clara's recently renovated bus station where,
in a cubby-hole partitioned off for tourists, a beautiful young woman laid
down the law with a charming smile: I must use Viazul and I could book a
seat now but I could buy my ticket only one hour before departure for
Camaguey at 2.00 p.m. on the morrow.

A bicitaxi took me to Immigration on the city's far side. Because Cuban
visas are granted for thirty days my five-week visit required an extension
for another thirty days. In Dublin I had asked the Cuban ambassador
(H.E. Noel Carrillo, a congenial and helpful character) if he could provide
me with two thirty-day visas to spare me another encounter with the
Ministry of the Interior. That, however, was impossible; the extension
must always be obtained within Cuba. But I could get it at any provincial
capital's Immigration Office on any date that suited me.

I have mixed feelings about bicitaxis. As a 'green' alternative and a
healthy source of income for many men put out of work by factory closures,
I applaud them. But, being myself a cyclist, I found it quite embarrassing
to sit behind the pedaller watching other legs transporting me. This chatty
young man was a vigorous pedaller who played baseball for Santa Clara
and paused en route to show me a photograph of his infant son.

The Ministry of the Interior occupies a 1920s villa on a street corner.

Across the road an off-duty bus horse was enjoying the lush grass of the verge and in the front garden a palm tree had shed glistening red berries to the delight of a toddler who was being warned not to touch them. Here was a short queue, relaxing on the verandah's two benches while the toddler's mother shadowed him around the garden. Through an open door we could see two tall, handsome mulatto officers in well-tailored brown uniforms doing their bureaucratic things in a drab little office. Their secretary was a dumpy woman of uncertain age, sharp-voiced and weary-looking.

The petitioner on my left was being summoned repeatedly into a side office; after each brief interview she looked more anxious. An overweight woman, her movements awkward, she had copper-dyed hair, a prominent nose, wide-set grey eyes. Having been recently widowed, she wished to live with her daughter in Havana but some arcane regulation was blocking the mandatory 'change of residence' permit. Her final interview, on the verandah, was with a tall young woman, stylishly dressed in mufti, who spoke to her kindly but could offer no reprieve. She hurried to the gate with head bowed, holding back tears. Then, as she passed along the pavement, I could see her face crumpling and hear anguished sobs. This denial of the 'human right' to move house does smell of dictatorship.

When my turn came the junior officer spent thirteen minutes (there was a wall-clock above his desk) filling in a form which the senior officer, after a quick glance, pronounced '*invalido*'. My visa could not be extended until 15 October, two weeks before its expiry. So much for the ambassador's illusion . . .

I walked the three miles back to Parque Vidal – slowly, with rest stops, being bludgeoned by the heat. I had long since abandoned my plan to trek from Holguin to Biran (Fidel's birthplace). I would get there, but not on foot.

Near Immigration the city's main open-air food market covers acres of uneven ground and by midday was uncrowded. I admired the day's left-overs which to me looked like prize-winners; Santa Clara prides itself on being a pioneer of Cuba's *organoponico* movement. As Tania boasted, 'When overseas people talked about the Revolution collapsing, its spirit was being revived here in this city by the new challenge of having to feed ourselves'. Those revivalists had Marx on their side. In *Das Kapital* he noted: 'Capitalist production . . . disturbs the metabolic interaction between man and the earth, it prevents the return to the soil of its constituent elements consumed by man in the form of food and clothing.

All progress in capitalist agriculture is a progress in the art, not only of robbing the workers, but of robbing the soil.'

By now Cuba is famous for the multi-faceted triumphs of its organic agriculture to which the Californian red earthworm energetically contributes. 'Lumbri culture,' explained Tania, 'has made our urban food-growing possible.' Whereupon she took the lid off her barrel of 'assistants' – as she affectionately called them – to reveal Californian reds in a state of perpetual motion as they converted waste matter to fabulously enriching fertiliser.

Indulgence in Coppelia seemed an appropriate reward for my sweltering walk. After a twenty-minute pavement queue came a ten-minute cash-desk queue followed by a twenty-five-minute wait to be served, while staff members chatted together, their backs turned to the patient customers. Were one even slightly in a hurry, this would be unacceptable. But Cuba's ice-cream addicts never appear to be in a hurry and I always enjoyed Coppelia's non-profit-making ambience.

In Havana one of my genuine dissident friends (that circle had widened) gave me a letter to deliver to a fellow-dissident in Santa Clara University. Boarding an early students' bus, I was puzzled to find it almost empty. Then I remembered the date: 10 October is not only Clodagh's birthday (Ten Today!) but a Cuban national holiday, the anniversary of Cespedes's launching of the first War of Independence in 1868. To celebrate, government offices and educational institutions have the day off and I found those miles of campus deserted, all doors locked; but perhaps someone would appear a little later. For more than an hour I ambled around the green spaces between the blocks – park-like and tree-rich, the silence broken only by bird song. I needed the silence and solitude; I had been too long (twelve days!) in cites. Worryingly, no one appeared – and I had a bus to catch at 2.00 p.m. So what to do with that letter? Entrust it to Tania? Or return to sender? The latter, I decided: which says something about my relationship with the Revolution.

That relationship has to be ambiguous. Mario explained why in Key West. 'I left for the same reason you, as a writer, would have left. You wouldn't be happy in a country where you couldn't express all your true thoughts and feelings. So I sailed away not hating *el comandante* but seeing no space for me in his world.' If born a Cuban, would I have had the courage of my socialist convictions and remained loyal to Castroism at the cost of my freedom to write and to travel? I doubt it. The real Heroes of the Revolution are the considerable minority who made that sacrifice to benefit the majority.

On the half-full Viazul bus I rescinded all scornful references to 'air-conditioned luxury'; in that cool coach I could feel myself coming back to life. Our five-hour journey was agreeable enough, the driver taking the pot-holed roads slowly and allowing two longish stops, in Sancti Spiritus and Ciego de Avila.

My only fellow-tourist was a Finnish OAP with a bald pate and a long white beard who had been holidaying annually in Cuba since 2001. He was uneasy about the Rapid Reaction militia. Was it not dangerous to train all the young how to fight with guns? Supposing another Bay of Pigs when Fidel dies – might not big numbers rise against Raul's regime? Wanting their share of tourism benefits, having been taught the Revolution is all about equality . . . Was it not stupid to expect them to go on accepting the dual currency's inequality? I suggested thinking more positively; such an uprising seems unlikely, however discontented the have-nots. Contemporary Cubans are disinclined to shed each other's blood though they have been conditioned to shed any amount of invaders' blood should that prove necessary.

At first our road wound through low irregular hills: the ground broken, few *bohios*, little cultivation, patches of woodland, much scrub. Then came the fertile flatness of Camaguey province – Cuba's largest, long famous as a source of enormous wealth (cattle and sugar cane). However, between Cuba's Wars of Independence the international sugar crisis shattered the social superstructure of old *latifundista* families; in 1958 not one mill was owned by the descendants of a Spanish grantee. A few aristocratic Camaguey clans, like the Betancourts and Agromontes, retained shrunken cattle ranches but the largest and richest estates belonged to US companies.

When the Revolution rather ham-fistedly appropriated about one-third of a million Camaguey acres (one hundred and thirty-one ranches), opposition to Agrarian Reform was unusually vigorous. In August 1959 the dispossessed tried to bribe two army majors to join a conspiracy to set up a provisional administration run by ranchers. Feigning enthusiasm for this plan, the majors assembled fifty armed men at Trinidad airport where the plot leaders were appalled to see Fidel sitting under a mango tree. Within hours hundreds of conspirators had been arrested, all over Cuba.

A month later internal dissension fractured the Rebel Army when Huber Matos, a multi-talented and popular guerrilla leader, resigned as Camaguey's provincial governor and military commander. He objected to the Revolution being infiltrated by Communists and to the manner in which Agrarian Reform was being implemented – though not to the Reform itself. Fourteen other officers resigned with him. In a touching and dignified letter of resignation he warned *el comandante*: 'It is right, however, to recall to you that great men begin to decline when they cease to be just.' Fidel then labelled him 'a traitor who has obstructed Agrarian Reform' and on 20 October travelled to Camaguey personally to supervise Matos's arrest – the *compañero* who less than a year before had been fighting beside him in the Sierra Maestra.

Matos's trial, in December, brought him a twenty-year sentence and the officers who had resigned with him received between seven and two years. The ensuing controversy threatened for a time to destroy the unity of Fidel's following; the Camaguey newspaper, *Adelante*, supported Matos, defending both the validity of his criticism of Agrarian Reform blunders and his right to voice them. However, this self-inflicted injury soon healed; already most Cubans were benefiting from their fast-moving Revolution. For the first time in history what had been promised to the Cuban poor was being delivered.

By mid-afternoon we were driving towards a dense mass of low black cloud – and then we were driving through it and my Finnish friend exclaimed, 'Is like submarine travel!' That torrential downpour lasted for seventy-two hours, slightly modifying the heat.

Camaguey, one of the seven original Spanish settlements, was known until 1903 as Santa Maria del Puerto del Principe (Puerto Principe for short). In 1514/15 it replaced a large indigenous village whose inhabitants were briskly slaughtered to make space for farmers who arrived from Seville in 1516. During the seventeenth century it became city-sized, its development often interrupted but not much slowed by pirate raids. In 1668 Henry Morgan, the English 'terror of the Caribbean', occupied Camaguey for a week or so while his buccaneers were collecting jewels and gold from the homes of already wealthy cattle ranchers. To induce them to reveal their treasures' hiding-places he locked them into the cathedral without food or water. Eleven years later the French pirate, Francois de Granmont, took over the city for four weeks, sacked it comprehensively and departed with fourteen women captives, all later released unharmed – hence his nickname, El Caballero. By the nineteenth century Camaguey was Cuba's second largest city (since overtaken by Santiago) and always it was predominantly white – and noted, pre-Revolution, for its strict segregation policies.

Alina and Max had invited me to stay in their *casa non-particulare*. I didn't ask why they felt free to entertain a foreign guest; they were friends of Juan (let's call him) with whom I had that important though so inconvenient appointment for the thirteenth. At the bus station Alina awaited me with outstretched umbrella and we ran to an unlicenced taxi which cautiously negotiated dark narrow streets racing with water. Near the former Plaza de Armas (now the Parque Agramonte) Max opened a massive hall door flanked by carved granite pillars and leading directly into a high-ceilinged drawing-room. There the TV set and computer looked incongruous amidst an abundance of imperial mahogany chairs and chests, frail rosewood occasional tables and an escritoire inlaid with gold leaf.

All the one-storey colonial mansions on this cobbled street have misleading façades: only two windows to one side of the entrance. In fact they extend far back and beyond my room were the dining-room, a smallish kitchen, a large *banyo* and four other bedrooms. This was a three-generation family: two *abuelas*, the young couple, nine-year-old Lydia, five-year-old Patricio. An aloof smoky Persian was on bad terms with a furry golden mongrel (cocker terrier?) who answered to the name of Guzzie when so minded.

From the drawing-room Alina led me down a long corridor-cum-patio, the former roofed, the latter a jungle of shrubs, cacti, creepers, ferns and young trees, now being thoroughly washed through wire netting to Alina's gratification. Superb tiles, brought from Spain in the eighteenth century but still unchipped, brightened both floor and wainscoting. Antique copper bracket lamps lit all the main rooms and delicately wrought grills protected the windows. The ten-foot-high doorways were narrow in proportion – the effect elegant, with finely carved wooden screens filling each doorway's middle section, allowing air to circulate in the windowless bedrooms. Alina warned me that my 1940s air-conditioning didn't respond for eight minutes after the switch being pressed – then it came on with multiple thuds, like an elephant step-dancing, before settling down to a rattle-and-whine duet. I sweated instead. Just outside my door a giant *tinajone* was still in use beneath a gutter. These bulbous clay jars, up to five feet tall and ten feet in diameter, are to be seen all over Camaguey – though usually, now, as ornaments. Invented to store oil, wine or grain, the Spaniards imported them to this drought-prone city for water storage; when half-buried in the earth their contents remain cool and fresh. In the seventeenth century Camaguey began to make its own *tinajones* and soon a family's wealth was being judged by the quantity and quality of its water-jars.

Non-stop rain, accompanied by hours of deafening thunder and blinding lightening, transformed me into a dutiful tourist. Instead of rambling for a day around this unknown city I 'did' the Iglesia Nuestra Senora de la Soledad (rebuilt 1776, faded baroque frescoes), the Iglesia del Sagrado Corazon de Jesus (1920, neo-Gothic, too much gilt and marble), the Convento y Hospital de San Juan de Dios (1728, superb arcaded cloisters), the Catedral Metropolitana de Nuestra Senora de Candelaria (1864, to replace Camaguey's first church, built in 1530 but demolished by an earthquake) and Casa Natal Ignacio Agramonte, the war hero's home, a solidly dignified eighteenth-century mansion furnished in a style made possible by large cattle ranches. Between churches I saw a man naked to the waist cycling fast through the downpour balancing a birthday cake in one hand with a dachshund, wrapped in a transparent plastic bag, sitting upright in his wire handlebar basket.

Camaguey, though noticeably poorer than Havana or Santa Clara, has its quota of *tiendas*, their stock restricted by local demand. In one I queued with four tins of Buccanero and found myself shivering. Are these stores kept so very cold to reinforce their 'affluent' image? Such abrupt and extreme changes of temperature must endanger public health, apart from wasting energy. I began to sneeze when the young woman ahead of me caused a logjam by paying for a CP30 purchase with a CP100 note. All her ID details, and the note's ID details, had to be handwritten in a ledger, which she and the assistant signed before the latter entrusted them to a computer together with details of the purchases (three children's garments). For twenty minutes I stood waiting while behind me the queue lengthened and for once was not patient. But nobody blamed the system; the young woman was at fault for not having changed her note at the *Cambio* across the street.

By a happy coincidence this imprisoning weather converged with a Cuban rarity, a short shelf of English books belonging to Irma, Alina's mother, who had been nun-schooled in Philadelphia and became a Rose Macaulay fan. While rain loudly lashed the patio jungle I lay on my bed, sweat trickling steadily, and took refuge in three volumes of cool, supple prose. These transported me to a 1920s London where young married couples had two house servants and farthings were legal currency and Sudanese visitors were referred to as 'fuzzies'. Not for the first time, I reflected that phrases hinting at sexual excitement can be more erotic than paragraphs describing orgasms.

Twice Irma invited me into her shadowy bed-sitter, stuffed with heavy dark furniture. 'I like to practise my English while I tell you my thoughts for Cuba's future. We must mend fences with Washington, it's for our gain. We're always America-oriented, even before 1898. Talking about a love-hate relationship is silly, it's not that complicated. We only hate what all US administrations have done and tried to do. I remember how it was when thousands of Soviet helpers lived in ghettoes, more than twelve thousand technicians and soldiers with families. All stayed separate – schools, apart-ment blocks, restaurants, sports and social clubs – no dating or inter-marriage. Even the children couldn't bother to learn Spanish, we had to learn Russian or use interpreters. All the Party's "eternal friendship" rhetoric got very boring. If those helpers were *Yanquis*, and Washington respected us, we'd have made real friends. See our young now, loving US films, music, clothes, IT gear – food if they could get it! But don't be fooled, they'd not like the flavour of a US puppet government. That's the message the State Department can't hear.'

Irma had high hopes of Carlos Lage Davila as a fence-mender. 'He's a good sort of age, mid-fifties, experienced but vigorous. A physician by training but by nature a very smart economist – and in touch with public feeling. He knows millions of Cubans are just dying to set up private enterprises and Cuba needs them all. Too bad if some people get richer than others – that's the way of the world though Fidel won't have it.'

I felt a little buzz of shock as on touching a defective lamp switch. To hear *el comandante* named in a sentence implying censure is extremely unusual; in my case it happened twice in four months. As though to prove herself a sound nationalist Irma added, 'Martí believed a country of small property-owners is a truly rich country. I agree, I'm not wanting the corporations back.'

Juan arrived early on the Saturday morning, bringing sunshine with him, and after breakfast we strolled in Casino Campestre, Cuba's biggest city park, blessed by two rivers – the Juan del Torro and the Hatibonico – and magnificently wooded. Each mighty tree is meticulously labelled in Spanish and Latin and many of the thick contorted roots extend twenty or thirty feet overground, seeming quite separate from their trunk. One set coiled down to the narrow Hatibonico – then reappeared on the far bank. Monuments to local notables abound and parents wishing to relax in the *cerveza* tent may safely dump children in an immense playground, carefully fenced. A vigilant superintendent sits in a wooden hut by the only entrance gate and allows small children to leave only with the adults who deposited them.

Juan had lived in English-speaking countries for several years and our mutual friend had described him as 'a new breed of dissident, over-loyal to Revolutionary ideals'. When his criticisms of certain 'joint ventures' with foreign investors were too widely repeated, he was asked to retire early. He knew exactly where he would like to see the 'new Cuba' going and lamented its already being off in the opposite direction.

Listening to Juan's development of this theme, I understood why our mutual friend had identified us as kindred spirits. He longed for a Cuba that looked ahead, recognising the long-term significance of the Special Period's achievements.

'We've been there,' said Juan. 'We're an important example because we've survived. We've proved a people thrown back on their own resources, without warning or outsiders' aid, *can* survive. The Revolution's greatest achievement was not ousting Batista but quietly making an alternative plan after the Soviet collapse. We've adapted to having to go backwards, which is how even the US will have to go one day not so far off.'

'But,' I objected, 'you weren't really without warning. Fidel foresaw the collapse ahead of most world leaders. And isn't tourism outside aid? And how many Cubans are willing to continue going backwards? Adapting to a temporary crisis is different.'

Juan believed that the majority could be educated to accept a permanently 'green' society. 'If Fidel had twenty more years he could make them proud of that!' In 2006, when the World Wildlife Fund singled Cuba out as 'the only country now developing sustainably', Juan was not surprised. Obviously horse-buses and ox-ploughs can contribute more to solving the world's environmental problems than 'new technologies'. We agreed that the technologists who made so much of the mess can't reasonably be expected to clean it up while maintaining the value of shares. Do the world's corporate and political leaders really believe that this is possible? 'Maybe they have to fool themselves,' said Juan, 'or they'd get scared. Going backwards doesn't protect power and profit!'

By then we had retreated to the *cerveza* tent though its few torpid table fans did nothing to relieve the humidity. Opening our Buccaneros, Juan deplored the nature of Venzuela's industrial aid: a petro-chemical factory, a monster cement factory, an expanded nickel-smelting plant – 'How will our sustainability look in 2010?' Given the urgent need for more consumer goods, to replace essentials worn out or broken, President Chavez's petro-dollars should be used, argued Juan, to set up little factories, here and there around the island, providing jobs for redundant sugar workers.

In Casino Campestre, as elsewhere, T-shirts saying 'VIVA Chavez!' and baseball caps inscribed 'Venezuela', were now popular amongst all age groups. Juan commented on Cuba's feeling much less isolated in recent years, partly as a result of Fidel's reception (an unprecedented demonstration of affectionate respect) at the momentous Mercosur summit ten days before his illness struck. Latin American leaders are, understandably, better informed than any others about Cuba's revolution and the reasons why its humane social policies go with varying degrees of repressive authoritarianism. Juan added, 'Ché should be here to feel how the Latin American currents are moving – even after his death he stayed powerful. Who said "You can kill a man but not an idea"? It's a favourite Fidel quote, I should remember the source.'

We talked then about the adjective 'communist' as incessantly deployed to confine Cuba to an ideological territory despised throughout the capitalist world. Even now its Cold War accretions make the average reader/listener/viewer recoil, while putting a gloss on anti-Castroism per se. I recalled how my generation grew up hating and fearing Communism; the Cold War distorted international relations for most of my lifetime – beginning when I was fourteen, ending when I was sixty. In Roman Catholic Ireland it was easy to instil a loathing of atheistic Russia where churches were desecrated, children taught to revile God, priests and nuns slaughtered and raped ('violated' was the 1950s word). We didn't hear anything about the Russian Orthodox Church's sometimes lethal detestation of Roman Catholicism: that would have spoiled the picture. Personally I had decided by the age of eighteen that Christianity (or any institutional religion) was not for me; yet I abhorred Soviet Russian's dogmatic and brutal atheism. (Fidel was surely right – 'Every people in the history of the human race has had some diffused religiousness'.) Then, with the Cold War's ending, came a persistent sleight-of-tongue campaign. 'Socialism' was disgraced, defeated, dead; deliberately 'communism' and 'socialism' were and are used as synonyms – confusing a generation, making them all the more reluctant to challenge the morality of Capitalism Rampant.

With sudden vehemence Juan exclaimed, 'There was *no* Cold War! It was an arms race that only the richest could win. And communism wasn't defeated in Russia – like Gandhi said about Christianity, it would be a great system if someone tried it.'

'That depends,' I said, 'on what you mean by "communism". But I agree the Cold War was phoney.' And then we marvelled at the Western public's gullibility – its sheer want of common sense – throughout those decades. Picture the Soviet Union in 1945, gutted by its contribution to defeating Nazism – at least twenty million dead, the economy in ruins. The notion that within the foreseeable future that country could – or would want – to invade Western Europe or anywhere else was insane. But it was a notion dear to the military-industrial complex's heart, the best possible fertiliser to keep 'defence budgets' growing.

Juan described Cuban Socialism as 'a more authentic popular movement' then the Soviet version ever was. Yet even friends of the Revolution, he complained, didn't recognise – or misinterpreted – its genuinely populist foundation while critics ascribed Fidel's mass support to authoritarian manipulation. 'It's the other way round,' asserted Juan. 'Fidel's mass support gave a permit for authoritarianism – or what looks like it.'

My negative reaction to the word 'populist' brought a quick assurance that Fidel was a populist leader in the best sense, the ordinary Cubans' spokesman and facilitator, someone so directly linked to the populace and who empathises so strongly with them that he can voice their deepest wishes and often unexpressed thoughts. When Juan asked, 'Do you know Ernesto Laclau?' I shook my head.

'You should read him, an Argentine political theorist, I did my thesis on him. He says there can be no socialism without populism and the highest form of populism can only be socialist. I believe that.'

Scornfully Juan dismissed those who make fun of Fidel's long speeches. Such oratorical marathons were, he insisted, an essential ingredient of a populist leader's relationship with his followers. Mysteriously, over the years, those apparent monologues had had the effect of dialogues, strengthening the bond between speaker and audience while creating a powerful collective identity among vast crowds. Moreover, outsiders didn't appreciate how often Fidel's speeches from podiums or on TV were reinforced by leisurely conversations with ordinary individual workers or small groups. Until shortly before his illness, he regularly toured all the provinces, listening to the populace no less attentively than he used to listen, in his guerrilla days, to the Sierra Maestra *campesiños*. 'Remember,' said Juan, 'we're not talking about blind, stupid followers. The populist leader and the populace are interdependent. That's why Gaitan said, "I am not a Man, I am the People".'

Soon after Jorge Gaitan's famous declaration, in April 1948, the Columbian oligarchy used assassination to abort his revolution. Then Argentina's Colonel Peron foretold, 'That country will not return to normality for fifty years'. An understatement, as Juan pointed out. 'It's now sixty years and no normality in sight.'

Juan was an unusual Cuban in several respects, not least in his willingness to speculate with a foreigner about the future of Cuban Socialism.

'So where,' I wondered, 'does all you've said leave Castroism post-Fidel?'

Juan didn't feign optimism. He had a sharp-edged (or simplistic?) vision of the Revolution as a noble project demeaned by Sovietisation. '*Communism* wasn't – isn't – our problem. *Sovietisation* is still holding us back.' This idiosyncratic *fidelista* went on to define Sovietisation as a worse handicap, during Cuba's present critical transition stage, than the US embargo which only has practical consequences. He diagnosed 'intellectual paralysis' within the Sovietised bureaucracy, just when new thinking is needed to protect the Revolution's gains and build on the unity Fidel's populism achieved. He condemned the habitual use of stale Soviet-speak – a considerable irritant to the younger generation, a signal that their leaders feared to 'think new'. Meanwhile they were 'acting new', compromising with capital, openly looking to China as their model. At that point Juan shuddered – visibly, physically shuddered. After a moment's pause he said, 'China mixes the worse of both worlds, capitalist greed with communist tyranny. Odd how we don't hear Washington demanding "free and fair elections" before trading with those tyrants.'

Plainly Juan's recent 'career change' had inflicted a deep wound, been traumatic enough to distort his perception of Cuba on the cusp, a country with no alternative but to compromise Revolutionary ideals. I urged him to look on the bright side. What Washington had been dreading for years – a smooth transfer of power to Fidel's designated successors – was now a *fait accompli*. The friends I had contacted since my return spoke of their new collective leadership with pride; even those most critical of corruption, inefficiency, bureaucracy and chronic shortages were not at all eager for US 'help'. The 'intellectual paralysis' could, I suggested, be overcome in time by the new leadership. Professor Fred Halliday, an occasional advisor to the Cuban Foreign Ministry since the early 1980s, described in 2000 'an impressive group: witnesses of four decades of revolutionary upheaval and international drama, familiar with the leaders and inner workings of the Cuban state, well-travelled, committed to the broad aims of the Cuban revolution, sceptical of much of what passed for Marxist or radical writing in the west, and devoid of the kind of rhetorical posturing that so often characterises officials of such regimes.'

Repressing my own pessimism, I argued that the current compromise with capitalism didn't have to lead to the abandonment of Castroism, only its modification. Capitalism Rampant is now being exposed as inherently unstable, dependent for its survival on the use of high-tech military power – therefore doomed eventually to be defeated by the Majority World's low-tech resistance. And it could be that Cuba's experiment will serve, throughout the bloodiness, to hearten those who believe in people before profit.

The Camaguey Ballet Company, founded in 1967, is a close second to Cuba's Ballet Nacional which leaves foreign audiences breathless when it goes on tour. Juan had planned a *Giselle* evening at the Teatro Principal; he knew the Director who might wish to meet an Irish member of the CSC. The Birmingham and London Royal Ballets regularly donate shoes to Cuba's ballet schools, their transport organised by CSC's Music Fund. Astonishingly, Cuba has eleven provincial dance schools, in addition to the National School, and all performances draw wildly enthusiastic mass audiences – though before the Revolution classical ballet was unknown on the island.

At Sadler's Wells in 1952 Alicia Alonso's dancing in *Swan Lake* so enchanted me that I spent all my food money on a repeat performance. A few years later this prima ballerina returned to Cuba in Messianic mode and personally funded a small company, with foreign dancers. Here the narrative has a fairly-tale tinge. Fidel was intent on providing culture as well as food and medicine and one day he appeared without warning at Alicia's side. Would she help the Revolution by founding a state ballet company? Fidel made two hundred thousand dollars available – at that date a powerful sum – and added a colonial mansion as headquarters.

Alicia immediately set about training local dancers while introducing the population to ballet. The latter task took her to many factories, collective farms, military barracks, universities and hospitals: everywhere she demonstrated her art under the most taxing conditions. (No wonder she and Fidel became life-long friends!) Recruiting pupils was not difficult; most Cubans respond to rhythm like trees to the wind and dance spon-taneously as soon as they can toddle.

In parks and plazas I had often been puzzled by little groups of boys, aged perhaps ten to sixteen, practising turning very fast on a curved wooden board. Now Juan explained: they were striving to master double-figure pirouettes. Because ballet dancing is not mocked as an effete profession, Cuba produces an abundance of male talent. When Carlos Acosta was a very naughty nine-year-old his truck-driver father reckoned a discipline-plus-fun ballet school would sort him out – and so a star was born.

Alicia danced on stage into her mid-seventies but most ballerinas retire much earlier, then coach their juniors. Cuban ballet dancers' dedication to their art is single-minded; it puzzles them to hear of retired dancers in other countries seeking second careers.

The bad news came at 5.30 in a note to Juan; rain-damage to the Teatro had forced a postponement of *Giselle*. However, compensation was just around the corner in Casa Agramonte's gracious courtyard – chamber music with a programme I might have chosen myself: Beethoven's 'Archduke Trio' and 'Spring Sonata', Mozart's 'Piano Trio in G Major', Schubert's 'Death and the Maiden' Quartet.

At 8.00 a.m. next day I was back in Casino Campestre because five-year-old Patricio insisted on taking me to the zoo, a routine Sunday treat and his elders seemed relieved to have a stand-in. Supplied with bread for the flamingos and biscuits for the monkeys we paid, respectively, half a national peso and quarter of a national peso, sums too minuscule for a euro conversion. This ordeal was even more harrowing than expected, the centre-piece a deep lion-pit recalling Dante's *Inferno* as illustrated by Doré. An adult lion and three lionesses were confined in a stinking enclosure, some twenty yards by ten, with brick walls and stone paving – not a blade of grass to be seen. A jaguar and a puma, both alone, endured much smaller enclosures. The bedraggled flamingos shared their opaque lake and muddy islet with a variety of ducks, the only healthy-looking creatures around. Two baboons, a chimpanzee and several smaller monkeys seemed less unhappy, being fed by their regular visitors. A few children were allowed to tease them, which shocked Patricio; I couldn't help hoping for nipped fingers. Desperate to escape, I offered three goat-cart rides – a successful bribe.

On the way home the streets were bicycle-busy as families pedalled to Sunday gatherings. Maximum load: pappa with three on board – handle-bars, cross-bar, carrier. Mamma followed with a prone infant roped to her carrier.

Glancing into the churches we passed, I saw meagre congregations and octogenarian priests. In one simple, half-restored small church eleven women and one man were standing in front of the tabernacle fervently reciting the rosary aloud. In an otherwise empty side-chapel of de la Soledad, Patricio lit a candle while I watched a semi-crippled elderly woman receiving some odd treatment from a stalwart forty-ish mulatta – much use of hands but they never touched the body, being slowly moved over its contours with murmured incantations. Throughout the city many Santería devotees were to-ing and fro-ing, recognisable by their all-white garb.

The open-air cafeteria where I was to meet Juan at noon overlooked an unprotected railway crossing on a main street and one could watch Neanderthal goods wagons indecisively shunting backwards and forwards. Tourists were scarce in Camaguey but two fat elderly Irishmen and one trim white-haired Canadian sat at this bar and had each acquired an early teenage *jinetera* – slim, honey-skinned, glossy-haired girls wearing very short shorts and bikini tops, expertly stroking and nuzzling their sex-expeditioners. Why can't I ever take this commonplace scene in my stride? Am I laughably out of synch with the real world? Those six were the only other customers. Then I saw Juan's face as he came through the vine-draped entrance archway to find himself beside them. Obviously he, too, was out of synch. Grimly I remarked that we were looking at part of the cost of Cuba's recovery from the Special Period – a part overlooked the day before as Juan dwelt on the island's self-sufficiency.

By now I felt able to question Juan about the criticisms I had heard of Cuba's 'humanitarian internationalism'. A few people had hinted that not all the teams sent to work in remote regions are enthusiastic volunteers. Others had dismissed these missions as mere propaganda stunts, arguing that the money thus spent is needed at home, could improve housing and agriculture, could be spent on essential imports. Even those who seemed proud of Cuba's capacity to help the victims of callous capitalism doubted if such programmes could continue, because the idealism fuelling them belongs to Cuba's isolated past and can't be expected to survive its con-tamination by free-marketeers.

The coercion hint infuriated Juan, on the whole an equable chap. How could thousands of Cubans, dispersed across three continents, possibly be controlled from Havana? 'As for "propaganda",' said Juan, 'even if our intervention is a sort of stunt, isn't it a more civilised way of "power projection" than militarism? If the *Yanquis* sent medical brigades to Afghanistan instead of bombers – inoculations instead of stealth missiles – they'd have friends all over the country helping them against the Taliban! Our "power projection" shows poor people what anti-capitalism means down on the ground, in their *barrios* and villages. That way, we do menace the neo-liberals. In the US, with money you get every best medical advance, without money you're left to die.'

'It is very extraordinary,' said I, 'that this small country is able to offer so much help to so many.'

Juan referred me to Fidel's speech at the international medical brigades' launch in 1998, immediately after Hurricane Mitch's devastation of Central America. I easily located it and the punch lines were:

> Graduating as a doctor is like opening a door to a long road leading to the noblest action that a human being can do for others . . . Not once, throughout the selfless history of the Revolution, have our people failed to offer its supportive medical assistance to other nations in need of this aid at times when catastrophes have hit them, regardless of wide ideological and political differences.

An ignoble scepticism tinges one's reaction to such sentiments – then one feels ashamed. Has our profit-driven world corrupted us all to the extent that we can hardly believe in genuine altruism? Looking back, is there much difference between Cuba's roving medical and educational teams and those countless Christian missionaries who spent uncomfortable lifetimes in isolated places ('hardship posts', in UN-speak) providing services for no material reward? But of course I'm overlooking a crucial difference: the missionaries were confident of a post-mortem reward, not on offer to Cubans.

Juan observed, 'There's a lot about Cuba capitalists can't understand so they say it's not true – like Fidel being honest, having nothing stashed away. They think leaders must get very rich very quick.'

We chuckled then over the *Forbes* boomerang episode. In June 2006 that magazine rashly listed Fidel as a billionaire and the global media gleefully circulated this misinformation, not even the *Guardian* pausing to check before playing Mr Forbes's game. The shrewd Fidel offered to resign at once if anyone could find a single dollar belonging to him in any financial hidey-hole in any country. When no such dollar appeared *Forbes* had to admit that their guesstimate of Fidel's personal wealth was based on the assumed value of Cuba's state-owned assets. Now that Fidel's indifference to money had to be recognised, it became a major character flaw, ruinous for Cuba's economy. The media quoted such critics as Fred

Halliday – 'He remains the prisoner of a moralistic hostility to material wealth'. And Angel Tomas Gonzalez – 'Fidel's problem is that he genuinely dislikes money. That's why there was no problem between him and Pope John Paul.'

How many people believe what they read in *Forbes?* Malcolm Forbes, its owner (rich beyond computing and often described as 'McCarthy incarnate') was once a wannabe White House tenant. On 12 December 2005 his magazine recommended Israel as 'the go-to country for anti-terrorism technologies'.

Without bluntly questioning Juan about Raul, I could sense a hostile strand in his attitude to Cuba's then Acting-President. However, he approved of the recent release of sixty-five 'dissident' prisoners, a move interpreted by some as a concession to US demands. Those freed included Armando Betancourt Reina, a journalist employed by Nueva Prensa Cuba, a Miami-based website, who had served fifteen months for concocting a story about a Camaguey dissident family's eviction from their home – the sort of story US-funded journalists are paid to write. 'Those agents have to be punished,' said Juan, 'but fifteen months is long enough.'

Back in Casa Max, we all sat around the TV to watch that morning's Ché commemorations at Santa Clara. Fidel, participating from his convalescent quarters, looked gaunt but cheerful, his voice sounded a trifle shaky – and yet, as Alina put it, 'There's not a marble missing!'

The Venezuelan President's prominent role at these ceremonies evoked interesting reactions; in this bourgeois-tainted household Hugo Chavez seemed much less popular than among Cuba's masses.

Irma complained, 'That man is too demagogic. And too clever at using Fidel. Why is he cheered all over the hemisphere? Because we back him! I don't understand why he's treated like a favourite son and honoured guest – getting to see Fidel in hospital when no one else could!'

Alina, speaking English for my benefit, said to her mother, 'Can't you see, now it's Fidel needing *him*! His public worshipping makes it look like our Revolution still leads the poor against the rich. And don't forget oil! For any sort of normal living everyone needs this demagogue!'

Max spoke no English but Alina translated his brief remark. The bartering of fully equipped medical brigades for oil pleased him, he wouldn't want Cuba to be accepting 'aid' from 'that man'.

Juan had other concerns. He asked me, 'Did you get what Chavez was saying? About possibly being able to give us some political help – I don't like it! What does he mean? Some sort of formal alliance? Think how the

Yanquis could manipulate that sort of talk! We've enough problems with them, we don't need Washington-Caracas hostility polluting our space.'

As we were saying 'adios', out on the pavement, Juan murmured, 'Some people don't like Chavez because he's a lower class mulatto. The Revolution couldn't civilise everyone!'

In the railway station's obscure little office for foreign passengers I was invited to sit on the spare stool while a tall, wide-smiling, bushy-haired young woman wrote all my details into a massive ledger before storing them on her computer. This belt-and-braces routine intrigued me; evidently official Cuba has not yet put its faith in the new technology. Departure time was 2.00 p.m.

At 1.00 I joined the long confirmation queue; at 1.40 we were told that the track to Holguin had 'become broken'. A replacement bus would collect us, perhaps within an hour or two. The long, wide, crowded waiting-room had unglazed windows on either side yet no current of air moved through. The sky was half-overcast, the humidity extreme; almost everybody carried a much-used sweat-rag.

As the hours passed I could feel myself becoming zombified. From a nearby stall the peckish bought NP10 pizzas – stodge with a thin tomato and cheese topping. I ate a NP8 avocado, rugger ball-sized, and wondered why Cubans don't snack off fruits instead of stuffing themselves with carbohydrates.

A small TV set, high on one end wall, showed a quartet of senior government ministers and President Chavez signing fourteen trade agreements. The ministers wore well-tailored white tropical suits, Hugo looked relaxed and informal in a loose red shirt. Raul also wore civvies, was being the Acting-President rather than the Minister of Defence. He spoke in a dreary monotone and seemed an insignificant little figure, not just in contrast to Fidel but by any standards. A misleading impression; on the revolutionary scene Little Brother has never been insignificant. No doubt this was an historic occasion but the solemn signing and counter-signing and exchanging of fourteen documents, however momentous, has limited entertainment value. Between each document there was much apparently affectionate hugging and kissing and at least one long speech. Nobody around me looked even slightly interested until Hugo took over at the end and began to crack jokes, greatly appreciated by the crowd. (Would Irma have laughed? Somehow I think not.)

By 4.30 the clouds had thickened and darkened and an earth-shaking thunder clap directly overhead made most people jump and/or exclaim. Torrential rain followed a dazzling display of jagged lightning. At 5.15 we were told to 'confirm': the bus was on its way. Another ledger demanded everyone's details before our train tickets could be stamped on the back (twice, by different clerks) for bus use. When the Astro coach arrived at 6.40 the torrent had dwindled to a trickle – just enough to dampen the next queue, by the bus door. On a front seat sat the conductress, a uni-formed middle-aged mulatta whose task it was to enter all our details in her mini-ledger before admitting us. As I waited, poised on the lowest step, she queried two ID photographs and long arguments ensued. (One beard had disappeared, one shaven head had grown hair). While my details were being inscribed I stowed my rucksack on the overhead rack where it fitted easily. But the conductress insisted it must go in the hold, at which point my adaptability to the Cuban way of travelling was almost over-taxed. I wanted to stamp my feet and shout at this bully. Around the open hold passengers were queuing to have their luggage tagged, a reasonable security precaution. One ancient man had a battered cardboard carton in a plastic sack tied with twine. The tag wouldn't stick to the plastic and it took his trembling fingers several minutes to undo the knots – during which time the driver refused to tag anyone else. We departed at 7.05 and ten minutes later, at a traffic lights pause, two men boarded, slipped the driver a NP10 note and took empty seats at the back – unregistered and ticketless.

We were allowed a twenty-minute break in Guaimaro where Cuba's first constitution was devised in April 1869, as a roadside billboard reminded us. This event tends to be over-glorified in the revolutionary history books; in fact it involved certain awkward compromises. The convention voted for annexation, a devisive issue which illustrated the reformist movement's inner uncertainties. Cespedes was nominated as president of the notional republic. He had already freed his own slaves but was hoping for support from the super-rich Matanzas cane-planters – therefore the constitution, while declaring 'all inhabitants of the republic absolutely free', stipulated that emancipated slaves must remain with their masters as paid workers. This dissatisfied everyone, especially the black rebels fighting with Cespedes and led by the twenty-year-old mulatto Antonio Maceo. Of the one hundred *centrales* operating around Camaguey in 1868 only one remained unburnt in 1878. Reluctantly Cespedes con-doned this strategy – 'It would be better for Cuba to be free, even if we have to burn every vestige of civilization'. Meanwhile Agramonte's rebel followers had gladly abolished slavery throughout their area; ranching is not labour-intensive.

On our way out of Guaimaro an Inspector waved his STOP sign and jumped aboard – a tall young black, handsome and self-important. Detecting the two skivers delighted him; at once the driver was ordered out of the bus and his mate (asleep on the seat in front of mine) took over. To my uncharitable satisfaction the conductress was severely reprimanded and given a docket – but afterwards she had many passengers on her side. No doubt Cuba's compulsive/obsessional recording of travellers' details has to do with knowing where everybody is on any given date – but can three sets of details really be needed for a three-hour bus journey?

From Holguin railway station – deserted at 10.30 p.m. – a talkative, elderly man, whose bicitaxi rattled and squealed, slowly pedalled me to my *casa particulare* on the far side of the city: a spacious H-shaped 1980s bungalow, with 1950s décor, set in a small garden near the base of Loma de la Cruz.

Immigration's demands on *casa particulares* are inconsistent; in Bayamo and Holguin provinces the register must be shown at once, elsewhere a day or so may be allowed to elapse. When Hector heard that my visa needed renewal he offered me a lift in his 1957 Buick and for twenty minutes we drove along tree-lined colonial streets to a residential area opposite a spacious park. In a bright airy office a cheerful young woman greeted Hector with a kiss, saw to his register, turned to me – and had a problem. My e-mail return ticket was *invalido*; I must produce a *real* airline ticket . . . With difficulty Hector persuaded her that e-mail tickets have become the norm outside of Cuba. Still looking perplexed, she gave me a chit authorising my purchase of a visa stamp at a specified bank far away in the centre. Poor Hector, who had a heavy cold, refused to desert me; happily there was no bank queue. Back at Immigration he stayed in the car while I endured a Santa Clara rerun. Holguin's senior Immigration officer, an exceptionally nasty woman, pronounced that visas must be renewed within the forty-eight hours before expiry – confirming my suspicion that these ghouls make it up as they go along. Hector and Yamila were furious on my behalf.

The region around Holguin was densely populated when Columbus landed nearby; half a century later Captain Garcia Holguin, one of Mexico's conquerors, had cleared the land of trees and savages before setting up one of Oriente's earliest cattle ranches. The town was founded one hundred and fifty years later, in 1720, on the standard Spanish colonial grid plan. During the nineteenth century it prospered: much sugar production, some fruit growing, limited tobacco estates. The Revolution added factories, engineering plants, Cuba's biggest brewery and Soviet-style apartment blocks which enhance no country but in Cuba look extra-vile. Now Holguin is chiefly remarkable for its exceptionally friendly people, an unusual number of red-heads and beautiful city parks.

The enormous main square, Plaza Calixto Garcia, is a marvel of ornamental green and pink marble shaded by many trees and dominated by General Calixto Iniguez Garcia, Commander-in-Chief of the Rebel Army during the Ten Years War. He was born on 4 August 1839, just around the corner from the Plaza, in a comfortable but unexciting house – now a museum of outstanding boredom. In 1872 he defeated the Spaniards and took control of Holguin but soon after was captured and imprisoned in Spain. When the second war of independence started he escaped to New York, then returned to Cuba to lead the rebel army in the battle for Santiago. Later that year he died suddenly during a visit to Washington.

In the very beautiful Plaza de la Maqueta (colonial architecture at its most pleasing) I got into conversation with two young men who gave me bad news. Cuba's baseball season traditionally opens in October and Juan had been confident that I could see a game in Holguin – but there would be no game. According to the local health authority, to play in such abnormal heat and humidity would be gratuitously risky. This disappoint-ment was obliquely consoling, as justification for my being reduced to comparative immobility.

Horse-buses took me to and from Holguin's homage to Ché, a monu-mental three-part sculpture in dark stone, standing alone on an open slope by the suburban Avenida de los Libertadores. The panels show Ché approaching in silhouette – arriving forcefully, seeming about to step out on to the grass – then receding in silhouette. Caridad Ramos, one of Cuba's most renowned sculptors, was in her early twenties when she created this powerful work, austere yet curiously touching. The daughter of poor *campesiños*, she has said, 'We had to share what little we had. Solidarity was essential. Thanks to the Revolution I had the opportunity to study which my mother never had.'

As the Special Period took hold, 'community culture' was used to fortify the threatened Revolution. Ileana Barrera, an historian who helped to found the Bonifacio Byrne Cultural Centre in 1991, explained – 'Because material goods were scarce, we thought cultural activities vitally important to offset the shortages and foster intellectual life'. At the time, outsiders scoffed. 'Cultural activities to offset hunger? More communist craziness!' But in a non-profit-making environment cultural activities have a value and meaning incomprehensible to such outsiders.

In 1995 Caridad Ramos worked hard to launch the Swallow Project which ran workshops (music, acting, plastic arts, puppetry) for ninety participants of all ages. In defiance of limited resources, the projects had seven art teachers and time was divided between traditional repertoires and daring experiments. This and many similar efforts were forerunners of what came to be known as 'the Battle of Ideas', often described as 'a revolution within the Revolution' and referred to by Juan in Camaguey as 'a repair job after the Special Period'.

In 2000, on Fidel's suggestion, Abel Prieto, Minister of Culture since 1998, established fifteen institutions throughout Cuba to train art instructors. (This well-chosen minister is the author of several scholarly works and of a semi-autobiographical novel entitled *The Flight of the Cat*.) Each province now has its Arts School, open to everyone from primary school-children to pensioners. But the Battle of Ideas involves much more than art schools; its programmes aim to revitalise all aspects of the national life.

The two young men with whom I had talked in the Plaza de la Maqueta were newly returned from Grenada where they had been leading a volunteer team deployed to change the island's light bulbs from incandescent to fluorescent. (Cuba, they proudly told me, is also donating thousands of fluorescent bulbs to other Caribbean countries.) These brothers, Roberto and Rolando, belonged to the local BUTS – Brigadas Universitas de Trabajo Social (University Social Work Brigades). Their more humdrum tasks included helping old people who live alone and encouraging school drop-outs to engage in community work, the reward a small stipend. They told me about Operation Alvaro Reinoso, which aims further to reduce sugar production by at least fifty per cent. ('You call it downsizing?' queried Rolando. Vigorously I shook my head.) In the village around a closed *centrale* BUTS works with SUMS – Sedes Universitarias Municipales (Municipal University Units), another Battle of Ideas creation. University graduates put out of work by Alvano Reinoso, or by other factory closures, are invited to become teachers in retraining programmes which provide a small wage for both teachers and students. The young who have never been able to find work are also given small stipends if they attend Integral Improvement Courses which usually lead on to university-level evening classes in the humanities, held in school buildings all over the island. Many retired academics, and other pensioners with specialist knowledge, have volunteered to work in these new faculties. On 26 May 2005 one such academic, Maria de la Vega Garcia, editor of the journal *Marx Ahora*, distilled the essence of the Battle of Ideas in a moving speech:

> A distinctive feature of the Universalisation of Higher Education – one of the most momentous and comprehensive of the Revolution's programmes within the context of the Battle of Ideas – is the formation of associate professorships to participate. This represents a contribution to the general culture of our people, and without doubt is also a new way to personal fulfilment . . . The relationships with university faculties, and with the institutions and organisations of the municipalities that support such educational work, broaden our horizons . . . We come to realise that we are doing much more than implementing a programme or offering to share our knowledge of a particular discipline. It is – without doubt – a closer acquaintance with the personal lives of our students, their families and their social and work environments that establishes strong emotional links as the only way to a fruitful academic orientation, while also contributing to the students' human development, awakening in them their sensibilities to the advances of science, culture, and the history of their country and raising their self-esteem, often diminished through multiple and adverse factors. It is to discover and make shine the star that can exist in the heart of any human being.

By the end of 2005 sixty-three per cent of TV transmissions were educational and in the Battle's first six years seven hundred projects were completed including an Oldies' university, La Universidad del Adulto Mayor. By January 2008 one thousand twelve hundred more were nearing completion, half in the medical sector. This broadening of education will, it is hoped, to some extent inoculate Cuban society against the more deleterious effects of global pop 'culture'. But in Camaguey Juan had sadly described the Battle as 'Fidel's last stand', an unwinnable battle. Raul's compromises would, he predicted, undermine the attitudes that make such shoestring campaigns possible – and attractive to people lacking material goods. I remembered his words when I heard the spokesman for some Washington think-tank commenting, 'Raul is more tolerant of the social costs of accepting market mechanisms to which his brother would never agree' (BBC World Service, 18 December 2007).

As one strolls and sits and observes, it's obvious that Holguin has been hard hit by the closure of several factories and provincial *centrales*. I saw three ragged old men, pickled in alcohol, wandering unsteadily around the parks (in Cuba a very unusual sight) and a dozen seedy young men lounged on benches sharing bottles of rum before noon. In the city's main bar – open-air, separated from the pavement by a trellis supporting a creeper laden with fragrant white blossoms – I was tentatively approached by two respectably dressed woman beggars; they reminded me of Siberia's destitute pensioners in 2002 and 2004, victims of the Soviet Union's collapse. However, in a capitalist-run city afflicted by Holguin's recent misfortunes one would see considerably more poverty and distress.

For someone who eats only once a day, *casa particulare* breakfasts are made to measure. Example: large jugs of fresh mango and guava juice, three cups of milky coffee, two toasted ham and cheese sandwiches, a two-egg omelette, a pyramid of crisp oven-warm rolls with imported (from Germany) butter and local honey. Thus fuelled, I turned towards Holguin's tourist challenge, Loma de la Cruz. Its four hundred and fifty-eight steps – wide, concrete, shadeless, heat-reflecting – did not tempt me though the reward is a panoramic view (say the guide-books) and a thatched restaurant. At the bottom of the steps I turned right to follow a rough track through a sprawling village on ledges of mountain overlooking the city. This was a post-Revolution settlement of terraced concrete block housing: one-storey, white- or pink-washed, unglazed windows barred, outside spiral stairways giving access to flat roofs with laundry-lines and herb gardens. Soon the track became a steep boulder-path (a stream bed after heavy rain), climbing between hedges of neatly clipped candelabra cactus and fiery crotons. Beyond the settlement, around a shoulder, a track descended to an invisible motor-road past a colossal obsolete water-storage tank (obsolete for lack of pumping fuel). Another path would have taken me past clusters of *bohios* on the opposite slope. More tempting was a barely discernible pathlet zig-zagging upwards through high, thick grass. This was an easy climb, the wet grass cooling and bushy shade available at intervals. Only crowing cocks, grunting pigs and frequent bird calls broke the silence. The last stage was a scramble over smooth boulders, then I was looking directly across a shrub-filled valley to the mini-fort and restaurant on Loma de la Cruz and could enjoy the panoramic view without having toiled up those four hundred and fifty-eight steps.

During the descent I realised that the strong grass, through which I had to push my way, wielded a secret weapon – minute barbs that lodged tormentingly in one's garments. Having extracted the two-inch stalks, it is very difficult to find and pluck out the barbs. This task occupied me for hours, using a borrowed pair of tweezers – work suited to the midday heat, demanding neither physical nor mental energy.

Later I met Roberto and Rolando in the bar and sought their advice about transport to Biran, the village nearest Fidel's birthplace. Hitch-hiking they wrote off; in this thinly populated region motor vehicles are a novelty. There might be an occasional bus from Mayari to Biran though they doubted that. Probably I'd have to take a taxi. Inwardly I winced – what a test of my *fidelismo*! The nearest main road village to Biran is La Guira – taxiless according to my advisors. But in Mayari, the municipal centre, about twenty-seven miles north-east of Biran, I could certainly find an unofficial taxi. That figure made me grumpy – only twenty-seven miles! An enjoyable day's walk had the weather conditions been otherwise.

Chapter 20

A four-mile walk, begun in darkness, took me beyond a road junction to the relevant *punto embarcacion*, a small open-ended shelter with concrete seating for a dozen or so. When two Transporte officers came on duty at 8.00 a.m. I told them I would settle for any vehicle going to Mayari. My companions looked sympathetic; most who wait at that *punto* are en route to closer destinations.

A mother and two high-spirited schoolgirls, aged perhaps four and six, were awaiting a horse-bus. As the children played happily – racing around the seats, swinging on the railings – I was puzzled by their total silence. Could it be part of the game? But that age-group is not noted for silent games, even when playing hide-and-seek. Then their mother communicated with them, in sign language, and they fluently responded. Both were deaf and dumb, attending a special school and already well equipped to cope with their handicap. I moved to sit beside their mother who explained – as the horse-bus approached – that special schooling starts at the age of two and special arrangements, varying with the circumstances, are made for rural dwellers.

A century or so ago the German psychiatrist, Emil Kraepelin, judged that 'The development of a country can be measured by the manner in which it treats its handicapped and its mentally impaired'. Cuba's internationally praised Psychiatric Hospital, near Havana, has about two thousand five hundred beds and a staff of seven hundred and eighty-five psychiatrists, physicians and nurses. On its one hundred and fifty-five acres some patients live in bungalows with flower and vegetable gardens, cultivated as part of their therapy. The list of occupational therapies is long: painting and drawing, handicrafts, computer studies to assist memory training, music, psycho-ballet, theatre and sports – the last including riding around the grounds, if appropriate. The hospital has its own theatre and stages frequent shows. It also has its own railway station for the convenience of family and friends. (In Ireland some of the families and friends of long-term patients, in any hospital, can't easily afford the high car-park charges.) Child visitors are encouraged because so many patients find it easier to communicate with them than with fellow-adults. The hospital's motto is: 'With love and affection one achieves more than with medicines'.

At 12.15 my Transporte guardian beckoned me and held out his STOP sign; the approaching vehicle would pass Mayari on its way to the nickel-smelting town of Moa. Incredulously I stared at this smart and only moderately over-crowded coach – a gift from Scandinavia with reclining seats and well-polished picture windows. The fare for this fifty-mile journey was less than two euro cents.

Around Holguin several hillsides have been reforested quite recently. Then comes flatter terrain: cane and pasture. At the little town of Cueto we crossed a significant railway, built to serve the port of Antilla in securely sheltered Nipe Bay. For some reason the Spaniards had never systematically developed this corner of Cuba but its US colonisers moved fast. In 1901 and 1904 the United Fruit Company's gigantic sugar mills, Boston and Preston, began operations – only made possible by the Cuban Railroad Company's line to Antilla. Until 1959 four major US companies controlled this whole region. The Munson shipping line ran a fortnightly service from Antilla to New York. The expat workers had a polo club, swimming pools, US-stocked shops. The Rural Guards barracks and the post office were on United Fruit Company's land and the company employed twenty mercenary soldiers licensed to carry arms. Between 1899 and 1953 the population of Mayari municipality increased tenfold while Biran and its hinterland went from five hundred and twenty-nine to eight thousand three hundred and five. The 1953 census revealed that very few of Mayari's hundred and fifteen thousand houses enjoyed indoor 'sanitary facilities'. Only one per cent of the adults were university graduates and more than fifty per cent hadn't even reached the first grade in primary school. Into this US dependency Fidel was born in 1927 – or 1926, if you accept his altered birth certificate.

At the turn-off for Moa I disembarked alone. A twenty-minute walk past Mayari's post-Revolution hospital, clinic, schools, municipal offices and five-storey apartment blocks left me heat exhausted. The old town, founded in 1757, struggles amidst much greenery on the banks of the Rio Mayari and was the Castro family's metropolis, though too far away to be regularly visited. Most guidebooks ignore the place, yet I found it attractive, short of 'grand colonial' architecture but with a pleasing symmetry about its shabby streets and shaded, *bohio*-lined laneways. It has scarcely begun to recover from the Special Period. The Bitiri, a large motel surrounded by dignified trees and lavishly flowering shrubs, is now in ruins from which 'home-improving' locals have helped themselves. Previously it catered for Cuban holiday makers drawn by the nearby

Taino caves and pine-forested mountains. For three months in 1967 José Yglesias lived here while collecting material for his classic *In the Fist of the Revolution*.

I hadn't expected to find a *casa particulare* but in 2003 Casa Eduardo opened – very much my sort of place. Behind his cramped dwelling on the edge of the town Eduardo has contrived a cave-like bedroom, stone-walled and windowless with a tiny *banyo* of unpredictable plumbing. The open-air dining-room is a circular palm-thatched space – ancient tree roots writhing in one corner, the table and benches of rough-hewn palm trunks. That evening was overcast with humidity off the scale and thunder rumbling for hours around the Sierra Cristal. Here I encountered the first mosquitoes of this journey, as active within my room as outside. Although I didn't complain Eduardo heard me slapping my flesh and before I could intervene he had drenched my room from a giant can of spray – a frighteningly effective mix.

Eduardo then telephoned his friend Diego who next morning would be my taxi-driver. We planned to leave at daybreak, for climatic reasons.

Anti-Castroites often refer, misleadingly, to the circumstances of Fidel's birth. Ed Vulliamy, for instance, writing in the *Observer* (21 January 2007) – 'Born out of wedlock on a sugar plantation on 13 August, his father was the owner, his mother was the housemaid.' Those English phrases suggest a certain sort of background (lecherous gentleman has his way with cowed skivvy) far removed from the facts.

There is some irony in Fidel's ancestry: the man who established Cuba's independence is only half-Cuban, as two of Ireland's best known revolutionary leaders were only half-Irish (Patrick Pearse and Eamon de Valera). In 1998 'an important US magazine' – unnamed by Fidel – accused him of being 'the son of a Spanish soldier who fought on the wrong side during the war of independence' (1895–98). Fidel then angrily defended his father, a Galician peasant 'who could barely read and write' and 'had been sent to Cuba as a teenage conscript to suppress the insurrection'. Declared Fidel, 'My father fought on the right side, with the Spaniards . . . If he had fought on the Cuban side he would have been on the wrong side because that was not his country. He knew nothing about it. He could not understand what the Cubans were fighting for . . . When the war ended he was repatriated to Spain and he came back to Cuba a little later to work as a farmhand.'

From Galicia, one of Spain's poorest regions, thousands emigrated to

Cuba where labourers (but *not* more blacks, thank you!) were urgently needed. The US settlers who had bought large estates at bargain prices from the departing Spaniards were planning to expand them. And US companies, as we have seen, were clearing enormous tracts of virgin land around Mayari. For the enterprising Angel Castro, Cuba proved an island of ever-expanding opportunities. Soon he was pushing a handcart through plantations and forests, selling barrels of homemade lemonade to cane-cutters and loggers. Then he got a job with United Fruit's Railroad Company, saved his wages for a few years, opened a general store serving the *campesiños*, saved his profits until he could lease some land from United Fruits, employed a team of peasants recently arrived from Spain, set up a sawmill, sold wood to neighbouring sugar mills, continued single-mindedly to save and eventually bought about a thousand hectares (two thousand five hundred acres) of flat fertile land near Biran. Later he leased another ten thousand hectares, grew maize as well as cane, bred cattle, pigs and poultry of various sorts and built a small wooden house – on stilts, Galicia style, with stabling underneath.

Then came a late marriage, to Maria Luisa Argota, a schoolteacher who bore him two children before being supplanted by Lina Ruz, one of the numerous children of a very poor peasant from Pinar del Rio. The Ruz family had travelled more than seven hundred miles by ox-cart to the Biran area where they scraped a living by carting cane to the mills. When Lina was fifteen, Cuba got a lucky break: her father begged the forty-five-year-old Angel to employ her and the third of their seven children was Fidel.

Diego arrived with the first of the light wearing a 'Venezuela' baseball cap and a 'Viva Chavez!' T-shirt. Both his doctor daughters were earning oil for Cuba by serving with their brigade in some village near the Columbian border. His Lada had long since lost its side windows and door handles, an idiosyncrasy to which I was becoming accustomed, and its windscreen was in four pieces taped together. When a dense sunrise mist reduced visibility to about twenty yards Diego apologised for having no wiper. After the mist had risen a long, low bank of orange-brown cloud remained lying along the horizon above the coast and this threatening smoke from Moa's nickel-smelting plants bothered Diego. A Canadian company wanted to set up another plant which Raul seemed to favour but the locals were vociferously against it . . . That evening Eduardo commented that given the region's poverty Moa can't afford not to have it: the old, old story, heard on all continents in relation to profitable environmental destruction.

I didn't have to feel to guilty about emitting carbon to gratify my Biran whim. We never had fewer than three passengers, sometimes five, and at one stage five adults in the back plus two toddlers on my lap. Hereabouts Cuba's transport problems reach their nadir: no buses, few *camiones*, fewer cars. Between the main road and Biran no vehicle of any sort appeared. Even bicycles are rare in this area where some *campesiños* wear ragged garments – a sight unusual enough to be shocking. Much of the main Mayari-Holguin road is a series of 'volcanic craters', as Diego resignedly complained, but bumping along at fifteen miles per hour suited me. On the minor road to Biran a knobbly surface kept our speed below ten miles per hour because the thirty-year-old Lada needed t.l.c. Diego and I agreed that Fidel certainly travelled by helicopter when visiting Finca Las Manacas. Diego added, only half in jest, 'Soon Chavez will fix *all* our roads!'

As yet Operation Alvaro Reinoso has made no mark on this landscape and we drove through mile after mile of level canefields, bounded to the east by a long, irregular ridge – the Altiplanicie de Nipe where, during school holidays, Fidel roamed happily, climbing escarpments and hunting with his dogs. Visually sugarcane is an unattractive crop – apart from one's subliminal associations of it with the worst horrors of slavery. In 1840 one young *cafetale*-owner, the writer Anselmo Suarez y Romero, wrote to a friend:

> I do not like the *ingenios*. To have seen one is to have seen them all. Nothing more than vast light-green cane fields, divided into squares by straight boundaries, at whose edges are not seen – as one sees in the *cafetales* – the wide tree-tops, nor the mamey, nor the honey berry, nor the avocado; nor do they exude the citron flower fragrance of the lemon and orange trees.

I don't know when the Moors brought cane to Spain but by the time Velasquez introduced it to Cuba, in 1512, it was among Europe's most precious commodities – 'white gold'. Diego, who had worked all his life as a boiler repair man, told me that one ton of cane produces about two hundred and twenty pounds of sugar. During the *zafra*, *centrales* operate twenty-four hours a day and nothing is wasted. The mud from the clarifier, in which cane juice is initially boiled, makes an excellent fertiliser. Rum arises from the molasses. The pulpy fibres go to feed cattle, or make cardboard or wallboard, or fuel *centrale* boilers.

Several people waved at Diego as we jolted through Biran, a scattered village owned by the United Fruit Company until the nationalisation of the sugar industry in 1960. Approaching Finca Las Manacas, on a narrow winding road, the canefields were replaced by more broken terrain – grassy patches, bushy patches, dwarf palms and a merry, sparkling stream where we paused to view Fidel's boyhood bathing pool, overhung by fig trees. Into old age, swimming has remained his favourite form of regular exercise.

As we continued, Diego informed me (boastfully, as though speaking of a relative or friend) that at the age of forty-eight Fidel had stopped smoking – having puffed through half a box of cigars per diem all his adult life. This feat was much publicised when he insisted on anti-smoking lectures being included in Cuba's preventative healthcare programme: an admirable if 'double standards' stance for a leader whose country exports cigars as a valuable source of revenue. Nor did Fidel do anything to promote rum; for years his daily alcohol ration was one glass of whisky, sipped so daintily that it lasted for hours. Although something of a gourmet, his eating was equally controlled – of necessity, given a tendency to corpulence. According to Diego, and other of my Cuban friends, their leader's reputation for self-discipline greatly enhanced his moral authority, putting him in a strong position to urge that virtue on the whole population 'for the sake of the Revolution'.

Previously the public were excluded from Finca Las Manacas unless given a special pass by the Communist Party headquarters in Holguin, a pass not readily issued. Visitors could only stand outside the gate and stare towards a cluster of buildings mostly hidden within a wood planted by Angel. Only recently was it decided to open *el comandante*'s birthplace to tourists, a 'personality cult' gesture Fidel has always opposed. The entrance fee was CP10 and the same again for permission to photograph.

We were welcomed by a charming Interior Ministry officer, young and chubby-faced; to meet a charming individual in that uniform was a new experience. Two others (equally agreeable, scarcely out of their teens) hung around at a little distance keeping me within sight whenever I was out of doors – surely a superfluous precaution?

Finca Las Manacas has always been unfenced and unwalled, merging into the surrounding countryside, the small gate a mere token. An elegant young woman named Ruth led me past a rope barrier and at once my gaze was drawn to the tall, slender, long-winged angel who with bowed head looks sorrowfully down at the simple stone slabs of the family graves. Around them grows a profusion of wild flowers – red, white, yellow – while wreaths of artificial flowers drape the little headstones. Angel Castro died in November 1956 when Fidel was in Mexico organising the Granma expedition. A few weeks later, after the shipwreck, his mother was reading government-directed press reports that Fidel and Raul Castro Ruz were both dead. Lina was sceptical and told a journalist, 'I suffer as a mother of soldiers and revolutionaries, but if Fidel and Raul decide to die, I pray that they may die with dignity.' She herself died suddenly at the end of July 1963, having seen the Revolution succeed. She had supported Agrarian Reform, though Fidel's landowning eldest brother then found the Finca reduced, like all others, to four hundred hectares.

Not far from the graves, dwarfed by majestic guayacan, baria and acuje trees, stands 'Escuela Rural Mixta: No. 15: BIRAN' – a clapboard, tin-roofed, one-room state school where the three-year-old Fidel began his education. Being the youngest he sat at the front of the class on a nursery chair and soon became a nuisance, restless and defiant. A score of ink-stained, penknife-scarred mini-desks fill the room and photographs of the young Fidel almost cover the walls. 'All is original,' Ruth assured me. 'Nothing changed only pictures added.' The twenty or so pupils, children of Angel's workers, were of different ages so some had to sit on the desk tops. Only Fidel and his siblings would go to another school; for the rest, once able to do manual work their studying days were over. That teacher must have been both patient and skilled; aged five, the disruptive Fidel could read, write and do his sums. A year later he and his eight-year-old sister, Angela, were despatched to faraway Santiago to be privately tutored in preparation for boarding-school. At this time Fidel and his siblings were baptised and their parents had a church wedding; both ceremonies were prerequisites for the children's acceptance into Roman Catholic schools.

Inevitably the Finca's present ambience is museum-like. Yet as Ruth led me through the house on stilts, to which rooms had been added as the babies came, I gained quite a vivid impression of the Castro family's lifestyle. Despite their prosperity (employing six hundred workers at harvest time and attaining 'Don' status in the Biran area) Angel and Lina were uninterested in 'upward mobility'. Fidel recalled, 'There was no feudal or bourgeois society in Biran. My father was an isolated landowner. Some-times a friend visited him but we hardly ever visited others. My parents usually stayed at home, they worked all the time.' A simple peasant life contented them: servants eating with the family, milking cows tethered under the house, wayward hens roosting in some of the permanently untidy rooms. The antique telephone and wireless set took me back to my own early childhood. No other inessentials went to the furnishing and equipment of this home. The most expensive-looking possessions were the saddles and tack habitually used by Angel and Lina, kept well oiled and burnished. However, those frugal parents willingly paid high school fees to ensure that their children had the best possible education.

Surprisingly, Ruth restrained me from photographing the parental bedchamber, a smallish room resembling a side-chapel, crowded with statues, crucifixes, holy pictures, candlesticks and votive offerings with a strong Santería flavour. I asked, 'Why no pictures?' and was told 'It's disrespectful to religion'. A bizarre notion and Ruth herself didn't seem convinced by it. Could this ban be to do with lingering Communist Party prejudice?

In one of his famous conversations with the Brazilian Dominican, Frei Betto, Fidel remembered his mother as 'a very religious woman, a deeply religious woman, more religious than my father but not because she'd received any religious training . . . She was practically illiterate. She learned how to read and write all by herself. With great effort, she tried to learn. She couldn't attend school or church, there wasn't any church where I was born, far from any city. I think her religious beliefs had their origin in some family tradition for her parents were also very religious.'

In that same conversation Fidel looked back, with gratitude, to his years at Belen College. 'The Spanish Jesuits inculcated a strong sense of personal dignity – regardless of their political ideas . . . They valued character, rectitude, honesty, courage and the ability to make sacrifices. Teachers definitely have an influence and the Jesuits influenced me with their strict organisation, their discipline and their values.'

Outside, we sauntered across wide expanses of short green grass, kept cropped by several horses and bullocks, all in fine condition. Remote Finca Las Manacas soon grew to be a private hamlet, the family home surrounded by numerous thatched *bohios*, a shop, a post office, a bar, a school, a teacher's house (one-roomed), a wooden dower-bungalow built for Lina after Angel's death and a circular cock-pit with a superbly crafted roof and wooden tiered seating for two hundred. I tried to imagine the scene when Angel was running his busy estate: Haitians cooking supper outside their huts, children dawdling to and from school, customers thronging around the shop on pay-day, week-end gamblers converging on the cock-pit where reckless men often lost their week's wages. (Raul is said to be addicted still.)

When Fidel was born, Don Angel was fifty-two and too focused on estate matters to form close relationships with any of his children. But in a distant way he treated them kindly. And Fidel (politically minded from the age of ten) noted approvingly his father's comparatively humane attitude to the poorest workers. Between harvests, the Haitian cane-cutters on US-owned plantations were jobless and destitute; Fidel often heard their hungry children crying and never forgot that sound. Don Angel heard it too and hired many of those men to weed canefields not in need of weeding. Fidel reminisced, 'I can't recall his ever failing to find a solution when somebody came to him for help. Sometimes he grumbled and complained but his generosity always got the upper hand.'

When Ruth noticed my heat-exhaustion, as we returned to Diego and his Lada, she reproved me for not wearing a hat. I explained that in Cuba I couldn't find one to fit my extra-large (fat) head. 'Then you buy a *sombrilla* (parasol),' said she. I should have listened . . .

My signature was the first in the Visitors' Register – a school exercise book. As we drove away Diego calculated the Finca will only take off as a tourist attraction after Chavez has fixed the province's roads. I'm glad I saw the place before its tranquillity is shattered and its authenticity eroded by a café, a souvenir shop, public conveniences, a Visitors' Centre, a kitsch coloured map of the region and a tarred car park.

Perhaps Fidel's background – isolated home, unsociable parents – partly explains his distaste for private parties. His friend Gabriel Garcia Marquez has noted, 'He is one of the rare Cubans who neither sings nor dances'. For recreation he reads and he has admitted 'In my next reincarnation I want to be a writer'. His letters from the Isle of Pines prison (not written for publication) reveal an extraordinary depth and breadth of reading for a man in his middle twenties. Discussing books kept him a happy prisoner – Shakespeare and Thackeray, Kant and Freud, Turgenev and Dostoyevsky, Descartes and Marx, Varela and Martí, Cervantes and Plutarch. From dawn to dusk he read, mentioning in a letter dated 18 March 1954, 'I fell asleep finishing *The Transcendental Aesthetics of Space and Time*'. Most of us would have fallen asleep beginning it.

In the late afternoon a slow walk on a rough muddy track took me beyond Mayari to where much reeking garbage is indiscriminately dumped on open ground. Then, strolling between banana groves, I reflected on Fidel's various writings, read over the past three years, and found myself re-gretting, as do many *fidelistas*, that he sometimes leaves himself open to ridicule by pronouncing on international matters of which he has a limited understanding. He hands his enemies a whole arsenal of weapons by, for example, sounding naïve (the EU), or wildly over-emotional (Serbia) or ill-informed (Tibet). He is (or chooses to seem?) unaware of the EU's funda-mental flaws – breeding bureaucrats on a scandalous scale, condoning gross internal corruption even after it has been exposed to public view, enabling those transnational corporations he so detests to have their way regardless of individual member country's real economic/social needs and long-term environmental welfare. Maybe the EU does constitute a threat to US global hegemony, but it's certainly no threat to the free marketeers' stranglehold over member states.

NATO's 1999 attack on Serbia was the sort of 'asymmetrical conflict' we've since become accustomed to in Afghanistan, Iraq, Palestine and Lebanon. Why does Fidel describe it as a 'war'? Not one NATO life was lost during that shameful and ruthless bombing of a country that posed no threat to the bombers. Yet this was no 'genocidal' attack on the Serbs, as he alleges. It directly served particular US interests in the Balkans and was incidentally useful for the testing of new US weaponry – a motive Fidel identifies while distorting the main motive.

As for Tibet – in a speech made in Havana on 11 June 1999, coinciding with the end of that 'humanitarian intervention' in Serbia/Kosovo, Fidel considered the implications of NATO's playing a new role, far beyond the North Atlantic, and concluded:

> If they feel like it, the imperialists and their allies could declare any incident that occurs in China – and that becomes a bone of contention – a massive violation of human rights. Buddhist Tibet, for instance, is mentioned and certain Muslim minorities in the northwest. We closely follow China's constant harassment by the West. Of course, the Chinese are wise politicians . . . They would not invade a country to take it over. They are, indeed, very zealous in matters relating to their own affairs. They strictly follow the principle of non-interference in the internal affairs of other countries.

Tell that to the Tibetans!

I returned to Casa Eduardo by a different route. Along the high river embankment old men dozed in the shade of even older ceibas while children romped in a spacious playground, some of its elaborate equip-ment needing replacement. In a big bookshop half the dusty shelves were empty and the stock, priced in national pesos, consisted mainly of Party publications, their pages yellowing. Behind the counter two middle-aged women were trying to mend a dented electric kettle. They explained that new books, priced in convertible pesos, didn't sell in Mayari.

Vigorous hymn-singing drew me to a Methodist Friday service being briskly taken by a mulatta minister in a partially restored church originally built in 1926 for United Fruit Company employees. (During the pseudo-Republic many US churches expanded into Cuba.) There was much joking interaction between the minister and her congregation of a hundred or so and several new pews had been installed for the hundreds more who worship on the Sabbath. The nearby Roman Catholic church was firmly locked, its grounds neglected. Attendance is poor, said Eduardo, an atheist who regarded all the imported US churches as 'subversive' and the Vatican as an ally of the imperialists in Washington.

I planned to spend Sunday 21 October – municipal elections day – in Manzanillo before continuing down the coast to Playa Las Coloradas. But how to get from Mayari to Manzanillo? Perhaps a return to Holguin (going in the wrong direction), then a bus to Bayamo, forty miles short of Manzanillo. But no one knew when a vehicle would leave for Holguin – and it might well miss the one daily service to Bayamo. When Diego offered to do the direct three and a half hour drive to Bayamo for CP50 – with a stop on the way to visit the remote Dos Rios Monumento Martí – I didn't hesitate. This journey is measured in time rather than distance because of the road's condition.

We were off before sunrise, accompanied by Diego's forester son, Carlos, who normally cycled the ten miles to his tree nursery job. He was an effervescent young man, proud of Cuba's reforestation programme and aware of its importance. An educated population can produce many young workers who feel so personally involved in their project that a sense of achievement compensates for low wages.

Everywhere colonists inflicted deforestation on their new properties but in Cuba the process went slowly. Columbus landed on an island eight-eight per cent forested; as late as 1774 that figure had been reduced by only five per cent. Two centuries later is was down to fifteen per cent. Then a vigorous reforestation programme, adhered to even during the Special Period, raised the wooded area to twenty per cent by 2005. 'And maybe twenty-one per cent by now!' said Carlos.

Our first hitch-hiker was a voluble policeman with a grievance about the unavailability of hinges for the wooden cupboard he was making as his sister's wedding present. Soon after leaving the main road we picked up a distraught young mother carrying a very sick baby. Her village doctor had diagnosed a condition needing specialist treatment and a Bayamo ambulance was on its way but precious time could be saved by our meeting it. This meant no détour to Monumento Martí. I had begun to feel jinxed. Thwarted by bureaucrats in Santa Clara, the Camaguey ballet cancelled by rain damage, the Holguin baseball match postponed by humidity, the Dos Rios interlude thwarted by a sick baby . . . And in fact there was worse to come.

Very slowly we traversed a wide plain, shimmering in the heat, its cane-fields eventually replaced by treeless pastureland where Brahmin cattle mingled with fine herds of multi-coloured goats. Passing Dos Rios I saluted Martí's ghost and wondered why such an intelligent man behaved so stupidly on meeting a small posse of Spaniards. Impulsively he charged them (wearing his black frock-coat and bowtie!) and was shot through the neck, becoming the war's first casualty. As a poet and philosopher, untrained for the battlefield, he should have stayed with the rearguard.

Soon after joining the Santiago-Bayamo road at Jiguani we met the ambulance, then picked up three more hitch-hikers. At Bayamo bus station I invited Diego to have a farewell Hatuey in the hidden peso bar where we heard that no buses left for Manzanillo on a Saturday. However, a *colectivo* was just then filling up and for CP3 I could have a seat.

More canefields separate Bayamo from the coast but on this newly repaired road our speed did something to relieve the asphyxiating midday heat. Beside me sat Alejandro, a stunningly handsome mulatto who spoke fluent if erratic English and described himself as a wind-power aficionado. An engineer, he was working on the construction of a windpark near Holguin and he urged me to take out my notebook and spread the gospel. Soon six 180-foot windmills would be generating 1,800 megawatts annually, saving Cuba about US$136,000 in oil at current prices. Using French technology, these windmills are designed to be quickly dissembled as hurricanes approach.

Showing admirable devotion to civic duty, Alejandro was going home to Manzanillo to vote next day. On discovering my interest in the election he generously offered to be my guide and interpreter; we would meet on Parque Cespedes at 9.00 a.m.

Chapter 21

By the late 1980s increasing public discontent with over-centralisation had prompted Fidel and his advisors to institute certain reforms. In 1992 a major constitutional change enhanced Poder Popular (people's power) by establishing a new electoral system allowing the direct election of all members of the provincial and national assemblies. (Municipal assembly members had always been directly elected.) This adjustment has been so successful that voter turnout is now high enough to provoke incredulous sneers among those to whom the Cubans' highly developed sense of community is incomprehensible.

Because voting is not compulsory in Cuba the 1993 election was widely regarded as a referendum on Castroism. Miami's hard-liners ran a Radio Marti campaign, thousands of hours long, urging Cubans to boycott the election. One of their most prominent allies was Florida's then governor, Lawton Chiles, who broadcast frequently, exhorting the Cubans to spoil their votes or stay at home. (Picture the reaction were a Cuban politician to urge US citizens to boycott an election – which almost half of them do anyway, having lost faith in their own version of democracy.) When Havana launched a counter-campaign, calling for a big turnout, Miami accused them of 'distorting the democratic process' and continued confidently to forecast 'fifty per cent spoiled or blank'.

On 24 February 1993 over a hundred journalists from twenty-one countries, and numerous foreign visitors, were free to observe both the voting and the counting. No one, anywhere, accused anyone of fraud. Support for Castroism came from eighty-eight per cent of the electorate, ninety-nine per cent of whom had voted – and this despite multiple external misfortunes and internal misjudgements having reduced the island to near-starvation point. Beyond doubt, the government had a renewed mandate. This was recognised even by Elizardo Sanchez, then President of the Cuban Commission for Human Rights and National Reconciliation and one of the government's best-known resident opponents. Five years later, after the 1998 election, he again acknowledged 'the renovation of the mandates and the legitimacy of the government'. In 2003 he made no comment when a ninety-seven per cent voter turnout gave Castroism ninety-one per cent support.

When Bush II rants on about 'liberating Cuba from the Communist tyranny of one-party rule' he is riding the wrong horse. The ideal of single-party rule, symbolising national unity, derives from Martí's thinking and is therefore respected by Cubans as no Soviet imposition would be. Martí's Cuban Revolutionary Party healed many of the wounds caused by faction fighting among Cuba's 'rebels' and also united the island's revolutionaries with their exiled supporters in the US and elsewhere.

After his exile in Spain, Martí lived for seven years in the US, working as a political journalist and studying US democracy. He had this to write in 1885:

> Capitalists, in exchange for laws that are favourable to their undertakings, support the party that offers those laws . . . Both parties govern equally abusively wherever they govern, for both are slices of the same people; since upon no major question do they differ, but are divided equally . . . Elections are quite costly. The capitalists and large companies help the needy candidates with their campaign expenses; once the candidates are elected, they pay with their slavish vote for the money laid out in advance.

By the 1880s multi-party politics was already distrusted in Cuba as a device used by the Spaniards to weaken the revolutionary movement. Nowadays the system is distrusted because US intervention (already planned and funded, as Caleb McCarry repeatedly informs us) could only return Cuba to the era when the US embassy selected candidates for all elections, assisted by special envoys sent from Washington. Caleb McCarry is not the first of his kind; several US Mafia leaders then living in Havana influenced the choice of candidates as no Cuban citizen could do. There is enough gruesome evidence strewn around the globe to prove the undesirability of importing US-style democracy-cum-free-marketeering.

The common assumption that 'the Red threat' ignited US hatred for 'Castro's Revolution' is wholly false. Two years before Fidel defined the Revolution as 'Socialist', and before the new Cuba had even established diplomatic relations with the Soviet Union, President Eisenhower signed the Pluto Plan, authorising the CIA to destabilise Cuba. Quite simply, Washington saw the island as US property – now stolen. In 1963 Robert Scheer and Maurice Zeitlin wrote:

> The tragic course of US-Cuba relations has been encouraged and accelerated by the US government's foreign policy towards Cuba. That policy acted both to change political attitudes among the Cuban leaders

and to increase the probability that men already holding Communist or pro-Soviet beliefs would move into positions of influence and power within the revolutionary movement.

The Revolution's first year saw an extraordinary upsurge of popular energy as control of workplaces and neighbourhoods was secured, without violence, by the ordinary people. Interim town councils replaced the *batistianos*. Every aspect of public life was quickly and bloodlessly transformed, something that could not possibly have been done without the support of the majority. Incredulously the world watched as Fidel and his *compañeros* issued one thousand five hundred (or so) laws and decrees in the first nine months of 1959 and formed a well-trained armed militia, ignoring the US State Department's increasingly angry shouts and the recall of the US ambassador. Never before in Latin America had a new government got away with calmly and methodically implementing its nationalist/reformist programme in opposition to US interests. Within eighteen months the old political parties had faded away, not repressed or intimidated but having accepted their irrelevance; the arrival of the *barbudos* really had marked a popular revolution, immune to civil disturbances or faction fighting. Meanwhile outsiders continued to expect the *barbudos* to be overthrown but at the Bay of Pigs those to whom that task had been delegated were themselves defeated – a victory which sealed the Revolution's triumph, filling the Cubans with pride, confidence and gratitude towards their leaders.

For several years Revolution-speak was innocent of tedious Communist formulae. The Movement's anti-oligarchic and popular character was emphasised but without mention of the proletariat or the working-class, per se. Fidel made it clear on 12 March 1959 that if the rich and privileged abandoned their privileges their contribution to the new Cuba would be much appreciated. 'The privileged will not be executed but privileges will be.' He warned the rich not to try to evade revolutionary measures through bribery and corruption. 'I ask everyone to make a sacrifice, to continue making a sacrifice for the country through this creative effort, because the Revolution doesn't preach hatred, the Revolution preaches justice . . . ' Two days later Fidel's little brother, the twenty-eight-year-old Raul, echoed him – 'To those who in miniscule numbers are against the Revolution, we tell them in good faith – because in principle we don't wish evil for anyone – we make a patriotic appeal to them to adjust to the new situation, to adapt to the brilliant process which began on the First of January.' In June

Fidel pointed out that those attempting to light the class fuse were the counter-revolutionaries. Addressing more than one thousand members of the Havana Bar Association, he demanded, 'What do they want? To provoke class war? To incite class hatred when it is our wish that the Revolution should be seen as the work of the whole nation?' Many in that audience heeded him and became essential props of a process that needed a whole flock of legal eagles to oversee its legitimate development.

Fidel has repeatedly been accused of hyper-duplicity because in March 1959 he spoke of elections within the next two years or so, when the new regime had settled down – while allegedly he was planning to consolidate his dictatorship. In a TV interview he replied to US journalists, 'We are favourable to elections, but elections that will really respect the people's will, by means of procedures which put an end to political machinations'. He spoke of the need for genuine democracy rather than elections. 'The government now is at the service of the people, not of political cliques or oligarchies. We have democracy today, for the first time in our history. What is really odd is that those who have no popular support talk about elections.' Unsurprisingly, given the people's memories of past elections, a June opinion poll, run by *Bohemia* magazine, showed sixty per cent against elections and ninety per cent in favour of their new government. Most Cubans clearly saw the difference between liberal multi-party democracy and their new revolutionary democracy. Hence their reaction to the First Havana Declaration, approved by more than a million people assembled in the Plaza de la Revolucion on 2 September 1960. Hostile historians dismiss this event as 'mob rule' or 'crowd hysteria', quoting no more than a phrase or two. In part, Fidel said:

> Close to the monument and the memory of José Martí, in Cuba, free territory of America, the people, in the full exercise of the inalienable powers that proceed from the true exercise of the sovereignty expressed in the direct, universal and public suffrage, has constituted itself in a National General Assembly.
>
> The National General Assembly of the People of Cuba expresses its conviction that democracy cannot consist only in an electoral vote, which is almost always fictitious and handled by big landholders and professional politicians, but in the rights of citizens to decide, as this Assembly of the People is now doing, their own destiny. Moreover, democracy will only exist in Latin America when its people are really free to choose, when the humble people are not reduced – by hunger,

social inequality, illiteracy and the judicial system – to the most degrading impotence. In short, the National General Assembly of the People of Cuba proclaims before America:

The right of peasants to the land; the right of workers to the fruit of their work; the right of children to education; the right of sick people to medical and hospital attention; the right of youth to work; the right of students to free, experimental and scientific education; the right of Negroes and Indians to 'the full dignity of man'; the right of women to civil, social and political equality; the right of the aged to a secure old age; the right of states to nationalise imperialist monopolies, thus rescuing their wealth and national resources . . .

Those hostile historians who jeer at 'crowd hysteria' fail to see the connection between that Plaza de la Revolucion Assembly and its Latin American background as elucidated by Professor D. L. Raby:

The idea of the people taking up arms to achieve liberation is central to Latin American political culture, and it by no means excludes other forms of struggle and participation. It is intimately linked to the concept of popular sovereignty, that sovereignty really does reside in the people as a whole and not in the propertied classes or in any hereditary group or privileged institution. The people, moreover, constitute themselves as political actors by collective mobilisation, not merely by passive reception of media messages or individualised voting. The secret ballot is undoubtedly regarded as essential, but as inadequate unless accompanied by mass organisation and mobilisation . . . Hence the resonance of the term 'revolution' tends to be positive, unlike in contemporary Europe or North America where it has come to be associated with irrational violence or dogmatic sectarianism. For the same reasons, 'democracy' in Latin America is popularly associated with collective rights and popular power, and not just repressive institutions and liberal pluralism.

Considering the functions of the provincial assemblies and the National Assembly, Isaac Saney has written:

The goal of achieving unity and consensus is central. The unanimous votes that occur are not indicative of a rubber-stamp mentality but of a consensus that is arrived at through extensive and intensive discussion, dialogue and debate that precedes the final vote in the National Assembly: the end-point of a long, conscientious and sometimes arduous process . . . A critical aspect of the Cuban political system is the integration of a variety of mass organisations into political activity. No new policy or legislation can be adopted or contemplated until the appropriate organisation or association representing the sector of society that would be directly affected has been consulted.

Castroist democracy has gradually evolved into something quite original, by means of various constitutional adjustments, and Arnold August describes Electoral Law No. 72 as 'At first sight . . . an incomprehensible labyrinth'. I do not intend to lead you there; suffice to say that the municipal elections are by far the most democratic. The Cuban municipality is like no other and not at all what the term suggests to our ears – a city authority. It may be part of a large city but according to Article 102 of the Constitution:

The municipality is the local society having, to all legal effects, a juridical personality. It is politically organised according to law, covering a surface area that is determined by the necessary economic and social relations of its population, and with the capacity to meet the minimum local needs.

Down on the ground (an important place) Cubans elected to run their municipality do a lot of serious decision-making. Delegates are elected for two and a half years, provincial assembly and National Assembly delegates for five years. Sixteen is the voting age, for all Cubans except convicts and those declared mentally disabled by a court. Any citizen over sixteen may be elected at municipal and provincial levels though delegates to the National Assembly must be over eighteen. No organisation is allowed to nominate a municipal candidate but any individual can nominate any other individual on the voters' list for that constituency. Approximately fifty per cent of National Assembly delegates, from whom the Council of State is chosen, start out as municipal delegates. The National Electoral Commission has no legal link with the state and candidates for any of the assemblies are ineligible to serve on it. Electoral Commissions must be established at least three months before polling days, voter registration being one of their main responsibilities. An unusual feature of Cuba's election season is the vast body of volunteers who for nine months devote much time and energy to ensuring orderly and efficient polling days and vote-counting.

To avoid the Soviet Union's unhealthy symbiosis, the Party is legally prohibited from intervening in municipal elections where delegate nomination is genuinely free. At the National Assembly level, the Party does control the membership in a roundabout but effective way. Only fifteen per cent of adults belong to the Party yet seventy per cent of National Assembly delegates are members. The other thirty per cent includes representatives of religious faiths and of the arts and sports world.

The keystone of Cuba's participatory democracy is the nomination of municipal candidates by a show of hands at small public meetings. Tens of thousands of these local gatherings take place, on average lasting no more than thirty minutes. Participation is not compulsory but about seventy per cent normally attend; on polling day the turn-out everywhere is in the late 90s. The procedure is, Alejandro assured me, a Cuban invention, uninfluenced by any foreign systems. It is extremely ingenious, and hermetically sealed against corruption/vote-rigging, but much too intricate to be presented in a résumé. Those deeply interested in psephology may find the details in Arnold August's *Democracy in Cuba* and Peter Roman's *People's Power*.

The Council of State, controlled by the Communist Party, takes all major decisions with island-wide implications. These are ratified by the National Assembly which meets only twice a year but staffs numerous specialist commissions to do a lot of necessary boring work. Occasionally, at Party level, democracy raises its pretty head and popular views, wishes and judgements are taken into account. In preparation for the 1992 Constitutional amendments small groups met and debated various issues in eighty-nine thousand workplaces, schools, universities and community halls. A distillation of their comments eventually reached the legislators and was respected. In 1993–94 a similar number of 'workers' parliaments' debated the major economic reforms then being proposed. The opinions voiced were synthesised and considered and those held by a majority caused legislative changes – notably of taxation.

To us this form of participatory democracy is a novel notion. Imagine a proportionate number of 'people's parliaments' gathering in Britain, by request of the government, to discuss, for instance, the Poll Tax, or closing mines or post offices, or the introduction of university fees, or an airport extension or new Tridents. Then try to imagine Britain's democratically elected government giving consideration to voters' views . . . But would we Minority Worlders appreciate this sort of collective involvement in running our countries? It requires a certain expenditure of mental energy – and time. Moreover, despite having regular access to 'free and fair elections', and complaining so often about governmental decisions, we seem to feel terminally disempowered in relation to decision-making. But enough of fantasy-land – let's return to Manzanillo.

Most Cuban cities share the background motifs of smugglers, sugar, slaves. Long before Manzanillo's founding in 1784 its natural harbour was a smuggler's favourite. During the nineteenth century it prospered as quite an important port and its wealthier citizens built mansions displaying a taste for whimsical Moorish flourishes. At sea-level one is scarcely aware of the Caribbean's nearness: just occasionally a patch of blue sparkles at the end of a street. But then, from the steep, densely populated hills that semi-encircle the colonial centre, one is overlooking the Gulf of Guacanayabo's dazzling expanse. Nowadays Manzanillo is chiefly renowned for its Rebel Army associations. Here Celia Sanchez, Fidel's right-hand woman, clandestinely set up the supply base without which the Rebels could not have survived.

The *colectivo* put me down at 3.15 when sun-scourged Manzanillo was not lively. In a shadeless open-air cafeteria, facing Parque Cespedes, the bar was closed – no one in sight. Eduardo in Mayari had recommended a *casa particulare* and provided a street sketch. I sat on an iron chair to consult this – then leaped up with a burnt bottom. Clutching that scrap of paper I crossed the park diagonally, pausing to admire the sphinx statues in each corner, the fake nineteenth-century lamps and the enchanting Glorieta Morisca, designed by a Granada architect, where the municipal band plays regularly and bridal couples pose for photographs. Most such Cuban agoras are in all-day use but here not even one bench was occupied. Although my *casa particulare* was quite close, I felt slightly dizzy on arrival.

An open street door led directly into the living-room and I gatecrashed a celebration; relatives and friends had gathered to drink the health of a new-born baby. I was enthusiastically received as another friend rather than the new p.g. Liqueur glasses of some powerful homemade alcohol, dark brown and syrupy, were being rapidly downed and refilled. The infant's plastic crib (made in China, very fancy with a nylon mosquito net) stood on high legs in the centre of the room. A three-year-old first born was having displacement problems and querulously demanding everyone's attention. On a low altar beside my bedroom door a black Virgen de Regla/Yemaya, clad in flowing blue and white robes, had to be included in the party; at intervals people offered her a sprinkle of that strange herb-flavoured potion, or a few peanuts, or a scrap of coloured thread or ribbon.

Later I got the family sorted out. Juana, the *abuela*, suffered from obesity and her daughter-in-law, Rita, was going in the same direction. Manuel, her English-speaking son, worked at the local ship repair yard and had a not unusual grievance. In 1994 his father and an uncle took off for Miami accompanied by Manuel's two sisters, then in their late teens. Father had promised to 'claim' his wife and thirteen-year-old son once he had 'settled'; instead, he was lost to view. In due course Juana presented Manuel with a step-father, Viktor, a wispy little man who seemed in danger of being suffocated in the marital bed should his wife roll over in her sleep. Viktor operated a horse-bus and his eighteen-year-old daughter, Margarita, a student nurse, was the fifth member of the household. The jolly scene I had witnessed on arrival was misleading. Placid Juana, who apparently loved everybody, was at the still centre of a maelstrom of animosities. Margarita criticised Rita for continuing to work part time as a free-market vegetable seller though she had a year's maternity leave on full pay. Rita insisted that the three-week-old baby was perfectly happy on his *abuela*'s lap sucking expressed mother's milk from a bottle. Viktor sided with his daughter which provoked Manuel to condemn him for overworking his horse. Rita objected to Manuel's gambling on cockfights which made it necessary for her to sell vegetables. Carlos, the first-born, reacted predictably to all these simmering (and often loudly overboiling) dissensions. He was the only unhappy child I met in Cuba.

Next morning I observed that in Manzanillo dawn comes twenty minutes earlier than in Havana. At 6.35 the first pale orange tint appeared above the horizon as I strolled through a run-down district of small, variously designed dwellings, many with dormer windows, lining laneways shaded by misshapen trees. Already polling stations were being unlocked and when I peered into one I was invited to come back later. In contrast to the exclusion of unlabelled solo travellers from public institutions, foreigners are positively encouraged to take a close look at Cuba's election processes – for obvious reasons.

In Havana I had first seen the only harbingers of this Election Day – A4 pages displayed in office and shop windows showing passport-type photographs of the candidates and listing their academic and/or practical achievements and the mass organisations to which they belong. These are drab little notices, impersonal, nobody claiming that they will do this or that if elected; nor are there any canvassing visits, posters, leaflets, loud-hailers, rallies, telephone calls or TV appearances. At no stage is money involved; the state provides the A4 notices. Winning or losing does not evoke the same emotions as in our world. Losing may be a personal disappointment – but no cash has been wasted. Winning is taken calmly, and not as Step One to prosperity; Cuba has no greasy pole on the political field. (I wouldn't know about the joint-venture field.) Those elected (who may be anything from lawyers and street-sweepers to factory hands and professors) continue in their jobs while working as unpaid public representatives. In local government only the president, vice-president and secretary of each municipal assembly – officials elected by the delegates – receive salaries. Twice a year, at accountability sessions, delegates must listen to *planteamientos* (suggestions and complaints of local importance) and representatives found unsatisfactory by their constituents may be 'recalled' (sacked) and replaced in what we would call a by-election. Municipal delegates are responsible for the day-to-day running of their neighbourhoods. They organise mini-brigades to build houses for the community, maintain *organoponicos* to feed the community, oversee local schools, polyclinics and factories – and participate, if trade unionists, in the planning and management of their enterprises. They are on duty twenty-four hours a day seven days a week and may be approached at any time by any constituent with any sort of problem from a family row to a burst water main.

At 7.00 a.m. precisely, all over Manzanillo (and all over Cuba) the national anthem, being quietly relayed by Radio Rebelde, signalled the opening of the polling stations, each catering for the residents of its immediate neighbourhood. A forty-minute walk took me past nine stations. This means an absence of queues or crowds; a tourist could have spent 21 October drifting around any Cuban city or town without realising it was Election Day. On arrival voters exchange their registration cards for ballot papers, then enter a tent-like enclosure set up in a corner where they are invisible while making their marks. Thus citizens may anonymously express disapproval of or hatred for the government by spoiling their paper. A few steps take the voter from tent to ballot box, guarded by two uniformed junior schoolchildren. I watched one opening ritual. Out on the pavement, an elderly CDR member held high an empty cardboard carton while inviting any passer-by to enter the station to witness its being sealed with glue and placed on a little table between its juvenile guardians.

After breakfast I met Alejandro who suggested our touring the hilltops 'before it gets too hot'. (In my estimation it was already very much too hot.) On steep slopes, Manzanillo's streets of stuccoed houses (1920s) become grass-verged tracks with open drains running down the centre. Narrow green valleys separate the hills and Alejandro pointed to once-fine villas set amidst still handsome trees. Other *barrios* have a quasi-rural character with livestock wandering around charmless utilitarian cottages (1960s) and closely fenced *organoponico* beds.

We were invited into polling stations improvised in a kindergarten, a *tienda*, a polyclinic, a cultural centre, two offices. The children's role fascinated me. As the folded ballot papers were pushed through the slits these Pioneers saluted smartly and together chanted – 'Voto!' It was important, said Alejandro, to educate young citizens about how Cuban-style democracy really works, to make them feel responsible for the boxes' integrity and proud of contributing to the election of the best represen-tatives to run *their* community. To prove that this involvement was genuine, not any sort of stunt or cosmetic gesture, Alejandro led me at 7.00 p.m. from a polling station to the nineteenth-century Asamblea Municipal del Poder Popular. As the polling station's box was being transported, opened and emptied on to a counters' table, two pairs of sharp little eyes watched every movement. According to Alejandro, this 'catch 'em young' policy explains why even today's teenagers vote eagerly in municipal elections. At which point I recalled Professor Raby's assessment:

> Revolutionary popular power can survive for decades even in a small country like Cuba . . . so long as the leadership remains committed to Socialist goals and closely linked to the mass popular movement . . . The problem for Cuba is that above the municipal level it has restricted political debate and participation and this, combined with the hardships imposed by the US blockade, has produced a dangerous sense of alienation among large sections of Cuban youth.

When Alejandro asked how Western democracies select candidates I explained the Irish system, then told him of the unease often voiced by Tony Benn (among many others) about decisions once made by govern-ments having been transferred to the EU, NATO, the unholy Trinity and the multinational corporations *'whom we do not elect and cannot remove'*. I added, borrowing a metaphor from the liberation theologian Franz Hin-kelammert, that Western parties now treat voters as consumers whose political choices can be swayed by market techniques. And Socialism, as one choice, is now excluded. According to my guide, 'All delegates must live in their own constituencies. If they don't help enough with local problems they won't get selected next time.'

I wondered why anybody should want to be re-selected for such a demanding unpaid job, then realised that this remark exposed my im-perfect understanding of Revolutionary thinking (and feeling). As David Beetham has put it:

Participation enhances people's own knowledge and competence as
they address practical problems in their communities . . . Being able to
see tangible outcomes from one's participation produces a sense of
empowerment, and an incentive to continue one's involvement.

By this stage we had retreated with a few Buccaneros to the shady
Andalusian courtyard of the Colonia Española club where wall tiles show
Columbus landing in Cuba and pensioners play dominoes all day and a
three-man band was rehearsing on a balcony. 'They play for their own joy,'
commented Alejandro. 'I like best this way of music.'

Some of the domino players were Rebel Army veterans in their eighties
and Alejandro introduced me to a nonagenarian in a bath-chair who had
twice descended to Manzanillo to fetch Ché's asthma medicine – easily
provided by Celia Sanchez the doctor's daughter.

By mid-afternoon we were touring again, stopping quite often for
Alejandro to talk at some length to friends and acquaintances. He seemed
not to notice that standing around in the sun exhausted the Irish *abuela*. I
remarked on the numbers of disabled voters we saw driving their buggies
into polling stations, the majority black men in their fifties. 'African vets,'
said Alejandro. 'For long years Cuba gave big sacrifices for Africa.' Those
veterans are members of an association for the handicapped. Proudly
Alejandro told me what I already knew: all Cubans belong to an
appropriate group. 'We have Committees to Defend the Revolution, the
Cuban Federation of Women, Federation of University Students, National
Association of Small Farmers, Confederation of Cuban Workers, groups of
lawyers, economists, athletes, artists, writers, musicians.' Representatives
from all those organisations make up the Electoral Commissions whose
Presidents are chosen by the Trade Unions, from the Confederation of
Cuban Workers. Anyone other than a Party member can serve on a Commission. Pericles would have approved: 'No one, so long as he has it in him
to be of service to the city, is kept in political obscurity because of poverty.'

All day there was not a soldier or a policeman to be seen; this 'People's
Election' needed no state supervision or regimentation and the uniformed
forces change into civvies before voting. According to Alejandro, everybody
knowing, personally, each individual on the candidates' list gave the whole
process a reassuring reality. Unmistakably these were keen voters, participating in something that mattered to them, not merely tolerating a
meaningless routine.

Later we watched the count for half an hour, all done with pencil and paper. Much double and treble checking, by the constituency electoral commission, is mandatory. After supper with Alejandro's family we were back at the Asamblea Municipal in time to see the list of those elected being posted outside – an astonishingly fast count because of each 'college' being so small.

Back at Casa Juana I retired feeling queasy and generally unwell, in an unfamiliar way.

Not long after my return to Ireland the following letter appeared in the *Irish Times*:

> Recently, in quite a remote Cuban town, my host found me semi-delirious at midnight on a Sunday, suffering from severe heat stroke. Hyperpyrexia, which can be fatal, needs immediate treatment.
>
> Fifteen minutes later the family doctor arrived, on his bicycle, to provide the appropriate isotonic saline and administer other treatments. Eight hours later he telephoned to check on my progress, which was satisfactory.
>
> Were I to fall ill (or have a serious accident) in my home town of Lismore, Co Waterford, between 6.00 p.m. on a Friday and 9.00 a.m. on a Monday, someone would have to telephone Caredoc's nurse in Carlow, eighty miles away, describing my symptoms or injuries and leaving it to the nurse to decide whether or not a doctor was needed.
>
> This grotesque arrangement assumes that the person contacting the nurse is knowledgeable enough to accurately interpret the symptoms. Should the nurse guess (it can only be a guess) that a doctor is needed, the Lismore patient must then be transported, by whatever vehicle his/her helper can provide, to the nearest doctor – fifteen miles away in Dungarvan.
>
> If the nurse in Carlow has somehow been persuaded that the patient in Lismore cannot or should not be moved, a doctor will *be driven* to Lismore by a chauffer who knows the territory so that no time is lost. But so much time has already been lost that were I, in Lismore, afflicted by a condition comparable to hyperpyrexia (say a stroke or a heart attack) I might well be dead before the doctor arrived. Viva Fidel!

Hyperpyrexia is so scary that I heeded the amiably authoritarian doctor, not long home from a two-year posting in a high Andean village. He prescribed forty-eight hours rest, then back to 'cool (!) Havana'. Playa Las Coloradas was even hotter than Manzanillo – transport was uncertain –

the *Granma* trail was long and exposed, through mangrove forest. He managed politely to imply that anyway *abuelas* should use Viazul coaches and stay in tourist hotels.

On the spacious flat roof, approached by a stairway from the patio, Juana had created a wondrous bower of white-blossomed vines. Here I obediently rested, drinking the prescribed gallons of water and dolefully abstaining from Buccaneros. This was a good vantage point from which to observe the rhythms of local life and I noted the prevalence of parasols and fans, used by both sexes. We associate fans with delicate Victorian ladies reclining on chaise longue, not with males whose biceps bulge and whose hairy chests are sweat-matted. And parasols go with fair maidens mincing through the Capability Brown groves of stately demesnes – not with men trying to give both their small bicycle passengers a safe share of the shade. Motor vehicles were rare, bicitaxis numerous – including some ingenious homemade models, with beach umbrellas wobbling over wooden sidecars and metal footrests welded to the solid bicycle frame.

The recent DIY conversion of Casa Juana to a *casa particulare* had demanded much bold experimentation on the plumbing and electrical fronts – the latter a serious health-hazard, given permanently sweat-wet hands. One morning I found my bathroom waterless and so it remained until Manuel returned from work. Sitting in my bower, I admired his gymnastics as he hung by his heels from a parapet doing something daring with the hose piping and electric wiring that supplied my room.

By then I had recovered from the Playa Las Coloradas disappointment and was contemplating my good fortune: adequate medical care provided within fifteen minutes at midnight! One can see how neo-liberalism's corrosion of the welfare state is insidiously weakening Western democracy. Voter turn-outs have remained highest where the welfare state has suffered least damage – e.g., Holland, Germany, Scandinavia. There is no one to protect it in countries like Britain and Ireland, stricken by the cancer of privatisation – q.v. Ireland's 'Caredoc' system. As Gunter Grass wrote in the *Guardian* in 2005:

> Democracy has become a pawn to the dictates of globally volatile capital ... Questions asked as to the reasons for the growing gap between rich and poor are dismissed as 'the politics of envy'. The desire for justice is ridiculed as utopian. The concept of solidarity is relegated to the dictionary's list of 'foreign words'.

The failure of central planning in the Soviet Union and its satellites left those régimes, unsustained by popular support, with no choice but to submit to Capitalism Rampant. When Fidel opposed the Gorbachev reforms, leaving himself open to charges of 'Stalinism', he knew that Cuba's Revolution still had the loyalty of most Cubans and could therefore survive the Special Period. But now . . . ?

In 2004 Aurelio Alonso, one of Cuba's shrewdest political thinkers, considered Castroism's future and wrote, 'It is not possible to speak of an alternative without also talking about power'. He advocated giving much more power to local community action because 'history has shown that capitalism can reproduce itself without democracy but socialism cannot'. Like other experienced observers, he believes that new socialist régimes will emerge from Latin America, régimes intent on independent development, founded on participatory democracy, explicitly challenging the morality of putting profit first. They would of course have to work with capitalist enterprises, as Cuba is now doing. However, by defending state power against the Unholy Trinity they could continue to promote social justice and economic sovereignty, with key industries nationalised and political leaderships supported *and monitored* by mass popular organisations. Capitalism Rampant shudders to think of such regimes evolving as the 'socialism of the twenty-first century', to which several Cuban leaders have referred in recent years. Transitologists are deaf to the likes of Ricardo Alarcon, president of the National Assembly, who emphasises, 'We do not want to be seen as a model. We respect the right of others to develop their own system just as strongly as we demand that ours be respected'.

Did Professor Raby coin the word 'transitology'? He notes that with the preaching of 'free trade and monetarist fundamentalism as the only economically acceptable policy . . . a vast academic literature has sprung up on "democratic transition" . . . Virtually all countries outside the North Atlantic core are assumed to be "in transition". The notion that the democratic will of the people might prefer to place restrictions on the unfettered rule of the market is scarcely even considered. The "transitology" literature is very revealing as to the true significance of neo-liberal orthodoxy on the issue of democracy . . . Particularly striking is the emphasis on markets and property rights and the absence of any mention of social justice or popular participation'.

Despite hyperpyrexia, I was glad to have had the opportunity to observe 'popular participation' in Manzanillo with Alejandro as my guide.

Chapter 22

Manzanillo's railway station is hardly a mile from Casa Juana but I had learned my lesson and at 1.00 p.m. Viktor's horse-bus picked me up. The Havana train would depart some time between 3.00 and 8.00 but tickets must be bought not later than 1.30. Even by Cuban standards this timing seemed inordinately vague and there was a sad explanation. A few days previously one of Cuba's worst train crashes had occurred at Yara, between Manzanillo and Bayamo, when a Santiago-Manzanillo train collided with a bus at a level crossing. 'Thirty people died at once,' said Manuel, 'and more may go – seventy injured, fifteen very much smashed up. Now time-tables are all confused.'

Viktor refused to believe that I was no longer convalescent; he insisted on carrying my rucksack into the waiting-room and telling the ticket clerk I was too old and ill to queue. Having stared me up and down she grunted unsympathetically, then said she wasn't authorised to deal in convertible pesos and handed me a NP5 ticket to Bayamo. There the tourists' ticket office would accept my CP25.50. Noting my alarm – the train might leave me behind – kind Viktor hurried away to seek the train's 'captain' who at once volunteered to buy the ticket if given my passport and cash.

When this railway was first constructed Manzanillo lacked road connec-tions – hence the enormous waiting-room. For the next five hours three TV sets, hung high on a long wall, showed children's cartoons interspersed with documentaries about soil erosion and dengue fever. There were no fans. There was no bar. My companions were few and various; as no one had the least idea when the service might depart people wandered in, sat around hopefully for a time, then strolled away.

Soon Marc arrived, a burly young creole wearing a Stars and Stripes T-shirt. Spotting the foreigner, he sat opposite me and spoke bluntly. Taxes on the new private enterprises were too high and restrictions too tight. His grandparents used to spend weekends in Miami before the Revolution; he'd been confined all his life to the island. Sellers of snacks and drinks on peso transport (buses and trains) were forbidden to charge more than street prices so their initiatives went unrewarded while those catering for Viazul passengers could charge what they liked. I remarked that it was consistent with the Revolutionary ethos not to penalise peso-dependent 'captive' consumers. And consistent with the capitalist ethos to charge tourists as much as they would pay, taking advantage of their captivity. Marc shrugged and looked at my watch and got up to go. A later train would not get him to Bayamo in time for his appointment; there was no bus until next day and he couldn't afford a collectivo. Friends told him transport was improving elsewhere in Cuba but Granma had always been a neglected region.

Later, when Francisco sat beside me, we pooled our linguistic resources and he told me about his eighteen months as a paramedic with the humanitarian brigade despatched to Iran by Fidel during the 1980s war. Saddam Hussein, then a cherished US ally, was using chemical weapons (some of their ingredients supplied by Donald Rumsfeld's corporation) and Francisco said he doesn't expect ever to recover from the horror of watching so many gassed youths slowly dying in extreme agony. At the time he asked himself why Cuba was helping a country that exposed many thousands of mid-teenagers to such a fate. Later he came to understand that the object of his mission was not to help the Iranian government but to help relieve the suffering of its innocent victims.

At 6.30 our train could be heard in the distance, jerkily reversing towards us. Pre-Revolution, its coaches must have been first class. The black leatherette seats, with headrests, were wide and soft and adjustable – but now involuntarily so, having come loose from their moorings. Compared with my Havana-Bayamo train of indelible memory this was indeed first class but it had its little idiosyncrasies. A cockroach Rapid Reaction Force swarmed just above my arm-rest, its divisional headquarters the crevices around the window, its reactions attuned to the opening of food parcels. Far worse were the mosquitoes; at sunset they zoomed hungrily through all the open windows and soon I felt like one big mosquito bite. Long before I needed the malodorous loo its defects were evident: a loudly banging unlockable door, a floor slithery with pee.

All the way to Bayamo the train's bucking was sensational, provoking much merriment. 'Same like as we rode a wild horse!' chuckled Francisco, sitting beside me. I thought it more like one of those dare-devil fun-fair machines that have you bouncing a foot off your seat but always landing safely. Between bounces Francisco reminisced about his only journey abroad, from Havana to Tehran via Newfoundland, Germany, Greece, Turkey. More than twenty years later he could remember exactly how long each stop had been, on both journeys, and what he had observed at each airport – one benefit of an uncrowded mental storehouse.

At Bayamo I looked anxiously for the captain, clutching my passport and convertible pesos, but he was nowhere to be seen; only then did I scent a scam. During the fifty-minute halt, overlooking a busy road junction, not one motor vehicle appeared. There were criss-crossing flows of cyclists, bicitaxis and various models of horse vehicles – including elegant carriages, Bayamo boasting the finest range in Cuba. (Soon I'd be at home, missing the clip-clop of hoofs . . .) How unpleasant that wait would have been – smelly, ugly, noisy – at a major junction in a 'normal' twenty-first-century city! Here everyone was getting where they wanted to go, quietly, comparatively slowly, without pollution. Car ownership in the Majority World used to worry Fidel years before it occurred to most other people. Yet scant thought is given to its social effects. In Cuba, for instance, how would it change the quality of neighbourhood life? At present Cubans vivaciously converse, play dominoes and chess, make music and dance in their homes or Casas de la Trova, exercise together in the local stadium, work together in the local *organoponico* – always aware of each other, rallying around in times of crisis. Where almost universal car ownership provides mobility, entrepreneurs provide entertainments as commodities. Individuals or 'nuclear' families habitually zoom off in different directions to do this or that and communities become fractured. Neighbourhoods matter less as restlessness takes over. People feel an urge to move simply because moving is possible and relatively expensive entertainments work their own black magic, making free pleasures seem inferior. Instead of a walk in the woods, 'caring' parents take their children to a theme park. If you have to pay for something, it must be more valuable – right?

At 10.20, when every seat had been filled, the engine whistled wheezily and we went on our jolting way. Then, by one of those improbable coincidences with which travellers are familiar, I discovered that the man across the aisle, in the other window seat, was a friend of the 'independent dissident' I had failed to contact at Santa Clara University. Moreover, Jesus already knew about my courier role which meant that he was someone to whom I could safely entrust that little packet, now in the depths of my rucksack. Extracting it on the carriage floor broke the monotony for my *compañeros* who exclaimed in awe as book after book emerged.

At Santa Clara Jesus was replaced by Ernesto, a young man with one of those faces that look like a cartoon come alive – elfin ears, a sharp nose, a pointed chin. Before long he had joined the ranks of the many who told me that 'all Cubans are trained how to fight, how to kill with guns and grenades and use camouflage'.

Around midnight, when the lights were off and most passengers asleep, the captain appeared beside me and whispered a request for my passport and CP25.50. Pocketing the latter, he made much of noting my details, by faint torchlight, in a copybook. No ticket was given me but this didn't matter; oddly enough, arriving passengers are not checked.

By moonlight central Cuba's wide flat spaces have a beauty denied them in sunlight. Gazing out at the black and silver tranquillity, I concluded that Fidel's experiment, despite having been so maimed by US enmity and Soviet friendship, had much to teach the free-marketeers, not least about social cohesion and participatory democracy. Yet I had no easy answer for those (well-disposed towards Castroism) who anxiously asked, 'How can the Cubans change their government?' Even now most of us regard this as democracy's acid test, though for decades its significance has been diminishing as all major political parties fall into line behind their corporate controllers.

The foundation stones for a viable Western-style democracy are generally taken to be: a) a stable *state* with a competent (more or less) administration and disciplined law enforcement agencies acceptable to (almost) everyone; b) a united *nation* within settled boundaries, its citizens in agreement on who 'belongs'; c) safeguards to prevent any religion from dictating legislation or policy; d) an economy sound enough to provide for the population's essential needs. (On point c, it has to be said, Ireland was flawed until 1971 when we altered our constitution to abolish the 'special position' of the Roman Catholic Church. And Britain does have all those Anglican bishops in the House of Lords . . .) Europe's senior democracies quarried their foundation stones gradually, over centuries, and had them in place long before full-blown democracy appeared. In contrast, throughout much of the Majority World they have only recently been carted from the quarry and remain not very securely laid. Yet the free-marketeers pretend 'democracy' can be quickly contrived wherever its façade seems likely to serve their purposes.

Some of my dissident friends argued that by now Cubans are better placed than most Majority Worlders to adopt multi-party democracy, Castroism having laid the foundations while securing their economic and social rights – without which all others are elusive, if not meaningless. (Minority Worlders tend to forget that the rights to free expression and association, or to seek election or found a political party, are not usable by illiterate citizens suffering from malnutrition, overcrowding and untreated illnesses.) It's unsurprising that such dissidents impatiently ask – 'Why not abandon Martí's misunderstood one-party ideal, which attracts so much criticism, and let us all off the leash?' But when I put this to Juan in Camaguey he countered that such an electoral venture could only succeed if undertaken by an unthreatened sovereign state. Which took us back to Mr Caleb McCarry and his Commission for Assistance to a Free Cuba.

In Ireland, if I protested against Fidel's being sweepingly dismissed as a dictator, my friends knew how to silence me. Home births are illegal in Cuba, women cannot choose where and how to deliver their babies. Having witnessed the Trio's arrivals as happy family events, free of the pressures exerted by medical 'birth-managers', I find the denial of this fundamental right enraging. Granted, to achieve a home birth on our islands a mother has to be doggedly assertive and lucky with attitudes at her local hospital; and in Ireland, relatively rich. She must ignore accusations of irresponsibility and challenge the medical profession, citing evidence that mothers with planned home births gain on all levels (physical, mental, emotional) by not being exposed to a hospital ambience at this rare and wondrous time in their lives. And she must ask, 'Where in the research is there evidence that a healthy woman who enjoys a normal pregnancy and labour is safer giving birth in hospital?' No one I met in Cuba seemed to remember that home births were standard practice in all countries until recently, when an expanding medical industry decided that pregnancy and childbirth are quasi-diseases requiring long-term high-tech surveillance followed by hospitalisation.

As clouds sailed swiftly from the north-west, coalescing to veil the moon, my mosquito bites grew itchier and the loo fumes became more acrid. Even light dozing was off the agenda and I continued to speculate about Cuba's future, recalling my three long journeys (1993-95) south of the Limpopo. South Africa was then in transition from white minority rule to what seemed like a model multi-party democracy furnished with a comprehensive Bill of Rights, an independent constitutional court, an all-party executive for the first five years, job security for the apartheid régime's civil servants and immunity from prosecution for crimes committed by members of the armed forces. Since 1990 Nelson Mandela had been tirelessly echoing Martí – 'Let everyone start from the premise that we are one country, one nation, whether we are white, Coloured, Indian or black'.

On the day after the new President's inauguration I wrote in my journal:

President Mandela will be one of the three most highly paid Heads of State in the world, earning R734,350 per annum. All parliamentary salaries and allowances have been set by the Melamet Committee at private-sector levels. This is rumoured to have been part of the 'deal' with Nats. South Africa however is not a profit-making corporation run to benefit shareholders. Most of its citizens lucky enough to have jobs earn about ten thousand rands per annum while millions of jobless go permanently hungry. Nor is this a naturally rich country; the whites' lifestyle gives a false impression . . .

Yesterday [10 May 1994] President Mandela spoke of the need 'to heal the wounds of the past' and construct 'a new order based on justice for all'. Those wounds were inflicted by whites in pursuit of wealth. And in 1994 the fragile national prosperity remains dependent on the exploitation of black labour. An increasing number of blacks will now have access to wealth but rich blacks are no more (sometimes less) sensitive to the needs of the poor than rich whites. Constructing a new order must involve wealth-sharing and that would sink the reconciliation boat. In the real world, 'justice for all' and Madiba's noble ideal of reconciliation are incompatible.

When *South from the Limpopo* appeared some critics reproved me for being insufficiently enthusiastic about South Africa's 'peaceful transition to democracy'. In 1995 I had ended that book with the words:

I do have hope (hope rather than faith) that eventually justice will prevail – though the mechanism whereby it could do so at present remains invisible. It would be good to return one day and discover that my doubts were not, after all, well-founded. Sometimes it is exhilarating to be proved wrong.

Unfortunately the fate of South Africa's blacks in the intervening years has proved me right. Whites have retained most of the fertile land and they share other lucrative assets with a minority of ruthless blacks. In 2005 more than half the black population continued to live far below the official poverty line, still enduring inadequate housing, schooling and health care. Meanwhile unemployment is being exacerbated by migrants from other 'democracies' – like Zimbabwe. In 1959 Fidel chose 'a new order based on justice for the majority' – Cuba's minority being allergic to reconciliation with the Revolution.

At 2.00 p.m., as we approached the coast at Matanzas, the dark clouds sank lower and a gale sent the royal palm fronds streaming eastwards. The storm broke as we dawdled into Havana station, the engine seeming exhausted after its twenty-hour journey. By then Ernesto and I had had some revealing conversations; he was proud of being an 'independent dissident'. Now he invited me to stay in his Vedado home – 'we have room and I like to talk English'.

A bicitaxi took us through an almost deserted Havana; on every street sheets of water rushed towards flooding gutters. To semi-shelter us, the young cyclist had rolled down two plastic sheets, tied to the canopy struts. He told us the storm was forecast to continue for at least thirty-six hours. Then, between thunder claps, he and Ernesto talked baseball.

We stopped outside a three-storeyed balconied villa with a large front garden where the potted palms had already been overturned. Inside, archways divided high, wide rooms and a white marble staircase led to the first floor flat where Mamma advanced to greet her son – then paused, exuding hostility to his foreign guest. She was a small, slight, chain-smoking woman with narrow hazel eyes and a permanently pursed mouth. I would have left immediately but for the deluge; I was far from No. 403 and my aged rucksack, containing those precious books, is no longer as waterproof as once it was.

A flustered Ernesto showed me to my room and explained, 'We've no licence and my mother is scared of the police. She hates Fidel and she thinks they know that and watch her. That's crazy, only family know. She goes to our CDR meetings and seems OK there, she acts well.'

I said, with a hint of reproach, 'But didn't you realise she'd be angry about me?'

Ernesto stared at his toes and replied, 'This is my home, too. I want to live another way, not scared, able to have foreign friends. The government wants millions of tourists and makes publicity about Cubans giving welcomes. That's good, but it's bad to need a licence to give welcomes.'

As Ernesto's foreign friend I was dual purpose – a symbol of his defiance of government regulations and a weapon in this mother-son conflict. He apologised then; he hadn't foreseen it would be so difficult . . . And it got worse. To my host's extreme mortification Mamma asserted that there was no food to spare for a guest and Ernesto naturally didn't believe my claiming never to eat in the evening.

The *banyo* was on the far side of a spacious living-room where an ancient, mildly senile *abuela* spent hours sitting in front of a soundless TV set, dim eyes fixed on meaningless images. Her son had long ago died in a car crash; Ernesto could scarcely remember him. I never saw Mamma again. Ernesto joined me for a time in my pleasant room, its french window leading to a square balcony furnished with a wrought-iron table and chairs. Our conversation was not lively; we both needed an early night.

Thunder, lightning, a gale force wind and torrential rain continued until 9.50 next morning, by which time Ernesto had left for the university in a colleague's Lada. It only half-surprised me that I was not offered a lift; Mamma would have blocked that courtesy. A black 'daily' let me out and between further heavy showers I walked to No.403 via the Malecón where the road was closed to traffic and a coconut hit me on the head. I was lucky, it might have been a stone; waves were hurling an awesome tonnage of litter over the wall and strewing it across the street – everything from planks of wood to bottle-tops. Interestingly, there was no broken glass: a valuable commodity, rarely discarded.

Next morning I watched small earth-movers pushing all this litter into piles which were then loaded on to lorries by men using shovels and brushes. This labour-intensive procedure left the Malecón immaculate. Two days later an even wilder storm, with still higher waves, threw up only a few stones, fish and clumps of seaweed.

I found many of my Havana friends seething because Bush II had just broken a four-year silence on Cuba to address that amorphous entity, 'the international community'. Said he:

Now is the time to look past Fidel Castro's rule and help Cubans prepare for a new democracy after communism. Now is the time to support the democratic movement growing on the island. Now is the time to stand with the Cuban people as they stand up for their liberty. And now is the time for the world to put aside its differences and prepare for Cubans' transition to a future of freedom and progress and promise. The dissidents of today will be tomorrow's leaders. And when freedom finally comes they will surely remember who stood with them. The horrors of Mr Castro's regime remain unknown to the rest of the world. Once revealed, they will shock the conscience of humanity and they will shame the regime's defenders and all those democracies that had been silent.

The President of the United States ended with a special message for the armed forces of another sovereign state:

You must ignore claims that the US is hostile towards Cubans and turn on Mr Castro. You may have once believed in the revolution. Now you can see its failure.

To this incitement to civil war Felipe Perez Roque, as Foreign Minister, responded calmly. He noted that Mr Bush wanted to reconquer Cuba by force but the notion of an internal uprising was 'a politically impossible fantasy'. Next day *Granma* published Fidel's latest essay – 'Bush, Hunger and Death' – in which Fidel wrote of the grim reality that 'The danger of a massive world famine is aggravated by Mr Bush's recent initiative to transform foods into fuel' – an abuse of fertile land that Fidel has been condemning since 1985.

As we fumed companionably about this latest Bush aberration one of my friends remarked, 'We surely have an ally in the State Department! Some guy who tells him what to say to bring dissidents back on side.'

We also fumed about Washington's recent refusal to permit an MEP delegation to visit the Miami Five, a decision described by Willy Meyer MEP as 'a violation of basic principles of justice' and excused on the grounds that the Europeans did not know the Five before their imprisonment. These men's ordeal had been often discussed during my Cuban journeys but I postponed outlining their case to this final chapter, hoping that by then they might have been released. Gerardo, Ramón, Antonio, Fernando, René – those names, accompanied by photographs large or small, are seen everywhere, from the foyers of luxury hotels to the gable ends of rural sheds, from garlanded wayside monuments to *barrio* façades and *tienda* check-out desks. Moreover, every Cuban seems familiar with the Five's family backgrounds and in 2007 a best-selling book of their collected letters and poems was published in Havana.

Between 1990 and 2007 numerous US citizens funded and organised, from US territory, fifty-six major acts of violence against Cuba. These included shelling new tourist hotels from off-shore 'fishing-boats', planting a bomb in José Martí airport and attacking Viazul buses. When Cuban protests to the US and the UN were consistently ignored, Havana's Ministry of the Interior deployed the Five to infiltrate the relevant gangs in Miami, as a safeguard against future attacks. Leonard Weinglass, the Five's lead attorney, had repeatedly made clear that 'By US law, no US citizen can take up arms against another country. And the classic definition of terrorism is: attacks directed against civilians to change policy'. Every country is entitled to use anti-terrorist agents to protect the homeland and the Five were breaking US federal laws only by failing to register as foreign agents (impractical, in the circumstances) and using false names – comparatively minor offences.

A MinInt statement explains:

In the face of increased terrorist activities during the '90s, in an en-
deavour to work jointly against this scourge, we provided the Federal
Bureau of Investigation with detailed information about violent plots
being hatched in Miami, together with video and audio tapes, and in-
depth personal information related to the organisers of these criminal
activities. Our Report did not state, although it was obvious, that the
only way of obtaining this information was via infiltration of these
terrorist groups. The political response of the US government was not
long in coming. Only three months after our meeting, on 12 September
1998, during an FBI operation carried out at dawn, Gerardo Hernandez
Nordelo, Ramón Labañino Salazar, Antonio Guerrero Rodriguez,
Fernando González Llort and René González Sehwerert were arrested
in their homes.

Four days later the Five were accused of 'conspiracy to commit espionage'.
A second conspiracy charge involved only Gerardo, who had successfully
infiltrated Brothers to the Rescue. Allegedly he had conspired with Cuban
air force officers to shoot down two Cessna aircraft belonging to this group,
killing four Cuban-Americans. Brothers to the Rescue had been founded in
1991 by José Basulto, a Bay of Pigs veteran, to help the minority of *balseros*
(rafters) who capsised while illegally crossing the Florida Straits in defiance
of the US Attorney-General's instructions. These Cessnas often entered
airspace to scatter seditious leaflets and in July 1995 *Granma* published
a warning:

Any vessel coming from abroad, which forcefully invades our sovereign
waters, could be sunk; and any plane shot down . . . The responsibility
for whatever happens will fall, exclusively, on those who encourage,
plan, execute, or tolerate these acts of piracy.

Richard Gott records:

The Miami pilots ignored the warning . . . When they again entered
Cuban air space in February 1996 the Cuban air force took action. Two
out of three Cessnas were shot down after several warnings had been
issued . . . American opinion was affronted by this drastic action, and
the incident caused such commotion that President Clinton felt obliged
to sign the Helms-Burton bill into law. This was an historic and fateful
step . . . Any possibility that Clinton, or some future President, might

order the lifting of economic sanctions now evaporated, to the irritation of America's trading partners, notably in the European Union, and of the farmers and manufacturers within the US who hoped for eventual access to the Cuban market. The EU took vigorous steps to oppose the legislation, perceiving it as a clear violation of international law . . .

The Five's case spawned many more violations of both US and international law. They did not resist arrest, were unarmed, had never been involved in damage to property or disturbances of any kind and were well regarded by their neighbours and workmates. Yet they were not allowed to apply for bail and spent seventeen months while awaiting trial in solitary confinement in cells reserved for 'dangerous prisoners' in maximum security jails hundreds of miles apart.

On the first day of their trial in a Miami court the Five readily identified themselves as agents of the Cuban state and Professor Lisandro Perez, Director of the Cuba Research Institute in the International University of Florida, observed, 'The possibility of selecting twelve citizens from Miami Dade county that would be impartial in a case like this that includes recognised Cuban government agents is practically zero'. Illustrating this point, the then South Florida District Attorney, Guy Lewis, insisted in a *Miami Herald* article (18 August 2000) that the Five 'had vowed to destroy the US'.

To prove the crime of espionage the law requires the acquisition of 'national defence information'. As expert witness, the Five's defence presented three high-ranking retired US officials, one of whom, Major-General Edward Atkinson, former Director of the CIA's military intelligence, closely examined over twenty thousand pages of correspondence between the accused and MinInt. He found no instruction for the Five to seek classified information or take any action that would be harmful to the US.

Another witness for the defence, Debbie McMullen, investigator in the Office of the Public Defender, testified to 'finding boats in the Miami River being prepared to take explosives to Cuba and the proposal of the accused Gerardo Hernández to pass on that information to the FBI via an anonymous telephone call'.

At the end of an almost seven-month trial, during which the jury heard seventy-four witnesses, they deliberated only briefly and submitted not one query before unanimously finding the Five guilty on all counts. This included finding Gerardo guilty of first-degree murder which intensified the procedure's aura of unreality; the prosecution, reckoning that that case 'presents an insurmountable hurdle for the US', had long since applied to withdraw the infamous Charge Three. Six months later (why so long?) Judge Joan A. Leonard imposed three life sentences – which in the US means *life* – and gave the others nineteen and fifteen years.

Five years later (long years, for the Five in their maximum security jails) the Eleventh Circuit Court of Appeals in Atlanta at last handed down its verdict – a ninety-three-page document. That panel of three judges reversed the Miami courts' convictions, already declared illegal by the Working Group on Arbitrary Detentions of the Human Rights Commission of the UN. Speaking for the Cuban government, Ricardo Alarcon said, 'While what took place in Miami was a charade that shames the American legal system Atlanta produced an example of professional ethics and rigour that goes beyond the bounds of the normal appeals process, to demonstrate the innocence of the five accused and expose the colossal injustice to which they fell victim.'

Although the Five had now been pronounced free men, against whom no legal sanction remained, they were not released. Soon Ricardo Alarcon was protesting bitterly, 'They are five kidnap victims of an administration that rides roughshod over the law everywhere. Not just in Abu Grahib and Guantanamo – within US territory as well.'

A few weeks later, on 30 August 2005, more than one thousand five hundred internationally respected philosophers, writers, artists and musicians, including six Nobel laureates, wrote an open letter to the then US Attorney General, Alberto Gonzalez. It ended:

> For the past seven years, these five young men have been held incommunicado in isolated cells for long periods of time and two of them have been denied the right to receive family visits . . . Considering the nullification of their sentences, nothing justifies their incarceration. This arbitrary situation which is extremely painful for them and their families cannot be allowed to continue. We, who have signed below, are demanding their immediate liberation.

Neither the three Atlanta judges nor all those distinguished sympathisers could influence the Five's enemies. A year later, on 9 August 2006, a majority of the full Atlanta Appeals Court of twelve judges ruled against the 2005 revocation, reinstated the Miami sentences, denied the Five a new trial and ordered the case back to the original three-judge panel for 'a consideration of nine outstanding issues'.

For how many more years must the Five remain 'kidnap victims'?

Even when the sea is boisterous groups of youths dive off the Malecón wall through dense spray – an apparently hazardous frolic but those lads know their shoreline. I paused to watch one group, including three girls who didn't dive, as they laughed and shouted while being tossed about in the heaving, seething water. Emerging unscathed on to those sharp volcanic rocks, when the waves are so bullying, demands a special skill. In our over-protective world most youngsters have no chance to develop such skills in a natural setting.

By midday on 1 November the sea was wilder than ever I'd seen it, a gusty force nine gale flinging the spray forty feet high. The Malecón was deserted, except for two young men standing on the wall, supporting each other, being showered. I first saw them at a little distance and as I drew closer another soaring fountain of spray enveloped them – then they were no longer visible, on wall or pavement. Immediately their disappearance was noticed by a policeman outside the Hotel Nacional on its high bluff directly above.

Within five minutes two ambulances had arrived, closely followed by a van marked 'Bombaderos' from which jumped four Navy divers in full kit. As they plunged into the tumultuous Atlantic a fire brigade arrived and hoisted two long ladders over the wall. Then a tiny lifeboat emerged from the port, looking futile as it rode the waves.

Meanwhile a small crowd had gathered, excited in a subdued way as such crowds tend to be. But the mood changed to shared anxiety when two parents joined us, a mother and a father of those reckless young men. Anxiety became grief as an hour became two hours. Eventually we saw that gallant little lifeboat returning to the distant port. Both bodies had been found, so injured by those jagged rocks that no attempt to swim would have been possible. An ambulance drove the parents to the lifeboat's berth.

All that afternoon the sun shone strongly between tropical downpours and once I sheltered on the café-terrace of the venerable Hotel Inglaterra, overlooking Parque Central. To celebrate this first visit to a Havana tourist hotel I decided to sample its cuisine and from a limited menu chose a ham and cheese sandwich. Forty minutes later an adolescent waiter placed a dinner plate in front of me; the 'sandwich' consisted of a stack of five slices of thick stale white bread separated by thin layers of ham and cheese (both items processed and imported) and rings of raw onion. Two 'airline' butter pats decorated the side of the plate. When I requested cutlery the youth looked peeved and returned after some time with a plastic fork wrapped in a square of loo paper. The young Austrian woman at the next table was not enjoying her anonymous jam imported from Spain. We agreed that these repellent foreign foods (part of inward investment deals) do a lot to maintain Cuba's reputation as a gourmet's hell. By then the sun was shining and in the park I could see an ancient man washing a sackful of plastic bottles in the fountain. Two days previously I had watched him collecting those bottles from amidst the litter thrown across the Malecón by the storm.

Helena from Vienna, a regular visitor to Cuba, was upset by Havana's increasingly obvious and persistent beggars. Victims of the bureaucracy, I suggested; having failed to cope with it they had become non-persons, probably through no fault of their own. For instance, that unfortunate widow in Santa Clara, who couldn't get a change-of-residence-permit, might find herself destitute were she to move illegally to live with her daughter. But why, wondered Helena, were officials not rounding such people up and returning them to whatever bureaucratic box they had fallen out of? Blatant begging contradicts what visitors expect of Fidel's Cuba. I reminded her that we were now living in Raul's Cuba, a not-so-subtly different place as several of my friends had pointed out since my return to the capital.

Overnight the wind dropped and Pedro sadistically informed me that my last three days would be 'calm, humid and all sunshine'.

Emerging from No. 403 at daybreak I saw at the far end of San Rafael a puzzling wall of white fog, luminous and thick. Soon I had identified it as an anti-mosquito chemical, being sprayed from two gigantic cylinders on the back of a rickety little truck, one of several that all morning moved at slow walking speed throughout Havana. This deadly vapour seemed to rasp at one's nose, throat and lungs but the *habaneros* consider such temporary (we hope) discomfort much preferable to haemorrhagic dengue fever – otherwise known as break-bone fever, so agonising are its symptoms.

This virus, usually transmitted by the *Aedes Aegypti* mosquito, is mainly confined to the indigenous populations of south-east Asia. However, since 1997 the non-haemorrhagic virus (common in tropical and sub-tropical regions and rarely a killer) has been spreading in the Western hemisphere, especially in Brazil and Cuba.

Haemorrhagic dengue first arrived in Cuba in 1981, appearing simultaneously in three regions about two hundred miles apart, to the epidemiologists' bewilderment. None of the countries with which the international brigades were then involved is a source of this virus. It spread quickly; more than three hundred and forty-four thousand sufferers over-crowded the hospitals and the US Treasury, loyal as ever to the embargo, delayed export permits of the specific insecticide so urgently needed. Yet only one hundred and fifty-eight died, of whom one hundred and one were children. In 1984 the epidemiologists' curiosity was satisfied when Eduardo Arocena, leader of the Cuban exile gang Omega 7, testified in New York's Federal Court while being tried on another matter, that towards the end of 1980 a ship sailed from Florida to Cuba with:

> a mission to carry some germs to introduce them in Cuba to be used against the Soviets and against the Cuban economy, to begin what was called chemical war, which later on produced results which were not what we expected, because we thought it was going to be used against the Soviet forces, and it was used against our own people, and with that we did not agree.

Evidently Arocena had some futuristic vision of genetically modified mosquitoes designed to bite Soviets only. Incidentally, Omega 7, based in Union City, New Jersey, was described by the FBI in 1980 as 'the most dangerous terrorist organisation in the US'.

New York's Federal Court may have been surprised by Arocena's confession but *Science* readers were not. According to that magazine, haemorrhagic dengue had been studied since 1967 at the US government centre in Fort Detrick, Maryland, being listed 'among those diseases regarded as potential biological warfare agents'. And where better than Cuba to do a test run?

In 1971 terrorists obtained from the CIA the African swine fever virus and within six weeks half a million Cuban pigs had to be slaughtered to prevent an island-wide epidemic. This was the Western hemisphere's first African swine fever infection and the Food and Agricultural Organisation of the UN ranked it a 'the most alarming event of the agricultural year'. Small wonder if some Cuban officials remain paranoid to this day about dissidents' potential.

To say '*adios*' to good friends I spent three days criss-crossing humid Havana – prudently, by bicitaxi. (A melancholy mission: we were unlikely to meet again.) Those concentrated conversations – some starting at 8.00 a.m., some ending at 1.00 a.m. – made me acutely aware of witnessing history: Cuba on the cusp. My contacts, though numerically limited, represented various social layers, from the sporadically employed victims of industrial collapse to the tourism-connected resurgent bourgeoisie to the securely employed but impoverished intelligentsia. Predictable hopes and fears were expressed, varying with an individual's circumstances, but everyone was quietly proud of the smooth transfer of power in August 2006, seen as a reassuring measure of national stability.

By then Raul and his team had been in charge for fifteen months yet Fidel remained very much present, continuing to communicate through his *Granma* essays – still being read by many, *pace* certain outside observers. There was a general expectation that after the Assembly elections in February 2008 Cuba would have its second President Castro, as has happened. No one mentioned faction fighting within the government but a few hinted that unity could fracture as preparations were being made for the Sixth Party Congress in 2009. This might well be a healthy development, said my dissident friends. It would surely make more space for the sort of discussions of public grievances that Raul had begun tentatively to encourage. Perhaps then my friends could publish the polemical journal for which *socialist* foreign friends had recently offered them funding.

Unlike Juan in Camaguey, all those *habaneros* were uncritical of the reforms being promoted or mooted by their Acting President. Yet a few of the more outspoken doubted his dexterity – could he carry them through without conceding that pure Castroism simply wouldn't work in the hostile global environment of the twenty-first century? He is reputed to be an adroit string-puller behind the scenes but leading a nation towards drastic modifications requires another sort of talent. It was generally agreed that in any event major reforms should happen gradually – and not only to avoid upsetting Fidel. As one young man pointed out, most Cubans have no memory of another way of being. Castroism has formed their world and however impatient some may be for change everyone will need time to adjust to socialism remoulded.

Taking off from José Martí airport my hopes were higher than on the flight home from Jo'burg in 1995. South Africa's problems were and are far more complex than Cuba's. In 1959 Fidel could lead a real revolution without risking countrywide bloodshed and so he was able to construct the sort of egalitarian society Madiba dared not attempt to build. It comforts me to think that recent developments may not have invalidated Juan Antonio Blanco's cautious prognosis. In the middle of the Special Period this remarkable Cuban – philosopher, historian, diplomat, radical and one-time rock singer – looked ahead and wrote:

There is no certain victory for the Revolution. Lloyds of London would not offer an insurance policy on this prospect. But its victory – which means preserving independence and social justice within a framework of ethical solidarity – is still possible . . . Cuba cannot – if it wishes to survive – be a museum for a dying socialism, but neither can it be the pastiche of Latin America's tragedy. Cuba has the human and material potential, in spite of the crisis, to become a successful social laboratory for a new model of authentically human and sustainable development. If it is possible to 'reinvent' socialism anywhere, then the conditions for doing so exist on this island.

Glossary

Abuela/o – grandmother/grandfather

Agromercado – farmers' market

Annexationist – Cuban advocating the island's annexation to the USA

Apagon – blackout/power cut

Apperrear – to throw to the dogs

Automovil – car

Autopista – motorway

Banyo – bathroom

Barbudos – bearded men (synonym for the Rebel Army)

Barrio – district/neighbourhood

Bohio – hut as built by indigenous Cubans

Burdel – brothel

Cabaña – hut, cabin

Cafetale – coffee farm

Caique – chief/local ruler

Campesiño – country-dweller, peasant

Camiones – lorries

Cena – supper

Cenagueros – swamp-dweller

Centrale – sugarcane plantation

Cerveza – beer

Colectivo – shared taxi

Compañero/a – companion

Creole – Cuban-born, but of European descent

Cubania – essence, spirit of Cuba/love of, pride in Cuba

Cucurucho – sweetmeat peculiar to Baracoa region

Fidelista – a supporter of Fidel Castro

Ingenio – sugar factory (earlier usage – sugarcane plantation)

Latifundo – big estate

Libreta – ration book

Marabu – thorny bush imported from Africa by accident

Mestizo – of mixed race

MinInt – the Ministry of the Interior

Mogote – geological oddity peculiar to Pinar del Rio

Mulatto/a – a person of mixed black and white ancestry

Peninsulare – Spanish-born Cuban resident (used throughout Latin America)

Peresto – government-subsidised shop

Playa – beach

SECSA – a private security firm

Tienda – shop accepting only convertible pesos (still known as 'dollar-shop')

Vagueros – tobacco farmer

Zafra – cane harvest

Bibliography

Acosta, Tomás Diez, *In the Threshold of Nuclear War: The 1962 Missile Crisis*, trans. Ornán José Batista Peñe, Instituto Cubano Del Libro, 2002

Ali, Tariq, *Pirates of the Caribbean: Axis of Hope*, Verso, 2006

Andrew, Christopher, and Mitrokhin, Vasili, *The Mitrokhin Archive II: The KGB and the World*, Penguin Group, 2005

Anson, Robert Sam, *"They've Killed the President!": The Search for the Murderers of John F. Kennedy*, Bantam Books, 1975

Arboleya, Jesús, *The Cuban Counterrevolution*, trans. Damián Donéstevez, Instituto Cubano Del Libro, 2002

—— *Havana-Miami: The US-Cuban Migration Conflict*, trans. Mary Todd, Ocean Press, 1996

Arenas, Reinaldo, *Before Night Falls: A Memoir*, trans. Dolores M. Koch, Penguin Group, 1994

August, Arnold, *Democracy in Cuba and the 1997–98 Elections*, Instituto Cubano Del Libro, 1999

Báez, Luis, *Absolved by History*, trans. Angie Todd, Instituto Cubano Del Libro, 2003

Baker, Christopher P., *National Geographic Traveler Cuba*, National Geographic Society, 2003

Benjamin, Medea, *Cuba: Talking About Revolution – Conversations with Juan Antonio Blanco*, Ocean Press, 1994

Bennis, Phyllis, *Calling the Shots: How Washington Dominates Today's UN*, Interlink Publishing Group, 1996

Beytout, Olivier and Missen, François, *Memories of Cuba*, Thunder's Mouth Press, 1998

Blackburn, Robin (ed.), *New Left Review 220: Che's Missing Year*, New Left Review, 1996

Blanco, Katiuska, and Perera, Alina, and Núñez, Alberto, *Witnesses to the Miracle*, trans. Adrián Martín Replanski, Abril Publishing House, 2004

Blum, William, *Killing Hope: US Military and CIA Interventions since World War II*, Zed Books, 2003

Bravo, Olga Miranda, *Undesirable Neighbors: The US Naval Base at Guantanamo*, Instituto Cubano Del Libro, 2001

Castro (Ruz), Fidel, *Capitalism in Crisis: Globalization and World Politics Today*, Ocean Press, 2000

—— *Cold War: Warnings for a Unipolar World*, Office of Publications, Cuban Council of State/Ocean Press, 2003

—— *Fidel: My Early Years*, eds. Deborah Shnookal & Pedro Álvarez Tabío, Ocean Press, 2005

—— *Fidel and Religion: Castro Talks on Revolution and Religion with Frei Betto*, trans. The Cuban Center, Simon & Schuster, 1988

—— (ed.), *My Life*, Ignacio Ramonet, trans. Andrew Hurley, Penguin Group, 2007

—— *2nd Congress of the Communist Party of Cuba Main Report*, Political Publishers, 1980

—— *We Will Never Kneel*, José Martí Publishing House, 1990

Chavarría, Daniel, *Adios Muchachos*, trans. Carlos López, Instituto Cubano Del Libro, 2003

Chávez, Ernesto Rodriguez, *Cuban Migration Today*, trans. María Luisa Hernández Garcilaso de la Vega, Instituto Cubano Del Libro, 1999

Chomsky, Noam, *Hegemony or Survival: America's Quest for Global Dominance*, Penguin Group, 2003

—— *World Orders, Old and New*, Pluto Press, 1994

—— and Herman, Edward S., *The Washington Connection and Third World Fascism*, South End Press, 1979

CIA Inspector General and Font, Fabian Escalante, *CIA Target's Fidel: The Secret Assassination Report*, Ocean Press, 1996

Coltman, Leycester, *The Real Fidel Castro*, Yale University Press, 2003

Corbett, Ben, *This is Cuba: An Outlaw Culture Survives*, Perseus Books Group, 2004

Cramer, Mark, *Culture Shock: Cuba*, Graphic Arts Publishing Company, 1998

Didion, Jean, *Miami*, Simon & Schuster, 1987

DK Eyewitness Travel Guides, *Cuba*, Dorling Kindersley, 2002

Eire, Carlos, *Waiting for Snow in Havana: Confessions of a Cuban Boy*, Simon & Schuster, 2003

Elizade, Rosa Miriam and Baez, Luis, *'The Dissidents': Cuban State Security Agents Reveal the True Story*, Editora Política, 2003

Bibliography

Escalante, Fabian, *The Cuba Project: CIA Covert Operations 1959–62*, Ocean Press, 2004

Estévez, Abilio, *Thine is the Kingdom*, trans. David Frye, Arcade Publishing, 1999

Farmer, Paul, *Pathologies of Power: Health, Human Rights, and the New War on the Poor*, University of California Press, 2003

Fernández, Luis Martínez, *Fighting Slavery in the Caribbean: The Life and Times of the British Family in Nineteenth-Century Havana*, M. E. Sharpe, 1998

Fisk, Robert, *Inside the Crusader Fortress*, Spokesman Books, 2005

Foss, Clive, *Fidel Castro*, Sutton Publishing, 2000

Gébler, Carlo, *Driving Through Cuba*, Hamish Hamilton, 1988

Geldof, Lynn, *Cubans: Voices of Change*, St Martins Press, 1991

Gleijeses, Piero, *Conflicting Missions: Havana, Washington, and Africa, 1959–1976*, The University of North Carolina Press, 2002

González, Aurelio Gutiérrez, *Trinidad*, Aurelio Gutiérrez, 1999

Gott, Richard, *Cuba: A New History*, Yale University Press, 2004

Gray, John, *Al Qaeda and What it Means to be Modern*, Faber and Faber, 2003

Guevera, Ernesto (Ché), *The African Dream: the Diaries of the Revolutionary War in the Congo*, trans. Patrick Camiller, Harvil Presss, 2000

—— *Ché Guevara Reader*, ed. David Deutschmann, Ocean Press, 2003

—— *The Complete Bolivian Diaries of Ché Guevara and Other Captured Documents*, George Allen & Unwin, 1968

—— *The Motorcycle Diaries: Notes on a Latin American Journey*, ed. and trans. Alexandra Keeble, Ocean Press, 2003

—— *Reminiscences of the Cuban Revolutionary War*, Monthly Review Press, 1968

Henríquez, Hugo Azcuy, *Human Rights: An Approach to a Political Issue*, trans. Fernando Nápoles Tapia, Instituto Cubano Del Libro, 1999

Horowitz, Irving Louis, and Castro, Josuéde, and Gerassi, John (eds.), *Latin American Radicalism: A Documentary Report on Left and Nationalist Movements*, Jonathan Cape, 1969

Kennedy, Robert F., *Thirteen Days: A Memoir of the Cuban Missile Crisis*, W. W. Norton & Company, 1999

Laffita, Graciela Chailloux, and Ocegnera, Rosa López, and Herrera, Silvio Baró, *Globalization and Cuba-U.S. Conflict*, trans. Frank Cabrera, Instituto Cubano Del Libro, 1999

Lamperti, John, *What Are We Afraid Of? An Assessment of the "Communist Threat" in Central America*, South End Press, 1988

Lamrani, Salim (ed.), *Superpower Principles: U.S. Terrorism Against Cuba*, Common Courage Press, 2005

Lechuga, Carlos, *In the Eye of the Storm: Castro, Khrushchev, Kennedy and the Missile Crisis*, trans. Mary Todd, Ocean Press, 1995

Luis, Julio García (ed.), *Cuban Revolution Reader: A Documentary History of 40 Key Moments of the Cuban Revolution*, Ocean Press, 2001

Lumsden, Ian, *Machos, Maricones, and Gays*, Temple University Press, 1996

McAuslan, Fiona and Norman, Matt, *The Rough Guide to Cuba*, Rough Guides, 2005

McCoy, Alfred W., *The Politics of Heroin: CIA Complicity in the Global Drug Trade*, Lawrence Hill Books, 1991

Machado, Miguel A. Castro, *Baracoa: Where Cuba Begins*, trans. and ed. Jo Anne Engelbert, Soledad McIntire, Ivan Schulman, S Augustine-Baracoa Friendship Association, 2001

Marshall, Peter, *Cuba Libre: Breaking the Chains*, Victor Gollancz, 1987

Mencía, Mario, *The Fertile Prison: Fidel Castro in Batista's Jails*, Ocean Press, 1993

Miller, Tom, *Trading with the Enemy: A Yankee Travels Through Castro's Cuba*, Perseus Books Group, 1992

Ogle, Maureen, *Key West: History of an Island of Dreams*, University Press of Florida, 2003

Ojito, Mirta, *Finding Mañana: A Memoir of a Cuban Exodus*, Penguin Group, 2005

Oppenheimer, Andres, *Castro's Final Hour: The Secret Behind the Coming Downfall of Communist Cuba*, Simon & Schuster, 1992

Ospina, Hernando Calvo, *Bacardí: The Hidden War*, trans. Stephen Wilkinson and Alasdair Holden, Pluto Press, 2002

Parry, Renée-Marie Croose, with Parry, Kenneth Croose, *The Political Name of Love*, New European Publications, 2007

Pérez, Eugenio Suárez, and Román, Acela A. Caner, *Fidel Castro: Birán to Cinco Palmas*, trans. Angie Todd, Instituto Cubano Del Libro, 2002

Pérez Jr., Louis A., *Winds of Change: Hurricanes & the Transformation of Nineteenth-Century Cuba*, The University of North Carolina Press, 2000

Pérez-Stable, Marifeli, *The Cuban Revolution*, Oxford University Press, 1993

Raby, D. L., *Democracy and Revolution: Latin America and Socialism Today*, Pluto Press/Between the Lines, 2006

Ray, Ellen and Schaap, William H. (eds.), *Covert Action: The Roots of Terrorism*, Ocean Press, 2003

Rodríguez, Enrique Del Risco, *Cuban Forests: Their History and Characteristics*, trans. Fernando Nápoles Tapia, Instituto Cubano Del Libro, 1999

Rogers, Paul, *Losing Control: Global Security in the Twenty-First Century*, Pluto Press, 2000

Rose, David, *Guantánamo: America's War on Human Rights*, Faber and Faber, 2004

Rosset, Peter, and Benjamin, Medea (eds.), *The Greening of the Revolution: Cuba's Experiment with Organic Agriculture*, Ocean Press, 1994

Ryan, Alan (ed.), *The Reader's Companion to Cuba*, Harcourt Brace & Company, 1997

Rysbridger, James, *The Intelligence Game: The Illusions and Delusions of International Espionage*, The Bodley Head Ltd, 1989

Salazar, Luis Suárez, *Cuba: Isolation or Reinsertion in a Changed World?*, trans. Carmen Gonzáles, Instituto Cubano Del Libro, 1999

Saney, Isaac, *Cuba: A Revolution in Motion*, Fernwood Publishing/Zed Books, 2004

Sarduy, Pedro Perez, and Stubbs, Jean (eds.), *AfroCuba: An Anthology of Cuban Writing on Race, Politics and Culture*, Ocean Press, 1993

Schwartz, Rosalie, *Pleasure Island: Tourism & Temptation in Cuba*, University of Nebraska Press, 1997

Singh, Patwant, *The World According to Washington: An Asian View*, Understanding Global Issues Ltd, 2004

Smith, Wally and Barbara, *Bicycling Cuba*, Backcountry Guides, 2002

Suchliki, Jaime, *Cuba from Columbus to Castro and Beyond*, Brassey's Inc, 2002

Talbot, David, *Brothers: The Hidden History of the Kennedy Years*, Simon & Schuster, 2007

Tejada, Aurelio Alonso, *Church and Politics in Revolutionary Cuba*, Instituto Cubano Del Libro, 1999

Thomas, Hugh, *The Cuban Revolution*, Harper & Row, 1971

UNESCO travelling exhibition, *The Arts of Latin America*, UNESCO, 1977

Valladares, Armando, *Against All Hope: The Prison Memoirs of Armando Valladares*, trans. Andrew Hurley, Alfred A. Knopf, 1986

Walzer, Michael, *Just and Unjust Wars: A Moral Argument with Historical Illustrations*, Perseus Book Group, 1977

West, Richard, *The Gringo in Latin America*, Jonathan Cape, 1967

Williams, Eric, *From Columbus to Castro: The History of the Caribbean 1492–1969*, André Deutsch, 1970

Wollaston, Nicholas, *Red Rumba: A Journey through the Caribbean and Central America*, Hodder & Stoughton, 1962

Yglesias, José, *In the Fist of a Revolution: Life in a Cuban Country Town*, Random House, 1968

Index

ELAND

61 Exmouth Market, London EC1R 4QL
Tel: 020 7833 0762   Fax: 020 7833 4434
Email: info@travelbooks.co.uk

Eland was started in 1982 to revive great travel books
which had fallen out of print. Although the list now includes new
books, biography and fiction, it is united by a quest to define the
spirit of place. These are books for travellers, and for those who are
content to travel in their own minds. Eland books open out our
understanding of other cultures, interpret the unknown and reveal
different environments as well as celebrating the humour and
occasional horrors of travel. We take immense trouble to select
only the most readable books and many readers
collect the entire series.

Extracts from each and every one of our books can be read
on our website, at www.travelbooks.co.uk. If you would like a free copy
of our catalogue, please contact us by phone,
email or in writing.